Civic Hope

Civic Hope is a history of what everyday Americans say – in their own words – about the government overseeing their lives. Based on a highly original analysis of 10,000 letters to the editor from 1948 to the present published in twelve US cities, the book overcomes the limitations of survey data by revealing the reasons for people's attitudes. While Hart identifies worrisome trends – including a decline in writers' abilities to explain what their opponents believe and their attachment to national touchstones – he also shows why the nation still thrives. *Civic Hope* makes a powerful case that the vitality of a democracy lies not in its strengths but in its weaknesses, and in the willingness of its people to address those weaknesses without surcease. The key, Hart argues, is to sustain a culture of argument at the grassroots level.

RODRICK P. HART holds the Shivers Chair in Communication and is Professor of Government at the University of Texas at Austin. Former dean of the Moody College of Communication and founding director of the Annette Strauss Institute for Civic Life, Hart is the author or editor of fifteen books, the most recent of which is *Political Tone: What Leaders Say and Why* (2013). Hart has been named a fellow of the International Communication Association and Distinguished Scholar by the National Communication Association, and received the Edelman Career Award from the American Political Science Association. He is also a member of the Academy of Distinguished Teachers at the University of Texas at Austin.

Communication, Society and Politics

Editors

W. Lance Bennett, University of Washington
Robert M. Entman, The George Washington University

Politics and relations among individuals in societies across the world are being transformed by new technologies for targeting individuals and sophisticated methods for shaping personalized messages. The new technologies challenge boundaries of many kinds – between news, information, entertainment, and advertising; between media, with the arrival of the World Wide Web; and even between nations. Communication, Society and Politics probes the political and social impacts of these new communication systems in national, comparative, and global perspective.

Other Books in the Series

Civic Hope

How Ordinary Americans Keep Democracy Alive

RODRICK P. HART
University of Texas at Austin

CAMBRIDGE
UNIVERSITY PRESS

CAMBRIDGE
UNIVERSITY PRESS

University Printing House, Cambridge CB2 8BS, United Kingdom

One Liberty Plaza, 20th Floor, New York, NY 10006, USA

477 Williamstown Road, Port Melbourne, VIC 3207, Australia

314–321, 3rd Floor, Plot 3, Splendor Forum, Jasola District Centre,
New Delhi – 110025, India

79 Anson Road, #06–04/06, Singapore 079906

Cambridge University Press is part of the University of Cambridge.

It furthers the University's mission by disseminating knowledge in the pursuit
of education, learning, and research at the highest international levels of excellence.

www.cambridge.org
Information on this title: www.cambridge.org/9781108422642
DOI: 10.1017/9781108525138

First published 2018

Printed in the United States of America by Sheridan Books, Inc.

A catalogue record for this publication is available from the British Library.

ISBN 978-1-108-42264-2 Hardback
ISBN 978-1-108-43562-8 Paperback

For my granddaughters,
Colleen, Elly, Jill, Meg, and Olive,
for whom my civic hope abides

Contents

Figures

Tables

Acknowledgments

This project began during the run-up to the Clinton/Dole presidential campaign of 1996, when it occurred to me that the voice of the American people was a colossal muffle. Was it possible, I asked myself, to write a modern history of what citizens were thinking about their government, and to do so in their own voices? I did not immediately think of using letters to the editor, but I quickly discovered that they were the only game in town. But where could I find such letters? If found, would they reasonably represent opinions in their communities? How might the letters be analyzed once gathered? When might I start such a project and when might I finish?

Much has happened in my life since those early thoughts. For one thing, I gathered 10,000 letters to the editor written (between 1948 and the present) by people living in twelve small American cities stretched from coast to coast. I visited each of these cities on multiple occasions and, in 2004, was ready to write the book. Then, unexpectedly, I was dragooned into becoming dean of the Moody College of Communication at the University of Texas at Austin. It would be another twelve years before the writing could commence.

In retrospect, this long interruption was more a blessing than a curse, allowing me to think harder about what the letter writers were saying. I took more than 250 flights for fundraising purposes during my time as dean, but I never left town without grabbing a new batch of letters to read on the plane. It was not easy being a scholar and an administrator, but the burden was lifted considerably by having colleagues with whom I could share my thoughts-in-the-making. Chief among them were Sharon Jarvis Hardesty, my colleague at the University of Texas, and Kathleen Hall

Jamieson of the University of Pennsylvania. They showered me with thoughtful kindness (the former) and stern remonstrance (the latter). I have profited from their gifts equally.

This project has taken me far afield, drawing as it does on diverse disciplines. I could not have responsibly embarked on it without reading the work of three magisterial scholars: Robert Lane, Robert Putnam, and Michael Walzer. Their rich conceptual insights and deft empirical observations are models of community scholarship. I am also indebted to the work of political scientists Lance Bennett, Kathy Cramer, Morris Fiorina, John Hibbing, Chris Karpowitz, Skip Lupia, Eric Oliver, and Wendy Rahn, as well as sociologists Nina Eliasoph, Andrew Perrin, Michael Schudson, Richard Sennett, and Theda Skocpol and psychologists Jamie Pennebaker and Rick Snyder. Equally, I have profited from the work of communication scholars Rob Asen, Pablo Boczkowski, Greg Dickinson, Daniel Kreiss, Nick Lemann, Sam McCormick, Rasmus Nielsen, Bill Reader, Brian Thornton, Karen Tracy, Graeme Turner, Barbie Zelizer, and, especially, Stephen Coleman and Karin Wahl-Jorgensen. Closer to home, I continue to be blessed by faculty colleagues who – for better or worse – also study media and politics. They include Bethany Albertson, Lucy Atkinson, Gina Chen, Tom Johnson, Bryan Jones, Bob Luskin, Susan Nold, Steve Reese, Daron Shaw, Bat Sparrow, Paul Stekler, Talia Stroud, Sean Theriault, and Chris Wleizen.

I have enjoyed the superb backing of university leaders, including Jay Bernhardt, Barry Brummett, Sheldon Ekland-Olson, Larry Faulkner, Greg Fenves, Steve Leslie, Bill Powers, Randa Safady, and Ellen Wartella. I am also indebted to my dear friends in the Texas journalism mafia who have taught me so much over the years, including Rosental Alves, R. B. Brenner, Jane Chesnutt, Jeff Cohen, Tracy Dahlby, Craig Dubow, Karen Elliott-House, Glenn Frankel, Elizabeth McCue, Kathryn McGarr, Kathleen Mc Elroy, Jim Moroney, Dan Rather, Evan Smith, Karen Tumulty, Mary Walsh, and my late friend Walter Cronkite.

Fifty years ago, I was lucky to have married a sociology major, Peggy Hart, who helped me understand the twelve cities when we traveled through them together. I am also indebted to Hank Hardesty and Mark Knapp for the greatest gift of all: They make me laugh.

The research for this book was complicated, and I could not have done it alone. I have depended heavily on three fine computer scientists (Laurence Brevard, Rob Crossman, and Shawn Spiars) and a cadre of administrative personnel who did work for me that was tedious, when it was not *remarkably* tedious. That they performed these labors cheerfully is a testament to the human condition. Thank you, Genevieve Bittson, Melissa Huebsch, Candice Prose, Anne Reed, Dian Sierra, Christie Smith, Margaret Surratt, and Kat Yerger.

The research on which this book is based – the interviews, the survey work, and the content coding of the letters – happened only because I was able to assemble (and reassemble, as the years went by) stalwart teams of research assistants. Since leaving my employ, some of these individuals have aged gracefully and others have aged fitfully because of their labors for me. Whether graceful or fitful, though, each is a personal treasure. The list includes Ana Aguilar, Heló Aruth, Vidula Bal, Emily Balanof, Laura Barberena, Sarah Blumberg, Jay Childers, Stacey Connaughton, Alex Curry, Lisa Densmore, Mary Dixson, Cindy Duquette-Smith, Lisa Foster, David Gilbert, Elizabeth Glowacki, Kristyn Goldberg, Hannah Gourgey, Stephanie Hamel, Soo-Hye Han, Bryant Hill, David Humphreys, Bill Jennings, Natasha Kovalyova, Becky Lavally, Colene Lind, John Lithgow, Marla Morton-Brown, Rachel Mourao, John Pauley, Radharani Ray, Jon Rutter, Kanan Sawyer, Josh Scacco, Juandalynn Taylor, Ori Tenenboim, Keri Thompson, Mary Triece, Claire Van Ens, Holly Waldren, Naomi Warren, Rick Webb, and Joel Wiggins.

I am especially grateful to the editorial staffers working for the newspapers in the twelve cities studied here. On three different occasions they took the time to explain what they did and why they did it. Some of these folks were grizzled veterans of the news business and some were newcomers, but all were exceedingly helpful to me. Also generous were those who reviewed *Civic Hope* prior to publication. I thank Sara Doskow, my editor, for her prompt, insightful, and professional comments, as well as the anonymous reviewers who provided detailed feedback. I have never received more helpful advice in all my years of writing books.

Ultimately, though, my greatest debt is to the American citizens who, year after year and issue after issue, contribute to letters columns in the nation's newspapers. I have grown to love and respect these people. They are opinionated, yes, and some of them are nasty even on their nicest days, but, to me, they sing the song of democracy in exactly the right key. All of us who care about our communities should join their chorus.

PART I

THE NEED FOR CIVIC HOPE

Can Politics Be Fixed?

Three days after the presidential election, Barb L. of Billings, Montana was still distraught. Her team had shockingly lost the 2016 campaign, a wound that was both cultural and political for her:

Good news, parents and teachers. Your job just got a whole lot easier. If you have a child who is rude, petty, vindictive, crass, bullying, doesn't work well with others, makes fun of the disabled and imperfect, and blames others for anything that goes wrong, no worries. In fact, rejoice. You've got presidential material on your hands.
(*Billings Gazette*, November 15, 2016)

A bit further east, in Duluth, Minnesota, Georgianna H. was also disconsolate, declaring that "someone has thrown acid on my psyche." Then came the admissions:

Yes, I am indeed a fat pig who used to have blood coming out of my wherever. That's true. It's also true that long, long ago when I was a cute, young woman certain men seemed to believe they had a total right to grope me in public as if my privates were public property. And that's just me. What about Hispanics, Muslims, Gold Star parents, disabled people, African-Americans, and all the other innocent people verbally assaulted for months by the now newly elected Leader of the Free World?
(*Duluth News Tribune*, November 12, 2016)

One of Georgianna's neighbors had a bigger problem – he was hallucinating:

The morning after I awoke and the world was different, alien even. It felt like an eerie episode of *The Twilight Zone* in which people wake up in the morning to discover their entire suburban neighborhood was transported to an alien planet where they were to become slaves.
(David T., *Duluth News Tribune*, November 13, 2016)

Elsewhere in the country, people were happier. Declared Roy B. of Wichita Falls, Texas:

What a historic victory not for Donald Trump, not for the Republican Party, but for these United States of America and its people. This is not a victory for just the next four or, hopefully, the next eight years but for generations to come because of the looming Supreme Court appointments that are sure to come during President Trump's tenure in office.

(*Wichita Falls Times Record News*, November 10, 2016)

Jeffery K. was of mixed minds about the campaign. Like Roy B., he was pleased that Donald Trump had won, but he was miffed by how badly his fellow Americans were behaving post-election. "When President Barack Obama was elected and re-elected, there was a lot of disappointment and fear," he opined, "but you did not see riots or beatings. Nor did you have CEOs telling people who supported Obama that they should resign. I ask: Who are the real fascists and haters?" (*Duluth News Tribune*, November 15, 2016)

After taking all of this in, Jason C. of Fall River, Massachusetts called for a moratorium on the tumult. "Now that the election is over," he observed, "let's take some time to open a dialogue with someone you disagree with." Then he got specific:

Open up Facebook, make a phone call, text, chat in the neighborhood watering hole or eateries. Start a conversation with someone you disagree with. But this time do it from a starting point of empathy, compassion, and respect. See if you can't find just one thing you both agree with, that you want to change.

(*Fall River Herald News*, November 12, 2016)

I reflect in this book on people like Jason, Barb, Roy, and other Americans who write letters to the editor. Sometimes these folks say obvious things, sometimes banal things, and they can often be irritating. They trace their roots to the earliest days of the country, when broadsides flitted about in the colonies. Those who contributed to them were saccharine, intemperate, preachy, or all three, as if someone had ordained them. Eventually, their postings would become letters to the editor, and today they can also be found in myriad online forums. This book is about these unquiet Americans.

Quiet Americans are another matter entirely, and they drove pollsters crazy in 2016. They were sometimes called "shy Trump supporters," and survey experts wondered if they existed at all. It turns out that they did. Reflecting on election-day polls predicting a resounding victory for Hillary Clinton, veteran Republican strategist Mike Murphy said: "I've believed in data for 30 years ... and data died tonight." The polling in 2016 was "a debacle on the order of Dewey defeats Truman," observed the University of Virginia's Larry Sabato. "The miss was far and wide," admitted NBC News political director Chuck Todd. Speaking of media reportage more broadly, ProPublica's Alec McGillis noted that "the media are so, so far removed from their country," centered as they are in New York and Washington, and that they missed the churning among blue-collar workers in Pennsylvania, Michigan, and Wisconsin – a group now credited with handing Donald Trump his unexpected victory.[1]

As it turns out, the polls better predicted the popular vote than the Electoral College's, but that gave surveyors little solace. Here I will ask whether paying more attention to letter writers might have picked up more of the angst afflicting voters in fly-over counties. Letter writers, I will argue, sound a bit like politicians, a bit like journalists, but they have their own sound too. They are confident, argumentative, mildly perturbed. Letter writers know what they know and have clarified their values. Their bravado, their insouciance, can be off-putting, but it can also attract readers like a moth to a flame, which is why the letters column is among the most widely read parts of any newspaper. Writers' idiosyncrasies often make readers feel superior to them, but that sense of superiority can become a narcotic, ensuring that readers return to the letters column for one more prediction, one more lamentation, one more suggestion for coping with life itself.

I use letters to the editor here to get at a mysterious concept: civic hope, or the ability to keep going when all seems bleak. On November 9, 2016, life was no longer worth living for many Americans. Protests, some of them violent, erupted in city after city. Feminists, African Americans, undocumented workers, and Muslims were beside themselves with worry, as were run-of-the-mill Democrats in areas such as Hoboken and Evanston. Almost immediately, though, counterintuitive possibilities began to be raised. The director of the University of Pennsylvania's Center for the Study of Race and Equity in Education, Shaun Harper, spoke of "the gift of Trump," of new avenues for dramatizing "the racial ugliness of our nation."[2] In a similar vein, *Washington Post* columnist E. J. Dionne imagined how young people would now realize that "the coming months and years will require new and creative forms of political witness and organization" because of the campaign's outcome.[3] Even more imaginatively, a *Denver Post* writer saw Trump's victory as potentially Pyrrhic: "If he governs as he's campaigned – if he tries to build the wall, if he blocks Muslims from entering the country, etc. – he may relegate Republicans to long-term minority status."[4]

Hope among the ruins. But why? And how? Hope, I will argue, is not optimism; it is deeper, more enigmatic. It is the product of intense struggle and it means nothing without that struggle. The letter writers I will profile here exemplify that. They become energized when life seems dark, when problems abound, when the arena beckons. What makes them different from their neighbors? Why do they care? Why do they persist? This book addresses those mysteries.

THE PEOPLE'S VOICE

Erma D. decided it was time to write a letter to the editor and so she did. Her letter was published in the *Trenton Times* and it went like this:

> I am 12 years old. I hear people shouting about having a military man for President. Who was the greatest President we ever had? Why, George Washington – a great soldier and a great General. He went through hardships, battles and sufferings; but he always came out victorious. General Eisenhower is the greatest soldier and General of our day. I know he follows in the footsteps of Washington, Father of Our Country, and will always be victorious.
>
> (Erma D., *Trenton Times*, September 25, 1952)

Erma's letter is coherent enough for a twelve-year-old and indisputably charming. More importantly, it has a buoyancy that seemed missing during the 2016 presidential election. Absent from her letter are the snarky comments made on Twitter about Jeb Bush or the barbs directed at Bernie Sanders's improbable brand of socialism. There is a naiveté in Erma's letter, a sensibility unsuited to the new millennium, which has turned its back on naiveté in all its forms. But there is something else in her letter that has also gone missing: civic hope.

I tracked down Erma D. sixty-three years after she wrote the only letter to the editor she would ever get published. When I spoke to her she was retired and living in Florida, a doting grandmother whose main political preoccupation consisted of watching Fox News (avidly, she admitted). She forgot that she had written her letter, and seeing it again brought tears to her eyes. When asked why she had taken pen to paper in 1952, Ms. D. imagined it was because two of her uncles had served in World War II (one of whom was wounded) but had returned home safely. That memory, too, brought tears to her eyes.

This book focuses on people like Erma D. It reports the results of a multi-year investigation of letters to the editor written in twelve American cities between 1948 and 2012, a timeline that foreshadows the stresses and strains visited upon the nation during the 2016 presidential campaign. All the letters examined dealt with politics in some manner – local, state, or national – and the database consists of some 10,000 letters. Each of the letters was subjected to a scientific procedure known as content analysis, whereby expert coders documented the themes and tonalities of each letter to identify trends related to time, place, personality, and circumstance. In addition, ten different surveys were administered in these cities during the past twenty years to learn more about those who write letters, those who read them, and those who edit the letters prior to publication. In-depth interviews were also conducted with a sample of the writers to discover why letter-writing was important to them.

Why pay such careful attention to ordinary people doing such ordinary things? This book answers that question by focusing on civic hope, an expectation: (1) that enlightened leadership is possible despite human foibles; (2) that productive forms of citizenship will result from cultural pluralism; (3) that democratic traditions will yield prudent governance; (4) but that none of this will happen without constant struggle. Even as these sentences are being written, H. L. Mencken rises from his grave to wave us away from "the optimists and chronic hopers of the world, the believers in men, ideas and things. It is the settled habit of such folk to give ear to whatever is comforting; it is their settled faith that whatever is desirable will come to pass. A caressing confidence – but one, unfortunately, that is not borne out by human experience."[5]

Is Mencken right? Can we comfortably ignore the Erma D.'s of the world? Does anyone believe in civic hope today? If so, who will admit to such beliefs in public, and are there enough such people to sustain a polity? Has civic hope become too idealistic a notion for an advanced, technological society? Have recent events – unwanted wars in Iraq and Afghanistan, a porous southern border leaking unwanted immigrants, campaigners spewing forth bilious stuff in 2016 – convinced Americans that politics is completely beneath them?

Thinkers from Thucydides to Rousseau, from Oakeshott to Dahl say that democratic citizenship is a great and good thing, but, then again, they never met Donald Trump. In an era of economic dislocations and tribal loyalties, suburban retrenchments and media trivialities, civic hope seems antediluvian. Never before, it would seem, have so many people been willing to do so little for so many others. Scandals in the United Way drive down contributions. Neighborhood hegemonies push homeless shelters to urban peripheries. Two-income lifestyles erode time for volunteerism. Voter turnout plummets. If enlightened citizenship now counts at all, it counts for little. Civic hope? Surely not.

It was not always this way. When she wrote her first letter to the editor, Ann P. of Utica, New York was a bit older than Erma D. and her politics were different. Said Ann P. in 1984:

I am 15 1/2 years old. If I had the right to vote this year I don't know who I would vote for. President Reagan has an itchy trigger finger. He tries to act like he cares about senior citizens but he has cut back on funding for them, always wanting more for defense. I'm not crazy about the Mondale-Ferraro ticket either. Mondale was an ineffective vice president so why would he make an effective president? The only reason Ferraro was put on the ticket was to get the women's vote.

(*Utica Observer-Dispatch*, September 21, 1984)

Reading a letter like Ann P.'s makes one feel old and young at the same time – old because her nascent beliefs here are so raw, so available, but young because her political energy is so infectious. Most powerful of all, however, are her demands that leadership be audited, that political motives be made transparent, and that institutional renewal be prioritized. There is guilelessness here but there is civic hope as well.

This book does what public opinion pollsters also do. After all, researchers at the National Election Studies of the University of Michigan and the National Opinion Research Center at the University of Chicago fan out across the nation every four years with a panoply of questionnaires, projective tests, and focus-group interviews to plumb the nation's soul, after which they formulate elaborate statistical models to understand political trends, so why not follow their lead?

Important though such work is, survey researchers cannot capture the *texture* of people's beliefs – the reasons underlying their opinions and the varied ways in which a given belief can be expressed. A book examining letters to the editor, alternatively, has no choice but to wrestle with these multiple layers of meaning. And so I will ask bolder questions than can be asked of public opinion polls: Have the cynicisms of our age sunk deep roots in the American populace, replacing old civic pieties with new forms of alienation? When ordinary citizens talk about politics, do they reproduce the news media's depressing agenda or do they imagine new, more hopeful possibilities? Do the children of the new millennium have less faith, or more faith, in the nation's democratic traditions than those who came before?

A CULTURE OF ARGUMENT

While surveys can tell us much about people's attitudes, letters to the editor reveal how those attitudes are *performed*. As I have listened to the people's voices over the years, I have noted their increasing frustrations but also their perseverance. Perhaps that is why letters columns are as lively today (and their editors as heavily solicited) as they were in the middle of the twentieth century – the starting point of this book. The people are happy ... and so they write. The people are angry ... and so they write. Civic hope is about hanging in, about keeping the pot stirred. It prizes a culture of argument that endures across time.

Perhaps that is what Tom L. had in mind when he wrote his first letter to the editor in 1968:

The people of the nation have loudly voiced a demand for change but neither party has answered with equal spirit. The political system in 1968 has malfunctioned – if not failed. No wonder youth like myself are so disillusioned with their initial contact with the system. I am 18 years old and I was enthusiastic in this political year of 1968. I thought that the United States was going to make major advances in both domestic and foreign policies by having the courage to make both rational and moral judgments on matters of importance like Vietnam. The results were nil. If I am not angry I am disillusioned and alienated from the present American political system. And I am not alone; hundreds of thousands of American young adults I am sure feel exactly the same. We are beginning to wonder what a true democracy is.

(*Utica Observer-Dispatch*, September 6, 1969)

Tom L.'s letter is thoughtful and passionate, and while it raises the specter of systemic disenchantment, his decision to write a letter – to turn citizenship into a performance – suggests that this would not be his last such act. Indeed, it was not. Tom L. went on to spend a lifetime in direct civic engagement, working in special education, overseeing a charter school, volunteering with men newly released from prison, consulting with emotionally disturbed students, and embracing every known aspect of the Quaker belief system. His letter in 1968 was a prologue to his life.

My hope is that this book will be a political history the American people can recognize as their own. It is based not on what elites have said – journalists, scholars, and pundits – but on what people next door have been saying. It will trace how geographical and partisan circumstances have changed between 1948 and the present and how the American people were changed as a result. Letters to the editor constitute a humble database, but that is its strength. People who write these letters

are not always the best informed, but they know what they know. I wrote
this book because I wanted to know what they know.

Democracy in the United States is an impossible thing. It lets people
with toxic attitudes vote and, worse, it lets them be elected to office. It lets
presidents and senators bicker with one another even as pressing matters
go unattended. It accepts new citizens without regard to their talents,
attitudes, or personal histories. It doles out public funds so that all can be
educated, even though many struggle to do so. It ministers to everyone in
its public hospitals (even those without health insurance) and it cozies up
to capitalism despite its shortcomings. After considerable pain, it lets
black people vote, gay people get married, and Hillary Clinton run for
president. What happens once those accommodations have been made?
More complaining.

The vitality of a democracy, that is, lies not in its strengths but in
its weaknesses, and in the willingness of its people to address those
weaknesses without surcease. It is the imperfections of democracy that
call forth a people. If democracies were not shot through with
unstable premises and unsteady compacts, their citizens would remain
quiet, removed from one another. Disagreements – endless, raucous
disagreements – draw them in, or at least enough of them to have a
debate. Therein lie the roots of civic hope. What is said in a letter is
obviously important, but the writing of the letter is even more
important.

Hence this book's thesis: *Creating and sustaining a culture of argument
at the grassroots level make democracy flourish*. There are several parts to
this claim:

1. *It takes work to create an argument.* Consider environmental
   issues, for example. My cache of letters finds no real mention of
   such matters until 1976. In 1992, however, they took a major jump
   in prominence, with an even more pronounced jump in 2000,
   probably because young people in the United States took up the
   cause as the years unfolded, eventually galvanizing their parents
   as well.
2. *It takes work to sustain an argument.* Feminism is a good example:
   Judging from my letters, it ramped up in the late 1970s and climbed
   throughout the 1980s, only to throttle back down in the 1990s,
   perhaps because young women began taking it for granted (inaug-
   urating the post-feminist era?) as the new millennium rolled
   around.

3. *An argument must be two-sided.* An issue cannot depend on the enthusiasm of just one pressure group to energize a polity. So, for example, the "keep Christ in Christmas" folks had their day, as did the "communist sympathizer" crowd, but they can no longer generate an opponent – a fate the "no more immigration" cadre has not suffered in recent years.

4. *The argument must stimulate people at the grassroots level.* Elites can be part of the discussion, of course, but a local dialectic is especially needed. I find, for example, that "wages and prices" peaked as a topic for letter writers in the 1948, 1980, and 2000 elections but then stair-stepped downward in between, indicating that, important though it is, "income inequality" cannot consistently displace the myriad other issues important to everyday Americans.

A decidedly humble example shows such forces at work. Joe D. was nineteen when he wrote his first letter to the editor. He had been arrested for running a stop sign in Fort Worth, Texas in 1956 and his letter was a long and angry one. But even a portion of it points up the person, and the citizen, he would become:

We were ... thrown into jail with a group of drunkards and a man who beat his wife. There was no window in our cell or any other part of the place where they put us. Also there was not any kind of bunk or bed to sleep on. We had to sleep on the concrete floor which was cold and hard. The cell was filled with the putrid odor of vomiting drunks. We were accused of drinking when it was very obvious that neither of us had indulged. We were also cursed and threatened by the officers who used violent and vulgar terms. After much pleading we were allowed to notify our parents of our whereabouts. The next day both of us had to pay $10 in order to get out of jail. The boy with the car had to pay $7.50 more in order to get back his car. Then, of course, we had to pay the traffic ticket.

(*Wichita Falls Times-Record-News*, April 13, 1956)

In a sense, young Mr. Joe D. discusses trivial matters here – a speeding ticket, a collection of drunks, some cursing, a deserved fine. Who is he to turn a simple traffic stop into a bulky Constitutional matter? He is, as it turns out, an American citizen who knows his rights, especially his right to express his rights. He fully understands that citizenship must be performed to have real meaning, so he attacked his argument as he attacked everything in his life – by over-performing. At age nineteen he was short and quick but also feisty. Despite having been brought up in blue-collar circumstances, he became a standout in track and field in college and then went on to create a track club that produced dozens of Olympic medals and numerous world records. Joe D. became a social entrepreneur but first he became a citizen.

How, then, are democracies preserved? Through historical determinism? Not really, for the long sweep of history finds far more theocracies, monarchies, and dictatorships than democracies. Via formal institutionalization? Executive and legislative branches surely help governments function but non-democratic systems depend on these same entities as well. As result of economic prosperity? USA Inc. has unquestionably been a thriving corporation but it has also experienced wars and recessions without sacrificing its freedoms. By means of formal acculturation? The nation's schools have turned out generations of little citizens but schooling is a transitory thing, too often a passive thing, and governance needs a constant influx of energy.

While these other forces have their impact, *a democracy is at its best when it becomes a culture of complaint; it needs argument to keep itself going.* Talk to anyone with a letter-to-the-editor habit and you will find the reservoir on which it depends. "I'm not at all sure I'm having an impact," says Harold E. of Billings, Montana, "but I've just got to write." "The people in this town are lunatics," says Bruno D. of Trenton, New Jersey; "someone's got to straighten them out." "The squeaky wheel gets the grease," argues Eddie D. of Wichita Falls, Texas, "so if I squeak maybe someone will listen."[6] Democrats like this perform civic hope each day. This book tells their story.

CURRENT CIRCUMSTANCES

Attractive though the concept of civic hope might be, it seemed a rare thing during the presidential primaries of 2016. "To listen to the way some Republicans tell it," says the *New York Times'* Jeremy Peters, "America is a pretty awful place these days." With Donald Trump describing the nation as a "hell hole" and with Ted Cruz decrying "tyranny" and "lawlessness" at every campaign stop, their somber notes resonated with voters already feeling "angry, alienated and under threat."[7] Years of stagnant incomes, same-sex marriages, and Muslim immigration had caused many Republicans to declare their country adrift. Traditional pols such as Jeb Bush, Marco Rubio, and John Kasich tried to buck up their spirits but few seemed to be listening.

John Kennedy's "new frontier," Ronald Reagan's "shining city on a hill," and Bill Clinton's "thinking about tomorrow" were antique concepts for Republicans after eight years of Barack Obama. But there was

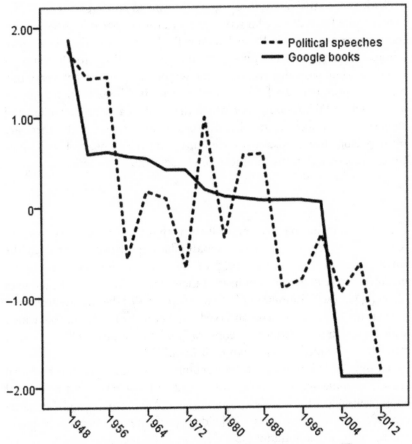

FIGURE I.I References to *Hope* in Different Genres over Time

something cultural afoot as well, as we see in Figure 1.1. Hope, it seems, has become less imaginable, or at least less discussable, for both authors and politicians.[8] Korea, Cuba, Vietnam, Iraq, and Afghanistan left emotional legacies for the United States, as did the economic recessions of the 1980s and thereafter. Collectively, these events may explain why politicians have become so dour. As far as authors are concerned, David Foster Wallace notes that postmodern cynicism "has become an end in itself, a measure of hip sophistication and literary savvy. Few artists dare to try to talk about ways of working toward redeeming what's wrong, because they'll look sentimental and naive to all the weary ironists."[9]

With politicians and authors now reluctant to speak of hope, can we expect more from those who write letters to the editor? It is, after all, one thing for youth such as Erma D., Ann P., Joe D., and Tom L. – all of whom wrote in ancient times – to imagine solutions to the nation's problems, but with the average letter writer being fifty-eight years old, can we expect as much from them? Perhaps civic hope is something we leave back in high school, after which the need to appear controlled and sophisticated dominates our lives. Issues of maturation aside, there are other reasons to suppose that civic hope is on the wane, and they range from the personal, to the political, to the societal.

Detachment

Benedict Anderson has written brilliantly about the imagination it takes for people to develop a sense of nationhood. "Members of even the smallest nation," said Anderson, "will never know most of their fellow-members, meet them, or even hear of them, yet in the minds of each lives the image of their communion."[10] The great wars of the twentieth century are extraordinary, Anderson observed, not because of "the unprecedented scale on which they permitted people to kill," but because of "the colossal numbers persuaded to lay down their lives."[11]

Turning individualism into community is getting harder for several reasons. People are now more mobile and so less likely to set down real roots. Self-help (if not self-love) movements have proliferated dramatically. Corporate rewards for "individual performers" marginalize team-work, as do telecommuting and other at-a-distance work routines that remove people from social spaces. We no longer belong "to a single well-defined group," says economist Daniel Klein, "but rather, increasingly, to many loosely defined groups, and those groups are increasingly of our own choosing." "We get used to 'knowing' many people of celebrity who do not know us," Klein continues, but we fail to meet "the fellow who lives next door. People pursue their own interests and communities freely ignore the vast social oceans that lap against the walls of their homes."[12]

Lewis Althusser has observed that "the citizen is the State in the private man,"[13] but given the flux and flow of modern life, we must ask how much State remains, especially since new technologies let us and our loyalties roam freely. Perhaps we have become digital nomads with increasingly cosmopolitan tastes (a dangerous example of which is the citizen-turned-terrorist via online modalities)? After all, domestic politics, like all merchandise, is now pitched to our individual smartphones and customized Web browsers instead of to families gathered around a television set. Traditional modes of civic engagement – volunteering, canvassing, petitioning – have also gone electronic. There is great efficiency in that but there is also a loss of group solidarity. Who, we must ask, can withstand these temptations to detachment?

Polarization

As the Obama administration drew to a close in 2016, virtually no legislation was proffered by the Republican congress unless, of course, it was designed to elicit an immediate veto and, hence, fresh meat for the campaign trail. Intense partisanship has often produced such antagonisms, but with gerrymandering having by now become a fine art, one must look hard to find a political district prone to a partisan shift. In 2012, for example, 90 percent of House incumbents and 91 percent of Senate incumbents who sought re-election were successful.[14] Under such circumstances only a fool would consider compromise.

Citizens are also caught up in these tides. A recent Pew study finds that the "tails" of the normal distribution have doubled over the past twenty years, meaning that people have gone from "disliking" their political opponents to describing them as "a threat to the nation's well-being."[15] Pew also reports that Americans now share a greater desire to live in a place "where people share my political views," meaning that "ideological silos" are now "common on both the left and the right." Not surprisingly, voters are increasingly getting their political news from a narrow set of sources, with 47 percent of consistent conservatives attending only to Fox News and with their liberal counterparts gravitating to MSNBC, CNN, NPR, and the *New York Times*.[16] People's Facebook friends can also be predicted by knowing their political beliefs.

These trends add up to what two political scientists, Neil Nevitte and Stephen White, have called a "democratic deficit" – a gap between citizens' expectations for governance and their evaluation of it. They found such gaps in virtually all the countries they studied. What accounts for these gaps? Economic marginalization, to be sure, but also excessive partisanship, social isolation, and even political idealism. That is, older and better-educated individuals – those with a clear view of how politics "should" function – were especially upset with the status quo. That was particularly true in the US among those who were "psychologically engaged" with politics. And so this book's question emerges in another form: Have the fragmentations of the age dismayed those who write letters to the editor or have they resisted them, buoyed up by a mysterious sense of civic hope?

Distrust

Logically speaking, detachment could be either the cause or the result of declining trust. So too with polarization: If politicians cannot trust one another, why should we trust them to protect our welfare? Tracking the causal arrow in politics is never easy, although the results are clear enough: Trust is now at an all-time low in the United States. Using a variety of different "feeling thermometers," scholars have documented consistent declines in political trust between 1958 and the present. Studies show that people become less trusting of politics as they age, as their financial profiles weaken, as their party of choice loses influence, as crime rates soar, as political scandals emerge, and as their media consumption increases.[17]

Evidence collected by Jean Twenge and her colleagues casts an even darker shadow: Trust in *people in general*, not just in politicians, has also declined in the United States since the 1970s, reaching an historic low in 2008.[18] That was true for persons in all age groups – from high school students to the elderly – thereby disappointing those who expected millennials to reverse the trend. Other studies find that citizens with especially high hopes for governance have lost the greatest amount of trust, as have those with the most formal education. Eri Bertsou of the London School of Economics finds three different kinds of distrust: technical ("people have failed at their jobs"), moral ("people have violated our shared values"), and personal ("people have forsaken our relationship").[19] All three types of distrust are displayed each evening on the national news, but they are displayed, too, in sitcoms, TV dramas, and reality shows. Lost trust has become the avatar of our age.

Political scientists John Hibbing and Elizabeth Theiss-Morse add an extra dimension to this discussion. It is true, they say, that voters distrust Congress more than ever, but this is not so much because they hate the ground politicians walk upon. Rather, it is because the current system permits so many violations of *procedural norms* (e.g., fair play, equal opportunity, open debate, etc.), thereby denying voters the chance for input.[20] That tune plays particularly well at Tea Party rallies, but progressives are also humming it, as Vermont senator Bernie Sanders proved during the 2016 Democratic primaries. While voters continue to have faith in the abstract principles of democracy, Hibbing and Theiss-Morse report, what they really want is a kind of "stealth democracy" that respects their priorities, that does so efficiently, and that otherwise leaves them alone.

Bystanding

Kate Krontiris, a social scientist at Harvard's Berkman Center, recently led a research team that studied political "bystanders." They found many of them. Bystanders, the team reports, "view politics as a source of conflict, and want to avoid experiencing that contentiousness with their friends or coworkers, either in person or online."[21] Bystanders are not active consumers of news, largely because they find it so upsetting.[22] Bystanders claim that local involvement is important but they only vote at the national level. When asked to describe some of their past political attitudes, bystanders often draw a blank. People like this are "immobilized," says Karin Wahl-Jorgensen of Cardiff University. Their descriptions of political life are "formulaic and uncreative" but also "shot through with a sense of disenchantment."[23]

Bystanders find "nothing natural about politics."[24] Although governments fight wars in which many are killed and although public agencies build highways over which millions travel each day, bystanders find governance a removed thing, devoid of human consequence. "Nobody is ever held to account for their mistakes," bystanders complain, even though that is massively untrue (just ask former congressman Anthony Weiner and many big-city mayors). "Everything happens behind closed doors," they complain further, a statement that is far less true than many believe (just ask those on the Watergate, Iran–Contra, and Clinton–Lewinsky hearing panels).

Despite these attitudes, bystanding apparently does not lead to systemic alienation. One set of researchers finds few signs that voters have "a declining faith either in the legitimacy of democracy ... or in the major institutions of society,"[25] although they are indeed distressed by the *political people* they see on television. It is true, says Stanford's Morris Fiorina, that the "political class" has become more dyspeptic, but even as that has happened, more and more Americans have moved to the center or declared themselves Independents.[26] Bystanding, it appears, largely leads to standing by – a societal problem, but not a fatal one.

And So?

Fragmentation, polarization, distrust, bystanding – conditions for a fraught politics. But might another, cheerier story be told? After all, even if one grants that survey researchers have interpreted their gloomy data correctly (and I certainly do), we are confronted with the superb fact that the US endures. How has that happened? What counterforce keeps the nation whole? It is the people and their infernal disagreements, I shall argue. The people, or at least some of them, act upon the fragmentation and intemperance they see even though many of them are distrustful as well. So what sustains them? Why don't they just stand by?

Those who write letters to the editor are but a speck on the wall of citizenship. Some of them are daffy and some self-important. But they can teach us much if we study them carefully. We can ask, for example, how they cope with polarization. We can ask what their hopes are for the commonweal, which of their historic rights they still treasure. We can ask what constitutes knowledge for them, what solutions they see for current problems, what risks they are willing to take to set the nation aright. Above all, we can ask if there still exists within them a reservoir of fellow-feeling, and, if it exists, we must measure its depth.

WRITING LETTERS

How to hear an electorate? I choose to listen to letter writers, but that may be putting an undue burden on them. Can such letters really be a stand-in for the "people's voice," one shared by 350 million Americans? Indeed, if such a voice existed, would it not be a cacophony, an unhearable, uninterpretable mess? It may indeed be just that but, then again, there is reality: Where else could one go to get a consistent, nuanced look at lay sentiment across a considerable expanse of time? Today, of course, one could examine Twitter feeds, Facebook postings, and comment strings to gauge what voters are thinking, but these are recent inventions and their lack of transparency and generalizability presents its own problems.[27] If gathering historical data were not so important, I could have followed those who visited with people in bars and restaurants to get their thoughts,[28] or who interviewed them in structured settings.[29] Other researchers have listened to citizens taking part in guided deliberations, in town meetings, or in radio call-in shows.[30] All of these studies have borne fruit, but understanding citizens-in-time required something else.

I settled on letters to the editor because they are part of a long-standing tradition and because they contain people's own, spontaneous words. It is one thing, after all, to oppose abortion. It is quite another to explain one's opposition in Biblical language, different again to express it in clinical, legal, economic, or familial language. Words give texture to an author's feelings, making them infinitely subtler and more interesting. Because that is so, people read letters columns for political expiation, for psychic liberation, for an informed dialectic, and, yes, for distraction and comic relief. But letters are nonetheless important, and I see three reasons why.

Authenticity

Keith V. of Lake Charles, Louisiana was transfixed by the nation's bicentennial celebration in 1976 but it is not clear why. Nevertheless, he spoke:

There has never been in the history of civilization on earth a nation as powerful or as unified. Only 2000 years ago, this country rose from the rubble of strife and anxiety to become the greatest sovereign nation of the planet. I cannot understand why the citizens are taking such a ho-hum attitude about a threat which is very real and so very dangerous from the USSR. Everyone is out to celebrate the Bicentennial and I see nothing wrong with that. But at the same time do your part to ensure its survival. Write your congressmen and tell them to get cracking. The time is now! Don't wait until tomorrow – tomorrow may be too late.
(*Lake Charles American Press*, July 4, 1976).

Keith V. is breathless here, so dire are the consequences of ... something. Although he overestimates the nation's founding by some seventeen hundred years (perhaps confusing it with the birth of Christianity), his point is made: People need to get cracking about ... something. Past and present collide here, as do growth and decline, torpor and energy. Long-standing American values – honoring the Founding, defending freedom, being prepared to act – are entwined from beginning to end. No professional politician would ever get things this convoluted and no journalist would ever be this nakedly axiological. But Keith V. is neither a politician nor a journalist. He is one of the nation's citizens and his voice is his own. Somehow, we catch his drift.

All written letters provide "a transitional space between public and private lives," says author Janet Maybin, thereby allowing people like Keith V. to venture forth.[31] When ordinary people get a chance to create content for public consumption, says the University of Queensland's Jean Burgess, they instinctively talk about "the serious business of the human experience – life, loss, belonging, hope for the future, friendship and love" instead of slavishly taking up the media's dominant discourse.[32] "Letters have the power to grant us a larger life," claims journalist Simon Garfield, "they reveal motivation and deepen understanding. They are evidential. They change lives and they rewrite history."[33]

Political scientist Taeku Lee observes that legislators once relied "on a diverse range of expressions of public opinion," including "local newspapers, visits with their constituents, letters from their districts, and interest groups," but are "now increasingly looking to opinion polls."[34] There is great danger in doing so, says Lee, since "letters capture an intensity of opinion and emotional pitch not easily and not often measured in opinion surveys."[35] Because each letter bears the unique stamp of its author, says Garfield, "a world without letters would surely be a world without oxygen."

Some years ago, historian David Thelen wrote a fine book on the Reagan administration's Iran–Contra scandal, using citizens' letters to Congress as his database. Too often, declared Thelen, the mass media have looked exclusively to "the opinion industries" to discover what people were feeling, thereby creating "drab public spaces where life's blacks and whites blur into grays, where data stand in for people and statistics for voices."[36] By paying exclusive attention to the chattering classes, Thelen concluded, journalists have ignored the voice of everyday experience, "of home remedies, folk wisdom, word of mouth, and first-hand experience, by which people have long made sense of life." All too often, said Thelen, "experts have concluded that everyday talk is ignorant. By narrowing the range of experience worth learning from, experts have simultaneously made only a tiny fraction of life visible and eroded the confidence people bring from their intimate worlds to public conversations."[37]

Even something as pedestrian as a letter to the editor, then, can generate what phenomenologists call "presence," which helps an author's way-with-the-world come across to readers. Such letters create "a window into how events of the day are seen by folks who don't pontificate for a living."[38] Letters of all types construct "an intended reader," says Swinburne University's Esther Milne, thereby invoking two separate worlds: "the here and now of the writer and the here and now of the reader."[39] For these reasons, researchers find that "astroturf letters" – those fashioned by national movement organizations or political parties for "planting" in local newspapers – are almost never published, especially in the small city newspapers examined in this book.[40] Editors in those locations are quick to detect inauthenticity, in part because they are adept literary critics and in part because they know how local people talk. No less an authority than Ralph Waldo Emerson noted this very phenomenon when describing the New England town meeting. "Every local feeling, every private grudge, every suggestion of petulance and ignorance were not less faithfully produced," in these meetings said Emerson.[41] The same can be said of letters to the editor.

Authority

To suggest that letters to the editor have "authority" may seem whimsical since their authors are just ordinary people. The fact that the letters are *published*, however, gives the letters at least a modicum of authority, even if the newspapers in which they appear are delivered to only 18,000 doorsteps a day. If all politics is local, all authority is as well, a point illustrated by Ruby E.:

As a Christian and a taxpayer I want to urge every parent, grandparent, and patriot of this country to write their congressmen and senators to kill the federal aid bill to schools and for teacher pay. Our freedom is surely slipping away and America is asleep at the switch. It would be too late to cry after the lambs and sheep have been stolen. Wake up America! Throw away your sleeping pills. Investigate!

(*Wichita Falls Times-Record-News*, February 11, 1960)

No think-tank studies are cited by Ruby E., no detailed examples provided. She seems to assume that her taxpaying and church-going are credentials enough and that the urgency of her voice connotes sufficient expertise. Ruby E. trades here on what psychologists call "funded experience." By declaring herself an American who cares about things, she opts for a certain walking-around authority. Although considerably younger than Benjamin Franklin, she also embodies the sort of education he once endorsed: "The Boys should be put on Writing Letters to each other on any common Occurrences ... In these they should be taught to express themselves clearly, concisely, and naturally, without affected Words, or high-flown Phrases."[42]

Letters-to-the-editor columns are said to be a "community's heartbeat," a "town meeting," "the loafer's bench on the courthouse square."[43] These designations result from the letters' oral style, a style that makes them "readerly" – colloquial, disclosive, transactional. That same style can make them sound proselytic, a blend of moral teachings, praise of the faithful, warnings of deceivers, narratives of consolation, and even prophecy.[44] Such letters draw on *lived authority*, a sensibility the *New York Times* once attributed to their

> multitude of views and moods. They abound in curious information. They consti-
> tute a debating society that never adjourns, in which everything knowable is
> discovered. A sodality of voluntary correspondents, approving, wrathful, critical,
> philosophical, humorous, full of admonition, reproof, instruction, miscellaneous
> knowledge has succeeded the long-winded Publicolas and Catos of our long-
> suffering ancestors.[45]

These same qualities, however, keep letters out of most canonical collections. Their sheer plentitude predicts that fate, as does the fact that they are written by unimportant authors addressing transitory matters. Why, then, are they read so heavily? Because creators of ephemera are often seen as "culturally courageous," says Professor Susan Miller of the University of Utah. They have given up their privacy because an issue is important to them.[46] The downside is that, once published, their letters cannot be retracted, thereby exposing them to potential ridicule. That is an unacceptable price to pay for most privacy-loving Americans, so letter writers get a certain grudging respect from readers in return. Because these missives operate at the intersection of the "everyday" and the "mediated," the newspapers in which they are published confer a bit of status on them as well.[47]

Letters also derive authority by being pitched to members of the local community. The use of direct address ("Head to the polls tomorrow!!") shows that an author has gone out of the way to confront a pressing problem. Because writers often juxtapose themselves against some peril-ous condition or practice, they can be seen as daring, intrepid. They can also be seen as blowhards, but scholarly research shows that people pay attention to those who know more and who care more about politics *even when disagreeing with them.*[48] In short, the sheer existence of the letters column says: (1) the people are watchful; (2) elites should not get too comfortable; and (3) democracy survives. All of these qualities give letters to the editor at least a bit of gravitas.

Idealism

Most citizens absorb political information one shard at a time. An item appears on their radar screens, they evaluate it, and then they dispatch with it without doing a lot of theorizing. But because the world of politics is so filled with hypotheticals – "how should we react to a more muscular North Korea?" "How can we deal with a new pandemic?" – theorizing is almost always required. As a result, normal people, grounded people, often tune politics out.

Letter writers live in an airier place. They are constantly in touch with abstract values and use them to process new data. Their letters bear the scars of pomposity as a result, or, to put it more positively, their letters can be seen as "principled." Bob E. of Roanoke, Virginia illustrates:

I once thought of Sen. John McCain as a sensible political moderate. His choice of Sarah Palin as his running mate dispelled that notion from my mind. Whatever he once was McCain has become a pawn of the *reactionary right*. He apparently has decided that in order to get elected he must fall on his knees to *corporate America* and those who believe that Americans should be compelled to live their private lives according to the beliefs of the religious right. I'm sorry, but I'm not going to take lectures or orders from *someone else's church pulpit*. Furthermore, McCain has forgotten or never learned what he should have about war during his ordeal at the Hanoi Hilton. What I *learned as a volunteer* in Vietnam is that we have the *finest military men and women* in the world and that they shouldn't be sent to sacrifice and die for the vanity of politicians or the greed of corporations. Iraq is only about oil and McCain knows that. *Experience* is of no value if what you learn from it is wrong. I'm voting for Sen. Barack Obama.

(*Roanoke Times*, September 11, 2008)

Although Bob E.'s letter is a straightforward comment on the 2008 presidential campaign, it also explains who he is without providing much biographical information. The phrases I have italicized reveal the scaffold of his values, the end-states that inform his beliefs and that warrant his arguments. By merging what Harvard's Michael Sandel calls "soulcraft" with "statecraft," Bob E. stretches further than the average citizen.[49] He knows where he is going; he has been there before.

One must avoid being too lyrical when describing letters to the editor. Many of them are poorly written and overly obvious. Although some commentators have described such letters as "bulletins on the temper of civilization,"[50] they can also be tedious. At the same time, though, they can expose a rich vein of public opinion too often missed by polling. Survey data, says communication scholar Stephen Coleman, can turn the public into a "bloodless aggregation," thereby missing its deeper sensibilities.[51] In contrast, because letter writers "live in and for the forum,"[52] they lay out the premises undergirding their conclusions and, in doing so, display their authors' deep-seated values.

Because such letters are meant for a popular audience, they can also shed light on a community's most basic beliefs. Letter writers appeal to those beliefs when fashioning their remarks, thereby exposing the nation's ideals. So we must ask: What are these ideals, these taken-for-granteds? Have they changed over time? Have the issues of the day worn them out or have they remained firm? These are complex questions but the ordinary philosophers who write letters to the editor hint at answers to them each day. It takes hermeneutic work to understand what the writers are saying but they are hardly foreigners. They live among us; they observe and react; they tell what they see; they judge. To my way of thinking, they have been ignored far too long.

CONCLUSION

Democracies churn. That is their nature. This book asks how one group of people – those who write letters to the editor – has reacted to the fragmentation, polarization, and distrust surrounding it. A number of options have been available to them – fear, lethargy, bystanding – but they have chosen to stand and fight. These writers are hardly omniscient but their willingness to discuss the affairs of the day has kept American democracy alive. They are, I believe, the nation's secret weapon.

This book will proceed as follows. Chapter 2 will lay out the challenge of maintaining an enlightened and engaged citizenry in the postmodern era, while Chapter 3 will detail the components and assessment of civic hope. Chapters 4 and 5 will report the results of several surveys inquiring into who writes letters, who reads them, and what newspaper personnel think of both. Chapter 5 describes the 12 mid-sized cities from which my data have been gathered, cities ranging from east (Fall River, MA; Trenton, NJ; and Utica, NY) to west (Provo, UT; Billings, MT; and Salinas, CA), and from north (Duluth, MN; St. Joseph, MO; and Springfield, OH) to south (Lake Charles, LA; Roanoke, VA; and Wichita Falls, TX). There is nothing special about these cities, which is why I chose them.

Chapters 6 and 7 are reciprocals, the former describing what readers enjoy about letters to the editor and the latter showing why they sometimes find them irritating. How civic hope has changed over time is described in Chapter 8, while Chapter 9 shows how writers have adapted to the issues of the day, the partisan environment, regional expectations, and the peculiarities of the election season. Chapter 10 asks if civic hope has a future. I believe that it does.

This book will touch on expected topics – political elections, the mass media, and civic engagement – but also the history of letter-writing, the psychology of hope, citizen journalism, studies of authorship, and theories of melancholy. My hope is that the writers' voices – rich voices, real voices, familiar voices, strange voices, impassioned voices – will offer an attractive alternative to today's political cynicism. My root assumption is that despite the febrile attractions of cable news ranting, online incivility, late-night savagery, and indecorous campaign debates, no democracy can sustain itself with defeatism as its only attendant. The good people who petition their fellow citizens in letters columns opt each day for something more salvific. My hope is to make their hope contagious.

In some ways, the inventory of values I will conduct here is similar to that conducted by Alexis de Tocqueville in the mid-1800s. Then, Tocqueville traveled widely among the American people, visiting their dram shops and hostelries and reporting on the peculiar temperaments of the people he met. The colonists, Tocqueville decided, were sane and decent but, mostly, they were voluble. They spoke their citizenship and did so brazenly. They hated wordiness, Tocqueville reports, but they hated minced wordiness even more.

And today? Does a civic temperament remain? Are we still Tocqueville's colonists? Do Americans still believe they have influence or is governance a chimera for them? Have they retained a sense of neighborhood or have the skepticisms of the age made marginals out of even the centrists among them? These are important questions and I will try to answer them by using Tocqueville's method: listening to what people say. Out of such ordinary stuff, I believe, much can be made.

Endnotes

1 For these and other observations on the 2016 campaign see Dylan Byers, "How politicians, pollsters and media missed Trump's groundswell," *CNN Media*, November 9, 2016. Accessed at http://money.cnn.com/2016/11/09/media/polling-media-missed-trump.

2 Sarah Brown, "A scholar of racial equity describes his 'painful gratitude' for Donald Trump," *Chronicle of Higher Education*, January, 20, 2017, p. A22.

3 E. J. Dionne, Jr., "The good that could come from a Trump presidency," *Washington Post*, December 28, 2016. Accessed at www.washingtonpost.com/opinions/the-good-that-could-come-from-a-trump-presidency/2016/12/28/63f5c82e-cdoe-11e6-a87f-b917067331bb_story.html?utm_term=.e08b97dff23e.

4 "It is Donald Trump's Washington now – what's next?" *Denver Post*, November 9, 2016. Accessed at www.denverpost.com/2016/11/09/how-donald-trump-won-and-why-the-media-missed-it/.

5 H. L. Mencken, "The cult of hope" in *Prejudices: Second Series* (New York: Alfred A. Knopf, 1920), p. 213.

6 These remarks are extracted from a series of interviews conducted with fifty individuals who wrote letters to the editor in the twelve cities profiled in this

book. Transcripts of the interviews (conducted between 2013 and 2016) can be obtained from the author upon request.

7 Jeremy W. Peters, "Gloomy Republican campaigns leave behind Reagan cheer," *New York Times*, September 12, 2015. Accessed at www.nytimes .com/2015/09/13/us/politics/gloomy-republican-campaigns-leave-behind-reagan-cheer.html.

8 These data have been normalized for comparative purposes. Values on the y-axis are based on a mean of 0 and a standard deviation of 1, so the figures indicate considerable dispersion from low to high. The occurrences of *Hope* in books were calculated from https://books.google.com/ngrams and those for political speeches from http://moody.utexas.edu/strauss/campaign-mapping-project.

9 Stephen Burn (ed.), *Conversations with David Foster Wallace* (Jackson: University Press of Mississippi, 2012), pp. 48–9.

10 Benedict Anderson, *Imagined Communities: Reflections on the Origin and Spread of Nationalism*, rev. edn. (London: Verso, 1991), p. 6.

11 Ibid, p. 144.

12 Daniel B. Klein, "The people's romance: why people love government (as much as they do)," *The Independent Review*, 10 (2005), 32.

13 Louis Althusser, *Politics and History: Montesquieu, Rousseau, Hegel and Marx* (London: NLB Press, 1972), p. 62.

14 Doug Mataconis, "38% of congressmen represent 'safe' districts," *Outside the Beltway*, October 7, 2013: 7. Accessed at www.outsidethebeltway.com/38-of-congressmen-represent-safe-districts/.

15 Pew Research Center, "Political polarization in the American public: how increasing ideological uniformity and partisan antipathy affect politics, compromise and everyday life," June 12, 2014. Accessed at www.people-press .org/2014/06/12/political-polarization-in-the-american-public/.

16 Amy Mitchell, Jeffrey Gottfried, Jocelyn Kiley, and Katerina Eva Matsa, *Political Polarization and Media Habits*. Pew Research Center, October 21, 2014. Accessed at www.journalism.org/2014/10/21/political-polarization-media-habits/.

17 See April K. Clark, "Rethinking the decline in social capital," *American Politics Research*, 43(4) (2015), 569–601; Margaret Levi and Laura Stoker, "Political trust and trustworthiness," *Annual Review of Political Science*, 3 (2000), 475–507; Samantha Luks, "Stability of citizenship values over time and the life cycle." Paper presented at the annual meeting of the Midwest Political Science Association, San Francisco, April 1996; Sofie Marien, Marc Hooghe, and Jenifer Oser, "Great expectations: the effect of democratic ideals and evaluations on political trust: a comparative investigation of the 2012 European Social Survey." Paper presented at the annual meeting of the Midwest Political Science Association, Chicago, April 2015; Miwa Nakajo, "The role of civic engagement in local political trust." Paper presented at the annual meeting of the Midwest Political Science Association, Chicago, April 2015; and Paul Taylor, *The Next America: Boomers, Millennials, and the Looming Generational Showdown* (New York: Public Affairs, 2014).

18 Jean M. Twenge, W. Keith Campbell, and Nathan T. Carter, "Decline in trust in others and confidence in institutions among American adults and late adolescents, 1972–2012," *Psychological Science*, 25(10) (2014), 1914–1923.

19 Eri Bertsou, "Disentangling political distrust: what do citizens *mean* and *think* when expressing distrust towards political institutions and politicians?" Paper presented at the annual meeting of the Midwest Political Science Association, Chicago, April 2014.

20 John R. Hibbing and Elizabeth Theiss-Morse, *Congress as Public Enemy: Public Attitudes toward American Political Institutions* (Cambridge: Cambridge University Press, 1995).

21 Kate Krontiris, John Webb, Charlotte Krontiris, and Chris Chapman, "Understanding America's 'interested bystander': a complicated relationship with civic duty," p. 14. Accessed at http://googlepolitics.blogspot.com/2015/06/understanding-americas-interested.html.

22 Ibid, p. 25.

23 Karin Wahl-Jorgensen, "Coping with the meaninglessness of politics: citizen-speak in the 2001 British general elections." Paper presented at the annual meeting of the International Communication Association, Seoul, South Korea, July 2002, p. 8.

24 Geoff Mulgan, *Politics in an Antipolitical Age* (Cambridge: Polity Press, 1994), p. 27.

25 Max Kaase, Kenneth Newton, and Elinor Scarbrough, "A look at the beliefs in government study," *Political Science & Politics*, 29 (1996), 226.

26 Alan I. Abramowitz and Morris P. Fiorina. "Polarized or sorted? Just what's wrong with our politics anyway?" *The American Interest* (2013). Accessed at www.the-american-interest.com/2013/03/11/polarized-or-sorted-just-whats-wrong-with-our-politics-anyway/.

27 Among the better studies in this genre are those by Richard Davis, *Politics Online: Blogs, Chatrooms, and Discussion Groups in American Democracy* (New York: Routledge, 2005) and Joseph Reagle, *Reading the Comments: Likers, Haters and Manipulators at the Bottom of the Web* (Cambridge: MIT Press, 2015).

28 See Julie Lindquist, *A Place to Stand: Politics and Persuasion in a Working-Class Bar* (New York: Oxford University Press, 2002) and Katherine Cramer Walsh, *Talking about Politics: Informal Groups and Social Identity in American Life* (Chicago: University of Chicago Press, 2004).

29 See, for example, Hibbing and Theiss-Morse, *Congress as Public Enemy*.

30 Among the best studies examining the politics of everyday life are: Frank M. Bryan, *Real Democracy: The New England Town Meeting and How It Works* (Chicago: University of Chicago Press, 2004); Stephen Coleman, *How Voters Feel* (New York: Cambridge University Press, 2013); Greg Dickinson, *Suburban Dreams: Imaging and Building the Good Life* (Tuscaloosa: University of Alabama Press, 2015); Christopher F. Karpowitz and Tali Mendelberg, *The Silent Sex: Gender, Deliberation, and Institutions* (Princeton: Princeton University Press, 2014); Casey Klofstad, *Civic Talk: Peers, Politics, and the Future of Democracy* (Philadelphia: Temple University Press, 2011); Andrew J. Perrin, *American Democracy: From Tocqueville to Town Halls to Twitter*

(London: Polity Press, 2014); Karen Tracy, *Challenges of Ordinary Democracy: A Case Study in Deliberation and Dissent* (University Park: Penn State University Press, 2010); and Katherine Cramer, *The Politics of Resentment: Rural Consciousness in Wisconsin and the Rise of Scott Walker* (Chicago: University of Chicago Press, 2016). Two additional studies of note have looked at letters sent to public officials by citizens. These include Taeku Lee, *Mobilizing Public Opinion: Black Insurgency and Racial Attitudes in the Civil Rights Era* (Chicago: University of Chicago Press, 2002) and George I. Lovell, *This Is Not Civil Rights: Discovering Rights Talk in 1939 America*, (Chicago: University of Chicago Press, 2012).

31 Janet Maybin, "Death row penfriends" in David Barton and Nigel Hall (eds.), *Letter Writing as a Social Practice* (Philadelphia: John Benjamins, 1999), p. 163.

32 Jean Burgess, "Hearing ordinary voices: cultural studies, vernacular creativity and digital storytelling," *Continuum: Journal of Media & Culture Studies*, 20 (2006), 211–12.

33 Simon Garfield, *To the Letter: A Celebration of the Lost Art of Letter Writing* (New York: Gotham, 2013) 19.

34 Lee, *Mobilizing Public Opinion*, p. 81. For a rich, theoretical treatment of the dangers associated with excessive reliance on polling see Susan Herbst, *Reading Public Opinion: How Political Actors View the Democratic Process* (Chicago: University of Chicago Press, 1998).

35 Lee, *Mobilizing Public Opinion*, p. 104.

36 David Thelen, *Becoming Citizens in the Age of Television: How Americans Challenged the Media and Seized Political Initiative during the Iran-Contra Debate* (Chicago: University of Chicago Press, 1996), p. 172.

37 Ibid, p. 171.

38 Gilbert Cranberg, "Genuine letters help democratize our debate: letters give a window into how regular folks see the events of the day," *The Masthead*, September 2004.

39 Esther Milne, *Letters, Postcards, Email Technologies of Presence* (New York: Routledge, 2010), p. 58.

40 See, for example, Ron Dzwonkowski, "It's a cheap form of propaganda: now they are offering prizes to people who trick newspapers into publishing fake letters," *The Masthead* (56), September 22, 2004. Accessed at www.highbeam.com/doc/1G1-123078809.html; Dan Radmacher, "A look at the perpetrators: the list of interest groups encouraging 'astroturf' is as long as the list of interest groups," *The Masthead* (56), September 22, 2004. Accessed at www.thefreelibrary.com/A+look+at+the+perpetrators%3A+the+list+of+interest+groups+encouraging...-a0123078810; Bill Reader, "Who's really writing those 'canned' letters to the editor?" *Newspaper Research Journal*, 26 (2005), 43–56; and Jim Frisinger and Luanne Traud, "An e-mail conversation: how to deal with letter-planters; let's try the town square rule for determining legitimate letters," *The Masthead* (2004), September 22, 2004. Accessed at www.highbeam.com/doc/1G1-123078816.html.

41 Ralph Waldo Emerson, "Second centennial of concord" in J. E. Cabot (ed.), *Emerson's Complete Works: Miscellanies* (Boston: Houghton Mifflin, 1883), p. 43.

42 As quoted in Lucille M. Schultz, "Letter-writing instruction in 19th century schools in the United States" in David Barton and Nigel Hall (eds.), *Letter Writing as a Social Practice* (Philadelphia: John Benjamins, 1999), p. 109.

43 As quoted in Karin Wahl-Jorgensen, "Letters to the editor," *Peace Review*, 11 (1999), 56.

44 For additional such analyses see Charles Bazerman, "Letters and the social grounding of genres" in David Barton and Nigel Hall (eds.), *Letter Writing as a Social Practice* (Philadelphia: John Benjamins, 1999), pp. 18–19.

45 As quoted in Ralph Nader and Steven Gold, "Letters to the editor: how about a little down-home glasnost?" *Columbia Journalism Review*, 27 (1988), 53–4.

46 Susan Miller, *Assuming the Positions: Cultural Pedagogy and the Politics of Commonplace Writing* (Pittsburgh: University of Pittsburgh Press, 1998), p. 48.

47 See John E. Richardson, "'Now is the time to put an end to all this': argumentative discourse theory and 'letters to the editor,'" *Discourse & Society*, 12 (2001), 148.

48 T. K. Ahn, Robert Huckfeldt, Alexander K. Mayer, and John Barry Ryan, "Expertise and bias in political communication networks," *American Journal of Political Science*, 57(2) (2013), 370.

49 Michael J. Sandel, "America's search for a new public philosophy," *The Atlantic Monthly*, March (1996), 70.

50 K. Gregory as quoted in Michael Bromley, "'Watching the watchdogs'? The role of readers' letters in calling the press to account" in Hugh Stephenson and Michael Bromley (eds.), *Sex, Lies and Democracy: The Press and the Public* (London: Routledge, 1998), p. 150.

51 Stephen Coleman, "Beyond the po-faced public sphere" in Stephen Coleman, Giles Moss, Katy Parry, John Halperin, and Michael Ryan (eds.), *Can the Media Serve Democracy? Essays in Honor of Jay G. Blumler* (London: Palgrave, 2015), pp. 185, 186.

52 This is Judith Shklar's description of the *vox populi*. See *American Citizenship: The Quest for Inclusion* (Cambridge: Harvard University Press, 1991), p. 11.

2

Can Citizenship Be Revived?

Some years ago, Jerry Stropnicky and several other members of the Bloomsburg (PA) Theatre Ensemble combed through two hundred years of letters to the editors published in that community's newspapers. Then they did a curious thing: They performed the letters out loud to audiences far and near, replete with staging, lighting, and costuming – an enterprise underwritten by several arts endowments. Their performance included such segments as "Kids and Dogs," "Marriage," "The President," "Out of Towners," "Human Nature," "Progress," and "Standards of Behavior." By carefully selecting the letters to be performed, Mr. Stropnicky and his colleagues reasoned, they could shed light on Bloomsburg's most basic values. "Again and again," the Ensemble concluded, "we found citizens speaking freely and from their hearts, recording a personal yet public diary of our community."[1] The Ensemble also noted that "implied in every word these authors wrote to their local newspapers is the hope that things can get better. That hope defines America."[2]

Did Stropnicky and co. get things right here? Were the letter writers they studied paragons or egotistical bores? More generally, how many Americans today are real citizens and how many just residents? And what does it mean to call someone a "real citizen"? Is that a factual designation? A legal designation? A social designation? Or is it merely an honorific, along the lines of the sort of thing Harry Truman said when leaving the White House: "I'm not leaving the highest office of the land. I'm assuming the highest office, that of citizen"? If some Americans are real citizens and some cosmetic citizens, how can one tell the difference? Is it a difference worth noting?

This chapter looks at letter writers through the lens of citizenship. Judging from the presidential election of 2016, using that lens has never been more important – or more popular. Donald Trump and Jeb Bush squared off over citizenship during the primaries, an old refrain for Mr. Trump, who had polished his nativist skills by hounding Barack Obama about his parentage four years earlier. Marco Rubio and Ted Cruz also went toe-to-toe. Their skirmish was confusing, though, since the Miami-born Rubio took a somewhat progressive stance toward citizenship while the Canadian-born Cruz joined Trump's hunt for illegals. Establishment Republicans such as John Kasich eschewed the immigrant-baiting altogether, as did South Carolina governor Nikki Haley. That distinguished her from former governor of Louisiana Bobby Jindal, who, like Haley, was a minority group member, but who, unlike Haley, salivated at the thought of shutting down the southern border.

Thoughts about citizenship have ebbed and flowed throughout the nation's history. "Citizenship" has been spoken of provisionally and reverentially, has been used as a shibboleth and a bludgeon. Michael Walzer finds within the concept a basic binary: Citizenship is a duty; citizenship is a right. Says Walzer: "The first describes citizenship as an office, a responsibility, a burden proudly assumed; the second describes citizenship as a status, an entitlement, a right or set of rights passively enjoyed."[3] Walzer's is no mere academic distinction, for within these two understandings lie entirely different worldviews. Here, for example, is what people's arguments look like when citizenship is treated as a right:

[We can] ensure a fair election by requiring some type of proof of citizenship before voting. I find it absurd that you have to show an ID to put money in your own bank account but not for voting which is a privilege of the American citizen.
(Buck C., *Wichita Falls Times-Record-News*, August 26, 2012)

* * * * *

[Barack Hussein Obama's] middle name alone strikes terror into the hearts and minds of the Tea Party, Rush Limbaugh, Glenn Beck, and many Republicans. Vile invectives pour from their lips. I even had an acquaintance tell me that he simply could not vote for a man with such a name.
(Peter B., *Utica Observer-Dispatch*, September 18, 2012)

Citizenship-as-a-right produces a muscular discourse, one that comes and goes but never goes forever. Day-to-day politics perpetuates this cycle but so too does Hollywood's love of the immigrant story: *Scarface* in 1983; *The Promise* in 1996; *Gangs of New York* in 2002; *Crossing Over* in 2009. Hollywood makes other movies that lionize citizenship-as-duty. *Mr. Smith Goes to Washington* gave that story special poignancy in 1939, a story that was retold ironically by *Dave* in 1993, cynically by *Bob Roberts* in 1992, and hilariously by *Idiocracy* in 2006. Political scientist Robert Lane notes that citizenship contains an inherent existential tension, a reminder that politics is not free. Acting like a citizen always costs somebody something:

The pains of democratic processes are mostly inherent in democracy: pains of internal distress and external conflict arising when fundamental social values are referred to democratic governments; pains incurred when one finds one's government is an opponent; pains experienced when governments protect unpopular causes and enforce the rights of people one loathes; and, finally, the moderate, unconscious distress occasioned when democracies enforce ethical codes running counter to our inherited biograms."[4]

Despite these challenges, some people – Sam F. of Utica, New York, for example – persevere:

By what right do "two-thirds of so-called Americans" have the right to avoid a good citizens "'duty" to be active and responsible, to support America vitally? ... To dodge ones' responsive citizenship duties is to condemn liberty, equal justice under the law, and to cause democracy to work for the few, the greedy. "Passing the buck" is a cheap shot, "cowardly" in the refusal to accept the duties of citizenship. Like it or not politics is everybody's business.

(*Utica Observer-Dispatch*, October 26, 1996)

Sam F. speaks liturgically here, but what does it take to be the sort of citizen he envisions? What attitudes, what behaviors, what sensitivities? Why risk personal exposure and potential censure by engaging others on this topic? If Robert Lane is correct, writing a letter to the editor involves political pain. What sort of pain is political pain? Where does one hurt when feeling it? Writing a letter requires people to ask themselves why they believe this and not that, which values are precious to them and which others are not. Writing a letter to the editor: What sort of citizenship is that?

THE REWARDS OF CITIZENSHIP

Several years ago, Bryan Turner called attention to something that often slips by us. Citizenship, said Turner, is a modern idea that disrupts both family and tribe in service of something vaguer – The Public. Citizenship criticizes "particularistic and private commitments," says Turner, demanding that people manage "assets in a fashion which is disinterested and accountable" even though they must abandon their privacy to do so.[5] Soon enough, The Public turns into The State, an even more unnatural thing. It is thus a miracle, says Sidney Verba, that people put up with politics at all. So why do they? For largely intangible reasons: They feel patriotic; certain issues are important to them; they reap the esteem of others; it feels good.[6] Active citizens get no filthy lucre but they do get a sense of self.

Identity

The good citizen, says social scientist Michael Schudson, has been defined in various ways over time. Depending on the era, good citizens have been said to vote regularly, trust in government, resist alien values, care for minorities and the poor, confront rank injustice, or participate in public dialogue.[7] This is too much work for most Americans, so they tell their elected leaders this: "I have little interest in political matters; consider this disinterest as license for you to move freely about your business of governing, subject to certain minimal controls."[8] This ceding of rights and responsibilities may seem censorious but it also makes sense. We are all by nature ineluctably alone, says poet Emily Dickinson – individuals from our beginnings to our endings. Because that is so, she once admonished a friend who had sent her a joint missive to "send no union letters." "The soul must go by Death alone," writes Dickinson, "so it must by life if it is a soul."[9] Group letters – emblems of the nation-state, not of poetry.

Political identity is a fabrication, a coarse and common thing that projects outward from the individual. When talking politics, one becomes a new person to oneself, especially when making politics a habit. Political identity tempts people out of their aloneness, inspiring them to preach:

Americans have the right to vote for whom they choose to represent them in our representative form of government. They also have the duty, a responsibility, to use their right to vote and to familiarize themselves with the candidates and the issues up for decision on Election Day.
(Albert D., *Lake Charles American Press*, November 2, 2008).

* * * * *

Should George Bush have read *The Times* on Oct. 24 and browsed the letters to the editor the message should have been clear and concise: Read our words George ... take a hike. As voters it is our duty to see to it that his journey out of Washington commences Tuesday.
(Gary G., *Trenton Times*, October 31, 1992).

Several duties are alluded to here – moral duties, intellectual duties, partisan duties, occupational duties – and the writers do not equivocate. Occasionally, an individual will send the same political recommendation during each election cycle. His or her very being requires it. At other times, writers will be leisurely and exploratory until, suddenly, they make a mad dash to the quotidian – "Trust me. This bond election stinks." If letter writers are philosophers, they are philosophers in a hurry.

Community

Literary scholar Michael Warner observes that those who organized the American revolution were "men of letters" who had risen to positions of influence in their respective colonies via the spoken word. But it was print discourse, Warner says, that "made it possible to imagine a people that could act as a people and in distinction from the state."[10] Warner says that the *published word* became a "political condition of utterance."[11] "The Constitution's printedness," Warner adds, "allows it to emanate from no one in particular, and thus from the people."[12] Similarly, the very existence of the letters column signals that there is "a people." It reminds us that we do not live alone.

Philosopher Paul Ricoeur has observed that "man cannot evade politics under penalty of evading his humanity. Throughout history, and by means of politics, man is faced with *his* grandeur and *his* culpability."[13] This is not how people in Billings, Montana talk, but the letter writers there would get Ricoeur's point: They must oversee their communities. That is a presumptuous thought but so be it. Their letters are typically uncomplicated, as if their motivations were beyond question:

Let us before we vote this Fall make sure that we have an intelligent understanding concerning the character of the different candidates and the issues involved. Our Johnson and Mr. Goldwater are both good Americans and it is my belief that each one in his own way and with his own belief have the best interests of the people at heart. You vote according to your belief and I will do the same and no matter which one is elected let us shake hands and join together as good Americans should work together to build "The Great Society" of which President Johnson so often speaks.

(Clyde W., *Springfield News-Sun*, September 25, 1964) .

A committed postmodernist such as comedian Bill Maher would find Mr. Whalen's style banal. That is because the rhetoric of community struggles mightily against the rhetoric of individualism. Critic Toby Miller explains that "the modern city provided the first comparatively open site for people to meet promiscuously,"[14] but those meetings instantly became complicated because of rugged individualism. TV ads hawking pickup trucks still contain semiotic references to macho independence, references that Alexis De Tocqueville noted three centuries ago. "The first language of liberty [was spoken] by men," said Tocqueville, and it almost always trumped the country's second language, the language of community, a language "spoken by women."[15]

Perhaps because it is a second language, the rhetoric of community is thick with nostalgia, making many letters to the editor seem quaint. But nostalgia should not be dismissed as an "evil or a false instinct," says Robert Fowler,[16] because it serves broadly therapeutic functions during crises, as it did in the United States after 9/11 and in France after the *Charlie Hebdo* shootings. But community-for-the-sake-of-community has its limits. Communitarians are too ready, says Fowler, to abandon formal structures and duly elected authorities in behalf of a mystical coming-together. Fowler argues that communitarianism too often produces "a practice that 'quietens and calms'" and that "leads away from the conflicts inherent in politics."[17] Contrastingly, says David Matthews, "when citizens rename problems and frame issues in their own terms" (as they do when writing letters), "they increase their power" even as they turn community into a political force.[18]

Passion

People write letters to the editor because of identity issues ("I *am* civil rights," "I *am* the NRA") and because of the call to community ("I am my brother's keeper"), but mostly because they have no other choice. They must talk and they must be heard. That is what the vernacular provides – a naturally produced, locally intelligible, demonstrative mode of speech.[19] For this reason, letters columns are usually lightly edited, as editors try to keep argument and arguer conjoined, and reason and emotion conjoined as well. But, given the unpredictability of emotions, "it is hard to fault people for keeping their political opinions hidden from the views of others."[20] Letter writers, people incapable of hiding, are clearly an exception to the rule.

Political scientist George Marcus has thought a great deal about this matter of political emotion. "Rather than being antagonistic or detrimental to citizenship," he and Michael MacKuen report, "emotion enhances the ability of voters to perform their citizenly duties."[21] Marcus and MacKuen find that heightened emotion – even when generated by attack ads on television – spurs information processing and can increase voter turnout as well. Anxious people pay more attention to the platforms of their opponents, Marcus finds, and make better decisions than when they are tranquil.[22] "Democratic politics cannot be solely a space of calm deliberation," Marcus concludes; "it must also be a sensational place, one that attracts and engages spectators".[23]

In these terms, the letters column becomes both a purgational and a problem-solving outlet. In the language of David Hume, it is a place where reason is enslaved by desire. But this talk of passion makes many Americans nervous. Most people "have no deep commitment to a creed or party and only about half of them bother to vote," says Michael Walzer. "Beyond that, they are wrapped up in their private affairs and committed to the orderliness and proprieties of the private realm."[24] Walzer goes on to say that "this makes life hard for the smaller number of citizens who are intermittently moved by some public issue and who seek to move their fellows. It may help explain the frenetic quality of their zeal."[25]

Sandi S. would object to being called frenetic but she might be comfortable with the charge of zealotry. Rather suddenly, politics had become personal for her:

Recently I walked into the Carilion E.R. with my 72-year-old mother bent over in excruciating pain with a kidney stone. We were told we would be seen as soon as possible. Not only was the triage so cursory as to be insulting it was clear that the nurse was simply not interested in patient care. We waited in that uncomfortable waiting room for more than five hours before they had a bed. The irony of a hospital with no beds abounds but that was the excuse we were given.

I was shocked and appalled at such a second-rate facility at the largest hospital in this area but how do you avoid it in such an emergency? For people who believe Obamacare will make the medical care in this nation worse I can only ask: How? Would we then wait eight hours? Not be seen at all? Have less than one doctor for eight beds? I am angry and I am well aware that my mom is not the first to suffer but don't even try to tell me we have world-class health care now. We simply don't.

(*Roanoke Times*, August 10, 2012)

Sandi S. was neither a community activist nor a member of the city council, but she was her mother's daughter, and so she wrote a letter. Her mother's illness tapped into her political identity and stirred her. But she also felt the need to warn others, to make them rethink the new healthcare system. So she became what George Marcus terms a "sentimental citizen," a call too loud for her to resist.[26]

THE PATHWAYS TO CITIZENSHIP

Sandi S.'s case is an obvious one. A beloved family member was at risk and the local medical staff had let her down, so she wrote a letter to the editor. A number of other options were available to her: showing up at the next meeting of the local medical board, starting a protest group, lobbying a member of Congress, besieging the Koch Brothers for help, using social media to get the hospital director fired, or becoming a lonely picketer. In selecting the "literary" route, she chose but one way of entering the public sphere.

What predicts who will become politically engaged? Chapter 4 describes the dispositions of the letter writers I studied, but what do we know about people in general? Researchers do not yet have all the answers, but some have examined what psychologists call "the Big Five" personality traits to find out. Peter Dinesen and his colleagues in Denmark, for example, ran subjects through a battery of tests to see which personality markers correlated with citizenship norms. Among other things, they found that people high on the "neuroticism" scale – those with an "anxious and uneasy nature" and very little political trust – were especially inclined to "keep watch on the actions of public authorities."[27]

Other researchers have looked at a wider array of predictors. Aaron Weinschenk of the University of Wisconsin-Green Bay, for example, observes that some people simply have a greater "sense of civic duty" than others. These individuals are usually older, better educated, more religious, and more highly compensated than those who eschew political activity.[28] People with a high sense of civic duty— a description that surely includes letter writers – have a special need to stay informed about public affairs. Sidney Verba and Norman Nie report that there now exists in the United States a wide variety of "lay specialists": community volunteers, partisan fieldworkers, NGO activists, letter writers, and many more. Ironically, say Verba and Nie, these individuals are often drawn from the upper middle class, leading to an unusual paradox: "those who may need governmental assistance the least participate the most."[29]

Other studies of engagement focus on political communication. Michael Neblo of Ohio State University reports that people's "willingness to deliberate is much higher than research in political behavior might suggest."[30] It is not the case, says Neblo and his colleagues, that Americans are universally alienated from public life. If asked to take part in public deliberations, they often accept willingly. Then why don't more of them participate? For a variety of reasons: they hate conflict; they are uninformed; they feel that political problems are insoluble; and, importantly, nobody has invited them to do so. Sean Gray adds to this list by noting that many citizens report being too busy, some are already satisfied with the status quo, and others have had unhappy prior experiences with government agencies.[31] But the most important points to note are that (1) "silent citizenship" is not one thing but many things, and (2) silence holds as much promise for the polity as it does peril.

And then there is Ronald W. of St. Joseph, Missouri, who worries a good deal. He is also an icon for the sort of civic participation that Professors Dinesen, Weinschenk, Verba, Nie, Neblo, and Gray champion. Ronald W. is a treble participant – involved in his local precinct, concerned about political absenteeism, and willing to upbraid his fellow citizens for their misdeeds. He also writes letters to the editor:

Tuesday night, I decided to attend my Democratic caucus ward mass meeting to become more involved at the grassroots level of our political system. At these ward meetings, any registered Democrat may express his or her opinion in regard to preference for Democratic presidential candidates and vote for delegates in the county convention.

I know how many citizens attended the Third Ward caucus. If you can believe it, only three persons were present – the committeewoman and two registered voters. I would like to say that if the citizens of this country do not take a more active role in selecting the people they choose to lead them, we are in a sad state of affairs.

(*St. Joseph News-Press*, April 24, 1980)

People like this live in the world of "ordinary democracy," a sphere located somewhere between public deliberation (with all its formalities) and everyday talk (with its social conventions and taboos).[32] Like a moth to a flame, they are drawn to problems and cannot let them go – for psychological reasons, for political reasons, for unknown reasons. Scholars who study town meetings find that the most active participants possess a kind of insulation that lets them admonish others without fear of retribution, which is perhaps why such meetings sometimes become quite testy.[33] Contrary to popular stereotypes, though, meeting activists are not too different from their neighbors.[34] Also contrary to popular stereotypes, they offer up facts (sometimes even statistics) when making arguments, they appeal to broad moral principles, they tell interesting personal vignettes, and they generally avoid making off-topic or threatening comments. They also respect conversational norms during discussion and largely eschew extremism.[35] In short, those who study *typical* town meetings find them to be far more benign than the ugly affairs that attract eyeballs on the nightly news.

Not all Americans are well-behaved, of course, and they become the objects of gossip and part of the nation's folklore (e.g., Mel Gibson's crazed character in the movie *Conspiracy Theory*). Although he notes that town meetings still have their problems (too many people playing to the crowd, too many not listening, too many expressing biases related to gender and class), Christopher Karpowitz of Brigham Young University concludes from his extensive research that "public meetings are vulnerable to the same inequalities of voice that typify other forms of political participation, but the worst fears of critics are probably overstated."[36] Diana Carlin and her colleagues agree. When comparing online to face-to-face discussions, they found the latter proved significantly better at achieving the "normative ideal" of democratic discussion.[37] When citizens choose to be at their best, they often succeed.

Although similar in many ways to other civic participants, letter writers bring something special to the table. In fact, they bring several such things to the table:

- *Knowability*: As community residents, writers have built-in authority, unless, of course, they make foolish arguments or say something beyond the pale.
- *Sharability* : A letter to the editor is a tangible thing. Once published, it exists forever and can be passed around. Today, it can be passed around digitally.
- *Simultaneity*: Writers are rooted in the present even though they sometimes trace the present to its historical roots. Until tomorrow happens, writers have the last word.
- *Dependability*: The letters column is created anew each day and readers come to expect it. Letters help stitch together a community-in-time by their regularity.
- *Idiosyncrasy*: A letter bears the irrepressible stamp of its author. Each is the product of a unique personality. Collectively, the letters become a carnival of opinions.
- *Antagonism*: Letter writers nurse vexations large and small. They resist hegemonies and conventional wisdom. Resistance is their drug; it attracts readers as well.
- *Incompleteness*: New issues arise and the world never stops. Even a brilliant letter cannot say all that must be said, nor can it be said perfectly. As a result, the public stays tuned.[38]

Those who write letters to the editor are a special kind of civic participant. Some are active in the local community and some even run for office. Some join the PTA or the VFW, some the Sierra Club; and all of them hate the cable company. But many of them are just observers – people who scan the horizon looking for trouble. They are often judgmental but they are not ashamed of that condition. Because they are special in these ways, politicians often pay attention to them even if they do not know what to make of them.[39]

THE TRIALS OF CITIZENSHIP

Comparatively few people write letters to the editor. Why is that? It is because politics is painful. Everyone wants to drive on smooth roads but the Public Works Department is broke. The old mayor could have fixed the problem but the affair with his assistant became public and he had to resign. The new mayor offers possibilities but the minority community distrusts him. All of this is enough to make one want to write a letter to the editor – or become depressed.

Or melancholy. Far removed from the hills of Fall River, Massachusetts and the waterways of Lake Charles, Louisiana, Charles Baudelaire once declared: "I can barely conceive a type of beauty in which there is no melancholy." "Depression is melancholy minus its charms," adds Susan Sontag. "There's a special quality to the loneliness of dusk, a melancholy more brooding than the night's," says Ed Gorman. "Melancholy is sadness that has taken on lightness," remarked Italo Calvino. Thoughtful comments all. But it is commentator John Derbyshire who best explains the letter writer's sensibility: "I preach that odd defiant melancholy that sees the dreadful loneliness of the human soul and the pitiful disaster of human life as ever redeemable and redeemed by compassion, friendship and love."[40]

Historically, two different discourses about melancholy have emerged, one psychological and the other aesthetic. Freud explained the first type as a "profoundly painful dejection" that inspires a "cessation of interest in the outside world, loss of the capacity to love, inhibition of all activity, and a lowering of the self-regarding feelings to a degree that finds utterance in self-reproaches and self-revilings and culminates in a delusional expectation of punishment."[41] Cessation of interest? Inhibition of activity? A lowering of self-regard? Self-revilings? Freud was obviously not talking about people who write letters to the editor.

But a less psychiatric view of melancholy sheds greater light on them. Some melancholics, observes Judith Shklar, are "wordless sufferers," while others "broadcast their blues."[42] Whereas mourning targets a specific loss, says Matthew Wolf-Meyer, melancholy is distinguished by a certain *longing*, a diffuse sense that the love object – better highways, fewer prisons – is close-but-far. In the aesthetic tradition, melancholy "involves the pleasure of reflection and contemplation of things we love and long for, so that the hope of having them adds a touch of sweetness that makes melancholy bearable."[43] This is too florid a description of those writing letters about clogged sewer lines, but the dialectic Wolf-Meyer mentions does characterize their letters, as Caroline J. of Duluth illustrates:

Elected officials like Becky Lourey, with their ultraliberal ideas, have allowed the slaughter of 1.5 million unborn babies each year. *We all had a chance to make a difference by voting pro-life in the Sept. 10 primary* but too few took the time to make a difference. Now we can see the sad results.

Wake up America before it's too late. This silence has allowed the government to use our tax money to promote homosexuality to schoolchildren, prayer to be outlawed from our schools, and tens of millions of our tax dollars given to organizations like Planned Parenthood which is the largest U.S. provider of abortion services.

This will either be the year we finally reclaim our nation for the moral virtues that built our great nation or a year of missed opportunities and crushing disappointment. Please don't miss this chance to be an active participant in the most important election of our lifetime.

(*Duluth Herald*, September 29, 1996)

Ms. Johnson is upset here but, as the italicized phrases show, her love object keeps showing up: One election went south but another is in the offing; silence (sleep) has slowed us down but we can still wake up; the future looks grim but the storied past contains solutions. Melancholics are "always mournful of a dying epoch," says sociologist Scott Lasch, because they have "a chronic inability to forget."[44] As a result, they practice not a "hermeneutics of suspicion" but a "hermeneutics of retrieval,"[45] an instinct Caroline J. amply illustrates here.

As we will see throughout this book, a shadow of melancholy is cast over most of the letters because their authors are idealists, attuned to lofty goals and to life's "blockages." These blockages include a loss of order, the forfeiting of bourgeois opportunity, a utopia misplaced.[46] That the writers choose to *act* under such conditions shows them to be progressives of a sort. But why not abandon politics? Walter Benjamin hints at the answer when noting that melancholy can either "arm" an individual or "cause sorrow."[47] For writers, it is often modernity itself – more organization, more production, more technology, more speed, more change, more efficiency, more openness – that keeps them going. They are, after all, Americans.

The letter writers I studied believe in the American creed and constantly look for ways of making practical improvements. That makes them different from those inhabiting the blogosphere, who, according to cultural scholar Michael Keren, produce a "politics of melancholy" characterized by a preference for virtual reality, a close-knit community of fellow bloggers, and, ultimately, a "resentful detachment" leading to political passivity.[48] The blogosphere, Keren believes, has a "tendency to wait for evil forces to disappear rather than search for the strategy needed to defeat them."[49]

The letter writers I studied are not, to be sure, deeply philosophical. They are practical people with a take on life. But because their world is so dialectical, they understand what literary scholar Eric Wilson meant when he said "you can experience beauty only when you have a melancholy foreboding that all things in this world die. It is the transience of an object that makes it beautiful." Obamacare may not have been adorable but it got people arguing. The fact that it did so is, from the standpoint of citizenship, ineluctably beautiful.

CONCLUSION

Except in the smallest of burgs, most people do not know all of their neighbors, and some people know none of them. It is a small miracle, then, that countless Americans become civically engaged. Some do so heroically, serving as volunteer fire fighters or working in homeless shelters or delicately managing interfaith meetings. Others do so regularly, coaching Little League, delivering Meals on Wheels, organizing events for the Junior League. Still others do so ferociously, protesting at city council meetings, marching on MLK day, and sleeping uneasily when sit-ins become camp-ins. And others do so quietly, writing letters to the editors.

Each of these activities is a boon in its own way. Letter-writing is surely not heroic, but it helps a community stay in touch with itself. But, according to sociologist Bryan Turner, that is becoming harder to do. Says Turner: "The idea of a 'face to face society' in which everybody knows everybody else and where decisions in a time of crisis are taken collectively, is a thing of the past" because of suburbanization, global economics, social mobility, etc.[50] All of that may be true, but, almost as a counterargument, people canvas for the Humane Society and then draft letters calling for more funding for cancer research when they get home. Democracy moves forward when they do so.

Many of those who write letters to the editor never hear from their readers. Others hear all too often, as, for example, when someone deconstructs the letter they had published in the paper last Tuesday. Either way, letter writers are congenital strugglers, struggling to stay cheerful. After all, as soon as one social problem is solved, another – another dozen – pops up to replace it. So civic participation is a rare thing and, because it is rare, it is a treasure. For their own melancholy reasons, some Americans argue like citizens. It is a blessing that they do.

Endnotes

1 Gerard Stropnicky, "Foreword," In Gerard Stropnicky, Tom Byrn, James Goode, and Jerry Matheny (eds.), *Letters to the Editor: Two Hundred Years in the Life of an American Town* (New York: Simon and Schuster, 1998), p. iii.
2 Ibid.
3 Michael Walzer, "Citizenship," in Terence Ball, James Farr, and Russell L. Hanson (eds.), *Political Innovation and Conceptual Change* (New York: Cambridge University Press, 1989), p. 216.
4 Robert E. Lane, "The joyless polity: contributions of democratic process to ill-being," in Stephen L. Elkin and Karol Edward Soltan (eds.), *Citizen Competence and Democratic Institutions* (University Park: Pennsylvania State University Press, 1999), p. 356.
5 Bryan S. Turner, "Outline of the theory of human rights," in Bryan S. Turner (ed.), *Citizenship and Social Theory* (London: Sage, 1993), p. 177.
6 Sidney Verba, "Culture, calculation, and being a pretty good citizen: alternative interpretations of civil engagement," Eckstein Lecture, University of California, Irvine (January 2001), p. 2.
7 Michael Schudson, *The Good Citizen: A History of American Civic Life* (New York: Free Press, 1998).
8 Robert J. Pranger, *The Eclipse of Citizenship: Power and Participation in Contemporary Politics* (New York: Holt, 1968), p. 51.
9 Quoted in Daria Donnelly, "The power to die: Emily Dickinson's letters of consolation," in Rebecca Earle (ed.), *Epistolary Selves: Letters and Letter-Writers, 1600–1945* (Farnham: Ashgate, 1999), p. 143.
10 Michael Warner, *The Letters of the Republic: Publications and the Public Sphere in Eighteenth-Century America* (Cambridge: Harvard University Press, 1990), p. xiii.
11 Ibid, 8.
12 Ibid, 108.

13 Paul Ricoeur, "The political paradox," in Hwa Yol Jung (ed.), *Existential Phenomenology and Political Theory: A Reader* (Chicago: Henry Regnery, 1972), p. 355.

14 Toby Miller, *The Well-Tempered Self: Citizenship, Culture and the Postmodern Subject* (Baltimore: Johns Hopkins University Press, 1993), p. 19.

15 As paraphrased by Robert Booth Fowler, *The Dance with Community: The Contemporary Debate in American Political Thought* (Lawrence: University of Kansas Press, 1991), p. 36. See also Robert N. Bellah, Richard Madsen, William M. Sullivan, Ann Swidler, and Steven M. Tipton, *Habits of the Heart: Individualism and Commitment in American Life* (Berkeley: University of California Press, 2007).

16 Fowler, *The Dance with Community*, p. 152.

17 Ibid.

18 David Matthews, *Politics for People: Finding a Responsible Public Voice* (Urbana: University of Illinois Press, 1994), p. 189.

19 For more on these matters see Chris Ingraham, "Talking (about) the elite and mass: vernacular rhetoric and discursive status," *Philosophy & Rhetoric*, 46 (2013), 14; Samuel McCormick, "Neighbors and citizens: local speakers in the now of their recognizability," *Philosophy & Rhetoric*, 44 (2011), 424–45.

20 Andrew F. Hayes, Dietram A. Scheufele, and Michael E. Huge, "Nonparticipation as self-censorship: publicly observable political activity in a polarized opinion climate," *Political Behavior*, 28 (2006), 260–1.

21 George E. Marcus and Michael B. MacKuen, "Anxiety, enthusiasm, and the vote: the emotional underpinnings of learning and involvement during presidential campaigns," *American Political Science Review*, 87 (1993), 681.

22 George E. Marcus, *The Sentimental Citizen: Emotion in Democratic Politics* (University Park: Pennsylvania State University Press, 2002), p. 111.

23 Ibid, 148.

24 Michael Walzer, "Civility and civic virtue in contemporary America," *Social Research*, 41 (1974), 605.

25 Ibid.

26 Marcus, *The Sentimental Citizen*, p. 141.

27 Peter Thisted Dinesen, Aasbjørn Sonne Nørgaard, and Robert Klemmensen, "The civic personality: personality and democratic citizenship," *Political Studies*, 62(1) (2014), 145.

28 Aaron C. Weinschenk, "Personality traits and the sense of civic duty," *American Politics Research*, 42 (2014), 101. André Blais adds that such individuals are also more likely to be women than men. See André Blais, *To Vote or Not to Vote? The Merits and Limits of Rational Choice Theory* (Pittsburgh: University of Pittsburgh Press, 2000).

29 Sidney Verba and Norman H. Nie, *Participation in America: Political Democracy and Social Equality* (New York: Harper, 1972), p. 12.

30 Michael A. Neblo, Kevin M. Esterling Ryan P. Kennedy, David M. J. Lazer, and Anand E. Sokhey, "Who wants to deliberate – and why?" Working paper, Harvard University, John F. Kennedy School of Government, 2009, 35.

31 Sean W. D. Gray, "Mapping silent citizenship: how democratic theory hears citizens' silence and why it matters," *Citizenship Studies*, 19(5) (2015), 474–91.

32 For more on this matter see McCormick, "Neighbors and citizens," 441.

33 Rebecca M. Townsend, "Town meeting as a communication event: democracy's act sequence," *Research on Language and Social Interaction*, 42 (2009), 87.

34 Christopher F. Karpowitz, "Extremists or good citizens? The political psychology of public meetings and the dark side of civic engagement." Paper presented at the annual meeting of the Midwest Political Science Associate, Chicago, April 2006.

35 Christopher F. Karpowitz, "Men, Women, and Wal-Mart: Citizen Discourse at Local Public Hearings." Paper presented at the annual meeting of the American Political Science Association, Chicago, September 2007.

36 Christopher F. Karpowitz, "A theory of local public talk and deliberative reform." Paper presented at the annual meeting of the American Political Science Association, Washington, DC, September 2005.

37 Diana B. Carlin, Dan Schill, David G. Levasseur and Anthony S. King, "The post-9/11 public sphere: citizen talk about the 2004 presidential debates," *Rhetoric & Public Affairs*, 8 (2005), 632.

38 For an enormously thoughtful discussion of letter-writing in general see Warner, *The Letters of the Republic*.

39 For more on the impact of citizen-generated content see Jennifer L. Brookhart and Alexander Moss Tahk, "The origin of ideas." Paper presented to the 72rd Annual Meeting of the Midwest Political Science Association, Chicago, April 2015 and Julie Firmstone and Stephen Coleman, "Rethinking local communicative spaces: implications of digital media and citizen journalism for the role of local journalism in engaging citizens," in Rasmus K. Nielsen (ed.), *Local Journalism: The Decline of Newspapers and the Rise of Digital Media* (London: Tauris & Co., 2015), pp. 117–40.

40 This medley of comments on melancholy – and many more – can be found online on the *Brainy Quotes* website: www.brainyquote.com/.

41 Sigmund Freud, "Mourning and melancholia," in James Strachey (trans.), *Complete Psychological Works of Sigmund Freud*, vol. 14 (London: Hogarth Press, 2016), p. 244.

42 Judith N. Shklar, *American Citizenship: The Quest for Inclusion* (Cambridge: Harvard University Press, 1991), p. vii.

43 Emily Brady and Arto Haapala, "Melancholy as an aesthetic emotion," *Contemporary Aesthetics*, 1 (2003), 10. Accessed at http://hdl.handle.net/2027/spo.7523862.0001.006.

44 Scott Lash, "Being after time: towards a politics of melancholy," *Cultural Values*, 2 (1998), 316, 318.

45 Ibid, 317.

46 Wolf Lepenies, *Melancholy and Society*, trans. Jeremy Gaines and Doris Jones (Cambridge: Howard University Press, 1992), pp. 10, 141.

47 Quoted in Johnathan Flatley, *Affective Mapping: Melancholia and the Politics of Modernism* (Cambridge: Harvard University Press, 2008), p. 3.
48 Michael Keren, "Blogging and the politics of melancholy," *Canadian Journal of Communication*, 29 (2004), 5, 21.
49 Keren 18.
50 Bryan S. Turner, "Silent citizens: reflections on community, habit, and the silent majority in political life," *Citizenship Studies*, 19(5) (2015), 515.

3

Is Civic Hope the Answer?

Writing a book about civic hope during the 2016 presidential campaign required a strong constitution. Suggesting that any American was hopeful during that wretched time exposed one to charges of lunacy. Wherever one turned, whatever one read, vitriol burst forth. "The American People Have Finally Had Enough," pronounced the *Daily Kos*. "Voters are Angry, and Shoes May Fly," declared the normally placid *Sacramento Bee*. Other news organs were more interrogative: "Angry Voters: Who Will They Support?" asked *Real Clear Politics*. The *Indianapolis Star* tried to explain "How Iowa Caucuses Got So Angry" (it was because people detested a "rigged" system, the paper concluded). Horserace commentators were naturally attracted to the floating dyspepsia: "Embracing 'Angry' Voters May Help Trump Win Nomination," pronounced *Breitbart*. The (conservative) *National Journal* licked its lips when calculating the strategic value of voter dismay – "Angry Voters Aren't Going Away," it warned – but even the (progressive) *New York Times* found its share of misery as the Obama administration drew to a close: "To Angry Voters, Washington Comes Out the Biggest Loser."

Voter dismay in 2016 was not universal, but it was broad-based and indiscriminate. Longshots such as Rick Santorum and Martin O'Malley felt its lash, but so too did well-financed candidates such as Jeb Bush and Hillary Clinton. Even politicians who were riding high in early 2016 – people such as Donald Trump, Ted Cruz, and Bernie Sanders – were just as likely to be pilloried as admired. Anger also took a postmodern turn in 2016, with people supporting certain candidates because they detested all politicians. Voters turned out in droves in the Iowa caucuses to register their disgust with politics itself. To be happy was to be naïve; to be angry was to be really happy. Jim Schmidt, a citizen in Johnson County, Iowa whose eleven-year-old son wore a bumper sticker proclaiming "Bomb the shit out of ISIS," fully embraced the zeitgeist: "I'm angry but I love it and enjoy it."[1]

All of the foregoing sounds strange for a nation often caricatured as hopelessly upbeat. "The United States is one of the few countries on earth in which optimism is almost a state ideology," says the United Kingdom's Terry Eagleton.[2] Americans have an "optimism bias," reports political scientist David Niven. They think "they are more likely than the average person to enjoy positive future events – and less likely than the average person to suffer from negative outcomes."[3] Others disagree. "Optimism and pessimism have always competed in the American character," says the American Enterprise Institute's Arthur C. Brooks. "Think of it as Horatio Alger versus the Zombie Apocalypse."[4] Indeed, optimism and pessimism weave a tangled web. "Negative information appears to have more weight in people's thinking than comparable positive information," says Niven. But here is a reciprocal: "The more optimistic the respondent, the less enthusiastic they are about government."[5]

This chapter, and this book, is not about optimism. It is about hope – and they are fundamentally different. Optimism is an emotional state, whereas hope is an emotional state gone behavioral. Optimists smile, but hopeful people often grimace because they have so much to do. Optimists expect good things to happen with or without confirming evidence. Hopeful individuals squint a good deal; only cold, hard evidence alters their heartbeats. Such people can, of course, imagine happy outcomes, but only after they have performed the necessary calculations. Trust comes slowly to such people because their memory banks are filled with broken promises and unfulfilled expectations. Because politics takes so much work, hope can die aborning.

Hope "is not the conviction that something will turn out well," says former Czech president and philosopher Vaclav Havel, "but the certainty that something makes sense, regardless of how it turns out."[6] Cornel West, a prominent public intellectual, also distinguishes hope from optimism, but he does so with considerably more anguish:

Hope has nothing to do with optimism. I am in no way optimistic about America, nor am I optimistic about the plight of the human species on this globe. There is simply not enough evidence that allows me to infer that things are going to get better. That has been the perennial state and condition of not simply black people in America, but all self-conscious human beings who are sensitive to the forms of evil around them. We can be prisoners of hope even as we call optimism into question.

To be part of the democratic tradition is to be a prisoner of hope. And you cannot be a prisoner of hope without engaging in a form of struggle in the present moment that keeps the best of the past alive.[7]

What does Professor West mean here? Presumably, he means that the African-American experience in the United States has been an endless succession of miseries. To ask for optimism from Cornel West would be to insult him. The best one can expect from him, the best he can expect from himself, is that the fundaments of American democracy – justice for all; equality of opportunity; one person, one vote – will remain a theoretical possibility and, eventually, will be practiced as well as preached. In the meantime, no smiling.

Those who wrote the letters to the editor I studied were neither as august as Vaclav Havel nor as learned as Cornel West, but they too were prisoners of hope. They sent in letters, had them rejected, and sent in two more. Sometimes they did so for ego reasons, but more often because there was so much work to do, work they had relegated to themselves. The best way to understand such people is to read what they write, and this chapter shows how I did so. I explain a systematic way of measuring civic hope's depth and show how some 10,000 letters to the editor were categorized, tagged, and interpreted by my team of researchers. Such labors were an admixture of art and science, because language is complex and because it resists easy interpretations. So I approached the texts from multiple perspectives to see what hope they contained.

Most people who read letters to the editor do not think of their authors as hopeful. Letter writers complain a great deal – often colorfully, never briefly. But they are also fixers by nature, the types of people H. L. Mencken called "half-baked ecclesiastics," "obscene vice crusaders," and "fantoddish old suffragettes." "It is difficult for the American mind to grasp the concept of insolubility," concluded Mencken, or to convince people they are no closer to getting their problems solved "than they were in the time of Ramses."[8]

Perhaps. But in 2016, at least, I found no nihilistic letters to the editor. Not one. Many of the letters I read were tortured and many were sulfurous, castigating income inequality, gay marriage, Wall Street greed, and Muslims everywhere. But nobody recommended throwing in the towel. Some writers were cynical and many of them smarmy, but none suggested decamping for Cuba. Instead, they universally urged people to vote. They did so not because they trusted the candidates running for office but because they believed in the perfectibility of democratic institutions. They mostly understood what Nietzsche meant when he declared hope "the worst of all evils because it prolongs the torments of man."[9] That may be true, the letter writers reasoned, but if the Anschluss could be prolonged until just after November 8, something better might happen. This odd mentality, this toleration of incomplete solutions, looks nothing like optimism. It looks like civic hope. This chapter explains what that means.

SOURCES OF HOPE

"The presence of doubt," says philosopher Darrell Moellendorf, "is destructive of belief [but] it is not destructive of hope."[10] "Hope can only take root," says Gabriel Marcel, "when perdition is a possibility."[11] "We mustn't limit our hopes," says the old adage, "for if we do we shall never find what lies beyond them."[12] So many searching phrases, so many elusive thoughts. Who can possibly find hope when hope is so hard to describe?

To understand hope, one must examine its roots. For me, hope comes from four places: memory, imagination, rationality, and energy. Each of these properties reinforces, and complicates, the other. When tragedy strikes, for example, our emotions often override our reasoning. We think too much about a problem, or not enough, and as a result our energies become sapped and comfort hard to find. As Terry Eagleton notes, when we suddenly feel the need for hope, "the unpalatable has already happened."[13]

Memory

The past can be a source of hope but it can also be a torment, a "night-mare weighing on the brains of the living."[14] "It is not dreams of liberated grandchildren which spur men and women to revolt," says German philosopher Walter Benjamin, "but memories of oppressed ancestors."[15] Because the past is a repository for our basic values and telling experiences (good as well as bad), it can help us sort through the options before us. Consider, for example, how two different letter writers deployed the past:

I was one of the poor Missouri boys facing the draft. I had a deferment because I was a sole surviving son of a World War II combat veteran killed in action but I enlisted. I loved my country then and now. Today there are roughly

42,000 surviving Vietnam Veterans in the U.S. who served in a political war that cost dearly in terms of human life. Perhaps if more national leaders were veterans, future threats of war would be a last resort. There are some things combat veterans will never forget: The dead and maimed buddies; Jane Fonda in Hanoi entertaining the Cong as G.I.'s perished; and politicians who beat the draft and now strive for votes.

(John S., *St. Joseph News-Press*, March 12, 1992)

* * * * *

Charity begins at home not in foreign countries but President Bush does not believe this. Why does he give $10 million a year to Israel? This should stop. The American people are in need of help. They are losing their jobs and many are going hungry. How can such neglect happen in a country of such great wealth? I was born of parents who came from the old country and when I was a little boy growing up I saw things happen that I will never forget. We were poor and times were rough and many were in the same condition but we made it to this day. Many have passed away but some are still around.

(Louis K., *Fall River Herald News*, March 23, 1992)

In many ways, the past has not stopped for these writers, and therein lies their chance for hope. Citizens such as these are "process philosophers" who pay close attention to current events because, in a way, they have witnessed them before. As a result, their letters are unhurried. They go back in time to core principles and to the nation's "collective imaginary" (i.e., the Vietnam War for John S. and early twentieth-century immigration for Louis K.).[16] It is said that great athletes also have this ability to "slow down" the blur of a game. They stand firm against the tumult, waiting until just the right moment to make their play. Such people "come from somewhere," so new events are not as new for them as they are for others. Hope provides "transitional value" for the civically involved; it sustains them "during the political process of the construction of a more just order."[17]

Imagination

But letter writers do not just wait around. "Hope involves a kind of plotting or projecting," says Terry Eagleton, "in the sense of an imaginative articulation of present and future."[18] Because hopeful people operate from a relatively clear basis of belief, they are "able to peer into the abyss of potential disaster, which the optimist is generally reluctant to do."[19] "The mere act of being able to imagine an alternative future may distance and relativize the present," says Eagleton, "loosening its grip upon us to the point where the future in question becomes more possible."[20] This "openness to time, to the future possible,"[21] lets hopeful people act and act now.

For these reasons, letter writers often seem odd to others. "How can these writers make such confident predictions?" their critics ask. "After all, they live their lives one moment at a time as do I." Well, in many ways, the writers do not; they live in the present-to-be. They are not utopians, though, at least not most of them. Their futures typically look like a better version of the present: "To reach our goals, we just need to drive the Democrats/Republicans/Socialists/Tea Partiers out of business." Letter writers are tiresome in these ways. They are not imaginative in any grand metaphysical sense; instead, they provide stock answers to complex questions and short-term answers to long-term problems. They do so, however, with the forcefulness of a soothsayer.

German philosopher Ernst Bloch tells us that "time expands" for the hopeful, that it "is the product of experience, failure, and resistance to an everyday acceptance of reality."[22] That is why the distinction between optimism and hope is so crucial. People who write letters to the editor are well aware of life's travails (indeed, they often obsess over them). At the same time, though, they can fashion new unfoldings out of their prior experiences and ideological commitments. Psychologist Tali Sharot reports that hopeful people live longer than pessimists because they act on imagined possibilities (e.g., by writing letters).[23] It also helps when they "mutually orchestrate" their imaginings, as they do, for example, in religious, social, and political groupings.[24]

Rationality

Although it is common to think of hope in emotional terms, hope is primarily the product of reasoned calculation. That is why letters to the editor often seem so trite, filled as they are with easy answers, leaden prose, and a tacky sort of confidence. To wit:

- "It's time to *hope* again. *Bill Clinton* has a plan to get our economy back on track! Vote Clinton on November 3." (Patricia S., *Springfield News-Sun*, October 29, 1992)
- "With *Republicans* there is *hope* of reducing taxes and spending. With liberal Slick Willie and Company there is no hope." (Joe P., *Duluth News Tribune*, September 9, 1992)

- "I *hope* that the leaders of the world, especially our *religious leaders*, would point out more often that being prejudiced is wrong and perhaps one day put an end to the stupidity." (Brian M., *Trenton Times*, September 25, 2008)
- "I *hope* that all pettiness will be put aside as *delegates* are elected and *platforms* are adopted reflecting the desires of our people." (Merrill G., *Provo Daily Herald*, July 17, 1964)
- "After hearing the presidential debates, I *hope* we will all *go to the library* and look up the records of those campaigning and find out for ourselves what their records show and make an intelligent decision on who we vote for." (Martha D., *Provo Daily Herald*, October 15, 2004)
- "I *hope* the *people of Fall River* will check them out as closely as possible to be sure these candidates will be working for the people's best interest and not the mayor's." (Barbara T., *Fall River Herald News*, October 12, 1972)

In the excerpts above, hope becomes a workhorse. It reduces taxes, confronts bias, and protects the citizenry. Hope is not an abstraction in these letters, nor is it a solitary actor. Its partners include, respectively, a presidential candidate, a political party, religious leaders, institutional mechanisms, library research, and the people themselves. To call such prose trite is to highlight these quotidian linkages of people and procedure.

Hope requires "peer scaffolding," says Simon Fraser University's Victoria McGeer. That means trusting others to become "the keepers of our hope until we are enabled, by their hope in us, to become agents of hope in our own right."[25] Hope is social in these ways, which may be why some people read letters to the editor avidly even while regarding them as mild diversions. But they are not diversions in the way that poetry, music, and theatre are diversions. After all, in the excerpts above, readers are directed to highly specific goals and remedies (lower taxes, responsive politicians, etc.). In these ways, hope is as much a strategy as an emotion.[26]

Researchers find that hopeful people are good at identifying "alternative pathways to their goals, especially when the path they try is first blocked."[27] They have learned to think in strategic ways and the people most important to them (friends, family, co-workers, etc.) come to depend on their hopefulness. Such people "lean into the future ready to act when actions can do some good," says McGeer – a mentality that lets them become "agents of potential as well as agents in fact."[28] Unless hope is "underpinned by reasons," says Eagleton, it becomes rather "like being convinced that there is an octopus under your bed."

Energy

This book is about people who *act* upon events with their leftover time. Nobody asks them to write letters, but they do, propelled by what psychotherapist Albert Ellis calls "the negative path to happiness." Like the Stoic philosophers of ancient Greece, such people find that "the best way to address an uncertain future is to focus not on the best-case scenario but on the worst."[29] Functionally, this "premeditation of evils" saps "the future of its anxiety-producing power" and thus empowers people.[30] To be future-worried in this way is to be in the game, to become both a dispenser of hope and its beneficiary.

Writing a letter to the editor may not amount to much in the grand scheme of things but it can be a useful start. It can move us out of our comfort zones, energize our ideas (and those of others), and mobilize people to think as we do. Outcomes like these can reinforce our sense of self and add purpose to our lives. "Hoping has something in common with prayer," says the University of Colorado's Luc Bovens, because "it builds on an illusion of causal agency."[31]

Now here is an interesting thing: Scholar Kimberly Gross and her colleagues found that the terrorist attacks of 9/11 led to increased confidence in many of the people they surveyed – not to depression, not to resignation.[32] Hope, which they term a "forward-looking emotion," was the only measure predicting long-term confidence in others. Presumably, such traumatic events do not lead to a mystical sort of hope but to hoping activities – commiserating with co-workers, assuaging children's worries, becoming informed about geopolitics. Hoping keeps people busy – planning a course of action, adjusting to the needs of others, preparing counterarguments, and persisting despite setbacks. "Hopefulness can smile with joy," says Rhodes College's Patrick Shade, "but it can also grit its teeth in the face of life's messiest, most painful, circumstances."[33]

Hope takes work. What is especially needed, says Shade, are habits of hope, the very sorts of thing found among those who write letters to the editor. While some of these writers are interested only in getting personal attention, most have a larger, or at least a broader, purpose. They ask necessary questions and the letters column becomes their testament to engaging with the world. They are amateurs when doing so, which is to say, they are citizens.

HOPE'S REQUIREMENTS

Some people are congenitally hopeful and some are not. What distinguishes them? For Karl Marx, that would be a silly question. Unless the lords of capital smile in your direction, he would observe, you have no hope for hope. For Jesus Christ, hope lay solely in the Trinity and in its promise of life everlasting. Between Marx and Jesus lie a thousand other prophets of hope: Jeremiah, Jeremy Bentham, Mahatma Gandhi, Martin Luther King, Jr., Norman Vincent Peale, Tony Robbins, America's Got Talent. But while many people line up for hope, real hope requires effort, and some are better suited to the quest than others. Hope is easier to find when three conditions are present: conceptual focus, cooperative relationships, and an available language.

Conceptual Focus

The late scholar Rick Snyder did pioneering work in the area of social hope. He spent much of his career identifying the tools of hope and determining what sorts of person used them best. "Hope, as I was coming to define it," said Snyder, "was primarily a way of thinking, with feelings playing an important, albeit contributory role."[34] Viewing hope in cognitive terms opened up an important stream of research that led Snyder to identify three features of hopeful individuals: (1) they easily identify *goals* to pursue; (2) they look for alternative *pathways* to solving a problem; and (3) they see themselves as *agents* of change, not its victims. Over the years, Snyder and his students built paper-and-pencil measures to tap all three dimensions and launched a small research industry within the field of social psychology.

High-hope persons, said Snyder, were especially good at "producing alternative routes" to accomplish a goal.[35] Compared to the general population, such people were more successful in school, physically and mentally healthier, better adjusted socially, more flexible when pursuing their goals, and more likely to have high self-worth. Low-hope people, in contrast, tended to set absurdly high goals for themselves and became depressed easily. "Cognitive resolve," as a result, turned out to be hope's leading indicator. Hope's "fixity of purpose," says Princeton's Philip Pettit, "represents the only way of retaining our identity and selfhood, of not losing ourselves to the turmoil of brute, disheartening fact."[36] Because hope also requires imagination, it has "an element of make-believe" that "does not amount to self-deception."[37] A fine line, that.

Contributors to letters columns do not get lost in rumination. Even when auditioning multiple viewpoints, they refuse to dither, usually seeing just two sides to a question, not three, not fourteen. While they, like all of us, have no idea what the future will bring, they can shake off doubts because of their self-mindedness. It is not surprising, then, that Knox College's Andrew Civettini found those scoring high on the hope scale paying more attention to politics, discussing it more frequently, becoming more involved in their communities, and even considering running for office more frequently than the broader population.[38] Focus, it seems clear, moves things forward.

Cooperative Relationships

In some people's eyes, politicians give hope a bad name. Every two to four years they trot out their wares, asking citizens to forget their past disappointments and embrace new possibilities. Politicians, says legal scholar Peter Drahos, "see hope as part of an exchange relationship in which it is traded for voters, favors, privileges, or money."[39] One would think that voters would quickly tire of this game and leave politics to the jivers and the shysters. But most do not. Political scientist Harold Zullow has documented (across a forty-year period) a quadrennial upsurge in optimism among US voters.[40] It goes up in August through November of the presidential election year, drops in the post-election year, and bottoms out in the mid-term election, only to rise again when the presidential candidates again come calling. Why? Perhaps because the American people have a special attachment to their chief executive, perhaps because campaigns tap into voters' needs to feel better about their own lives, or perhaps because a calendrical "fresh start" has become habitual for them.

Although most of those who write letters to the editor are skeptics, they are not immune to these enthusiasms. They too are members of a "historical community" possessed of value commitments, sacred rituals, and storied beliefs, all of which impact their levels of hope.[41] New events sometimes produce "hope without optimism," however, as when a political scandal hits the morning news. But even when politics dismays the writers, they seem unable to resist it. Hope "is called for when the world is not as we wish it, is not what it should be, when we are frustrated, insecure, anxious about the way things are, and eager to see them improved," says political philosopher Andrew Norris.[42] "Political hope does not build upon our pride in being democratic," continues Norris, "so much as it responds to our despair in not yet having realized our democracy."[43]

Australian scholar Valerie Braithwaite has tracked down the real-world consequences of such feelings. She found that people with a high sense of collective hope cooperate more readily with local taxing authorities because of their "shared desire for a better society, articulated through a broad set of agreed-upon goals and principles, developed and elaborated through socially inclusive dialogue."[44] That is, the "feel good" emotions afforded by group identity make it easier for people to part with their money. There is danger in that, of course, for such people can also be manipulated by the unscrupulous. But that sword cuts both ways: If politicians abuse their trust, collecting taxes will become harder. Relationships, that is, have consequences.

Available Language

Letter-writing is what J. L. Austin would call a "speech act," a text containing words, but words that *do something* because they have been made in public.[45] So, for example, the "I do" spoken at the altar sends a message of love but it also gets one married – legally and in front of witnesses. A letter to the editor is also an accomplishment, a sign that some new vexation has suddenly surfaced. No matter how poorly reasoned such a letter may be, the wise politician will scrutinize it carefully to see what act is being performed (e.g., unusual levels of resistance to the upcoming bond election).

The average person uses language to get work done ("please pass the salt") and to cement their relationships ("thank you, dear"). In contrast, says Chris Ingraham, elites *talk about* things.[46] Elites do not live in the world so much as they hover above it, looking down at what is happening. To talk about a thing is to grab it whole, to stop it in time, to turn it around in one's hands, to ponder it, to judge its essence, to imagine its implications. Everyday people have no time for such rarefied work.

Letter writers, though, are similar to elites in this way. They too talk about the world, thereby joining a cadre of politicians, teachers, journalists, and members of the clergy. Writers are presumptuous in doing so, of course: Who asked them to be community overseers? From the standpoint of citizenship, however, such people possess what Karol Soltan calls "cleverness," a refusal to let political life sweep past them *sans* scrutiny.[47] Richard Rorty defends such people as well, noting that "to retain social hope, members of ... society need to be able to tell themselves a story about how things might get better, and see no insufferable obstacles to this story's coming true."[48]

And so now we are in a better position to ask: What does hope look like when it is *civic*? I see three main components:

- *A values component – the democratic ideals being cherished*: As mentioned earlier, those with civic hope assume that enlightened leadership is possible despite human foibles, that productive citizenship results from cultural pluralism, and that democratic traditions produce wise governance. These are the core beliefs of civic hope but they are often not top-of-mind for individuals and they certainly are not static. Indeed, they are constantly being challenged by events of the day, which is why letter writers are often grumpy. What keeps them going is the sense that these end-states can be reached – somehow, at some time.

- *An action component – the willingness to defend such beliefs in public*: Those with civic hope are characterized by their constant vigilance and readiness to struggle over ideas. High-hope individuals are engaged in a never-ending search for new information to assess the changing political environment. They are willing to stand with their beliefs, and to do so in the public square with their names attached (via debate, boycotts, marches, etc.). This boldness, this acting-in-the-world, distinguishes them from those who can also recall grade-school civic lessons but who, for various reasons, shrink from the spotlight.

- *A depth component – how extensively the language of hope is used*: This is the rhetorical dimension of civic hope, a measure of people's ability to explicate the democratic verities. This chapter outlines a great many strategies for doing so, the operating assumption being that hope must be heard to stay viable (for speaker, for audience). Because hope is an inconstant thing, it is sometimes hard to see the light, to keep the struggle going, to find the right words. Keying on this depth component, Chapters 6–9 conduct an audit of the letters, asking which strategies have been deployed over the years and how well.

Under this three-part formulation, not all letters to the editor can be considered agencies of civic hope. Even when sincerely touting democratic principles (the belief component) and doing so forcefully (the action component), the letters may fail to maximize their potential because of ill-chosen words. And so we must ask: How do letter writers perform the business of citizenship? Do they find their primary meanings in the past or does the future drive them forward? Who among them speak as agents, as empowered citizens; which complain of fecklessness, of political drift? Do the writers focus on tangible outcomes, things to be completed next Tuesday, or do they wander in the wilderness, chattering to themselves? Which issues, which aspects of time and location, make civic hope more obvious, or less obvious? When does civic hope abide, and via which strategies?

MEASURING HOPE

At least 600 letters were gathered from each city, but to represent their differential "political energy," as many as 900 letters were collected in the most active locations (Duluth, Roanoke, Billings, and Trenton). Because presidential elections inevitably summon up a nation's most contentious issues, most of the letters selected were published between August 15 and November 15 of presidential election years (1948 through 2012), although a smaller cache of letters (15 percent of the total) was gathered during presidential primaries (largely February through May). In all, 80 percent of the letters dealt with presidential politics (65 percent with the campaign itself and 15 percent with public policy matters), with the remaining 20 percent focusing on city and state affairs.

All of the letters were signed by their authors and averaged 230 words in length. Roughly 10 percent of the letters ran more than 400 words (most of which were published in the early years of this study), the longest of which (1,174 words) was submitted by Frederick F. to the *Roanoke Times* on September 1, 2004. In it, he quoted Shakespeare, Pogo, and Jesus Christ and discussed fast food joints, modern advertising, blood chemistry, cyberspace, university archives, the mayor of New Orleans, minority groups, campaign practices, human psychology, and Oprah Winfrey. The shortest letter in the collection was submitted to the *Springfield News-Sun* by Dorothy K. on August 24, 1980, and read thusly: "The Democratic National Convention – four days of total baloney."

Dorothy K. and Frederick F. represent the alpha and omega of taciturnity and we tried to capture this difference in our coding instrument. The "we" consisted of a team of doctoral students who worked with me on the Campaign Mapping Project between 1992 and 2016 by gathering letters and analyzing them via the Civic Hope Codebook. Because the project unfolded over so many years, five different teams of coders participated in the Project. This required constant checks to ensure that the same textual features were being coded in the same way from year to year.

The actual coding of a letter began by recording its local identifiers, feeding the letter into a digital template (see Appendix A), calling up the first coding category, highlighting any textual fragments meeting the category's definition, and then "depositing" it in the databank.[49] The coding system allowed a given statement to be slotted into as many coding categories as made sense. This was an intentional decision, but one that would be unsettling to social scientists preferring discrete categories (because of the potential intercorrelations among variables). The defense of my approach is simple: Human language is rarely discrete; it says multiple things simultaneously. For example, a statement like "Hillary Clinton – an experienced leader who cares deeply about people" references both professional and personal qualities in the former First Lady. I wanted to capture this depth, this multiplicity of layers, thereby honoring the complex human beings who write letters to the editor.[50]

When developing the coding scheme, I made the assumption that civic hope involves (1) the pursuit of specific goals (2) by identifiable actors who (3) make political attributions within (4) a polity beset by tensions. All four of these concepts point to the problems – and possibilities – of democratic governance and show why something like civic hope is needed if a nation is to stay on kilter. The famed German philosopher Jürgen Habermas reminds us that such matters were much simpler when citizens were connected by tribal, ethnic, or religious bonds. "Citizenship was never tied to national identity," says Habermas, but when the nation-state was invented, especially when it was invented in diverse cultural, political, and geographical circumstances, something else – civic hope, I suggest – was needed to keep the confection together.[51] My claim throughout this book is that such confections depend on ordinary people engaging in a culture of argument. Elites must help, of course, but unless acts of citizenship are performed locally, the cake will fall. My coding scheme measures how well letter writers ward off such possibilities.

Goals

Political scientist David Matthews notes that simply being able to articulate a democratic ideal is critical to achieving it.[52] Without a game plan, Matthews notes, a nation flounders. It is also true, however, that while the American people have traditionally had high agreement about the abstract principles of democracy, "consensus breaks down completely" when concrete applications are mentioned, a fine example of which is the unending contretemps in the United States over Second Amendment rights.[53] Nonetheless, public ceremonies, corporate advertising, the volunteer community, sporting activities, and the military reinforce these superordinate goals. The aim of keeping the abstract principles of democracy fresh is further advanced when ordinary people get involved.[54]

Attitudes toward time are also important. Because the past is, well, past, it must be continually recreated if a nation is to stay connected to its most primitive beliefs. Too much concentration on the past can, of course, stifle a nation's progress (which often happens in monarchical societies), but even a pluralistic democracy like the United States needs its past to work overtime. Sociologist Robert Bellah notes that "communities of memory"[55] such as the family, the church, and the State are critical to identifying the common good even if the memories they preserve are sometimes faulty or overblown. People-in-the-present are often conflicted, but their shared past can bring them together when reinforcing agents (the president, civic leaders, or local community members) pitch in.

The problem with being human is that we are locked in the present. A fellow might eventually win the lottery, but today he is a plumber. The past gives us some breathing room (e.g., the plumber who remembers his days as a high school baseball star) but, right now, the valves are leaking. Because of these circumstances, the future compels us – especially when it is dramatized, an example of which occurs when blue-collar workers get hooked on the lottery because of state-sponsored advertising campaigns. Some see this sort of future-making as exploitative, but who can stifle a dream? Larger social groups need a future too, and political rhetoric obliges ("the lift of a driving dream" and all that). It is especially powerful when everyday citizens lay out a common future in deep and compelling ways. To see how the writers framed democratic goals, in our project, three sets of probes were used:

- *National Touchstones: enduring truths that guide a polity.* This is perhaps the most direct measure of civic hope. It asks if the nation's core beliefs still inform how Americans talk about politics. Are basic democratic elements such as due process, lay control of the military, and mass enfranchisement still invoked? Are writers respectful of civic volunteerism, public education, and the Judeo-Christian heritage? Do the nation's intellectual traditions (e.g., scientific progress and free-market capitalism) still have political punch?

- *Political Memory: past events bearing on current realities.* The past constantly affects the present but the past is also dynamic, changed by those reinterpreting it. To have a sense of community, citizens must recognize their shared experiences and the political traditions to which they are heirs. Was the past a time of destitution (no food on the table, high gas prices) and dishonor (rampant immorality, Communist infiltration)? Or was the past a halcyon period (superior leaders, high moral standards), a time of broad consensus (comity among nations, no ethnic strife)?
- *Civic Forecasting: where society is headed for good or ill.* This category includes a writer's specific or implied predictions about the nation's political future. Will peace and safety reign or will it be an unsafe and dangerous time? An age of enlightenment or one of ignorance? A time of freedom or injustice? Writers sometimes make "factual" assertions to support their predictions but, just as often, they make hortatory or injunctive claims implying that a certain future is foreordained.

Actors

There is no other way to say it: letter writers are fascinated by people. In an age of digital dissemination and always-on media, political gossip is now their birthright. Television, particularly, abets such tendencies. In an earlier work, I explained how television has constructed almost therapeutic relationships between citizens and their leaders.[56] The insides of politicians – her heart, his lusts, their insecurities – now seem more important than their outsides – how they will pay for another war in the Middle East. What else could explain how people reacted to vice-president Edmund Muskie crying in the snows of New Hampshire, or former Texas governor Rick Perry forgetting the third of his three points during a debate, or Senator Marco Rubio repeating himself in robotic style in the 2016 campaign? These human faults (if faults they be) compromised them, even though nobody went broke or was maimed because the candidates bungled a minor rhetorical assignment.

This is not to say, of course, that citizens should refrain from being skeptical about their leaders. But are they using the right *criteria* when evaluating those who will lead them? Are they paying attention to important things (such as financial wisdom) or to trivial matters (such as how they part their hair)? Do they have a substantive, long-term notion of leadership or are they compelled by the trendy and the tawdry? Has the culture of celebrity won them over, calling too little attention to the brilliance of George Washington and Abraham Lincoln and too much to the former's distillery and the latter's mournful looks?

Groups are also important in politics. In an era of super-PACs and pressure groups, NGOs and political parties, grassroots movements and labor unions, lobbying organizations and international alliances, business leagues and private foundations, politics in the United States has become a network of networks. Some of these groups have wealth defying the imagination, while others do such humble work as house-to-house canvassing. Some voters forget how powerful groups can be (perhaps because many of them are quite stealthy), but other voters are quick to point out the web of special interests enmeshing their leaders.

To track how keenly attuned the letter writers were to these interpersonal aspects of politics, two sets of probes were used:

- *Agents of Hope/Agents of Decline: individuals who advance or retard democracy.* Includes all persons designated by name (or via pronomial reference) who are said to influence the political process. Who, specifically, can society depend upon? Public officials? Professional educators? Ordinary citizens? Are historical personages still invoked in political discussion or has social power shifted to contemporary figures? Are members of the press, movement leaders, or heads of corporations credited with advancing the national agenda?
- *Helpful Groups/Unhelpful Groups: groups that advance or retard democracy.* A democracy often reduces to a confederation of interest groups, so one must ask: Which is trusted and which is feared? Which has influence and which is wasting their time? Can activist groups such as the NAACP or the National Rifle Association be depended upon? How about demographic groups such as the elderly or Hispanics? Mythic groups (e.g., "bureaucrats in Washington," "the Radical Right") sometimes worry people, but so too do empirical entities such as the National Education Association or "corporate America."

Attributions

There is no escaping the fact that politics is a judgmental business. The news media constantly evaluate politicians, as do corporate and nonprofit officials, as do religious, educational, military, governmental, and medical institutions. Their assessments are often characterological in nature, focusing on which political leaders have the right stuff personality-wise. Eri Bertsou of the London School of Economics says that political judgments often follow three other paths as well: technical (has the politician made errors of calculation?), moral (has the politician violated shared values?), and congruence (has the politician violated "our" relationship?).[57] Bertsou notes that citizens pay special attention to politicians' word–deed disjunctions as well as to abuses of power. Letter writers are heavily invested in this sort of judgment-making as well.

While politicians are a common object of scrutiny, citizens sometimes turn the gaze back on themselves as well. The electorate's understanding of itself has a little noticed but potentially important impact on political judgments. For example, Alec McGillis of the *New York Times* notes that the Obamacare controversy sometimes produced odd disjunctures: People who had actually benefited from the system came to resent it because *other people* were (in their eyes) gaming the system.[58] Somehow, those who profited from the program could "detach" themselves from their privileges even as they lambasted other beneficiaries quite like themselves. Thus, how the electorate views itself can have political impact. Letter writers often give evidence of that when constructing – and invoking – their fellow citizens ("the people of this country have got to learn that..."). They may not realize they are doing so, but their sociological commentaries "leak out" nonetheless.

Writers also manage their own presence in a text. Some writers stand back coolly, sounding clinical and dispassionate. Others invest themselves fully, drawing on their personal experiences and prejudices. Some write with altruism in mind, while others nag their readers. These self-management strategies affect the tone of a text: Do the writers display a reflexive humility or do they command the stage? Do they position themselves as fellow travelers or as people who can lead others out of the wilderness? Are they tightly wound or unemotional, respectful or threatening?[59]

To capture how the writers made attributions about themselves, their audiences, and their leaders, the following probes were used:

- *Positive Leadership Traits/Negative Leadership Traits: qualities in political leaders considered worthy or reprehensible.* A democracy needs good leaders but, equally, it needs agreement about the criteria for assessing leadership. Have these criteria changed over the years? Do writers now report a leadership vacuum, with elected officials seeking excessive financial gain or overweening ego gratification? Do writers emphasize doctrinal fidelity, canny strategic behavior, or political backbone? What is the balance between psychological characterizations of leaders versus their intellectual, social, and moral qualities?

- *Voter Perceptions: "we" statements that characterize the broader polity.* This category tracks authors' social projections, what they think of those with whom they share the world. Via such statements, authors often reveal what they take for granted: The extent to which Americans agree with one another, their intelligence about political affairs, their support for the military, their financial resolve, how they differ from non-Americans, and their willingness to battle against the odds.

- *Author Declarations: disclosure of personal experiences or values.* This probe tabulates writers' self-references, including comments about their feeling states, knowledge levels, behavioral inclinations, and even their personal dreams. This category sometimes reveals alienation effects – the distance between the author and the electorate (e.g., "I know what I'm about to say is unpopular but...") – or the author's deepest commitments ("I can't possibly endure another four years with the incumbent"). This category also records references to prior experience and personal confidence.

Tensions

Politics, they say, is not patty cakes, and this final set of probes captures its faultlines. In some elections, for example, people vote against a candidate rather than for his or her opponent. Such tensions often lead to anomalous effects: Some voters have no idea what their opponents stand for, but they despise them nonetheless. Other voters sound like political almanacs but jumble things when drawing practical conclusions. Still others see life from a cramped perspective, showing no ability to take the perspective of another or to express sympathy for their misfortunes. Fox News devotees may watch the news five hours a day but be unable to spell the word "Democrat," a fate shared by MSNBC stalwarts whose spelling problems pivot in the opposite direction. Political tensions, that is, can be blinding.

How do people explain such tensions? There is some evidence, for example, that US voters now have a less coherent understanding of the nation than they did in prior years. Partisan groups have become so fragmented and special interest camps so widely distributed that politics no longer makes sense to many Americans.[60] In the current age, if a bipartisan bill miraculously slipped through both houses of Congress and was happily signed by the president, nobody would believe it. Not surprisingly, then, most polls find equivalent antipathy for both political parties.[61] For these reasons, says Daniel Klein, the war metaphor – the war on drugs, the war on crime, the war on poverty – is the only family of metaphors that can move people.[62] Everyone is at war; we just don't know with whom.

All of these tensions come to the fore at election time. Disparities of income become the watchword for Democrats, diminished freedoms for Republicans. Tensions related to race, gender, region, and religion are also magnified, making contemporary campaigns toxic for many Americans. "The Left, the party of hope, sees our country's moral identity as still to be achieved, rather than as needing to be preserved," said the late Richard Rorty, while "the Right thinks that our country already has a moral identity, and hopes to keep that identity intact."[63] These deep-seated value differences have always been there, of course, but the ante has been upped because of how modern campaigns are conducted: push polls, character assassinations, negative advertising, and dirty tricks with social media. Many Americans cannot decide which they hate more: political outcomes or political processes.

To get a handle on this medley of tensions, three final sets of probes were developed:

- *Oppositional Literacy: people's capacity to explain what their opponents think.* Conflict is inevitable in a democracy, so it is important that disputants understand one another even when disagreeing with one another. This probe assesses writers' ability to explain their opponents' positions. Do they do so skeletally, purposefully, or not at all? This probe records direct quotations or paraphrases made by others, but it also looks for innuendo ("here's what they meant by that") and hypothetical statements (e.g., "The next thing they'll say is...").
- *Evidence of Coordination/Evidence of Disunity: who gets along with whom.* This category keys on (positive or negative) indicators of mutuality and interdependence. It assumes that even a cynical comment (e.g., "all pols scratch one another's backs") shows functionality, if not desirability, because people are at least working with one another. All polities need such linkages – between politicians and interest groups, between citizens and the press, between Congress and the courts, etc. A society's greatest challenge, of course, is to match this functionality with desired political outcomes.

• *Campaign Advice/Campaign Complaints: explanation for why campaigns succeed or fail.* Letter writers constantly make suggestions for improving campaigns, often identifying the baneful effects of partisan, regional, and media variables. But they also trace bad campaigns to incumbency abuses and an assortment of personality flaws. Writers are particularly upset with laws enshrining questionable funding practices, gerrymandered districts, and ethical breaches (mud-slinging, name-calling, payoffs, etc.).

Considering that letters to the editor average only a couple of hundred words in length, using sixteen separate probes to sort them out may seem like overkill. My defense is that while understandings of "public opinion" are now quite advanced because of survey studies, the study of "public opinions" – how ordinary people talk about politics without being prompted – is in its infancy. Also, because hope is an elusive concept, the sort of thing everyone intuitively understands until asked to explain it, I felt the need to attack the concept in as many grounded ways as possible. Ultimately, of course, the value of my approach will be determined by whether or not it reveals something important. I believe that it does.[64]

CONCLUSION

My assumption throughout this book is that the very existence of the letters column is a talisman of hope. The letters column is not a sign that solutions have been found or that grand possibilities are guaranteed. It is, however, a sign that people feel they have some answers. They are often wrong, of course, but their "hoping activities" send a message of possibility. And when readers read such letters, especially when they do so habitually, they become co-conspirators. Together, writers and readers thumb their noses at Euripides, who called hope "a curse on humanity," and Pascal, who described it as "a hollow-cheeked harlot," and Aquinas, who recommended hope only to youths, drunks, fools, and others "lacking deliberation."[65]

The existence of the letters column is a sign that a broad, inclusive, and enlightened democracy is still under construction, so no hosannas should be sung just yet. But hoping activities send another signal as well – that some creed, cultural tradition, network of human energies, or newly arrived leader may have answers heretofore unconsidered. As a result, working on hope "frees up energy that might otherwise be absorbed by resistance and denial."[66] As the environmentalist Paul Hawken tells us, "hope only makes sense when it doesn't make sense to be hopeful."[67]

In a perfect world, the work of hope can become contagious, perhaps even a legacy, which returns us to the 2016 presidential election. As I watched the fury and resentment being spit out by Ted Cruz's hardliners, Donald Trump's nativists, and Chris Christie's bitter minions, I kept wondering why the TV networks loved them so much. These devotees of the candidates were rarely eloquent, but that seemed to make little difference. Their faces were angry and television loves angry faces. Naturally, a political candidate should be outraged when people's jobs, religions, or neighborhoods are being threatened, but then there are the children: "Look, honey, Daddy's on TV ... shrieking." This, too, is a legacy. The quieter form of civic hope displayed by the letter writers in this book is, I believe, a better way. It is also easier on the kids.

Endnotes

1 Ginger Gibson and Chris Kahn, "America's angry voters divvied by Trump and Sanders: poll," *Reuters*, January 30, 2016. Accessed at www.reuters.com/article/us-usa-election-anger-idUSMTZSAPEC1USEXIB3.

2 Terry Eagleton, *Hope without Optimism* (Charlottesville: University of Virginia Press, 2015), p. 10.

3 David Niven, "The other side of optimism: high expectations and the rejection of status quo politics," *Political Behavior*, 22(1) (2000), 74.

4 Arthur C. Brooks, "We need optimists," *New York Times*, July 25, 2015. Accessed at www.nytimes.com/2015/07/26/opinion/sunday/arthur-c-brooks-we-need-optimists.html?_r=0.

5 Niven, "The other side of optimism," 74, 77.

6 Quoted in Paul Rogat Loeb, "Hope, voting and creating the world you want to live in: getting to the polls is just the first step," *The Nation*, September 10, 2014, 7. Accessed at www.thenation.com/article/hope-voting-and-creating-world-you-want-live/.

7 Cornel West, "The moral obligations of living in a democratic society," in David Bartstone and Eduardo Mendieta (eds.), *The Good Citizen* (New York: Routledge, 1999), p. 12.

8 H. L. Mencken, *Prejudices: Second Series* (New York: Alfred A. Knopf, 1920), pp. 211–18.

9 Friedrich Nietzsche, *Human, All Too Human: A Book for Free Spirits*, trans. Marion Faber and Stephan Lehmann (Lincoln, NB: Bison Books, 1996), section 70.

10 Darrel Moellendorf, "Hope as a political virtue," *Philosophical Papers*, 35 (2006), 416.

11 Gabriel Marcel, quoted in Eagleton, *Hope without Optimism*, p. 72.

12 Quoted in Patrick Shade, *Habits of Hope: A Pragmatic Theory* (Nashville: Vanderbilt University Press, 2001), p. 6.

13 Eagleton, *Hope without Optimism*, p. 5.

14 Ibid, 16.

15 Quoted in ibid, 32.

16 This is Scott Lash's term. See "Being after time: towards a politics of melancholy," *Cultural Values*, 2 (1998), 315. For more on these matters see Peter Thompson, "Religion, utopia and the metaphysics of contingency," in Peter Thompson and Slavoj Žižek (eds.), *The Privatization of Hope: Ernst Bloch and the Future of Utopia* (Durham: Duke University Press, 2013), pp. 82–105 and Wayne Hudson, "Bloch and a philosophy of the proterior," in Peter Thompson and Slavoj Žižek (eds.), *The Privatization of Hope: Ernst Bloch and the Future of Utopia* (Durham: Duke University Press, 2013), pp. 21–36.

17 Moellendorf, "Hope as a political virtue," 426.

18 Eagleton, *Hope without Optimism*, p.61.

19 Ibid, 58.

20 Ibid, 85.

21 Loren Goldman, "What is political hope? Kantian reflections on practical philosophy." Paper presented at the annual meeting of the Midwest Political Science Association, Chicago, April 2008, 8.

22 This is Slavoj Žižek's interpretation of Bloch's concept of hope. See "Preface: Bloch's ontology of not-yet-being," in Peter Thompson and Slavoj Žižek (eds.), *The Privatization of Hope: Ernst Bloch and the Future of Utopia* (Durham: Duke University Press, 2013), p. 7.

23 Tali Sharot, *The Optimism Bias: A Tour of the Irrationally Positive Brain* (New York: Pantheon Books, 2011), p. 57.

24 See Goldman, "What is political hope," 9.

25 Victoria McGeer, "The art of good hope," *The Annals of the American Academy of Political and Social Science*, 592 (2004), 108.

26 In this way, hope differs from what Jonathan Haidt calls "elevation," a more self-contained and less cognitive construct. See Jonathan Haidt, "The positive emotion of elevation," *Prevention & Treatment*, 3 (2000), 1–5.

27 John Braithwaite, "Emancipation and hope," *The Annals of the American Academy of Political and Social Science*, 592 (2004), 82.

28 McGeer, "The art of good hope," 104, 105.

29 Oliver Burkeman, "The power of negative thinking: both ancient philosophy and modern psychology suggest that darker thoughts can make us happier," *Wall Street Journal*, December 7, 2012, 5. Accessed at www.wsj.com/articles/SB10001424127887324705104578147333270637790.

30 Ibid, 8.

31 Luc Bovens, "The value of hope," *Philosophy and Phenomenological Research*, 59 (1999), 679.

32 Kimberly Gross, Paul R. Brewer, and Sean Aday, "Confidence in government and emotional responses to terrorism after September 11, 2001," *American Politics Research*, 37 (2009), 107–28.

33 Shade, *Habits of Hope*, p. 135.

34 Charles Richard Snyder, "Hope theory: rainbows in the mind," *Psychological Inquiry*, 13 (2002), 249.

35 Ibid, 250.

36 Philip Pettit, "Hope and its place in mind," *The Annals of the American Academy of Political and Social Science*, 592 (2004), 161.

37 Ibid, 162.

38 Andrew J. W. Civettini, "Hope and voting: exploring the usefulness of hope scales in examining political participation." Paper presented at the Annual Meeting of the Midwest Political Science Association, Chicago, 2010.

39 Peter Drahos, "Trading in public hope," *The Annals of the American Academy of Political and Social Science*, 592 (2004), 20.

40 Harold M. Zullow, "American exceptionalism and the quadrennial peak in optimism," in Arthur H. Miller and Bruce E. Gronbeck (eds.), *Presidential Campaigns and American Self-Images* (Boulder: Westview, 1994), p. 994.

41 Bernard P. Dauenhauer, "The place of hope in responsible political practice," in Jaklin A. Eliott (ed.) *Interdisciplinary Perspectives on Hope* (New York: Nova Science Publishers, 2005), p. 88.

42 Andrew Norris, "Becoming who we are: democracy and the political problem of hope," *Critical Horizons: A Journal of Philosophy and Social Theory*, 9 (2008), 80.

43 Ibid, 86.

44 Valerie Braithwaite, "The hope process and social inclusion," *The Annals of the American Academy of Political and Social Science*, 592 (2004), 146.

45 J. L. Austin, *How to Do Things with Words*, 2nd edn. (Cambridge: Harvard University Press, 1975).

46 Chris Ingraham, "Talking (about) the elite and mass: vernacular rhetoric and discursive status," *Philosophy and Rhetoric*, 46 (2013), 6.

47 Karol Edward Soltan, "Civic competence, attractiveness, and maturity," in Stephen L. Elkin and Karol Edward Soltan (eds.), *Citizen Competence and Democratic Institutions* (University Park: Pennsylvania State University Press, 1999), p. 20.

48 Richard Rorty, *Contingency, Irony and Solidarity* (Cambridge: Harvard University Press, 1989), p. 86.

49 Each time a deposit was made, a Frequency of 1 was recorded, as well as a Density count (i.e., the total number of words comprising the segment). The Frequency data indicated which topics were being introduced by the writers, while the Density data revealed the writers' rhetorical flourish: Did they address a given matter cursorily or expansively? The overall picture of civic hope provided by Frequency vs. Density data was not materially different. After examining both scores in considerable depth, I decided to concentrate on the Density data in this book because it captured more of the writers' individual styles and rhetorical predilections.

50 Surprisingly, even though all sixteen variables were allowed to mingle in these ways, the correlations among them were usually slight. Of the variables, four correlated with none of the other twelve; the remaining variables correlated with only one or two others, and even then only at .20 and .30 levels. As a result, I feel we have captured the writers' remarks in all of their complexity.

51 Jürgen Habermas, "Citizenship and national identity," in Bart Van Steenbergen (ed.), *The Condition of Citizenship* (London: Sage, 1994), p. 23.

52 David Matthews, *Politics for People: Finding a Responsible Public Voice* (Urbana: University of Illinois Press, 1994), p. 194.

53 James W. Prothro and Charles M. Grigg, "Fundamental principles of democracy: bases of agreement and disagreement," *Journal of Politics*, 22 (1960), 285. See also John R. Hibbing and Elizabeth Theiss-Morse, *Congress as Public Enemy: Public Attitudes toward American Political Institutions* (Cambridge: Cambridge University Press, 1995), p. 125.

54 For more on this matter see Michael Skey, "The mediation of nationhood: communicating the world as a world of nations," *Communication Theory*, 24 (2014), 1–20.

55 Robert N. Bellah, "Citizenship, diversity, and the search for the common good," in Robert E. Calvert (ed.), *"The Constitution of the People": Reflections on Citizens and Civil Society* (Lawrence: University Press of Kansas, 1991), p. 59.

56 Roderick P. Hart, *Seducing America: How Television Charms the Modern Voter* (New York: Oxford, 1994).

57 Eri Bertsou, "Disentangling political distrust: what do citizens mean and think when expressing distrust towards political institutions and politicians?" Paper presented at the annual meeting of the Midwest Political Science Association, Chicago, April 2014.

58 Alec McGillis, "Who turned my blue state red: why poor areas vote for politicians who want to slash the safety net," *New York Times*, November 20, 2015. Accessed at www.nytimes.com/2015/11/22/opinion/sunday/who-turned-my-blue-state-red.html?_r=0.

59 For more on these matters of tone see Stephen Hart, *Cultural Dilemmas of Progressive Politics: Styles of Engagement among Grassroots Activists* (Chicago: University of Chicago Press, 2001); Lee Edwards, "Accommodating agency and reflexivity in Bourdieu's analysis of language and discourse." Paper presented at the annual meeting of the International Communication Association, Boston, May 2011 and Dana Chabot, "In defense of 'moderate' relativism and 'skeptical' citizenship." Paper presented at the annual convention of the American Political Science Association, Washington, DC, 1993.

60 For more on these matters see W. Lance Bennett, "The uncivic culture: communication, identity, and the rise of lifestyle politics," *PS: Political Science and Politics*, 31 (1998), 740–61.

61 Frank Newport, Lydia Saad, and Michael Traugott, "Informed Americans rate both parties in Congress worse," *Gallup*, October 5, 2015. Accessed at www.gallup.com/poll/186011/informed-americans-rate-parties-congress-worse.aspx.

62 Daniel B. Klein, "The people's romance: why people love government (as much as they do)," *The Independent Review*, 10 (2005), 21.

63 Rorty, *Contingency, Irony and Solidarity*, p. 31.

64 Three additional points about our coding system are worth mentioning: (1) *Coding additivity*: Given the size and complexity of the Codebook, combining its various measures into a single grand index of civic hope was a temptation. I resisted that temptation, however, deciding that no good theoretical structure existed to guide such combinatorial work. Because the concept

of civic hope is new and because my measures had never been used before, I decided to let the individual indices tell their own stories. Descriptive statistics will be provided throughout this book as well as some straightforward tests of difference and, occasionally, some factor analysis. No statistical modeling will be tempted, however, although doing so in subsequent years is surely possible.

(2) *Coding specificity*: When coding a passage, many content analysts start by inspecting a text and then applying their category system to it. We operated in precisely the opposite fashion. Coders began the process by calling up one of our categories (or subcategories) and then asking if a match could be found in the text itself. By applying the tag to the text rather than the text to the tag, our analysts kept from being overly inventive (i.e., imagining that something was present in a letter when it was not). Coders were told that if no evidence of their tags could be found in the text, recording a 0 was more than appropriate. This approach had the benefit of boosting coders' confidence and also keeping them from being too fussy. In addition, rather than asking coders to become familiar with all sixteen variables in the Codebook, each coder focused on only four, a procedure that made training coders infinitely easier and that dramatically raised the reliability statistics for the overall coding protocol.

(3) *Coding reliability*: As mentioned earlier, the data reported here were gathered over a considerable period of time, which required frequent retraining as the various coders cycled in and out of the project. (Luckily, there was always at least a 33–50 percent overlap among the coding teams.) Fortunately, the Codebook proved to be straightforward enough and specific enough to make the training fairly efficient. Also, because the coders had to master only four coding categories, they were able to get up to speed quickly. We set .80 as the desired reliability level for moving coders from the training routine to the coding routine; we had no difficulty in exceeding that threshold over the years. Continual spot-checks were used throughout the project to ensure that the tags were continuously applied in appropriate ways.

65 Quoted in Eagleton, *Hope without Optimism*, 43.

66 Judith Andre, "Open hope as a civic virtue: Ernst Bloch and Lord Buddha," *Social Philosophy Today*, 29 (2013), 97.

67 Paul Hawken, "You are brilliant and the earth is hiring," in Paul Loeb (ed.). *The Impossible Will Take a Little While: Perseverance and Hope in Troubled Times* (New York: Basic Books, 2014), p. 59.

PART II

THE SEARCH FOR CIVIC HOPE

4

People Who Write Letters

For twenty years or so, Kenneth Gregory published a series of books reproducing letters to the editor from the *London Times*. When doing so, Gregory luxuriantly sampled, among the *Times*' correspondents from 1900 through 1996, a list that included George Bernard Shaw, Neville Chamberlain, T. S. Eliot, Iris Murdoch, John le Carré, Evelyn Waugh, Arthur Conan Doyle, and other notables. Most of the letters, though, were submitted by ordinary citizens such as Mr. P. A. Williams of Sussex and Mr. Ernest Bradbury of Yorkshire. The letters Mr. Gregory anthologized were both long and short, pedestrian and profound, witty and foreboding. Distributed as they were among myriad topics, the letters provided a shirt-sleeved history of modern Britain, including how its people faced two world wars, dealt with various waves of immigration, and handled one political crisis after another. But the letters also contained reflections on sporting contests, fashion, culinary tastes, the rise of television, irksome train schedules, and religion, and several hundred disquisitions on politesse.

Charming though the Gregory compendia are, their titles command special attention, beginning with *The First Cuckoo*, traveling through the Second and Third Cuckoos, and ending twice, with *The Next to Last Cuckoo* and finally *The Last Cuckoo*. The Brits love their ornithology, of course, so that may explain the titles. But one also senses that Mr. Gregory had a satisfied smirk on his face when deciding which letters to include and which to leave entombed in the *Times*'s archives.

Crackpots. Curmudgeons. Busybodies. Dilettantes. Blowhards. Suitable descriptions of those who write letters to the editor? This chapter confronts that question by detailing a series of surveys conducted between 1993 and

2013 in the twelve US cities studied here. Without foreshadowing too much of this book, I can assure the reader that none of the writers would be candidates for *The Elite Yankee Cuckoo*, should Kenneth Gregory decide to jump across the pond and have another go at it. Although some of the letters I examined were erudite and many impeccably reasoned, they did not dally about. These were *American* letters, after all, authored by people who had neither time nor words to waste. Some of the writers were sardonic but not in a British sort of way. When using irony, they used it as a bludgeon; when skewering someone, they disemboweled them for good measure. No P. G. Wodehouses in my collection.

The best estimates available suggest that between 5 percent and 12 percent of the American people will write, or have written, a letter to the editor of their local newspaper.[1] Why do they do so? Political scientists, many of whom embrace the "rational actor perspective" (which holds that people act exclusively to advance their bottom lines), are perplexed by letter writers, since writing a letter "costs" people both time and privacy. Why not opt for a "free ride" and let others oversee the polity? Sidney Verba and his colleagues did not really answer that question but they did speculate that affect, not demographics, best explains civic engagement.[2] Communication scholars James Dillard and S. J. Backhaus agree, arguing that emotion is "a mediating force between civic deliberation and political involvement."[3] For some Americans, political involvement simply feels right. But why?

The surveys and interviews discussed in this chapter provide some answers to that question. My overall argument is that letter writers are ordinary in most ways, but that they also have some surprising characteristics. One gets a sense of those qualities in an interview we conducted with Paul S. of Provo, Utah:

Q: How do you think letter writers are regarded in your community?
A: Well, I have heard both sides. I've heard people say they would never write a letter to the editor; the only supposition you can draw from that statement is that only crackpot-type people – fanatics, zealots – write letters to the editor. The other point of view is that people who are concerned sincerely about pressing issues of the day take the time and trouble and do the research to write letters to the editor and that those doing so perform a public service.
Q: How do those opinions make you feel?
A: I know that the electorate ... covers a wide spectrum of viewpoints that ranges from ultra-liberal to right-wing fanaticism, so I have no

problem with the fact that people may disagree or have looked upon my particular letters – some people, at least – negatively. I'm just doing what I regard as a citizen's responsibility. It's something that people can do, like voting on Election Day.

Such earnestness is fairly typical of the writers we sampled. Paul S. knows who he is and why he does what he does. He has a remarkably generous understanding of what others may think of him and he admits, with neither grandiosity nor defensiveness, that they are entitled to their opinions. The online environment obliges, with one recent comment string discussing letter writers in the digital age:

- **Ima Fish**, Aug 23rd, 2008 @ 8:11am
  You're totally missing the point. The point is that people used to write well-thought-out and well-articulated letters to the editors. Now they're emailing crap. It's not really about whether they're on paper or sent via email. It's that they're unprintable because they're so poorly written.
- **ixelsid**, Aug 23rd, 2008 @ 4:11pm
  You sound like my dad complaining about how typewriters used to work so much better than keyboards. People have and always will write crap, paper letters or otherwise. The fact that you posted your piece of subjective garbage is proof of that. Go back to bed grandma.
- **Anonymous Coward**, Aug 25th, 2008 @ 4:38am
  People still write letters to the editor. The problem is they're all crazy people.
- **Pope Ratzo**, Aug 25th, 2008 @ 6:11am
  If you were to read the op-ed pages of the *New York Times* or *Washington Post*, you would find that indeed people still do write letters to the editor. The problem is, they are all employees of Right-Wing think tanks, *National Review* wankers or conservative talk-show hosts.
- **Anonymous Coward**, Aug 25th, 2008 @ 7:12am
  You really believe that newspaper writers as a whole are good writers and care much about good journalism and commentary? Wow, are you deluded.[4]

There are more than enough hypotheses here to guide any discussion of letter writers. We will consider such attitudes in this chapter, providing empirical answers to a set of questions posed some years ago by journalism historian Emmett Buell, who noted that letter writers are often seen as ersatz citizens – lonely, disaffected, apart from others. As a result, says Buell, they are often ignored by researchers because they are "numerically insignificant, methodologically troublesome and ... theoretically uninteresting."[5]

While one cannot increase letter writers' numbers by fiat, one can study them carefully. As for letter writers being theoretically uninteresting, I disagree completely. For me, letter writing is a special sort of civic investment. It represents more commitment to politics than most citizens possess and yet it is also a quiet activity (no door-to-door canvassing, no late-night meetings). As such, it represents a middle ground of involvement, requiring energy, but energy that is neither determinative nor injunctive. I shall argue that letter writers are thus a multiplicity: (1) committed skeptics, (2) daily auditors, (3) watchful residents, and (4) political advocates. They stand somewhere between the ordinary voter and the impassioned activist and hence can tell us much about the politics of our times.

WRITERS AS SKEPTICS

During the past twenty years, we conducted three surveys of letter writers and non-letter writers in the study's twelve cities. Mail surveys were used in in all cases, with 642 solicitations made of letter writers and 6,183 sent to a random sample of non-writers drawn from local phone books. Each respondent received an individually addressed envelope, and no financial incentive was provided for completing the questionnaire. When unreachable residents were subtracted from these totals, and after two reminder postcards were issued, 350 writers and 1,068 non-writers responded to the surveys, representing usable response rates of 54.5 percent and 17.3 percent respectively.[6] No doubt, the latter figure results from our having sent out a (1) long, (2) mailed, (3) site-specific, (4) uncompensated survey. The former figure, though, is measurably higher, indicating letter writers' special interest in politics as well as their consummate curiosity.

The survey instrument consisted of forty questions, most of which required five-choice, Likert-type responses. In addition to the usual demographic questions, the respondents were asked to estimate their attentiveness to the most recent presidential campaign, their overall media habits, and their evaluation of news coverage. We also inquired into their political efficacy – whether they felt they had an impact on public decision-making and whether political officials paid attention to people like them. Finally, respondents were asked to report how much they trusted governing institutions.[7] Appendix B contains the survey administered.

The overall sample of roughly 1,500 souls was divided fairly equally among the twelve cities (an average of 124 respondents/city), with a few more surveys returned from the South and West, a bit fewer from the East and Midwest. Of the respondents, 37 percent were women and 63 percent men. Most were employed, most had lived in the target city for two to three decades, most owned their own homes, most (79 percent) had completed a year or more of post-high school education. Managers, teachers, office workers, and retirees made up 70 percent of the sample, with the remainder toiling away at pink-collar and blue-collar jobs. Of those completing our surveys, 40 percent were Republicans, 45 percent Democrats, and 15 percent Independents, "others," or non-disclosers. Finally, 60 percent subscribed to the local newspaper. Overall, then, our sample differed from a random cross-section of Americans, but it was a fairly good representation of voters in Salinas, Lake Charles, and cities of their ilk.

In addition to the paper-and-pencil measures, fifty in-depth phone interviews were conducted (in 2015–16) with letter writers in the same twelve cities. The interviewees were drawn from a list of the writers who had filled out prior surveys for us and had declared continued interest in our study. These discussions were particularly valuable, with our interviewees offering layered observations of the letter-writing craft. Most were aware of why they wrote letters, the responses they hoped for (and received), and how their letters figured into the larger civic enterprise. Several told us they were frustrated with their local newspaper, decrying the limits placed on the length of their letters, how frequently they were published, and the heavy-handedness of some editors. The interviews reinforced what the paper-and-pencil surveys hinted at: letter writers are both colorful and irrepressible.

Overall Trends

Our surveys echoed in many ways what other researchers have found.[8] The letter writers were overwhelmingly Anglo (93 percent), imbalanced by gender (69 percent males, 31 percent females), a bit older than non-writers (sixty-three vs. fifty-seven years old), somewhat better educated (one extra year of post-high school education), and, naturally, they were more faithful newspaper subscribers (77 percent vs. 56 percent for non-writers).[9] On the other hand, there were no differences between writers and non-writers in terms of party ID, home ownership, family income, longevity in the state, media attentiveness, or media satisfaction.[10] While 99 percent of the writers voted during the recent presidential election,

93 percent of the non-writers did so as well. This latter figure is much higher than what one would expect in a random sample of the American people, a sign that voters in my twelve cities were exceedingly generous about filling out surveys received in the mail without being paid to do so and that non-voters declined to participate.[11]

Three pieces of anecdotal data tell us something interesting about letter writers. As mentioned above, the response rates for writers were starkly higher than for non-writers, clearly indicating the former's special interest in politics. Second, I found that while 45 percent of the writers voted Democrat in 1992 and 49.3 percent did so in 2012, only 31 percent of the writers voted Democrat in 1997. These findings confirm a long-standing piece of folk wisdom: Republicans become more engaged when a Democrat sits in the White House, while Ds pick up the slack when their party is out of power. These data suggest that letter-writing is a contrarian's enterprise, a supposition reinforced with a third piece of evidence: When the surveys were returned, we noticed that some contained hand-written scrawls. These included wry observations about the questions asked, speculations about the researcher's motives, and corrections of spelling and syntax (100 percent of which were incorrect!). We began recording these emendations, dubbing them "volunteered commentary." Unsurprisingly, the letter writers provided *three times* as many unrequested comments as non-writers, once again attesting to the former's garrulousness.[12]

One of the most dramatic differences between the writers and non-writers lay in their differential political investments. While some commentators complain that letter writers are lethargic except when taking potshots at public officials, that is manifestly untrue. We asked nine separate questions about the respondents' activities during the recent election and found major differences on each dimension. Writers were far more likely to have worked on campaigns (31 percent vs. 6 percent) or to have made political contributions (61 percent vs. 24 percent) than non-writers. They watched party conventions more regularly (98.8 percent vs. 75.2 percent), as well as debates (94.2 percent vs. 86.0 percent); they also consumed more political ads (75 percent vs. 56 percent) and news broadcasts (98.5 percent vs. 48.0 percent), and spent more hours listening to talk radio (49.7 percent vs. 35.2 percent) and TV talk shows (57.9 percent vs. 43.7 percent), than non-writers. Finally, the writers discussed politics with their friends more regularly (96.3 percent) than did non-writers (84.1 percent).[13] These data reinforce what Emmett Buell discovered forty years ago: "letter-writing is not the work of a 'crank,' but the logical activity of the political activist."[14]

Political Efficacy

The most unexpected finding in our surveys was also the most intriguing: As we have just seen, writers had far higher scores on Political Involvement (a composite variable built from the nine subaltern questions) than nonwriters. But the surveys also showed that they had significantly *lower* scores on External Efficacy (perceived governmental responsiveness to the citizenry), and *dramatically lower* Internal Efficacy scores (voters' felt capacities for effecting political change).[15] These findings seem profoundly backward, or at least counterintuitive. Shouldn't politically active people have a heightened self-image? Expect to be heard? Be empowered by their letter-writing? Perhaps they should, but our data point in the opposite direction: Writers do not feel efficacious ... and so they write. Writers do not think that governmental agents behave properly ... and so they write. People with such a low sense of efficacy should, if logic prevailed, abandon politics and pursue more personal goals. But they do not.[16]

These findings fly in the face of common sense, and also fly in the face of prior research with people in general. Completely separate studies conducted over a twenty-year period by researchers at the University of Virginia, the University of Connecticut, the University of Central Florida, the University of Florida, Costal Carolina University, and Texas A&M University have sung in chorus: People who feel that they matter, who sense that democratic institutions serve them well, participate in the political process, while those low in efficacy do not.[17]

These studies report a kind of "retreating skepticism" that steers people away from the political arena. Letter writers, in contrast, embrace a "motivating skepticism." Although they did not focus on letter writers, political scientists Joseph Gershtenson and Dennis Plane found similar attitudes among political activists. These individuals were "healthy skeptics," constantly vigilant; when they saw something wrong, they worked to correct it.[18] People like this lean forward, say John Gastil and Michael Xenos, even though doing so does not eliminate their political distrust.[19] According to John Hibbing and Elizabeth Theiss-Morse, too much faith in the political system can actually inhibit participation.[20] Communication scholar Jack McLeod and his colleague at the University of Wisconsin found exactly the same thing: People participate in community forums when they *do not* feel empowered.[21] Letter writers feel this way as well, or so our surveys suggest.

This research shows the difference between cynicism and skepticism. Confronted with an immovable object, the cynic quits the scene but the skeptic places a different bet: One more letter, perhaps two, will awaken the gods of change. The psychology of letter-writing is therefore complex, feeding off negativity to advance the author's political goals. Writing a letter becomes not just a compositional exercise but a way of acting in the world. "Of course they're not listening," the letter writer reasons, "so I must speak." "Things are still broken," the writer reasons further, "so I must speak again." Who can understand such reasoning? Fans of the Cleveland Browns, perhaps.

Writer Individuality

What else, other than skepticism, explains why writers write? Figure 4.1 reports the network of relationships found among the demographic and attitudinal variables, but the picture it paints is not particularly satisfying. It shows that older writers watch more TV than younger ones; the more education a writer has, the more money he or she makes; efficacious writers are more politically trusting; older writers feel more empowered than younger ones (because the former are naïve and the latter worldly wise?); educated writers tend to be more recent city arrivals and, perhaps as a result, feel less political efficacy; and writers who are displeased with the media are displeased with government as well.

Most of this seems logical enough, but nothing really explains why letter writers get politically involved. One could easily imagine that better educated, wealthier writers would see the wisdom of becoming engaged, but my data do not show that. It would also make sense for politically trusting people to write letters (since they could anticipate a satisfying response), but that explanation does not hold. Efficacious people, too, should become politically active; if not, what does efficacy mean? And yet the only clear explanation of the writers' political involvement is that those who are unhappy with the media scrutinize political campaigns more carefully. Otherwise, Political Involvement remains a lonely variable.

Only pure individuality, I submit, explains letter writers. *Writers write for a variety of reasons but, mostly, for their own reasons.* They are iconoclasts. They listen to the beat within. A heightened sense of obligation pushes them forward. Some writers write because they are angry, others because they are healers. Some are doyens of the community, some rebels. Some hate government, some seek its salvation. In other words, it is the *absence of relationships* between political involvement and the other variables in Figure 4.1 that tells the richest story. Scratch a letter writer and you will find independence.

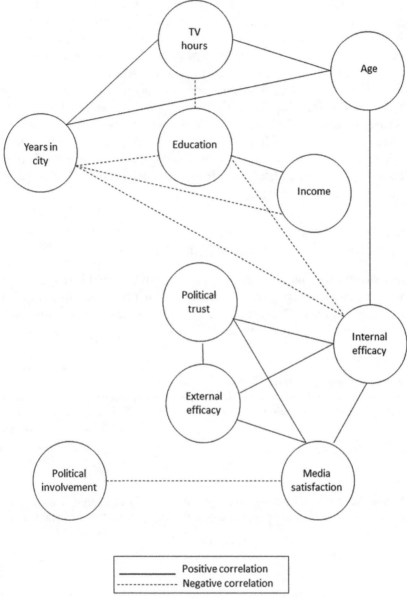

FIGURE 4.1 Political Involvement: The Lonely Variable (writers only, n = 328)

We pursued this lead further by examining all of the variables simultaneously through a grouping procedure known as factor analysis. This approach identified three fairly distinct types of writers: *Blue-Collar Believers* (older, long-time residents who were less well-off but who felt highly efficacious and who were politically trusting); *Busy Trustees* (younger, recent residents of the city with high Media Satisfaction and Internal/External Efficacy but low Political Involvement); and *Skeptical Patricians* (well-educated and well-paid residents with low senses of efficacy and low Political Involvement as well). Republicans were slightly more likely to be Busy Trustees; more Democrats (and men) could be found among the Skeptical Patricians; and Independents (and women) were more likely to be Blue-Collar Believers.[22] But while it is possible to identify subsets of writers in this way, the larger point remains: Writers write letters on schedules of their own making for reasons of their own choosing. One could pick a letter from our database at random to verify the truth of that claim.

Imagined Impact

The surveys we conducted were helpful in getting a broad-based view of who the letter writers were (and were not), but the interviews revealed how they reasoned. One of our guiding questions was this: "Do you think your letters are having an impact?" Some of the writers responded with a sense of derring-do:

People occasionally will stop and make a comment to me in the drugstore or the synagogue. And when I visited with the mayor over an issue of public prayer, he indicated that my name was not unknown to him.

(*Beston A., Trenton*)

* * * * * *

I know that the deputy county attorney [noticed my letter] because he was, again, a friend of my son's and he made a comment. I imagine they do have impact.

(*Patricia B., Billings*)

* * * * * *

Yes, I've been contacted by local officials when it affected, you know, some of their operations.

(*Dave G., Duluth*)

* * * * * *

I got a phone call about a week later from somebody I had never heard of or never met. He had somehow googled me and found my phone number and he called me to tell me how happy he was that I'd written that letter.

(Eileen L., St. Joseph)

These were the exceptions, though. The majority of our interviewees seemed surprised by our question, as if "impact" were an extraterrestrial construct for them. When answering, it was as if they were posing the question to themselves for the first time:

I would imagine that maybe they do. I don't know, but I've never had a comment that would get me to think that they do, but I would think if they're very smart, they would read any letters that go into the editor.

(Peggy B., St. Joseph)

* * * * * *

I'm not sure. I'm not sure. Although I have, after I wrote letters, received feedback. But it was from colleagues and people who said, you know, "I agree with you" ... but you know, you hang around with people who are like-minded about social issues.

(Carol B., Roanoke)

* * * * * *

It's like the little boy down on the shore, you know, with the crabs. He doesn't save very many of them, but those he saves probably are very appreciative. So I send them out [anyway].

(Edmund K., St. Joseph)

* * * * * *

I don't know what the impact would be. It depends on what side of the fence you're on. Either you like me or you don't. Most of the time ... I get some comments like "great letter" [but] I don't know what the impact is. I really don't care.

(Hal N., Wichita Falls)

Hal N.'s last statement is the most intriguing. Despite his plucky beginning, he ends in a place common to the writers we interviewed. What impact are you having? "Well, if any, minimal, next to nothing," says Beston A. of Trenton; "I mean one doesn't influence public opinion by sending letters to the editor." What's the purpose of such letters, then?

"It's all a placebo, a fraud," says Larry S. of Duluth. Editors "don't care about the ideas and don't care about the proposals or the suggestions that are made in these letters." Then what keeps you going? "I don't write with the idea that I'm going to change anybody's mind," says Douglas O. of Billings; "I write just for my own edification." Well, if elected officials aren't paying attention, what about your fellow citizens? "I bet you couldn't probably peg it at about 5 to 10 percent of actual newspaper readers actually bother to read the editorial page," says Richard C. of Roanoke; "they just pass over it. They're looking at newspapers these days more as entertainment than they are as information."

So here is our paradox: Writers expend considerable effort to keep up with current affairs, to get involved, to write a letter, but with no guarantee of progress. And yet they journey on. There is a certain magic to their doing so, a remarkable resilience as well. Perhaps these people are self-absorbed and delusional, unwilling to see the folly of their ways. Is there a second explanation for why they write? Civic hope, perhaps.

Writer Subgroups

With only 350 writers in our survey pool, one must be careful when commenting on subsets of the sample. But there were some expectable differences, a few surprises as well. When the surveys from the 1990s were compared to that conducted in 2013, we found that recent writers were older than those surveyed earlier (sixty-seven vs. sixty-one years of age), a bit better educated, slightly wealthier, and had lived in the target cities somewhat longer. Democrats and Independents now write letters a bit more frequently than they did in the 1990s, but today's writers showed the same level of Political Involvement found within the earlier cohorts.[23]

Interestingly, recent non-writers had somewhat higher Internal and External Efficacy scores than those who filled out earlier surveys and they had higher Media Satisfaction as well.[24] But there were *no* such differences among the letter writers. Their attitudes toward the political enterprise contained the same mixture of approach and avoidance we found twenty years earlier. Across the surveys, the letter writers proved obdurate.

There were a few differences between male and female writers, but they amounted to little. Unsurprisingly, male writers were slightly better educated and had slightly higher incomes than women. Female writers had lived in their current city longer and, perhaps as a result, reported somewhat higher Internal Efficacy.[25] But male and female writers differed not a whit on External Efficacy, Political Involvement, Media Satisfaction, Political Trust, or party ID. As we will see in Chapter 9 of this volume, the letters they wrote were much alike, perhaps suggesting a new era in gender relations in the United States.

We found a few differences between Republican and Democratic letter writers, although they too were modest. Republican writers had slightly higher External Efficacy scores, more Media Satisfaction, and a bit more Political Trust than Democrats.[26] But their Political Involvement was almost identical, as was their sense of Internal Efficacy and of Media Awareness.

Overall, then, while letter writers differed from one another in several ways, they are far more interesting when viewed collectively. The surveys we conducted were modest but they identified what makes letter writers special: They are true individuals. We found no single psychological, sociological, or political variable to explain why they work so hard to stay informed or to be civically engaged. Perhaps such people can only be explained philosophically. With Rousseau, they hold that community concern should be fundamental to one's identity. With Locke, they hold that political rights can only be safeguarded by constant vigilance. With Mill, they hold that public debate ensures democratic vitality. Other Americans believe such things too, but not as vigorously. The letter writers are skeptics, yes, but skeptics in a different key.

WRITERS AS AUDITORS

Letter writers are haunted by information and are hermeneutical to the core. They consume more media products than most people, they evaluate them more thoroughly, and they distrust much of what they see and hear. For some writers, there is never enough information available. For others, the information they most desire – what governments know, for example – is never available to them in sufficient quantities and so they actively imagine such information, often over-actively imagining it. Letter writers both love and hate information. A fated romance, this.

What happens when you receive an education? You read the newspaper more often, say Michael Miller and his colleagues.[27] What happens when you read a newspaper? You learn more about politics, say Stacy Rhine and her colleagues.[28] What happens when you learn more about politics? You become more opinionated, report Joohan Kim et al.[29] What happens when you become more opinionated? You are better able to evaluate members of Congress, say Danny Hayes and Jennifer Lawless.[30] And what happens when you read your *local* newspaper with special fidelity? You participate more avidly in political affairs, says Patricia Moy's research team.[31] This cascade of effects descends with special force upon letter writers, thereby reinforcing what Stephen Bennett and his colleagues observed some years ago: "Reading is the core of civic literacy." It may also be the core of civic hope.

Letter writers are political creatures but, more important, they are curious. Pete B. of Duluth is one such person:

I write regularly. And I say regularly – sometimes weekly. But I don't always send them. Sometimes I just write them to clarify my thoughts and to get it off of me get closure, because I have kind of a social conscience, I think. And whether it's – my thinking – is right or not, I express my thoughts and then I, I do that kind of privately. But when I see something in print in particular that I don't agree with, or that I see differently, then I tend to write.

Pete B. summarizes here the internal/external tensions that letter writers consistently described to us. For each letter Pete sent to the *News Tribune*, he held back several more. He implicitly understood what sociologist Andrew Perrin argues, that "culture in the mind" – people's thoughts and values – is distinct from "culture in the world" – how they behave in public.[32] It is this distinction, says Perrin, that makes current voting routines so different from those of the nineteenth century, when one voted in the presence of both party officials and one's neighbors. Today, people are walled off from one another when casting their ballots. They are often walled off from alternative viewpoints as well. Except for letter writers.

"When I go to bed at night," says Patricia B. of Billings, "that's my best letter writing period. I do it in my head when I can't get to sleep." This kind of interiority, this wrestling with the world, is built on a foundation of dialectic. "It's far more interesting for me to read what the other guy is writing or thinking," says Beston A. of Trenton. "I don't know what other people do," said Carol B. of Roanoke, "but I read the letters and pick them off: 'This person's a crank. This person doesn't have sex right. This person has another agenda. This person listens to Fox News too much' ... I learn things about what other groups of people are thinking and I think that's important – to read things outside your comfort level."

But letter-writing is not just sociology. It can also be sternly corrective. "I mean, a lot of people have no idea who's Secretary of State, Secretary of Defense," says Eddie D. of Wichita Falls; "they have no freaking idea, because they keep their nose to these freaking reality shows rather than watching a news channel every once in a while just to find out what's going on around them." The letter writers we interviewed were not brilliantly conceptual but they were intellectually hungry. Some aligned themselves with fringe movements and others with exotic ideologies, but most were genuinely inquisitive:

Q: When was the last time that you wrote a letter to the editor?
A: Oh my goodness. You know, I'd have to look but I don't remember. It's probably been a year. I have another one that's ready to go whenever I think the time is right. Of course, the one thing that upsets me the most is I've been an independent all my life, and I voted for people on both parties. But the Republicans seem to – they've got their head stuck between their legs, and they can't seem to think beyond abortion issues. That comes up all the time, and I don't want you in my womb or my body or my bedroom. So I'll probably be sending another one before elections.
Q: So your letters tend to be about these abortion issues?
A: That and, of course, I was upset about the chicken situation. I think that's the last letter I wrote, where the US Department of Agriculture had OK'd the slaughter of chickens in the United States and shipping them to China to be processed and then shipped back here for you to eat. And I didn't think that was such a good idea. (*Jeannette F., Billings*)

In many ways, Jeannette F.'s interview harkens back to the origination of letter-writing itself, a time in the early nineteenth century when "women, denied access to public life, used the exchange of letters to try out and refine particular ideas and beliefs, develop a shared ideology, and create network links before becoming more active agents of social change and claiming a space in the public arena."[33] Entering the arena is one thing, but doing so competently is quite another. Our interviewees constantly stressed the importance of having epistolary standards. They resented gut-spilling and under-handedness, and especially this: "I don't go for anonymous," said Douglas O. of Billings; "you write it, you own it." "I am really glad the newspaper will call and make sure I'm a real person and I am who I say I am," declared David S. of Roanoke.

Most of our interviewees brought up the topic of craftsmanship – having the facts straight, eschewing showmanship. Said Elwood E. of Billings: "I've many times scribbled out something that I had some brilliant idea about and then waited until tomorrow and looked at it and said, nah, that's not worth it. That's not good, or that's going to make me look just run-of-the-mill politico or whatever. So I do take it seriously. If it's going to be printed, I want it to be something I'm willing to stand for."

As politically active people age, says political scientist Lance Bennett, they move from being "engaged citizens" to "dutiful citizens," shedding their group-based and class-based identities for a more communal self-understanding.[34]

Frank C. of St. Joseph understands dutifulness: "Sometimes I'll think about it and I decide I'm better off just not shooting off my mouth. If I don't know what I'm talking about for sure, I'd better think twice."

Older adults, says sociologist Tali Sharot, have a "decreased ability to take bad news into account," and hence may be especially good candidates for the call of civic hope.[35] What we sometimes attribute to blind conservativism in older adults, says Jerry Weaver of UCLA, may just be their penchant for care and deliberation.[36] Senior citizens often score higher on political knowledge quizzes, says political scientist Brittany Bramlett, not because they are brighter than young people, but because they are more careful.[37] Some years ago, Kent Jennings and George Marcus found a modest rise in "political sophistication" among older adults,[38] findings which dovetail with those of Stephen Bennett, who documented significant increases in political engagement among those over sixty-five.[39] It is hard to decide, says political psychologist Molly Andrews, if a painter is still a painter when he or she experiences loss of vision, or if athletes are still athletes when their physical dexterity diminishes. But old age "does not challenge but enhances" our social and political identities, says Andrews, thereby putting to work the storehouse of information built up over the life-course.[40]

Information is one thing and wisdom another. A wise letter to the editor shows judiciousness and finds the right rhetorical register. Says Kevin K. of Springfield: "What I like about social media is it's more immediate . . . I can get it out there in two or three lines," but "the beauty of a letter to the editor is that there is accountability. If your name is on it and your picture is on it, you're going to – you know, you're accountable." Knowing what you're talking about, defending your position, standing by it. But our interviewees stressed authenticity more than anything else:

Q: If you were the editor of the newspaper, what types of letters would you encourage people to write?
A: One that is reflective, close to their heart, rather than partisan politics, which I think is self-serving, short-sided, greedy, rapacious, unproductive, vicious. If people were to write what's really in their hearts rather than try to protect some silly self-interest, that's what I would encourage. (*Beston A., Trenton*)

For the letter writers we interviewed, wisdom results from informed content mixed with existential ownership of that content. Argument alone, and even passion alone, do not a wise letter make. Wisdom requires getting the facts straight and doing so in support of a position that improves the commonweal. Many of our interviewees were aware of these strictures and most took pride in the writing craft. Sometimes they wrote intemperate letters or said overly obvious things. Wisdom involves knowing when one has done so and not doing it again.

WRITERS AS RESIDENTS

The public opinion industry has grown increasingly sophisticated during the past hundred years, with survey researchers using phone-based and online techniques to tease out national trends. After gathering their data, surveyors build elaborate statistical models to calculate which opinions have congealed within the citizenry and which have dissipated on the winds of change. When reporting polling results, journalists often use street-corner interviews to humanize for viewers the mathematical trends discovered. So goes the science of public opinion.

Analyzing what people say in letters to the editor is a less scientific project, but it has one grand attraction: It deals with empirically observable matters – what was said and what was not said. Surveyors, in contrast, deal mostly with abstractions. "51 percent of the American people like skiing," the poll discovers, but questions immediately arise: Who are these people? Why do they want to ski? And what is wrong with the other 49 percent? Are they lazy, broke, or simply resistant to cold weather? And there is another possibility: perhaps only 35 percent of the American people really want to ski and the remaining 16 percent climbed aboard the Mountain Express so the pollster wouldn't think they were afraid of heights. That, too, is the science of public opinion.

Letter writers are not abstractions. They live somewhere. As they age, such places help define them. Although some people flit from town to town during their lives, many stay where they were first planted, and that has political effects. For example, 72 percent of the American people follow local news closely, a tendency that increases with age,[41] and 67 percent of them also agree with the local newspaper's political slant – a result of acculturation, or smart newspaper marketing, or both.[42] Minority group members pay more attention to local civic affairs than do Anglos, no doubt because they are so directly affected by close-at-hand decisions.[43] People who subscribe to local newspapers (1) vote more often,[44] (2) identify with their community more completely,[45] (3) volunteer more frequently,[46] (4) feel closer to their neighbors,[47] (5) are better informed about local issues,[48] (6) become increasingly open to new information,[49] (7) are more willing to pay for additional online news outlets,[50] and (8) are more politically sophisticated (and politically more active) than non-subscribers.[51] The longer one lives in a given community, the more powerful these effects become. That is trebly true for those who write letters to the editor.

Our interviews continued to evidence the intimate connection between where one lives and what one says. One of the most poignant interviews was with Richard C. of Roanoke. He began dispassionately enough, decrying the poor turnout in local elections:

I don't understand why people don't vote. It blows my mind. I mean, I don't miss an election. It's like I feel like you can't complain about what's going on at whatever level if you're not voting for these people. If you're not choosing who you want to represent you then, for all intents and purposes, you aren't represented ... We've had local elections where 7 percent of registered voters turned out. And I think that's horrendous when we look around the world at people who are actually risking their lives just in order to go to a polling place and check-off on a ballot.

Then Richard C.'s remarks became personal:

People are just, you know, "Oh, I've got something else to do," or this or that or the other. And it's like, you know, you're talking about electing somebody who's going to represent your state or your region or whatever. It needs to be considered a pretty serious part of your life to make that happen. And I've tried to instill that in my son. He's 17. He's already kind of excited about registering to vote when he turns 18. But him being 18, he's also going to have to register for the draft. So he wants some sort of say in who may or may not be sending him, you know, off to war.

This was Richard C's peroration: "If I can get somebody to feel that something is wrong with government – whether it's state, federal, local – that if they're not seeing anything in the paper they need to write so the people are aware of it. Become the pamphleteer. Become Thomas Paine. Express your point of view and get it out there."

It is easy enough to think of Richard C.'s homily as embroidery prose. Community ties are indeed often a breeding ground for sentimentality. The longer one stays in a particular place, the truer that becomes, which may be why our interviewees so often stressed the need for civility:

I get excited about a topic and I think, oh, I need to write something, but in today's world, I have to say, the exchange of – the free exchange of ideas – is becoming so polarized that the things that I truly feel, or would like to say or express, would incite anger and hatred and ... you know what I mean? Like, for example, the issue of gay marriage. I would love to write a letter about that and, yet, it's such a toxic subject right now that I just won't. I won't, sadly.

(*Linda N., Provo*)

Linda N. shows us how community ties can take the very words out of one's mouth. And things can get worse:

I would write more often, except I feel – I don't want to say "unsafe" – but the very first time I wrote a letter to the editor which was, I don't know, ten years ago, I got two postcards. And ... they were obviously from the same person. But they were very hateful and scary and so I didn't write again for a long time. And then during the last presidential election and then the congressional election, I [again] wrote letters.

(*Carol C., Duluth*)

Perhaps because the cities I studied were small enough to create a sense of community, Carol C.'s experience was atypical for our interviewees. Most of them tended to be what political psychologist George Marcus calls "civic entrepreneurs," people whose "initiative, action, reflection, learning, and cerebration" put into motion "a virtuous cycle in which social capital tends to produce collective success, which in turn encourages the generation of new social capital."[52] While letter writers often tell a tale of woe, many of them, like Jeanette F. of Billings, eventually find their way to a better place:

A: I guess I'm just so upset with the way the country is headed that I just, I think, I grew up when this country was at its peak ... I think there's more racism today than there's ever been, more hatred. You know, I'm all white and so is my husband. We have three children. I have grandchildren that are all white. I have grandchildren that are white and Indian. I have grandchildren that are white, Indian, and Mexican. I have grandchildren that are black and white. Now, is any one of them less lovable than the other? Hmm?

Q: No, of course not.

A: No, and why doesn't anybody else see that? Why do you hate someone just because they're not your race or your color? I find that hard to understand. I just do. I don't know, I don't have a good feeling about what's taking place anymore. But who knows? I guess. *You never know what tomorrow's going to bring* [my italics].

Such resoluteness dovetails with what researchers have long told us: "Those willing to work for change in the community not only subscribed to several newspapers, spent more time rereading in general, and were better able to recall what they read" than those who did not keep up with local news, an effect that increases the longer one lives in a given town or city.[53] For these reasons, many observers are now worried about declining newspaper subscription rates. While the Internet provides "a subjective sense of efficaciousness,"[54] it does not produce the kind of community awareness that reading a local newspaper does. Not surprisingly, such declines are "a threat to representation and accountability in local elections," according to Joshua Darr of LSU. Readers of local newspapers, Darr finds, are twice as likely as readers of national newspapers to know who is running for office in local congressional elections.[55] In addition, cable subscriptions and satellite TV access are *negatively* associated with local political knowledge, according to Princeton's Lee Shaker.[56]

These findings establish why it is so important to know what local letter writers are saying even if they are not a perfect replica of the American experience. One must look elsewhere – to survey research, one supposes – to find a "representative" sample of the citizenry. But such a sample can also mislead us because the average person does not care about politics, does not know much about it, and does not talk about politics except on rare occasions. Oddly enough, these know-little/careless citizens are often valorized by observers because "they are not contaminated with the corruption, collusion, and cynicism" of governance.[57] On the other hand, being "above politics" is also to be removed from the problems besetting real human beings.

Rooted in communities as they are, letter writers are different from the "average" citizen summoned up by pollsters. Their "gestures and idioms, colors and dialectics, and shapes and dictions" derive from the places they inhabit.[58] In contrast, says historian David Thelen, the "opinion industries" have created "drab public spaces where life's blacks and whites blur into grays, where data stand in for people and statistics for voices." "Journalists and pundits," Thelen continues, are now "so accustomed to thinking in terms of aggregation and typicality and objectivity, to looking for averages and denominators" that they have become less "interpreters" than "spectators," thereby distancing themselves from the people they seek to understand.[59] Reading a letter to the editor can help one narrow that distance.

WRITERS AS ADVOCATES

To suggest that people who write letters to the editor are interested in political matters is an understatement. Many are interested in nothing else. But letter writers are also a special kind of political animal. As we saw earlier, they participate actively in civic affairs but they are really not insurgents. The great majority of them exist in what political scientists Amy Gutman and Dennis Thompson call the land of "middle democracy," a place where people enjoy "arguing among themselves and listening to people with different points of view."[60] The modern letters column is a site for proto-politics, rather like the festivals surrounding the "men's circles" in eighteenth-century Geneva where citizens became, in Rousseau's terms, "a spectacle for themselves," using public discussion to build a common identity.[61] Binding actions were not taken in such arenas but information was shared and attitudes adjusted. Codicils and laws came later.

The letters column also bears some resemblance to what Ray Oldenburg calls "third spaces," a location "beyond the home or workplace where people can meet and interact informally."[62] Oldenburg has in mind physical places such as the English pub or the Parisian café. Given that orientation, he is worried that the modern "home delivery media system" is making "shut-ins of otherwise healthy individuals" and depoliticizing them as a consequence.[63] Letters columns, especially those in small city newspapers, perhaps exist somewhere between the pub and cyberspace. For Oldenburg, third spaces are (1) local, (2) neutral, (3) inclusive, (4) accessible, (5) inhabited by "regulars," (6) personally rewarding for those participating, and sometimes even (7) part of an otherwise commercial environment (such as the modern mall, for example). Such spaces produce "bridging social capital," says Oldenburg, giving people a chance to encounter strangers with peculiar ideas and opinions. Third spaces make us more flexible than we might become on our own. Simon Garfield sees this potential in what he calls "the lost art of letter writing." Says Garfield: "Letters have the power to grant us a larger life. They reveal motivation and deepen understanding. They are evidential. They change lives and they rewrite history . . . A world without letters would surely be a world without oxygen."[64]

Garfield is a bit flamboyant here, but throughout my interviews with the letter writers, I sensed that they had a "calling." It was as if some external force was extracting their opinions without their permission, thrusting them into the public square despite its hazards and required transparencies:

I can remember when I was a kid, my mother on occasion would call in to one of these radio talk shows. I'd think, "Good grief, mom. What're you thinking?" But, you know, here I am. I'm periodically writing when I'm bothered or stirred.

(Pete B., Duluth)

* * * * * *

I mean, a lot of people fuss with me because I get too emotional about some of the politics. My daughter especially. So I mean, there are a lot of issues that I guess I might feel passionately about, and maybe overly passionately. Some of my friends and family – they get a little outraged at the way I see the country going.

(*Merrell G., Roanoke*)

* * * * * *

I write [letters] when my muse and anger takes over with me. I have two I'm mulling around right now about outrageous things. I tend to respond to letters to the editor that other people have written that get me mad. And so then I'll start mulling around the thoughts and I have two thoughts I'm working on right now that might become a letter to the editor.

(*Marge K., Duluth*)

In a superb book, *How Voters Feel*, Stephen Coleman explores what voting means to people both cognitively and emotionally. Through a series of discussions with everyday citizens, he uncovered the taken-for-granted (and unacknowledged) feelings about voting. "Many people feel an obligation to vote," says Coleman, "even though they do not expect their votes to count for much." Nevertheless, voting became for them "a declaration of sorts, a call to be represented as a certain person on certain terms. It is, at the very least, an assertion that one considers oneself to be a person who should count in the world." The people Coleman interviewed often "muttered jokes about how the candidates were 'playing at polit-ics'" and how they could only "keep awake during the speeches by putting matchsticks in their eyes." Why vote, then? Because it offered a chance to "upset the odds and shake up the future in surprising ways."[65] An obligation. A pronouncement. An agony. A wager. If that is what voting has become for citizens in the United Kingdom, it has become that-plus-a-thousand for US letter writers. The people we interviewed continually observed that politics called them forth even as it repelled them. For many, says reporter Ron Dzwonkowski, letter-writing is "something of an addiction, encouraged by occasional publication."[66] And unlike the casting of a ballot (which is inevitably cloaked in darkness), a published letter exists for all to see. Letter writers may not wish to sally forth but they do; they may want to hold back but they cannot. Strong political beliefs will do that to a person, especially when the enemy approaches:

Q: People have different reasons for writing letters to the editor. What would you say is your main reason?

A: Just to kind of repudiate the propaganda that the left media puts out. A lot of it is just misleading and totally untrue. And that's generally what I get upset about.

Q: What do you hope to achieve when you write a letter to your newspaper?

A: Just mostly to straighten out the falsehoods that we get in much of the media, and particularly some of the local people that write just the talking points and the party line and much of that is just way off base. It's just pure propaganda. And I just can't not respond to that and put forth what I view to be the real truth about it. *(J.W.B., Wichita Falls)*

For reasons ranging from national security to diplomatic relations to industrial espionage, the political world is often a shadowy place. Citizens can never know all they wish to know about those who govern them. Grumpily, perhaps, most people accept these conditions and go on about their business. Not letter writers. The shadows irritate them; the shadows intrigue them:

Like I said, we've got Democrats that are acting like Republicans. They are spending money on things that really aren't improving the city and stuff, and they're very secretive about what they're doing. And I've exposed them in my letters for several lies that they've told, particularly involving the rezoning issue. They claimed that the school was old and no good and my son had been a student there the year before. So I was extremely familiar with the school. It's only two blocks from my house, you know, things of this nature.

(*Richard C., Roanoke*)

Some people seek out politics and, for others, politics is thrust upon them. The letter writers we interviewed fell equally into both camps. The Actives – those whose engines never throttled into low – used every available opportunity to get published. The Reluctants wrote only when the spirit moved them. For both groups, however, letter-writing was a deeply personal matter and they came alive during our interviews. They reported being unable to abide what most people learn to abide – that life is unfair, that dishonesty reigns supreme. So they get out of bed at three o'clock in the morning "to teach the state (and its agencies) what it cannot know by itself."[67] Something deep within them knows what Nancy Rosenblum knows, that speaking out is "a virtually automatic response to the indignation we feel in the face of flagrant, if small and ordinary, injustices."[68] Therein lies a reason to write.

CONCLUSION

People who write letters to the editor, at least those surveyed and interviewed by my team, are irredeemably ordinary. Statistically, they are
neither "average" nor "representative" of the populace, but they are
nonetheless ordinary. Politically, they are not as uninvolved or as reticent
as most Americans, but they are ordinary. Culturally, they are "everyday," "familiar" people, and hence ordinary. Socially, they are "regular,"
"normal" people, and hence ordinary. Emotionally, they are "sober" and
"conventional"; economically, they are "middle-class" and "bourgeois."
Letter writers are ordinary, at least the ones I studied.

So they are worth getting to know. Our surveys find letter writers to be
generally similar to their friends and neighbors, with two major exceptions: They care a great deal about public affairs and they enjoy sharing
their thoughts with others. When examined collectively, their letters
provide a reasonably complete, reasonably diverse reflection of lay American sentiments. Writers tell us what many people are thinking and their
letters have a special resonance for readers, in part because their authors
are colorful and also speculative:

We used to be a kind of a soup, where people would come into this country, look
around, and do almost everything they could to become American. And you'd get
kind of a smooth soup out of it. What has happened – and it is happening the last
few years more and more – is people are coming in mass groups, and they're coming
in little enclaves and setting up their own culture within the enclaves, using their
own languages, bringing in a lot of their own customs. So instead of being a smooth
soup, we're now a stew cooking. And these chunks tend to not get along very well
because they're not trying to be American, they're trying to be what they used to be.
(*Edmund K., St. Joseph*)

It is curious that people who work so hard to keep up with public affairs
do not feel particularly efficacious. How do they convert their "negative
energy" into forward movement? What insulates them from the much-
despised transactionalism of politics? For some writers, it seems to be the
challenge of documenting what has gone wrong. For others, it is the
opportunity to advance the historical record so that old mistakes are
not repeated. Still other writers are minimalists, trying to stay just one
step ahead of calamity. Eddie D. of Wichita Falls is one such person:

What's the latest voter turnout? You get 15 percent, you're lucky. And that's
registered voters. It's ridiculous that Americans take for granted so much. I fear it
may be lost before they realize it's gone. So only by making noise, you know, the
old saying the squeaky wheel gets the grease. Maybe if I can squeak enough,
somebody will listen.

There is a reason why Robert Lane's *Political Ideology*, written in 1952, became an instant classic. In it, he talked to only fifteen men in one American town, but he asked them thoughtful questions and listened carefully to the questions they asked themselves – questions that were fresh and deep. Given letter writers' political vigor, they deserve similar treatment. We do not need better data than the data they offer us. We just need to become as smart as possible about the data they provide. The findings reported in this chapter help us understand letter writers a bit better but, still, there are mysteries:

Q: Do you think you'll continue to write letters in the future?
A: Yeah, as long as I'm alive. (*Larry S., Duluth*)

Endnotes

1 The lower estimate is provided by Steven Rosenstone and John Mark Hansen, *Mobilization, Participation and Democracy in America* (New York: Macmillan, 1993) and the higher ones by Steve Pasternak and Suraj Kapoor, "The letters boom," *The Masthead* (Fall 1980), 23–25; *Times Mirror Survey, The Vocal Minority in American Politics* (Washington, DC: Times Mirror Center, 1993), and Aaron Smith, Kay Lehman Scholzman, Sidney Verba, and Henry Brady, "The current state of civic engagement in America," *Pew Research Center*, September 1, 2009. Accessed at www.pewinternet.org/2009/09/01/the-cur rent-state-of-civic-engagement-in-america.

2 Sidney Verba, Kay Lehman Schlozman, and Henry E. Brady, *Voice and Equality: Civic Voluntarism in American Politics* (Cambridge: Harvard University Press, 1995).

3 James Price Dillard and Steven J. Backhaus, "An exploration into emotion and civic deliberation." Paper presented at the annual meeting of the National Communication Association, Chicago, p. 18.

4 Mike Masnick, "Too much free time: do people still write letters to the editor?" Podcast hosted by TechDirt on August 22, 2008. Accessed at www.techdirt .com/articles/20080822/0140562057.shtml.

5 Emmett H. Buell, "Eccentrics or gladiators? People who write about politics in letters-to-the-editor," *Social Science Quarterly*, 56 (1975–6), 440.

6 For a useful discussion of response rates in social science research see Richard J. Fox, Melvin R. Crask, and Jonghoon Kim, "Mail survey response rate: a meta-analysis of selected techniques for inducing response," *Public Opinion Quarterly*, 52(4) (1988), 467–91; Timothy Johnson and Linda Owens, "Survey response rate reporting in the professional literature." Paper presented at the annual meeting of the American Association for Public Opinion Research, Nashville, May 2003. Accessed at www.srl.uic.edu/publist/Conference/rr_reporting.pdf; Yehuda Baruch and Brooks C. Holtom, "Survey response rate levels and trends in organizational research," *Human Relations*, 61(8) (2008), 1139–60.

7 The survey questions included the following: (1) *External Efficacy*: "The people of the U.S. have the final say about how the country is run, no matter who is in

office" and "If public officials don't care what people think, there is no way to make them listen." (2) *Internal Efficacy*: "I often don't feel sure of myself when talking to others about politics and government," "I feel I could do as good a job in public office as most other people," and "People like me really don't have a say about what government does." (3) *Political Trust*: "When government leaders make public statements to the American people, they often mislead them" and "The people we elect to public office usually keep the promises they make during the election." The wording for the latter question was adapted from John E. Newhagen, "Media use and political efficacy: the suburbanization of race and class." Paper presented at the annual meeting of the International Communication Association, Washington, DC, 1993.

8 These findings have been remarkably consistent in studies run between 1957 and 2004. See William D. Tarrant, "Who writes letters to the editor?" *Journalism Quarterly*, 34 (1957), 501–2; Gary L. Vacin, "A study of letter-writers," *Journalism Quarterly*, 42 (1965), 464–5, 510; Thomas J. Volgy, Margaret Krigbaum, Mary Kay Langan, and Vicky Moshier, "Some of my best friends are letter writers: eccentrics and gladiators revisited," *Social Science Quarterly*, 58 (1977), 321–7; Michael W. Singletary and Marianne Cowling, "Letters to the editor of the non-daily press," *Journalism Quarterly*, 56 (1979) 165–8; Bill Reader, Guido H. Stempel, and Douglass K. Daniel, "Age, wealth, education predict letters to the editor," *Newspaper Research Journal*, 25 (2004), 55–66.

9 Patterns for age: writers = 63.298; non-writers = 57.305; F [1, 1400] = 36.727, $p < .000$; education level: writers = 3.937; non-writers = 3.676; F [1, 1411] = 13.465, $p < .000$; newspaper subscriptions: writers (77.1 percent) vs. non-writers (56.1 percent): x^2 [1, N = 1,412] = 45.844, $p < .000$; gender: women writing (17.5 percent) vs. men writing (25.7 percent): x^2 [1, N = 1,417] = 11.600, $p < .000$.

10 Although several surveys have found letter writers to vote Republican more often than Democratic, I found no such tendencies in my twelve-city surveys, perhaps because they were conducted in working-class towns. Chapter 5 will provide additional insights along these lines.

11 Practitioners increasingly complain that survey response rates have been plummeting across all survey genres. That has been especially true for mailed surveys, and trebly true for site-specific surveys like ours. So, for example, corporate researchers note that while a survey may generate a 30–40 percent response rate among employees within a given corporation, sending that same survey by mailed post to external constituents will register only a 10–15 percent response. See Andrea Fryrear, "Survey response rates," *Survey Gizmo*, 27 July, 2015. Accessed at www.surveygizmo.com/survey-blog/survey-response-rates/.

12 Patterns for Volunteered Commentary: writers = 0.969; non-writers = 0.372; F [1, 1462] = 40.587, $p < .000$.

13 Building an overall measure of Political Involvement required my converting these individual measures into continuous variables prior to combining them (3 = yes, 2 = unsure, 1 = no). Patterns for Political Involvement: writers = 21.600; non-writers = 18.485; F [1, 1393] = 159.435, $p < .000$.

14 Buell, "Eccentrics or gladiators," 448. A large Roper survey (*n* = 40,564) conducted between 1973 and 1994 prefigured all of these differences in

political activity between writers and non-writers, with findings that proved true for Roper's overall sample as well as for a 13 percent subsample of "small, central cities" ($n = 5,359$) – the kinds of cities I studied as well. For additional data along these lines see *Roper Social and Political Trends Data, 1973–1994.* Accessed at http://ropercenter.cornell.edu/CFIDE/cf/action/cata log/abstract.cfm?Ext=1&Archno=USRoper1994-Trends.

15 Patterns for Internal Efficacy: writers = 5.067; non-writers = 6.471; F [1, 1385] = 101.943, p < .000. For External Efficacy: writers = 5.438; non-writers =5.931; F [1, 1398] = 16.094, p < .000.

16 Alan Kornberg and Harold D. Clarke have found that people tend to talk more about politics during election seasons, and that they feel more efficacious as well. My letter writers exhibit the former tendency but not the latter. See *Citizens and Community: Political Support in a Representative Democracy* (New York: Cambridge University Press, 1992).

17 Adam Chamberlain, "The (dis)connection between political culture and external efficacy," *American Politics Research*, 41(5) (2013), 761–82; Philip H. Pollock III, "The participatory consequences of internal and external political efficacy: a research note," *Western Political Quarterly*, 36(3) (1983), 400–9; Michael E. Morrell, "Survey and experimental evidence for a reliable and valid measure of internal political efficacy," *Public Opinion Quarterly*, 67 (2003), 589–602; Steven E. Finkel, "Reciprocal effects of participation and political efficacy: a panel analysis," *American Journal of Political Science*, 29 (1985), 891–913; Stephen C. Craig and Michael A. Maggiotto, "Measuring political efficacy," *Political Methodology*, 8 (1982) 85–109; Arnold Vedlitz and Eric P. Veblen, "Voting and contacting: two forms of political participation in a suburban community," *Urban Affairs Quarterly*, 16(1) (1980) 31–48.

18 Joseph Gershtenson and Dennis L. Plane, "In government we distrust: citizen skepticism and democracy in the United States," *The Forum*, 13(3) (2015), 481.

19 John Gastil and Michael Xenos, "Of attitudes and engagement: clarifying the reciprocal relationship between civic attitudes and political participation," *Journal of Communication*, 60 (2010), 318–43.

20 John R. Hibbing and Elizabeth Theiss-Morse, "Americans' desire for stealth democracy: how declining trust boosts political participation." Paper presented at the annual convention of the Midwest Political Science Association, Chicago, April 2001.

21 Jack M. McLeod, Dietram A. Scheufele, and Patricia Moy, "Community, communication, and participation: the role of mass media and interpersonal discussion in local political participation," *Political Communication*, 16 (1999) 315–336. My findings differ from those of James Lemert and Jerome Larkin, who found letter writers to be generally efficacious. The discrepancies between their study and mine may have resulted from the instruments used (phone vs. mail surveys), from the sample generated (one city vs. a national survey), from the era in which the surveys were run (1970s vs. the 1990s and 2013), or from the survey items used. See James B. Lemert and Jerome P. Larkin, "Some reasons why mobilizing information fails to be in letters to the editor," *Journalism Quarterly*, 56 (1979), 504–12.

22 Top-line results include Blue-Collar Believers including more women than men: F (1, 250) = 11.032, p < .000; Busy Trustees more likely to be

Republican vs. Democratic: $F (3, 246) = 16.452$, $p < .000$; Skeptical Patricians more likely to vote for Ds rather than Rs: $F (3, 246) = 8.128$, $p < .000$, and to include a few more men than women: $F (1, 250) = 4.928$, $p < .000$. Cellular details can be obtained from the author upon request.

23 Political Involvement: patterns for age: 1990s = 60.447; 2013 = 67.065; $F [1, 316] = 19.101$, $p < .000$; for education: 1990s = 3.754; 2013 = 4.183; $F [1, 318] = 12.345$, $p < .000$; for family income: 1990s = 4.547; 2013 = 6.531; $F [1, 303] = 48.109$, $p < .000$; for residential longevity: 1990s = 31.753; 2013 = 42.328; $F [1, 310] = 21.161$, $p < .000$; for party: more Democratic writers today (38.8 percent vs. 48.6 percent) and fewer Independent writers today (10.4 percent vs. 0.0 percent): $x^2 [3, N = 325] = 16.953$, $p < .000$.

24 Patterns for External Efficacy: 1990s = 5.598; 2013 = 6.133; $F [1, 1081] = 20.385$, $p < .000$; for Internal Efficacy: 1990s = 6.237; 2013 = 6.611; $F [1, 1091] = 7.353$, $p < .007$. In more recent years, non-writers report higher Media Satisfaction: 1990s = 12.850; 2013 = 14.482; $F [1, 1039] = 34.397$, $p < .000$ but lower Newspaper Subscriptions: 52.9 percent in the 1990s vs. 29 percent in 2013: $x^2 [1, N = 1,093] = 59.869$, $p < .000$.

25 Patterns for education: women = 3.623; men = 4.066; $F [1, 318] = 11.044$, $p < .001$; for family income: women = 4.702; men = 5.619; $F [1, 303] = 7.487$, $p < .007$; for residential longevity: women = 41.155; men = 34.324; $F [1, 310] = 7.082$, $p < .008$; for Internal Efficacy: women = 5.781; men = 4.792; $F [1, 311] = 15.353$, $p < .000$.

26 Patterns for External Efficacy: Democrats = 5.029; Republicans = 5.827; Independents = 5.315; $F [3, 311] = 3.929$, $p < .009$; for Media Satisfaction: Democrats = 10.903; Republicans = 17.482; Independents = 12.294; $F [3, 300] = 69.145$, $p < .000$; for Political Trust: Democrats = 6.444; Republicans = 7.429; Independents = 7.105; $F [3, 304] = 12.487$, $p < .000$.

27 Michael K. Miller, Guanchun Wang, Sanjeev R. Kulkarni, H. Vincent Poor, and Daniel N. Osherson, "Citizen forecasts of the 2008 U.S. presidential election," *Politics & Policy*, 40 (2012), 1019–52.

28 Staci Rhine, Stephen E. Bennett, and Richard Flickinger, "Patterns of media exposure in the U.S. and their impact on knowledge of foreign affairs." Paper presented at the annual meeting of the Midwest Political Science Association, Chicago, April 1996.

29 Joohan Kim, Robert O. Wyatt and Elihu Katz, "News, talk, opinion, participation: the part played by conversation in deliberative democracy," *Political Communication*, 16 (1999), 361–85.

30 Danny Hayes and Jennifer L. Lawless, "As local news goes, so goes citizen engagement: media, knowledge, and participation in U.S. house elections," *The Journal of Politics*, 77(2) (2015), 447–62.

31 Patricia Moy, Michael R. McCluskey, Kelley McCoy and Margaret A. Spratt, "Political correlates of local news media use," *Journal of Communication*, 54 (2004), 532–46.

32 Andrew J. Perrin, *American Democracy: From Tocqueville to Town Halls to Twitter* (London: Polity Press, 2014), p. 8.

33 Janet Maybin, "Death Row penfriends: some effects of letter writing on identity and relationships," in David Barton and Nigel Hall (eds.), *Letter Writing as a Social Practice* (Philadelphia: John Benjamins, 1999), p. 163.

34 W. Lance Bennett, "Changing citizenship in the digital age," in W. Lance Bennett (ed.), *Civic Life Online: Learning How Digital Media Can Engage Youth* (Cambridge: MIT Press, 2008), p. 14.

35 Tali Sharot, "Optimism bias: why the young and the old tend to look on the bright side," The *Washington Post*, December 31, 2012. Accessed at www.washingtonpost.com/national/health-science/optimism-bias-why-the-young-and-the-old-tend-to-look-on-the-bright-side/2012/12/28/ac4147de-37f8-11e2-a263-foebffed2f15_story.html.

36 Jerry L. Weaver, "The elderly as a political community: the case of national health policy," *Western Political Quarterly*, 29 (1976), 612.

37 Brittany H. Bramlett, "Aged communities and political knowledge," *American Politics Research*, 41 (2013), 674–98.

38 M. Kent Jennings and Gregory B. Markus, "Political involvement in the later years: a longitudinal survey," *American Journal of Political Science*, 32 (1988), 306.

39 Stephen Earl Bennett, *Apathy in America, 1960–1984: Causes and Consequences of Citizen Political Indifference* (Dobbs Ferry: Transnational, 1986), p. 76.

40 Molly Andrews, *Lifetimes of Commitment: Aging, Politics, Psychology* (Cambridge: Cambridge University Press, 1991), p. 271. For a fine summary of social science research focused on wisdom, see Monika Ardelt, "Wisdom as expert knowledge system: a critical review of a contemporary operationalization of an ancient concept," *Human Development*, 47 (2004), 257–85.

41 Manuel Goyanes, "The value of proximity: examining the willingness to pay for online local news," *International Journal of Communication*, 9 (2015), 1507.

42 Leo Bogart, "The public's use and perception of newspapers," *Public Opinion Quarterly*, 48 (1984), 715.

43 Amy Mitchell, Jesse Holcomb, and Dana Page, "Local news in a digital age," *Pew Research Center*, March 2015. Accessed at www.journalism.org/2015/03/05/local-news-in-a-digital-age/.

44 Stephen Knack and Martha E. Kropf, "For shame! The effect of community cooperative context on the probability of voting," *Political Psychology*, 19 (1998), 585–99.

45 Lindsay H. Hoffman and William P. Eveland Jr., "Assessing causality in the relationship between community attachment and local news media use," *Mass Communication and Society*, 13 (2010), 180; Leo W. Jeffres, Jean Dobos, and Mary Sweeney, "Communication and commitment to community," *Communication Research*, 14(6) (1987) 624; William B. Davidson and Patrick R. Cotter, "Psychological sense of community and newspaper readership," *Psychological Reports*, 80 (1997), 659–65.

46 Eric W. Rothenbuhler, Lawrence J. Mullen, Richard DeLaurell, and Choon Ryul Ryu, "Communication, community attachment, and involvement," *Journalism and Mass Communication Quarterly*, 73 (1996), 445–66.

47 Alex S. Edelstein and Otto N. Larsen, "The weekly press' contribution to a sense of urban community," *Journalism & Mass Communication Quarterly*, 37 (4), (1960), 489–98.

48 Dietram A. Scheufele, James Shanahan, and Sei-Hill Kim, "Who cares about local politics? media influences on local political involvement, issue awareness,

and attitude strength," *Journalism and Mass Communication Quarterly*, 79 (2002), 435.

49 Paul Hagner, Linda Maule, and Janine Alisa Parry, "Political culture and information supply and consumption." Paper presented at the annual meeting of the Midwest Political Science Association, Chicago, April 1996.

50 Goyanes, "The value of proximity," 1515.

51 Lee Shaker, "Citizens' local political knowledge and the role of media access," *Journalism & Mass Communication Quarterly*, 86 (2009), 817; Keith R. Stamm, *Newspaper Use and Community Ties: Toward a Dynamic Theory* (Norwood: Ablex, 1986), p. 96; Bruce E. Pinkleton and Erica Weintraub Austin, "Individual motivations, perceived media importance, and political disaffection," *Political Communication*, 18 (2001), 331.

52 Gregory B. Markus, "Causes and consequences of civic engagement in america: initial report of the civic engagement project." Paper presented at the annual convention of the Midwest Political Science Association, Chicago, IL, April 2001, 33.

53 Jeffres, Dobos, and Sweeney, "Communication and commitment," 624.

54 Dietram A. Scheufele and Matthew C. Nisbet, "Being a citizen online: new opportunities and dead ends," *International Journal of Press/Politics*, 7 (2002) 70.

55 Joshua P. Darr, "The news you use: political knowledge and the importance of local newspapers." Paper presented to the 73rd Annual Meeting of the Midwest Political Science Association, Chicago, April 2015, 26.

56 Shaker, "Citizens' local political knowledge," 817.

57 John Clarke, "Enrolling ordinary people: governmental strategies and the avoidance of politics?" *Citizenship Studies*, 14(6) (2010), 640. See also Catherine Neveu, "Of ordinariness and citizenship processes," *Citizenship Studies*, 19(2)(2015), 141–54.

58 James P. McDaniel and Bruce E. Gronbeck, "Through the looking glass and back: democratic theory, rhetoric, and Barbiegate," in Karen Tracy, James P. McDaniel, and Bruce E. Gronbeck (eds.), *The Prettier Doll: Rhetoric, Discourse, and Ordinary Democracy* (Tuscaloosa: University of Alabama Press, 2007), p. 33.

59 David Thelen, *Becoming Citizens in the Age of Television: How Americans Challenged the Media and Seized Political Initiative During the Iran-Contra Debate* (Chicago: University of Chicago Press, 1996), pp. 172, 198.

60 Amy Gutman and Dennis Thompson, *Democracy and Disagreement: Why Moral Conflict Cannot Be Avoided in Politics, and What Should Be Done About It* (Cambridge: Harvard University Press, 1996), p. 40.

61 Zev M. Trachtenberg, *Making Citizens: Rousseau's Political Theory of Culture* (London: Routledge, 1993), p. 195.

62 Ray Oldenburg, *The Great Good Place: Cafes, Coffee Shops, Bookstores, Bars, Hair Salons, and Other Hangouts at the Heart of a Community* (New York: Da Capo Press, 1999), p. 77.

63 Ibid.

64 Simon Garfield, *To the Letter: A Celebration of the Lost Art of Letter Writing* (New York: Gotham, 2013), p. 19.

65 Stephen Coleman, *How Voters Feel* (New York: Cambridge University Press, 2013), pp. 71, 113, 172, 207.
66 Ron Dzwonkowski, "It's a cheap form of propaganda: now they are offering prizes to people who trick newspapers into publishing fake letters," *The Masthead* (September, 2004), 12.
67 Clarke, "Enrolling ordinary people," 644.
68 Nancy L. Rosenblum, "Navigating pluralism: the democracy of everyday life (and where it is learned)," in Stephen L. Elkin and Karol Edward Soltan (eds.), *Citizen Competence and Democratic Institutions* (University Park: Pennsylvania State University Press, 1999), p. 79.

5

People Who Read Letters

If anonymity is determinism, signed letters to the editor may someday drift away. If so, their authors will not go quietly. Take Martin Wolfson, for example, who fired off some 2,000 letters to the editor between 1927 and 1969, some of which were actually printed. "Even if much of what I write is not used," opined Wolfson, "I think editors and others learn from it."[1] Impressed by Mr. Wolfson's pathology of expressiveness, the venerable *New York Times* offered a paean to him and his cohorts on its editorial page:

Letters to the editor are a valued part of every newspaper. Their variety of topic is endless. They correct – and make – errors. They reflect a multitude of views and moods. They abound in curious information. They constitute a debating society that never adjourns, in which everything knowable is discovered. A sodality of voluntary correspondents, approving, wrathful, critical, philosophical, humorous, full of admonition, reproof, instruction, miscellaneous knowledge has succeeded the long-winded Publicolas and Catos of our long-suffering ancestors.[2]

Chapter 4 described why writers write, but we must also ask why readers read. Some readers may seek out what the *Times* seeks out – wrath, reproof, and all that – and some may be just as consumed with politics as the writers. Most readers, though, are probably just curious – curious about what is going on in town, curious about where the country is headed, curious about their more opinionated neighbors. The letters column, says Rasmus Nielsen, director of the Reuters Institute for the Study of Journalism at Oxford, "exists somewhere between a private life devoid of politics and a political life devoid of citizens."[3]

Those who regularly read letters seem drawn to this middle zone of life, a place where one gets a taste of politics but not too much. Pakistani scholar Hina Ashraf offers another explanation: Letters attract people because of their cultural imprint. After examining letters from a variety of countries, Ashraf found that British letters were typically factual and understated, Polish letters were highly opinionated, letters from France emphasized the nobility of virtue, and Italian letters were filled with digressions. Pakistani letters, in contrast, showed profound discontent, as if their authors lived outside the country they lived inside of, thereby exposing a yawning gap between them and government officials.[4]

The Pakistani situation may just be an arch example of a more general problem – determining who "the people" really are, a democratic necessity if citizens are to recognize themselves in decisions made in their name. "The people as a source of action and authority is more often potential than actual," argues Cambridge University's Margaret Canovan; thus "the people" keep haunting the political imagination.[5] Are those who watch political ads "the people," or just those who pay for the ads? Can "the people" really be found in public opinion polls and TV interviews? Are legal residents who do not speak English part of "the people" in the United States and, if not, how about undocumented computer programmers? Do those on welfare number among "the people" and, at the other end of the Marxian continuum, how about credit default swappers on Wall Street? "Everyday politics," says Canovan, "is concerned with the things that divide us, not the things that unite us"[6] – and that makes citizens instinctively curious about power, rights, money, fairness, identity, and opportunity.

Each day, letter writers offer their versions of who the people are, so letters columns become a place where "society as a whole fashions a knowledge of itself."[7] In offering their diagnoses and prognostications, letter writers operate in the realm of pure conjecture, if not pure fantasy. Those who read letters understand these limitations, but where can they turn for surer knowledge? To distant experts, perhaps, but who are those people, and where do they live? To elected officials, perhaps, but who are those people, and what are their motives? And so many readers go local, with 50 percent of newspaper consumers reading the letters column each day. Newspaper editors and elected officials also treat letter writers as stand-ins for "the people," but not on all occasions.[8] Because nobody really knows who "the people" are, democracies are filled with guess-work. An online regular named "Anonymous Coward" seems to understand this principle and hence has developed his own metrics: "The ladder of coherency starts with 'texting,' then unsigned comments on various forums, next posts attached to one's name, then blog posts, and perhaps ending at the [newspaper] letter."[9]

This chapter reports on several surveys run among newspaper consumers. The surveys asked readers how they spent their time, what sort of media they took in, and what they thought of those who wrote letters to the editor. The chapter is also based on a series of interviews conducted over a twenty-year period with those who edit the letters columns. The interviews asked how many and what kinds of letters the editors received, what topics appeared most often, and which letters were accepted and which rejected. Sometimes the surveys and interviews reinforced conventional wisdom, but more often they showed how complex and changeful a political culture can be. Our respondents seemed to feel what John Steinbeck felt: that "our morning eyes describe a different world than do our afternoon eyes, and surely our wearied evening eyes can report only a weary evening world."[10]

Steinbeck's remarks can be found in *Travels with Charley in Search of America*, a magisterial work recounting his loping trip across the country with his beloved poodle. In his book, Steinbeck travels the byways of the nation, sharing coffee and fishing stories with the folks he encountered. Drawing on these exchanges, Steinbeck paints a textured picture of the United States and its inhabitants. By the time he set out on his trip, Steinbeck was based in New York City and was the author of *Cannery Row*, *Of Mice and Men*, and *East of Eden*, and winner of the Pulitzer Prize for *Grapes of Wrath*. Despite the plaudits he had received, Steinbeck felt he was losing touch with "the people," so he set out to find them. His trips took him to his home town of Salinas, California, one of the twelve cities forming the backbone of my project. Understanding Salinas – a farming community, a sometimes tortured community – helps one understand Steinbeck as well. Those who read letters to the editor are also the products of their geographies, so let us begin by investigating the places from which they hail.

WHERE READERS LIVE

A standard trope in the social sciences is that "all samples are samples," meaning that any selection of items from a population will have limitations and hence can never fully describe the population itself. So too with this study. I examined but twelve small cities and, while they spanned the country, they can only tell the story they can tell. Knowing that, I began with the story I knew best – my hometown of Fall River, Massachusetts, a place once called "the city of hills, mills, and pork pies." The pork pies were eaten by those who worked in its textile mills in the early 1900s, before the clothing industry moved to the Carolinas and, then, to China. The result today is a husk of a city, with Fall River's mills now populated by discount malls or by nothing.

Fall River sits sixty miles south of Boston, thirty miles west of Cape Cod, and thirty miles north of Newport, Rhode Island. Nearby though it is, Fall River has none of Boston's sophistication, none of the Cape's restaurants, none of Newport's money. Fall River is known for comparatively little except for Lizzie Borden, who allegedly took an axe to her prominent parents in August of 1892, but who was never imprisoned for the crime. Like Lloyd Warner's *Yankee City*, Fall River's hills are stratified – Yankees at the top, Irish and Italians in the middle, Portuguese and French in the lowlands. Over time, some groups have moved "up the hill," with Cape Verdeans and Puerto Ricans replacing them down below.

Fall River is what sociologists call a "third tier" city, a place of "residuals, waste and deficits."[11] Such cities are typically built on a single industry (textiles, in Fall River's case) and when that industry faces difficulties, "the social and economic consequences can be catastrophic."[12] Most such cities are removed from major metropolitan areas, although they remain connected to them via road (e.g., Duluth, Minnesota), rail (e.g., Trenton, New Jersey), or waterway (e.g., Utica, New York). For most of the nineteenth and half of the twentieth centuries, these transportation links spelled profitability for the cities, but, as those industries declined, abandoned factories, deserted downtowns, environmental problems, and declining populations followed.

Despite these travails, third-tier cities can be "enormously resonant in people's lives," according to communication researcher Tara Brabazon.[13] They are often the major population center in their region; they have active Chambers of Commerce and well-established civic and political groups; they are composed of multi-generational families nested in tightly connected religious communities; they almost always have a small college or regional state university within commuting distance; and their long-standing food and music festivals, antique shops, ethnic restaurants, and sporting events invite people to town on a regular basis. Third-tier cities are not well known outside of their regions unless they are adjacent to popular tourist destinations (e.g., Glacier National Park for Billings, Montana; the Gulf Coast for Lake Charles, Louisiana).

In 1980 (the mid-point of my timeline), there existed approximately 120 cities in the United States with populations between 75,000 and 100,000. Using Fall River as the prototype, I randomly selected eleven additional cities to study, ensuring only that they were distributed across the country and, as a group, were politically, socially, and culturally diverse. The cities I selected are "average" or, better, "ordinary" places. Appendix D provides a wealth of information comparing them to one another and to the nation as whole. These data show that, taken together, the cities have roughly the same number of whites, Hispanics, and African-Americans as the country overall, although the ratio among these groupings differs from city to city. The cities also track the nation in the number of people over sixty-five years of age, those living alone, those with multiple ancestries, those who are long-term residents, and those admitted to the hospital. The cities also represent the nation in terms of the number of high school diplomas granted, hospital personnel, house- holds with cable television, and those having construction, manufactur- ing, transportation, finance, and real estate jobs.

On the upside, the twelve cities studied here have a lower cost of living than the nation as a whole, shorter commuting times, generally better health reports, and lower poverty rates. But over the past forty years these cities have also lost more population than the country in general, they report lower median incomes and lower retail sales per capita, and they have fewer residents with college degrees and more modest library expenditures than the United States in general. Their crime rates are worrisome, renters are all too common, home values are low, and unemployment is uncomfortably high.

These twelve cities are traditional in many ways, with fewer women in the workforce, more English-only speakers, more "religious identifiers" (and, correspondingly, more private schools – usually Catholic schools), and higher newspaper subscription rates than the nation as a whole. Overall, then, my cities are fairly large but not metropolitan, and removed but not provincial. Some of them are a bit more Republican and some a bit more Democratic, but they tend toward the political mean when viewed collectively.

Figure 5.1 adds nuance to that claim. According to the *Huffington Post*, Crowdpac has built "a unique data set with a nonpartisan out- look."[14] Using a "data-driven formula developed by a Stanford University professor," the organization "draws from sources that include campaign contributions and public statements that place political candidates [and urban locations] on the traditional liberal-conservative spectrum on a variety of issues."[15] As we see in Figure 5.1, my cities are fairly well distributed across the continuum, thereby providing a useful amount of sample variation. At the same time, though, all twelve cities are rather tightly clustered around the mean when compared to the nation as a

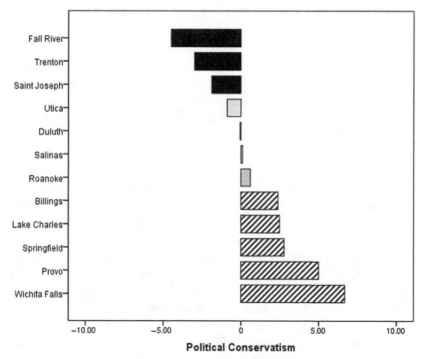

FIGURE 5.1 Crowdpac's 2015 Political Conservatism Rankings

whole. At the most conservative point (+10) on the continuum, one finds small cities such as Garden Grove, California and Grapeland, Texas, mixed in with larger cities such as Oklahoma City and Omaha.[16] At the least conservative point (−10), one finds small places such as Ridgefield Park, New Jersey and West Saint Paul, Minnesota, and bigger cities such as Seattle, Cambridge, and, of course, Berkeley.[17] When viewed in this light, then, my twelve cities provide enough political range to make things interesting, but are mainstream enough to represent the nation's central tendencies.

Partisan leanings aside, the twelve locations are "working-class cities." That distinguishes them from rural communities and small towns, from cosmopolitan urban environments, and from wealthy suburbs. Working-class cities are not identical to one another, but they do have several things in common:

- *They have an industrial history*: Most of the cities in my sample grew because of early twentieth-century technological demands. The need for iron ore built Duluth; the need for automobiles built Springfield. In his book *Triumph of the City: Invention Makes Us Richer, Smarter, Greener, Healthier, and Happier*, Edward Glaeser contends that the "age of the industrial city is over, at least in the West, and it will never return." Only "small-scale entrepreneurship and commerce" can ultimately revive such cities, Glaeser contends. More optimistically, Glaser notes that such cities "decline very slowly because people are loath to abandon something as valuable as a home."[18]

- *They have a regional mentality*: As the dominant players in their geographical area, the cities I studied report more community involvement, more neighborhood camaraderie, more information awareness, and somewhat less disillusionment with government.[19] It is often the case, says political scientist Katherine Cramer, that people's "social identities" – where they live, how they cluster demographically – are more important to them than their "partisan identities."[20] So, for example, in an attempt to emphasize its regional centrality, the *Fall River Herald News* has become the *Herald News*; a similar strategy has now been employed by almost all of the newspapers in my sample.[21]

- *They depend on local sources of information*: In the age of the Internet, few towns are as isolated as they once were, and that is true of my twelve cities as well. But distance has its consequences, and so "regional news cultures" also develop. The University of Illinois' Scott Althaus and his colleagues note that "even in a highly connected world where the mass in 'mass media' is larger than ever, the impressive subnational variation in media preference points to the tenacity and staying power of the local."[22] Because these local information channels can be quite powerful, say political scientists Robert Huckfeldt and John Sprague, "there is no single national electorate, but rather a multitude of subnational electorates."[23]

- *They are politically active*: My twelve cites tend to have higher turnout rates than larger and more diffuse metropolitan areas. There are several reasons for this effect: (1) because my cities are "well-bounded" by geography and have "clear borders," citizens learn to expect more from city officials;[24] (2) such cities also have low residential mobility, and so their residents develop a sense of common fate;[25] (3) they are diverse communities with sizeable population subsets, thereby facilitating political mobilization;[26] (4) because such cities have so many residents with deep roots in the community, pathways of social communication – via family members, via religious ties – are clear and functional.[27]

- *They are cities in transition*: Third-tier cities, argue economists Beth Siegel and Andy Waxman, are characterized by a shrinking tax base and fewer jobs.[28] Such cities are concentrated in the mid-Atlantic and Midwestern states but they can also be found throughout the country. With less capital investment and little philanthropic help, such cities must depend on enhanced amenities (e.g., Fall River's revived riverfront, Lake Charles' revived lakefront), local colleges and universities, strong civic associations, and greater interregional cooperation. Experiments such as these are now being run in all twelve locations, drawing on the cities' "useful histories" for new ideas – the Steinbeck Museum in Salinas, the Jesse James House in St. Joseph, the Norfolk and Western Train Museum in Roanoke. Renewal efforts like these depend on the cooperation of civic elites, including city council members, church and business leaders, newspaper editors, and community organizers.[29]

Some years ago, Wendell Berry argued that the national economy is making "colonies" out of all localities in the United States, dominating not only local businesses but also artistic, educational, and cultural productions.[30] Daniel Hopkins of Georgetown University adds politics to this argument, observing that, since 1980, it has been possible to predict the outcome of gubernatorial elections by consulting national political trends.[31] While it is too early to tell if the trends Berry and Hopkins identify will persist, urban cultures cannot be dismissed. "The city," says Richard Dagger, is the "true home of citizenship." Compared to the nation-state, it "is more accessible to its residents, more closely tied to their interests, and more likely to promote the sense of community which is usually associated with citizenship. Yet it is also large enough and sufficiently diverse in its composition to offer what the village cannot – a truly political environment."[32] Nothing I have learned about the twelve cities in my sample has caused me to doubt the wisdom of Dagger's claim.

While all twelve cities are "third-tier" in nature, there is considerable variation among them. One gets a sense of these differences in Table 5.1, which contains a randomly drawn headline from the *New York Times* for each city. It takes only a brief inspection of the table to see that Provo and Salinas are on the rise and that Springfield and Trenton are in decline. All twelve of my cities have experienced massive changes between 1948 and the present – some happy ones and some worrisome. Appendix D offers details on these matters but the overall picture is this: Four cities have made steady gains, five are functional but challenged, and three desperately need revitalization. Table 5.1 provides a glimpse of each city.

TABLE 5.1 *What Makes News in the* New York Times?

City	Headline	Date
Billings, MT	"Obama Takes Science Push to 'Mythbusters'"	October 18, 2010
Duluth, MN	"A Midwest Beer Tour to Cure Winter Blues"	February 4, 2011
Fall River, MA	"A Fresh Eye on Fall River, Mass."	January 2, 2014
Lake Charles, LA	"Religious and Public Stations Battle for Share of Radio Dial"	September 15, 2002
Provo, UT	"What Is the Next 'Next Silicon Valley'?"	March 5, 2015
Roanoke, VA	"With Bold Museum, a Virginia City Aims for Visibility"	December 29, 2007
Salinas, CA	"The Least Affordable Place to Live? Try Salinas"	May 7, 2006
Springfield, OH	"Surge in Jobs Mostly Bypasses the Factory Floor"	May 11, 2004
St. Joseph, MO	"Company News; Meadwestvaco Will Eliminate 600 Jobs to Cut Costs"	August 6, 2004
Trenton, NJ	"Trenton Budget Woes Imperil City Museum"	July 10, 2012
Utica, NY	"A City in Decline Fighting to Preserve Its 1800's Heritage"	July 14, 2006
Wichita Falls, TX	"Texans Getting Creative with Water Conservation"	October 11, 2014

Robust Cities

- *Roanoke, Virginia.* Formerly known as "Big Lick," Roanoke is located in the foothills of the Blue Ridge Mountains in southern Virginia and was once a dominant rail and manufacturing hub but is now centered on health care, retail, light manufacturing, and, increasingly, tourism. Roanoke College and Virginia Tech are nearby and the city has the second highest library circulation and the highest number of newspaper subscriptions per capita in my sample. The city core is populated by Democrats, union members, and African-Americans, with Republicans (especially Evangelical Protestants) living in the suburbs and rural areas.[33] Home to a number of music festivals, Roanoke is having some success revitalizing its downtown via restaurants, museums, and the arts.

- *Billings, Montana.* Billings is the largest city in Montana, surrounded by six mountain ranges and intersected by the Yellowstone River. Given its surrounding natural splendors (including Glacier National Park), tourism is a dominant industry, although oil and gas production have grown apace because of the Bakken formation and fracking. Lewis and Clark once passed through the Billings area (as did Calamity Jane) and the Little Bighorn Battlefield is sixty miles away. Billings has the lowest percentage of religious adherents in my sample, the best air quality, the highest number of women in the workforce, the most recent construction, and the lowest number of hospital admissions. Billings votes Republican, but not excessively so.
- *Provo, Utah.* The home of Brigham Young University, Provo is a rapidly growing city in a rapidly growing region focused heavily on the IT/digital economy. Overwhelmingly Mormon, eight in ten residents vote Republican, but education in all forms is prioritized. The Provo region is awash in beauty, with the Bridal Veil Falls attracting people who fly-fish in the morning and visit Robert Redford's Sundance Resort in the afternoon. Family-centered in all ways, Provo is the youngest city in my sample and has the most religious adherents, the lowest crime rate, and the fewest long-term residents. Obesity, smoking, and the Democratic Party are unheard of in Provo, which may explain its high scores on well-being, emotional health, and Twitter's happiness index.
- *Salinas, California.* Salinas has the lowest number of subscribers to its historical newspaper, *The Californian*, but that may be because 75 percent of its residents are Latinos, many of whom subscribe to *El Sol.* Salinas is a young, sun-drenched city with an agriculture-dominant economy and the Pacific Ocean thirty-seven miles to its west. Nicknamed "The Salad Bowl of the World," Salinas is the setting for one of John Steinbeck's masterpieces, *East of Eden.* Salinas is a complex place, with the highest median incomes and home values in my sample but also the highest number of uninsured, the lowest number of English-only speakers, and the fewest college graduates. Salinas has grown faster than any other city in my sample between 1948 and the present.

Challenged Cities

- *Fall River, Massachusetts.* A reliably Democratic city, Fall River is adjacent to the Atlantic Ocean and home to the dry-docked *USS*

Massachusetts. Interstate 95 cuts through the heart of the city, with City Hall perched atop it. Fall River's motto, "We'll Try," does not inspire a second great reawakening, but somehow the city endures, trying to turn its old mills into new enterprises. The city is proximate to several good colleges and has become a (distant) bedroom community for Boston. Overwhelmingly Catholic, it has the highest percentage of Anglos in my sample but the lowest number of English-only speakers, because of its mottled ethnicities. Fall River's relatively high median home values and personal incomes are a reflection of the larger Massachusetts economy combined with the state's liberal social services, but its environmental, exercise, stress, and emotional health indices are the lowest in my sample.

- *Duluth, Minnesota*. Perched across from Superior, Wisconsin and nestled along the shores of Lake Superior, Duluth sits halfway between Minneapolis and the Canadian border. Its once thriving iron ore and coal industries have gone by the boards, although some ocean-going shipping remains. Duluth, the home of Sinclair Lewis, Bob Dylan, and pie à la mode, has turned to tourism for a new lease on life and that seems to be working, albeit modestly. Duluth votes Democratic, is home to mostly English-only speakers, and is not especially religious. It has the highest number of construction workers in my sample and, conversely, the highest number of college graduates. It is cold in Duluth.

- *Lake Charles, Louisiana*. The climate is far more temperate in Lake Charles, where Mardi Gras is a year-round thing. The city not only sits on a lake but also has a deep-water channel leading to the Gulf of Mexico. Cajun culture, petrochemicals, casino gambling, soul food, and talk of LSU football swirl together in Lake Charles, a place where everyone goes to church on Sunday. Like the rest of Louisiana, politics is a contact sport in Lake Charles, a city where whites vote Republican and blacks vote Democrat. Lake Charles has the second highest proportion of African-Americans in my sample and, not surprisingly, the highest percentage of poverty and uninsured residents as well. More optimistically, it has the largest amount of new home construction.

- *Wichita Falls, Texas*. Wichita Falls was once known for its tornados and Democrats, but only the tornados remain. The city is home to Sheppard Air Force Base, which has an oversized impact on its economy now that the oil business has moved its ancillary operations elsewhere. Wichita Falls has been bedeviled by both floods and droughts, each of which has taken its toll on the city. Compared to other places in my sample, Wichita Falls boasts the shortest commuting time, one of the lowest costs of living, and the highest proportion of Evangelical Christians. Wichita Falls is home to Midwestern State University and the Hotter 'n Hell Hundred, the largest bicycle century race in the United States.

- *St. Joseph, Missouri.* Situated fifty-five miles north of Kansas City, St. Joe is 88 percent white but few of them live downtown, in the hardest-hit center city in my sample. Birthplace of the Pony Express and famed newscaster Walter Cronkite, St. Joe reached its peak in the late nineteenth century when it was a crossroads for shoes, dry goods, hardware, and anything else that could float down the Missouri River. Many of its Golden Age mansions now lie in ruins, although its suburbs are doing fairly well. Not surprisingly, St. Joe has the lowest cost of living in my sample and, as a result, one of the highest rates of home ownership. Politically, the city sports an even split between Democrats and Republicans, reflecting a broader trend found in Missouri itself.

Distressed Cities

- *Utica, New York.* All modes of transportation – road, rail, and river – have been part of Utica's history, but none seems relevant to a twenty-first-century economy. The city has hemorrhaged residents for years, although it has recently welcomed a surprising number of Bosnians, Burmese, Somalis, and Iraqis, justifying its sobriquet as the "second chance city." Utica's past has included gambling, prostitution, the Mafia, and both Republican and Democratic conventions, all of which were dutifully profiled by its Pulitzer Prize-winning newspaper. The city has the lowest median income and home value in my sample, the lowest well-being score, and the second highest proportion of elderly citizens. Despite all of this, downtown Utica today has a vibrancy that belies the tough times it has faced, and still faces.

- *Trenton, New Jersey.* Trenton's motto, "Trenton Makes, the World Takes," is emblazoned on a bridge spanning the Delaware River, but the motto has become a lie. Despite its Revolutionary War history, its status as the capital of New Jersey, and its once thriving rubber, ceramics, wire, and cigar industries, Trenton has come a cropper. Being situated halfway between Philadelphia and New York City on several major arteries only lets people bypass Trenton more quickly. The city has the highest rates of crime, unemployment, home vacancy, and population density in my sample. It also has the longest commuting

time, largely because white workers drive in from the suburbs. Somehow, though, Trenton has sustained not one but two good newspapers – *The Times* and *The Trentonian.*

- *Springfield, Ohio.* Springfield once had thriving agriculture and manufacturing industries, good race relations, a fine college (Wittenberg),
and a low crime rate, and was designated an All-America City by
Newsweek in 2004. Six years later, a Gallup poll labeled it "the
unhappiest city in the U.S." A high number of residential vacancies,
low median incomes and home values, and high obesity and poverty
rates make it hard for Springfield parents to entice their sons and
daughters back home once they graduate from college. Springfield's
current hope is that Navistar (formerly International Harvester),
Wright-Patterson Air Force Base, and a network of retail operations
will turn things around. In the meantime, chain restaurants dominate
the city.

Each of my twelve cities has its own story, its own history, its own
projections. Some cities have prospered over the years, although none is a
garden spot. All are working-class towns with almost no restaurants that
can be booked on OpenTable. But all of these cities are homes to industri-
ous people with dreams for their children. All of these cities are plagued
by street corner drugs and unhelpful interest rates, but they are also filled
with churches and VFW halls and ballfields and nicely landscaped city
halls. I chose these cities because they reflect a good portion of the United
States – at least its ordinary parts – and because I wanted to see if civic
hope can abide in places where the odds are long. I have visited each of
these towns at least three times over the years. I look forward to returning
to each someday.

WHAT READERS BELIEVE

Because so many stereotypes surround people who write letters to the
editor – they're intemperate; they're a bit loony – it seemed useful to
examine the relative popularity of these biases. Accordingly, in the spring
of 1994 and then again in the spring of 2014, we sent out mailed surveys
to 2,240 individuals living in the twelve cities just described (none of the
recipients had been approached for the writer-based surveys described in
Chapter 4). A total of 440 persons were solicited in 1994 and, because
survey response rates have dropped so much over the years, we surveyed
an additional 1,834 individuals in 2014. In all, 495 usable surveys were

returned, for an overall response rate of 21.8 percent (37.3 percent in 1994, 18.1 percent in 2014). The same instrument was used in both administrations of the survey and the cover letter framed it as an inquiry into respondents' media habits and preferences, including what sorts of television and radio programs they liked, how often they read the newspaper, and what they thought of various TV genres and personalities. Buried within these questions, however, were seven probes asking what the respondents thought of letter writers. The survey was rounded out by nine demographic questions (see Appendix C for the instrument used).

As can be seen in Table 5.2, respondents were generally middle-aged, long-term residents of their cities, with a good spread of income levels. The great majority had spent at least one year in some sort of college and almost all were white, with about 10 percent being members of minority groups. Men and women were equally represented, as were Republicans and Democrats; a full 20 percent of the respondents described themselves as Independents. Most were married, a quarter were retired, and both blue-collar and white-collar workers were well represented.

Over half the sample read the newspaper regularly and 64 percent of these faithful readers read the letters column each day. Surprisingly, almost 20 percent of the sample had written one or more letters to the editor over the years, double the number found in other surveys. Most of the respondents kept up with both national and local news, usually via television, and the longer they lived in the community the more likely they were to read letters to the editor. All of the above data were replicated from region to region, suggesting that our respondents' attitudes were similar to those held by Americans in general (or at least that subset of Americans kind enough to return survey forms).

To get a better feeling for people's attitudes toward letter writers, three collateral measures were developed from the individual questions asked: (1) *Writer Appreciation* – the sum of positively phrased questions (the writers are "better educated than most people," they "want to help the community," their views "are fairly similar to my own" and "fairly similar to people I know") minus negatively phrased questions ("they prefer sounding off to being constructive" and "they seem pretty egotistical to me"); (2) *Political Awareness* – a ten-part measure of respondents' attentiveness to local and national news (television, radio, and print), their interest in political call-in shows, and their reading of editorial columns, multiplied by the thoroughness with which they read the local newspaper; (3) *Media Disapproval* – a summation of the respondents' negative attitudes toward the mass media (e.g., "the people who call in to talk radio

TABLE 5.2 *Overall Characteristics of Survey Respondents (n = 493)*

Demographics	Mean age	54.7
	Mean years in current city	33.2
	% making $35K or less	29.2
	% making $36K–$65K	30.6
	% making $66K or more	31.4
	% with some college education	74.3
	% male	49.8
	% female	50.2
	% retired	26.9
	% blue-collar job	30.2
	% white-collar job	42.9
	% married	63.0
	% Democrats	32.9
	% Republicans	32.9
	% Independents	20.3
	% Other/not disclosed	14.3
	% Anglo	91.7
	% African-American	2.5
	% Asian	0.4
	% Native American	0.8
	% Hispanic & other	4.6
News Habits	% reading newspaper regularly	52.5
	% reading letters to the editor	47.7
	% writing letters to the editor	19.3
	% watching national news	65.5
	% watching local news	73.6
	% listening to news broadcasts	22.3
	% listening to political call-in shows	17.4
	% watching early morning shows	30.6
	% watching news magazines	38.5
	% watching political interview shows	20.1
Regular Letter Readers	% living in city for 10 or fewer years	34.3
	% living in city for 11–20 years	39.4
	% living in city for 21–29 years	45.8
	% living in city for 30 or more years	57.3

seem pretty unstable to me," "today's TV programs undermine the morals of the American people," etc.) minus their positive attitudes ("the publishers of my local newspaper are concerned about the community," "TV newscasters seem genuinely concerned about the American people," etc.).

Many of the findings reinforce common sense. Older persons, those who had lived in town longer, married individuals, and retirees scored higher on Political Awareness than their counterparts.[34] In terms of Media Disapproval, men were more disenchanted with the media than women, as were non-marrieds. Predictably, Republicans (and to a lesser extent Independents) were more irritated by the media than Democrats, who reported watching more television than either Republicans or Independents.[35] Also not surprising were the following findings: People who had previously written a letter to the editor were (1) more politically attentive than non-writers, (2) better educated, (3) more likely to be married, (4) more faithful news consumers (and more faithful letter readers), (5) more likely to have lived in the community longer, and, not surprisingly, (6) more familiar with letter writers than were non-writers.[36]

It is also not surprising that Politically Attentive individuals and those with low Media Disapproval also had somewhat higher scores on Writer Appreciation.[37] But the findings reported in Figure 5.2 are particularly interesting: Our respondents described the writers as similar to themselves and their friends, not especially egotistical, and generally assets to the community. On the negative side, our respondents felt that writers had a tendency to "sound off" and also felt they were not better educated than most people. Generally, though, Figure 5.2's graphs indicate that attitudes toward letter writers were normally distributed among the respondents, a finding that held true for those who had written letters as well as those who had not. Contrary to accepted folklore, then, no empirically demonstrable, psychologically consistent, or sociologically understandable stereotype of the political letter writer has organized the popular mind in these twelve cities.

This is not to say that individual citizens do not have strong opinions about letter writers but it is to say that people in general cannot agree on what they feel. Naturally, these findings may not hold true for the broad swathe of the American people or for particular subsets of them. Also, the folks in my cities may be more generous toward (or more confused about) letter writers than others. But the graphs in Figure 5.2 clearly show that locals "identify" with letter writers. Here is another important finding: no differences in Writer Appreciation can be attributed to respondents' partisan preferences or their age, education, income, occupation, gender, region, or longevity in the community. These data suggest that letters to the editor may well tap into what Americans-in-general are thinking. That, at least, is the conclusion I draw from these results.

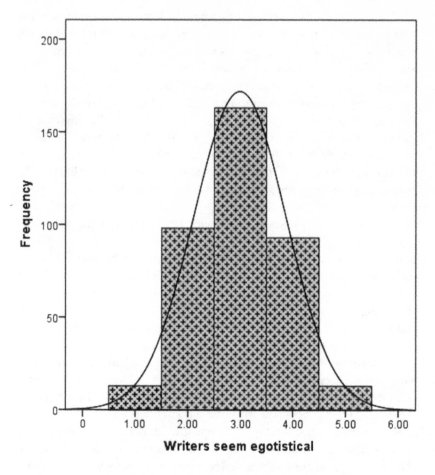

FIGURE 5.2 Writers' Perceived Characteristics (*n* = 493)

What about changes between 1994 and 2014? More recent respond-ents were considerably older (47.5 years of age vs. 58.5) and, sadly, less Politically Attentive and less likely to read the local newspaper.[38] On the other hand, there were no differences in Writer Appreciation over the years; readers' attitudes toward letter writers twenty years ago are the same as those today.[39] What are we to make of such findings? One possibility is that readers think of letter writers as rather special but cannot explain why. They may also find writers interesting because of their boldness and their willingness to take strong positions. Or perhaps they read what letter writers write not because they know them, but because they do not.

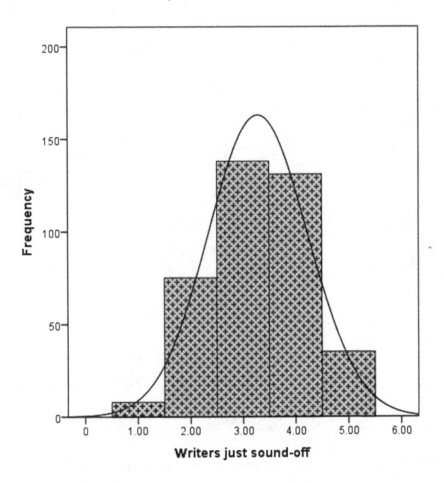

FIGURE 5.2 *(cont.)*

Ultimately, a short survey like this can only tell us so much. Additionally, respondents cannot answer questions they were never asked. But prior research contributes additional explanations for why reading letters to the editor is so common for so many, which now follow.

Letters Provide a Sense of Authenticity

In an age overwhelmed by eye-catching personalities and always-on media, letter writers are not going to win awards for flamboyance. But writers may open up ideas that readers cannot ignore. "Discovering what

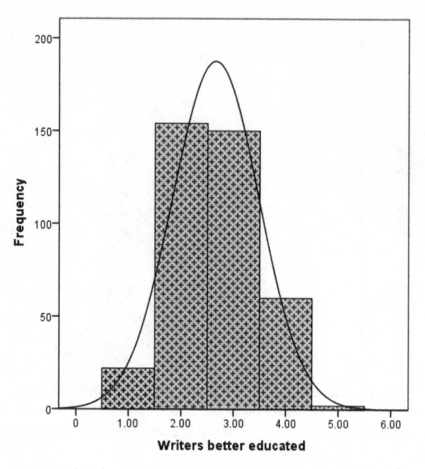

FIGURE 5.2 *(cont.)*

people have said in any setting intrigues us," says literary scholar Susan Miller, "because it seems to bring dead or muted voices into our presence."[40] Letters to the editor in small city newspapers may not have the elegance found in more exalted publications, but those deficiencies – because they are deficiencies – draw readers in. Research shows that, compared to many publications, letters are (1) less practiced,[41] (2) more energetic,[42] (3) more experiential,[43] and (4) more intense.[44] Not all letters have all of these qualities, but most of them have a narrative element ("this happened last week and it's an outrage") that taps into the author's life story, hence connoting authenticity.[45]

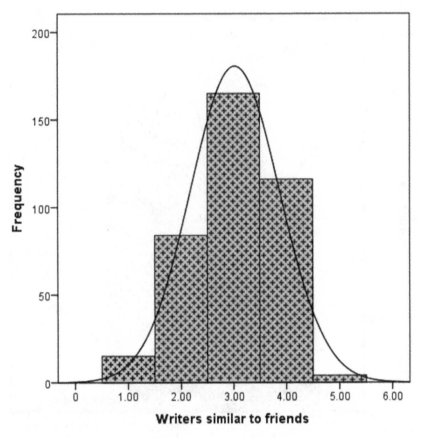

FIGURE 5.2 (*cont.*)

Letters Provide a Sense of Connection

The two most important words in a letter to the editor are "I" and "we." These two words support an ecology of engagement between author and reader. The "I" can sometimes be too dominant, but it is usually offset by a nod to the reader ("heed my warning, all ye good citizens"), the combination of which suggests a "conversation among absent friends."[46] Letters to the editor are part of an asynchronous public sphere where community conversations are interrupted by long periods of silence, but recommence when readers find time to read once again.[47] Letters to the editor give readers: (1) a common pool of factual references;[48] (2) an opportunity to celebrate shared values;[49] (3) a more respectful mode of interchange than

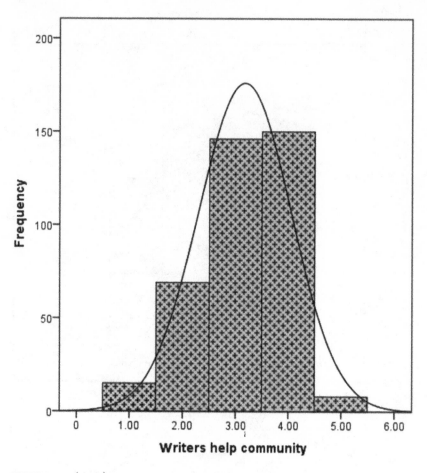

FIGURE 5.2 (*cont.*)

call-in radio;[50] (4) an opportunity to hear new, sometimes unpopular, voices;[51] and (5) the ability to connect to issues (e.g., distributive justice) under-reported by the mainstream media.[52] For these reasons, readers often find letters to be more reliable than other media products.[53]

Letters Provide a Sense of Novelty

Letters to the editor sometimes provide an early warning of what is on people's minds. When doing so, they can help editors "determine the

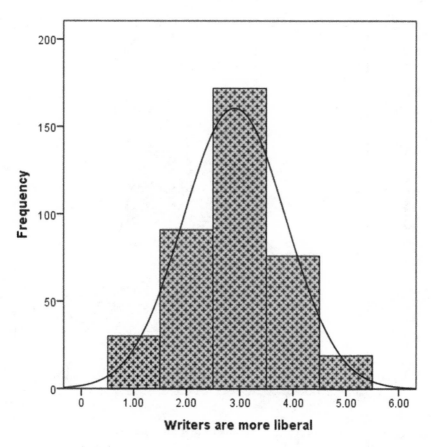

FIGURE 5.2 (*cont.*)

subject matter of the debate," says Lucy Atkinson of the University of Texas, and thereby affect the media's agenda.[54] If read carefully, letters sometimes reveal "an underlying discourse of powerlessness in [their] tone and organizational structure," indicating who feels left out in the current debate.[55] But letters can also be over-determined by established sources of power (the state, corporations, advertisers, etc.), so they must be read with care.[56] Political scientists Christopher Cooper and Gibbs Knotts have found that issues championed by female letter writers (e.g., education and health) differ sharply from those championed by men (e.g., national defense).[57] Partisanship can also play a role. Bill Reader and Dan Riffe of Ohio University found that highly polarized individuals (both

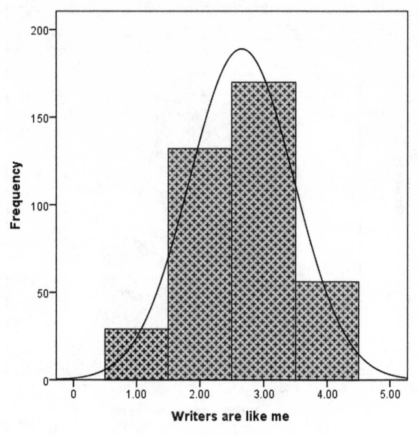

FIGURE 5.2 *(cont.)*

extreme Left and extreme Right) were especially attracted to the new, controversial matters discussed in letters columns.[58]

Letters Provide a Sense of Subversion

People who write letters to the editor in Billings, Montana are not going to be brought before the House UnAmerican Activities Committee for doing so, but such letters sometimes do push the envelope when attacking the newspaper itself.[59] A good example is provided by journalism scholar Brian Thornton, who found that editorials published in West Coast newspapers during the Japanese internments of World War II were "timid and pale" compared to letters submitted by ordinary readers.[60] In another study, Thornton found letters also setting the pace on women's liberation in the early years of that movement.[61] In a third study, Thornton determined that letters in the 1950s did not evidence "the bland homogeneity of the era's popular stereotypes" but contained "subterranean tremors of discontent" that led to the cultural explosion of the 1960s.[62] It is worth remembering, says historian Rebecca Earle, that newspapers themselves evolved out of letter-writing, so subversiveness was baked into them from the beginning.[63] Even letters written during colonial times in the United States constituted a kind of "print supervision" of political authorities, a mantle that letter writers continue to wear.[64]

The surveys reported here reveal that those who read letters to the editor identify with their authors, and that invites us to rethink our stereotypes. Letter writers have their peculiarities, to be sure, and it is not yet clear what makes them tick. I have speculated that letters are interesting because of their freshness, openness, and quiet rebelliousness, but it will take more research to validate these claims. Writers and readers are clearly drawn to one another, although it is still too early to say exactly why.

WHAT EDITORS THINK

We conducted phone interviews with the editorial-page editors from the twelve focal cities in 1993, in 1997, and again in 2014. In all, thirty-two individuals (89 percent of the sample) cooperated with us. The editors had held their positions for an average of six years. Our interviewees were typically expansive and the interviews averaged thirty-five minutes in length. Because editorial-page editors have sensitive jobs and because we wanted to guarantee as much candor as possible in our interviews, they will be referred to pseudonymously here.

The editors reported accepting 88.1 percent of the roughly 2,000 letters submitted per annum per paper, but they also noted a dramatic uptick in submissions during presidential elections.[65] While the topics discussed by their correspondents shifted a bit over the years, the hierarchy was clear: local and national politics (first and second respectively), and then the following in descending order of frequency: healthcare, religion, abortion, crime, gun control, the environment, and corporate spending. When asked why they rejected the few letters they did, the editors cited obscenity and libel as the main culprits. The remaining reasons included anonymity, excessive length, form letters, blatant inaccuracy, irrelevance (to local concerns), illegibility, and – mournfully – unsolicited poetry.

The editors' answers were remarkably consistent over the years, with one exception: When asked if the letters fairly represented local view-points, they agreed with that proposition only 35 percent of the time in the two early surveys. That number jumped to 70 percent in 2014. This disparity is echoed in the scholarly literature as well. Researchers who had, over the years, asked this same question of editors in quite different venues initially found what I found: Letter writers were thought to be living in a world of their own construction.[66] But other studies based on in-depth interviews found a growing sentiment that letter writers are the tip of the iceberg.[67] Social scientists comparing survey data to newspaper letters about the Equal Rights Amendment, the Vietnam War, and the Martin Luther King, Jr. holiday discovered a similar sort of consonance.[68] As one of our interviewees, Alex F. (East Coast), concluded, "People who take the time to write a letter to the editor are probably more active than an apathetic public would be, but I do tend to see that we do get a good cross-section of different ideas."

The twelve newspapers comprising my sample are lucky to have the editorial-page editors they do. They are true professionals, even though the pressures under which they labor have increased over the years because of disruptions in the newspaper industry. Nevertheless, long-standing journalistic values were evidenced throughout our interviews:

- *Ensuring ideological fairness*:
  - "They will write to me, and they will say, 'Hey, you know, over the last month you've run 60 Dems, 45 Republicans, what gives? We know you're left-leaning, but we didn't know you were that left-leaning.' It's very difficult to know what to do. Since our commit-ment is to run as many election letters as we can, that's what we do, which means that whatever we get that are respectful and accurate, we run. So sometimes there are letter writing campaigns for individ-ual candidates, and that can be a real pain in the neck." *(Donna G., East Coast)*
  - "We tell people it's an open forum. We do get kind of on-point to make sure that we're enforcing length limits, and things like that, commonly for everybody. But if one candidate gets 12 letters and one gets 2, we just publish what we've got, and we go to sleep at night and we'll tell people, 'Hey, we published what we had.'" *(Daniel E., Midwest)*

   o "I want people to feel that no matter where they stand on an issue that their opinions are welcome and that there's no set agenda that I'm trying to push, that everyone's ideas are welcome if they are able to express them in a respectful manner. I see the Opinion page as having an important role in community discourse and dialogue and debate, and whatever I can do to help facilitate that is something I want to do." *(Alex F., East Coast)*

- *Embracing community members:*
  - o "And I think a lot of papers have one or two, the regulars that everybody in the community knows from their letters, with the roll of the eyes, and 'Oh yeah, that guy.' And a couple of years ago, one of ours is a retired priest, and he's constantly, you know, he's very much a priest, and so his opinions are very tainted that way, to the chagrin of a lot of other writers, he's very anti-abortion, of course, things like that. And because people are always asking me about him and always writing, 'Why do you let this guy have the space?' Finally, we did a profile story on him, saying, 'You know what, you know the name, here's the person.' And I think that got a lot of reads. I think a lot of people appreciated that." *(Carl F., Midwest)*
  - o "We've had people who clumsily start writing, and they type in all caps, or they're typing in bulleted points without any real sentences and things, and we've actually gone back and forth with them to try to help them understand what we're going to do, and at the same time, publish those first or second offerings with some work on our end." *(Daniel E., Midwest)*
  - o "Sometimes we get something scribbled on a napkin or something. Not all the time, but sometimes we get things in unusual forms, and then sometimes people will write us what they think is a letter to the editor, but it's just page after page after page and just a script and very hard to read. And even then we sometimes at least try to figure out: Is there something we can do with that?" *(Katie N., southern United States)*
- *Maintaining compositional standards:*
  - o "[Sometimes] the grammar is embarrassing. It's kind of very telling about the comment, but that's across the board. I mean, grammar has gone out the window, as punctuation, you know, in the advent of texting and Facebooking and things like that. People don't pay attention to the language, which is kind of sad. I mean, that's just kind of a – it shows a deterioration of our society in a sense. People can't communicate anymore." *(Don D., East Coast)*

o   "[Correspondents] know that they're going to have to observe more of the decorum of a printed newspaper page, as opposed to the online world, and so they probably represent in the community usually a more credible response, a more credible person. They're a little more likely to go point by point, and frankly, if they're going to have their signed name, it's going to appear on our editorial page, we're going to read it." *(Daniel E., Midwest)*

o   "We try to find reasons to publish all of them. I mean, we will not publish ones that are longer than – we have a 300-word limit. We require that it's written by the writer. It can't be plagiarized in other words, and it needs to be exclusive to our paper. We just want that sort of content to be content that our readers can find only in our paper. And it has to be civil, and it has to be accurate. If we can tell that it's all garbage, we won't – we won't publish something that we know is not true." *(Carl F., Midwest)*

Situated as they are between publishers and advertisers on the one hand and feisty letter writers on the other, editorial-page editors do not have it easy. Letters columns are "untouchable," says Brazilian scholar Marisa Torres da Silva,[69] in part because they are popular (hence contributing to the newspaper's bottom line) and in part because free speech can be costly as well as noisy. But controversy also has its advantages. Researchers John Richardson and Bob Franklin report, for example, that publishers sometimes allow letters to become the stalking horse for divisive issues, thereby giving the newspaper a bit more time to frame its editorial position.[70]

When it comes to controversy, my twelve cities are well positioned. The cities are large enough to let a newspaper take strong stances on the issues of the day but small enough to sustain a sense of community.[71] "This is my city," says East Coast editor Donna G. "They are my people. I am their people. We're very close. I listen to the news on the radio and the TV, in the car. I'm always just keeping touch with what's going on." "After ten years," Donna G. continues, "a lot of them know me. They know my name. They know my family. I know theirs. I go to their funerals. It's all very, you know, we try to be as local as we possibly can, and we care." "So because I work on that basis," Donna G. concludes, "I can see, oh, you know, this is an issue that we just talked about, or this is an issue that so and so just called me about. I know that this is something that's fomenting in our area, so I'll run it, whether it's pro or con."

The letters column, observes journalism scholar Karin Wahl-Jorgenson, is an ideal place from which to observe "the clash between civility and provocation, between rationality and high blood-pressure, and between reason and passion," all of which affect how editors approach their jobs.[72] The letters column is also "one of the most dangerous pages in the newspaper because people can slip in the most diabolical things," says Wahl-Jorgenson.[73] All of this was true before editors were asked to add online comments to their oversight duties, a move that has made their jobs infinitely harder. Says editor Douglas E. of the western United States:

You know, I spent part of last week dealing with a really angry commenter who just was wanting to comment on everything, you know? [In doing so] I'm not defending my staff, I'm not doing anything that has to do with news, I'm just dealing with an online commenter who's really mad who, ten years ago, I would've never done. So is that a good thing? Probably not, but it's something that because it was on our website and because we're dealing with social media, it's just something that you deal with.

Editors, says Karin Wahl-Jorgenson, "parcel out entitlement for expression: they decide not merely who is allowed to speak, but how and why they may speak."[74] There is power there, but there is also responsibility. The editors we interviewed seemed equally aware of both. For example, right after describing his worries about online commentary, Douglas E. sounded a more upbeat note:

You know, I think to be truthful, [online commentary] is a really mixed thing because I started in journalism in 1996, and when I did we had the Internet, but it was really still in its infancy as it related to journalism. And so we didn't get feedback. In fact, we still put together stories and put out newspapers and we wonder what people thought of it. We were thinking: What would readers say if they could give us instant feedback? And so kind of what we have today is what we dreamed about having, which is that kind of instant feedback and knowing what readers were reading. And today we can do both of those things.

Wahl-Jorgenson observes that editors often use the "idiom of insanity" to describe letter writers, thereby distancing themselves from their correspondents and reinforcing their own superiority.[75] That may be true in more metropolitan papers, but I found none of that in the thirty-two interviews we conducted. I found, instead, dedicated professionals confronted by some writers trying to launch a vendetta against a local business and other trying to slip racist code words into their letters. And yet the editors revealed a grudging respect for the writers. Perhaps the size of the city – and hence the intimate contact between editor and writer – nurtured such attitudes. In any event, Douglas E., who had been in the newspaper game for thirty years, truly understood his calling. His remarks touched on all the themes discussed in this chapter and hence deserve to be quoted at length:

> You know, we get a lot of Tea Party letters. We get a lot of people who are not happy with their government, and we're a little different than some others. We kind of weigh that and say: "Well, maybe the people aren't happy; maybe our education is different or our life experience is different." We try not to just put our opinions in place of theirs.
>
> So there are a lot of people who, in this part of the world, don't want people taking their guns away. They don't want to be taxed. And they're short-sighted in some ways. If you don't want to pay taxes, how are you going to have decent roads and all that? So they kind of don't understand all the complexities, but I do think that the sentiments we see represented are genuine sentiments that people hold.
>
> And so to that extent, say you're a civic do-gooder and you want to get a new tax passed. You need to be aware that, gee, there's a whole undercurrent of people who are against this kind of thing and, you know what, they're represented right there on the [editorial] page. You know they exist. And so I think the newspaper helps in a way that it gives voice to those people and so everybody's more informed that that's the way our town works.

CONCLUSION

The cities chosen for this study are imperfect; the surveys we ran are also imperfect; the editors we interviewed add a third imperfection. Letters to the editor can only tell us what they can tell us but, as we will see in the next four chapters, reading the letters carefully can tell us much. Precisely because such letters are so ordinary, they can open up the world in strange yet familiar ways. Close but far, ordinary but enticing. There's utility in that.

Letters columns, says journalism historian Bill Reader, are "not the egalitarian, democratic forums many of us want them to be, but rather forums for the educated middle-class."[76] That is less true in the twelve cities I studied – cities where people are somewhat less educated and far more likely to be lower-middle-class. But letters columns are not as diverse as they need to be. That makes them rather like baseball, a "national pastime" that tugs at people's hearts and animates chatter in the union halls, but whose ballparks contain both sky boxes and bleachers. Ordinary people write letters and ordinary people sit in the bleachers, watching millionaires hit a baseball. As a result, journalism, like baseball, both reveals and conceals its essential truths. We need to learn more about both but, first, we must learn to respect them. Some critics worry that letters columns are being "colonized" by activists, PACs, and special interest groups, but the editors in my twelve cities are wise to that game and will have none of it.[77] Other critics worry that newspapers are becoming too partisan, but Daniel Butler and Emily Schofield find that the newspapers in their sample published more letters supporting the candidates they opposed than those they endorsed.[78] Some critics assume that people who write letters to the editor do so because they are angry at the newspaper, but that is also untrue. Professor of international journalism Michael Bromley finds that newspaper personnel do not constitute the letter writers' "imagined audience" and that their remarks are mostly pitched to their fellow citizens.[79]

Marc Dunkelman has written a fine book entitled *The Vanishing Neighbor: The Transformation of American Community*, in which he anguishes about the micro-homogenization of the United States, a nation in which people are living among those who think and look and act like them.[80] We seek out such people, says Dunkelman, to tell us we "belong." Americans now risk isolating themselves in these ways, he claims, clinging to "inner-ring" contacts (family and close friends) and "outer-ring" contacts (i.e., via television and the Web) and forsaking "middle-ring" possibilities – people who live near us but whom we do not know, whom we do not care to know. Despite Dunkelman's thoughtful analysis, he pays insufficient attention to middle-ring agents who challenge these modes of separation on a daily basis – schools, churches, civic groups, elected leaders, community-minded businesses ... and local news organizations. These institutions continue to call people forth, to call them together.

My twelve cities are especially dependent on these middle-ring resources, but time and tide have not been kind to them. All of these cities have been affected by unsettling economic trends, sociological shifts, and generational disruptions. These cities are not too big to fail but they are big enough to disrupt entire geographical regions if they do fail. On the plus side, each city has its own political culture, each has its plan for renewal, and each has enough local institutions to give it a chance for reinvention. Each city also has people who care about their communities and who are busy looking for answers. Some of these people are even brave enough to write letters to the editor – an excellent reason to examine what they have to say.

Endnotes

1 As quoted in Irving Rosenthal, "Who writes the 'letters to the editor'?" *Saturday Review*, September 13, 1969, 116.
2 Ibid.
3 Rasmus K. Nielsen, "Participation through letters to the editor: circulation, considerations, and genres in the letters institution," *Journalism*, 11 (2010), 34.
4 Hina Ashraf, "Letters to the editor: a resistant genre of unrepresented voices," *Discourse & Communication*, 1 (2013), 1–19.
5 Margaret Canovan, *The People* (Cambridge: Polity, 2005), p. 9.
6 Ibid, 128.
7 Karin Wahl-Jorgensen, *Journalists and the Public: Newsroom Culture, Letters to the Editor, and Democracy* (Cresskill: Hampton Press, 2007), p. 54.
8 See David Pritchard and Dan Berkowitz, "How readers' letters may influence editors and news emphasis: a content analysis of 10 newspapers, 1948–1978," *Journalism & Mass Communication Quarterly*, 68 (1991), 388–95; and Herbert Gans, *Middle American Individualism: The Future of Liberal Democracy* (New York: Free Press, 1988).
9 A contribution made by Anonymous Coward to a forum hosed by Mike Masnick, "Too much free time: do people still write letters to the editor?" *TechDirt*, August 22, 2008, 7:38 p.m. Accessed at www.techdirt.com/articles/20080822/0140562057.shtml.
10 John Steinbeck, *Travels with Charley in Search of America* (New York: Penguin, 1961), p. 60.
11 Tara Brabazon, *Unique Urbanity: Rethinking Third Tier Cities, Degeneration, Regeneration and Mobility* (London, Springer, 2015), p. 9.
12 Ibid, 16.
13 Tara Barbazon, *Unique Urbanity? Rethinking Third Tier Cities, Degeneration, Regeneration and Mobility* (Singapore: Springer, 2015), p. 42.
14 Paul Blumenthal, "Crowdpac helps small donors find a perfect match in politics," *Huffington Post*, October 7, 2014. Accessed at www.huffingtonpost.com/2014/10/07/crowdpac-donors_n_5943022.html.
15 Ibid, 2.
16 While Crowdpac uses different subscales for Democrats and Republicans, I folded them into a single scale here for the sake of illustration and simplicity.
17 For additional details see *Daily Data*, "The most liberal and conservative cities in America," December 15, 2015. Accessed at www.crowdpac.com/blog/the-most-liberal-and-conservative-cities-in-america.
18 Edward Glaeser, *Triumph of the City: How our Greatest Invention Makes Us Richer, Smarter, Greener, Healthier, and Happier* (New York: Penguin, 2011), p. 64.
19 Leo W. Jeffres, David Atkin, and Kimberly A. Neuendorf, "A model linking community activity and communication with political attitudes and involvement in neighborhoods," *Political Communication*, 19 (2002), 387–421.
20 See Katherine Cramer Walsh, "Putting inequality in its place: rural consciousness and the power of perspective," *American Political Science Review*, 106 (2012), 517–32.

21 For a particularly insightful discussion of such trends see Marcus Funk, "Imagined commodities? Analyzing local identity and place in American community newspaper website banners," *New Media & Society*, 15 (2013), 574–95.

22 Scott L. Althaus, Anne M. Cizmar, and James G. Gimpel, "Media supply, audience demand, and the geography of news consumption in the United States," *Political Communication*, 26 (2009), 249–77.

23 Robert Huckfeld and John Sprague, *Citizens, Politics, and Social Communication: Information and Influence in an Election Campaign* (New York: Cambridge, 1995), p. 283.

24 Sidney Verba and Norman H. Nie, *Participation in America: Political Democracy and Social Equality* (New York: Harper, 1972). See especially pp. 234–40, 332.

25 Robert J. Sampson, "Local friendship ties and community attachment in mass society: a multilevel systemic model," *American Sociology Review*, 53 (1988), 766–79.

26 Eric Oliver, "The influence of social context on patterns of political mobilization." Paper presented at the annual meeting of the American Political Science Association, San Francisco, August 1996.

27 See Sidney Verba, Kay Lehman Schlozman, and Henry E. Brady, *Voice and Equality: Civic Voluntarism in American Politics* (Cambridge: Harvard University Press, 1995), p. 460.

28 Beth Siegel and Andy Waxman, *Third-Tier Cities: Adjusting to the New Economy* (Washington, DC: US Economic Development Administration, 2001). Accessed at www.mtauburnassociates.com/pubs/Third_Tier_Cities.pdf.

29 Although he focuses largely on outer-ring suburbs, Eric Oliver's thoughts about the politics of local communities are especially trenchant and many of them apply to the kinds of third-tier cities studied here. See *Local Elections and the Politics of Small-Scale Democracy* (New Jersey: Princeton University Press, 2012).

30 Wendell Berry, *Home Economics* (San Francisco: North Point Press, 1987).

31 Dan J. Hopkins, "The increasingly United States." Paper prepared for the Annual Meeting of the American Political Science Association, Washington DC, August 2014.

32 Richard Dagger, "Metropolis, memory and citizenship," *American Journal of Political Science*, 25 (1981), 715.

33 This pattern – Democrats near the courthouse, Republicans in the suburbs – was repeated in most of the cities in my sample, thereby echoing what Jonathan Rodden found throughout the nation in small cities. See "This map will change how you think about American voters – especially small-town, heartland white voters," *Monkey Cage: The Washington Post*, October 31, 2016. Accessed at http://atlas.esri.com/Atlas/VoterAtlas.html?t=1&m=1& x=-94.69&y=38.62&l=5.

34 *Political Awareness* for married individuals = 25.014; single individuals = 19.519; $F_{(1, 447)} = 16.676$; $p < .000$; for working persons = 21.851; retired persons = 25.880; $F_{(1, 431)} = 6.994$; $p < .000$; for age 30 or younger = 15.818; 31–40 yrs. = 18.266; 41–50 yrs. = 23.076; 51–60 yrs. = 21.597;

61 and older = 27.172; F (4, 440) = 8.928, p < .000; residency of 10 yrs. or less = 17.833; 11 to 20 yrs. = 21.667; 21–30 yrs. = 25.932; 31 yrs. and longer = 26.265; F (3, 470) = 9.645, p < .000.

35 *Media Disapproval* for married individuals = 15.894; single individuals = 14.504; F (1, 363) = 12.180, p < .000, for females = 14.670; males = 16.121; F (1, 361) = 14.932, p < .000; for Democrats = 13.793; Republicans = 16.889; Independents = 15.614; F (3, 349) = 17.694, p < .000.

36 *Political Awareness* for non-writers = 20.928; writers = 31.446; F [1, 455] = 46.508, p < .000; *Writer Understanding* for non-writers = 0.123; writers = 0.305; F [1, 489] = 19.571, p < .000; *Newspaper Readership* for non-writers = 3.383; writers = 3.789; F [1, 461] = 5.944, p < .000; *Writer Education* for non-writers = 4.068; writers = 4.763; F [1, 483] = 18.875, p < .000; *Marital Status* for non-writers = 59.9 percent; writers = 76.1%; x^2 [1, N = 448] = 8.327, p <.004; *Residential Longevity* for non-writers = 32.185; writers =37.637; F [1, 472] = 4.555, p < .000.

37 Bivariate correlations between *Writer Appreciation* and *Media Disapproval* = −.345, p < .001, *n* = 347; between *Writer Appreciation* and *Political Awareness* = .125, p < .000, *n* = 347.

38 *Respondent Age* for 1994 = 47.53; 2013 = 58.46; F [1, 478] = 54.234, p < .000; *Political Awareness* for 1994 = 27.83; 2013 = 20.58; F [1, 448] = 29.805, p < .000; *Newspaper Consumption* for 1994 = 3.92; 2013 = 3.22; F [1, 461] = 25.848, p < .000.

39 There were also no differences in *Media Disapproval* between 1994 and 2014, although respondents now watch a bit more television and listen to a bit less radio than they did before. More recent respondents, naturally, make better salaries and have lived in the local city longer. Otherwise, there were very few across-time differences on any of the key variables.

40 Susan Miller, *Assuming the Positions: Cultural Pedagogy and the Politics of Commonplace Writing* (Pittsburgh: University of Pittsburgh Press, 1998), p. 2.

41 Mohsen Ghadessy, "Information structure in letters to the editor," *International Review of Applied Linguistics in Language Teaching*, 21 (1983), 46–56.

42 Kalman Seigel, *Talking Back to the New York Times: Letters to the Editor, 1851–1971* (New York: Quadrangle, 1972).

43 Daniela Landert and Andreas H. Jucker, "Private and public in mass media communication: from letters to the editor to online commentaries," *Journal of Pragmatics*, 43 (2011), 1422–1434.

44 Andrew J. Perrin, "'Since this is the editorial section I intend to express my opinion': inequality and expressivity in letters to the editor," *The Communication Review*, 19(1) (2016), 20.

45 For more on this quality see Gerard A. Hauser, *Vernacular Voices: The Rhetoric of Publics and Public Spheres* (Columbia: University of South Carolina Press, 1999).

46 Susan Whyman, "'Paper visits': the post-restoration letter as seen through the Verney family archive," in Rebecca Earle (ed.), *Epistolary Selves: Letters and Letter-Writers, 1600–1945* (Aldershot: Ashgate, 1999), p. 19. For more on the "I" and "we" see Monique Mémet, "Letters to the editor: a multi-faceted genre," *European Journal of English Studies*, 9 (2005), 75–90.

47 Andrew J. Perrin and Stephen Vaisey, "Parallel public spheres: distance and discourse in letters to the editor," *American Journal of Sociology*, 114 (2008), 781–810.

48 Rasmus K. Nielsen, "Introduction: the uncertain future of local journalism," in Rasmus K. Nielsen (ed.), *Local Journalism: The Decline of Newspapers and the Rise of Digital Media* (London: Tauris & Co., 2015), pp. 1–30.

49 Bill Reader and Kevin Moist, "Letters as indicators of community values: two case studies of alternative magazines," *Journalism & Mass Communication Quarterly*, 85 (2008), 830.

50 Michael Dupre and David Mackey, "Letters and phone-mails to the editor: a comparison of reader input," *Newspaper Research Journal*, 23 (2002), 142–7.

51 Paula Cozort Renfro, "Bias in selection of letters to editor," *Journalism Quarterly*, 56 (1979), 822–6. For more on this matter see a dated but still useful study: David L. Grey and Trevor R. Brown, "Letters to the editor: hazy reflections of public opinion," *Journalism and Mass Communication Quarterly*, 47 (1970), 452.

52 Katherine Cramer Walsh and David S. Lassen, "Rural vs. urban coverage in newspapers across an upper Midwestern state." Paper presented at the annual meeting of the Midwest Political Science Association, Chicago, April 2012.

53 Michael Singletary, "How public perceives letters to the editor," *Journalism and Mass Communication Quarterly*, 53 (1976), 535–7.

54 Lucy Atkinson, "The public sphere in print: do letters to the editor serve as a forum for rationale-critical debate?" Paper submitted to the Cultural and Critical Studies Division, Association for Education in Journalism & Mass Communication, Washington, DC, 2007.

55 Susana M. Sotillo and Dana Starace-Nastasi, "Political discourse of a working-class town," *Discourse and Society*, 10 (1999), 433.

56 Jackie Hogan, "Letters to the editor in the 'War on Terror': a cross-national study," *Mass Communication & Society*, 9 (2006), 63–83.

57 Christopher A. Cooper and H. Gibbs Knotts, "Voice of the people? Analyzing letters to the editor in North Carolina newspapers." Paper presented at the annual meeting of the American Political Science Association, Washington DC, September 2005. For more on gender differences in letters see Catherine Siebel, "Gender on the page: letters to the editor and the tobacco debate," *Feminist Media Studies*, 8 (2008), 418; and Christopher Cooper, H. Gibbs Knotts, and Moshe Haspel, "The content of political participation: letters to the editor and the people who write them," *Political Science & Politics*, 42(1) (2009), 131–7.

58 Bill Reader and Dan Riffe, "Survey supports publication of controversial letters," *Newspaper Research Journal*, 27 (2006), 74–90.

59 See, for example, Brian Thornton, "Telling it like it is: letters to the editor discuss journalism ethics in 10 American magazines, 1962–1972-1982–1992," *Journal of Magazine and New Media Research*, 1 (1999) 1–15.

60 Brian Thornton, "Heroic editors in short supply during Japanese internment," *Newspaper Research Journal*, 23 (2002), 109.

61 Brian Thornton, "Rejecting the eloquence of hate: 1972 magazine letters to the editor," *Journal of Magazine & New Media Research*, 12 (2011), 1–25.

62 Brian Thornton, "Subterranean days of rage: how magazine letters to the editor in 1952 foretold a generation of revolution," *American Journalism*, 24 (2007), 59–88. For an interesting adjunct to these findings, but in a radically different context – the world of professional science – see Anne Magnet and Didier Carnet, "Letters to the editor: still vigorous after all these years? A presentation of the discursive and linguistic features of the genre," *English for Specific Purposes*, 25 (2006), 173–99.

63 Rebecca Earle, "Introduction: letters, writers and the historian," in Rebecca Earle (ed.), *Epistolary Selves: Letters and Letter-Writers, 1600–1945* (Aldershot: Ashgate, 1999), p. 4.

64 Michael Warner, *The Letters of the Republic: Publication and the Public Sphere in Eighteenth-Century America* (Cambridge: Harvard University Press, 1990).

65 The 88.1 percent figure is a bit higher than the acceptance rates reported by other researchers for comparably sized newspapers, but not excessively so. See Karin Wahl-Jorgensen, "Understanding the conditions for public discourse: four rules for selecting letters to the editor," *Journalism Studies*, 3 (2002), 70; Steve Pasternak, "Editors and the risk of libel in letters," *Journalism and Mass Communication Quarterly*, 60 (1983), 314.

66 See Jaime Loke, "Old turf, new neighbors: journalists' perspectives on their new shared space," *Journalism Practice*, 6 (2012), 233–49; Suraj Kapoor and Carl Botan, "Editors' perceptions of the letters to the editor column." Paper presented at the annual meeting of the International Communication Association, San Francisco, May 1989; Brian Thornton, "Telling it like it is."

67 Sandra Stotsky, "Writing in a political context: the value of letters to legislators," *Written Communication*, 4 (1987), 395; Suraj Kapoor, "Most papers receive more letters," *The Masthead*, 47 (Summer 1995), 18–21.

68 David B. Hill, "Letter opinion on ERA: a test of the newspaper bias hypothesis," *Public Opinion Quarterly*, 45(3) (1981), 384–92; Lee Sigelman and Barbara J. Walkosz, "Letters to the editor as a public opinion thermometer: the Martin Luther King holiday vote in Arizona," *Social Science Quarterly*, 73 (1992), 938–46; Sidney Verba, Richard A. Brody, Edwin B. Parker, Norman H. Nie, Nelson W. Polsby, Paul Ekman, and Gordon S. Black, "Public opinion and the war in Vietnam," *American Political Science Review*, 61 (1967), 317–33.

69 Marisa Torres da Silva, "Newsroom practices and letters-to-the-editor: an analysis of selection criteria," *Journalism Practice*, 6 (2012), 256.

70 John E. Richardson and Bob Franklin, "'Dear editor': race, reader's letters and the local press," *The Political Quarterly*, 74 (2003), 184–92.

71 For more on these pressures see Mark Kelley, "For democracy and the bottom line: goals United States newspapers hold for their letters to the editor section." Paper presented at the Association for Education in Journalism and Mass Communication convention, San Francisco, August 2006; Francisco Vasquez and Thomas Eveslage. "Newspapers' letters to the editor as reflections of social structure." Paper presented at the annual meeting of the Association for Education in Journalism and Mass Communication, Corvallis, Oregon, August 1983.

72 Wahl-Jorgensen, *Journalists and the Public*, 91.

73 Karin Wahl-Jorgensen, "Letters to the editor in local and regional newspapers: giving voice to the readers," in Bob Franklin (ed.), *Local Journalism and Local Media: Making the Local News* (London: Routledge, 2006), p. 223.

74 Karin Wahl-Jorgensen, "Letters to the editor as a forum for public deliberation: modes of publicity and democratic debate," *Critical Studies in Media Communication*, 18 (2001), 310.

75 Wahl-Jorgensen, *Journalists and the Public*, p. 137. See also Marisa Torres da Silva, "Professional views on letters-to-the-editor as a means of audience participation," *Participations: Journal of Audience & Reception Studies*, 10 (2013), 430; and Karin Raeymaeckers, "Letters to the editor: a feedback opportunity turned into a marketing tool: an account of selection and editing practices in the Flemish daily press," *European Journal of Communication*, 20 (2005), 199–221.

76 Bill Reader, "New research on the nature of letters and their writers," *The Masthead* (June 22, 2005), 17.

77 See, for example, John E. Richardson and Bob Franklin, "Letters of intent: election campaigning and orchestrated public debate in local newspapers' letters to the editor," *Political Communication*, 21 (2004), 459–78.

78 Daniel M. Butler and Emily Schofield, "Were newspapers more interested in pro-Obama letters to the editor in 2008? evidence from a field experiment," *American Politics Research*, 38 (2010), 356–71.

79 Michael Bromley, "'Watching the watchdogs'? The role of readers' letters in calling the press to account," in Hugh Stephenson and Michael Bromley (eds.), *Sex, Lies and Democracy: The Press and the Public* (New York: Longman, 1998), pp. 147–62.

80 Marc Dunkelman, *The Vanishing Neighbor: The Transformation of American Community* (New York: Norton, 2014).

PART III

THE TEXTURE OF CIVIC HOPE

6

Why Letters Are Compelling

A great many people wish to be heard in US politics, and some are quite noisy. The chief executive, of course, is a dominant player, but the presidency is always a presidency-in-context. There are two other branches of government, after all, so the president must conduct his business in a contested sphere where everyone is jealous of everyone else. The president naturally wants Congress to do his bidding, a feat often hard to achieve even when the partisan vectors are well aligned. The Supreme Court is jealous, too, hoping that the president will mind his own business and that Congress will make philosophically and functionally consistent laws. Still other forces beckon: The press constantly stalks the president, no matter what he has done or failed to do. These two great rivals spit at each other constantly, trying to out-flank one another if not crush one another.

The Beltway contains still other actors, including a labyrinth of bureaus, agencies, and commissions employing tens of thousands of people who (literally) surround the White House, alternately reinforcing and frustrating the president's priorities. K Street is filled with still other rivals – lobbyists making the case for corporate America, think tanks producing uncomfortable facts and figures, advocacy groups that are almost always in a bad mood. To this political menagerie one can add entertainment outlets feasting on leaders' missteps, religious institutions with knee-jerk reactions to all things political, the nation's military branches exempting themselves from overt political entanglements but feeding their preferences to partisan friends throughout the District. The president's neighborhood is a busy place indeed.

Given the high profile of these players, it is easy to forget the people. But they too have preferences; they too have fears, anticipations, and lusts. Sometimes their sentiments find form in public opinion polls or TV documentaries, and sometimes voters speak for themselves via Twitter or Facebook. Equally often, though, the people's voice gets lost in an environment dominated by well-funded professionals. It is easy to forget that the people have a voice.

But what sort of voice is it? I and a colleague asked that question, wondering what would happen if the president, the press, and the people had a simulated conversation. From prior research, we knew that presidents use rhetoric to dramatize new policy proposals, to "prime" voters about impending Congressional initiatives, and to cut through the din of Washington, DC.[1] Presidents also use rhetoric to declare "mandates," implying that the nation's citizens endorsed their entire platform when electing them to office. Presidents also draw on the White House's hallowed past, embedding themselves in its traditions to generate forward movement.[2]

The press has a different voice. It has become less deferential over the years and, as a result, increasingly consequential.[3] Reporters compress politicians' sound bites, selectively decide which stories are worth telling, and remix the day's events to produce coherent narratives.[4] The news is a text more cordial to soft news than hard news, personalities vs. issues, immediate instead of long-term perspectives, and conflict above all else.[5] With presidents calling attention to this and not that, and with the press making small things seem large (e.g., where a president takes his vacation) and trivializing events the president thinks are important (e.g., what he says at a ribbon-cutting ceremony), things get complicated indeed.[6]

What do the people sound like? Alexander Curry and I decided to find out by gathering together some 5,000 political passages, 20,000 news segments, and the 10,000 letters to the editor being examined in this book. Taking a hint from the scholarly literature suggesting that presidents are typically upbeat and the press pessimistic, we used a computer program (DICTION) to compare their use of Promotional and Complaint language to that of letter writers.[7] The findings are presented in Figure 6.1.[8]

Across a wide array of topics and circumstances, we found a comparatively upbeat chief executive and a sour, stubbornly sour, group of journalists. This to-and-fro between the president and the press may reassure the nation that power is being kept in check, but letter writers also have their say. Across sixteen presidential elections, the writers split the difference between politicians and reporters, and they did so in eerily

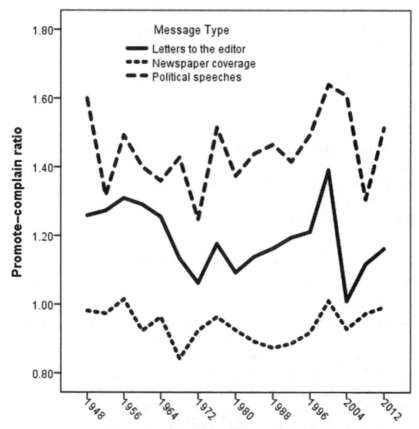

FIGURE 6.1 Promotional/Complaint Ratios across Time and Genre

consistent, eerily precise ways.[9] Given the size of this dataset (almost 40,000 passages sampled), the equidistant lines on the graph almost defy logic. Why do writers adopt the "middle way" so dependably? Why don't they throw in the towel and mimic the press's lamentations? Alternatively, why don't they cling to the nation's ideals like political leaders? Instead, writers weigh the good and the bad, as if they were referees in a tug-of-war. In some sense, they are.

These findings suggest that voters depend on presidents to protect the nation, wrangle with Congress, jet about the world, study public opinion polls, and light the Christmas tree. Simultaneously, they depend on reporters to get the facts straight, write decent prose, stand up to abuses of power, anticipate forthcoming events, and make sense of what it all means. And voters depend on themselves – or at least on their letter-writing neighbors – to keep the resulting dialectic active, refreshed, and balanced.

This chapter is the first of four exploring how writers make sense of the world, and our computer-based study raises several questions worth exploring: What expectations do readers have when approaching the letters column each day? How do they justify the time spent reading letters? What rhetorical features do they find particularly charming or off-putting? Why do they return to the opinion columns again and again? Letter writers, I will argue, offer three distinct enticements to readers. While letter writers do not speak for all Americans, they do call them forth with regularity. There is a Third Voice in American politics and it has an intriguing sound.

THE WRITER AS CARTOGRAPHER

For most Americans, letters to the editor are a common and unremarkable thing, rather like ants and peanut butter sandwiches. One pays no attention to the former until it invades the latter at a family picnic. Letters to the editor are so common, so unstudied, that they are hard to describe should one be asked to do so. They are letters, yes, but they are not love letters. They appear on the editorial page, but they are not ponderous like an editorial is ponderous. Letters to the editor are written by everyday people, but they are more formal than email notes – but not as formal as a letter of employment. Letters to the editor have a certain rhythm to them, but not a rhythm that inspires dancing.

Letters to the editor are best understood by examining what they are not. They are not, for example, blogs, although they do have a family resemblance. Like a blog, letters to the editor are written by people-with-names, people who represent only themselves and not some institution. Like a blog, letters to the editor are written by better educated, media-attentive, and politically concerned people.[10] Like a blog, letters to the editor are written for a general (vague?) audience, "serve no immediate practical purpose," and yet, for whatever reason, develop a loyal following.[11] And like so many blogs, letters to the editor wear their politics on their sleeves, which is not to say they are unmistakably partisan, but is to say they are passionate and concerned. Like blogs, letters to the editor are removed from the extant media infrastructure (and often take exception to it), but they depend on that infrastructure for their sustenance.[12]

But letters differ from blogs as well: Bloggers live in cyberspace, while letter writers live in Utica. Bloggers write about specialized topics in an attempt to develop a distinctive "brand," while letter writers discuss whatever irritates them at the moment. Bloggers tend to be younger, letter writers older; bloggers specialize in outrage, letter writers in potholes; bloggers insert new information into the media flow, trying to become a "tribune of the people," while letter writers offer opinions about last week's news.[13] But the main difference between bloggers and letter writers is that bloggers are part of an "ecosystem that is experienced primarily within the confines of their browsers," an ecosystem encouraging (1) fierce and endless jousts with other denizens of the Web and (2) great pressure to post each day, if not several times a day.[14] Letter writers, in contrast, are a more leisurely crowd. They are carefully regulated by their editors, so they have little opportunity for fisticuffs. They are typically prohibited, for example, from identifying by name the author of a letter with whom they disagree. A certain politesse prevails in letters columns.

The letter writers in my twelve cities can be thought of as cartographers, as persons who lay out the political terrain for their readers even though there is a certain presumptuousness in their doing so. When maps were first invented, after all, they were seen as heretical. What habit of mind, what carnal motive, would inspire a person to render in two dimensions God's three-dimensional world? Which nations would be mapped in such an enterprise? Which portions of which nations? Who would determine the accuracy of these maps? Who would reproduce them, for whom, and at what price? Why were they being made in the first place? To spread the gospel? To conquer heathen nations? To identify trade routes? To interrupt shipping lanes? Maps – humble things, dangerous things.[15]

Figure 6.2 maps my 10,000 letters in high relief.[16] It consists of just a few black bars on an ocean of white and it is reductionist to the core. But the tale it tells is easy to understand. For each pair of variables, the unhappy story is four times more powerful, or three times more powerful, or twice as powerful as the happy story. The figure shows that political individuals, political groups, and political processes are linked to one another in an unending tangle. Even though each of these variables was coded separately, they point in the same direction – to a fraught political system and to a near constant dialectic.

Figures 6.3 and 6.4 add specificity to this picture. Figure 6.3, for example, explains who counts in politics, with the width of the bars identifying the most important players: political parties first, then ideological groups and the federal government, followed by local government

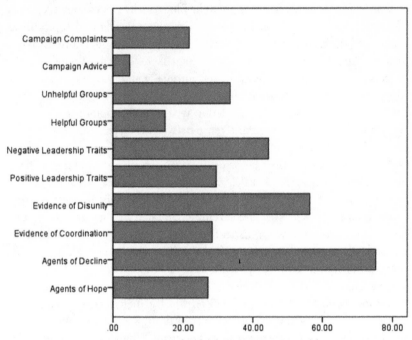

FIGURE 6.2 Use of Paired Civic Hope Variables

and the news media. All the remaining candidates come across as bit players, even though they are also found in the daily news feed. In the letters columns, however, *positionality* is the dominant force. Education, business, religion, volunteerism, the military, and geographical regions receive scant attention. The most positioned of all groups – political parties – receives the lion's share. In a recent column, *New York Times* columnist David Brooks bemoans that fact:

With fewer sources of ethnic and local identity, people ask politics to fill the void. Being a Democrat or a Republican becomes their ethnicity. People put politics at the center of their psychological, emotional and even spiritual life. This is asking too much of politics. Once politics becomes your ethnic and moral identity, it becomes impossible to compromise, because compromise becomes dishonor. If you put politics at the center of identity, you end up asking the state to eclipse every social authority but itself. Presidential campaigns become these gargantuan two-year national rituals that swallow everything else in national life.[17]

The letter writers also feature the parties as troublemakers. Figure 6.3 shows them tilting to the unhelpful side of the scale. The more institutionalized a group becomes, the more problems they create. Figure 6.4,

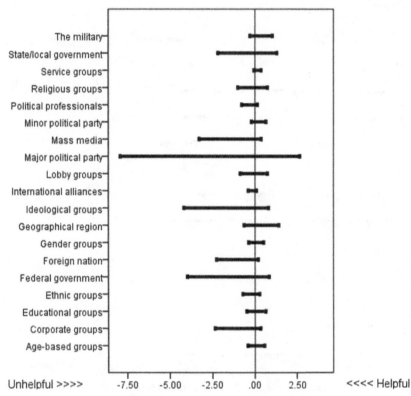

FIGURE 6.3 Mentions of Helpful and Unhelpful Groups

which tracks political relationships, adds nuance to this generalization. Elected officials are referenced frequently and almost always rancorously. Even if one had never read a letter to the editor, one could grasp its themes by quickly glancing at Figures 6.2 through 6.4. These figures show writers living in a tidy, circumscribed world containing a great many players, only a few of whom are significant. They also show (via the leftward tilt of the bars) that US politics is frequently in turmoil.

But there is a happier way of interpreting these data. The job of a cartographer, after all, is to present an accurate picture of the territory described, no matter what its imperfections. Letter writers perform that task by identifying who has power, what they do with it, and what happens as a result. Sometimes they go overboard when "updating" things in these ways but one cannot know the players without a scorecard. And so perusing a letter to the editor has a ceremonial aspect to it.

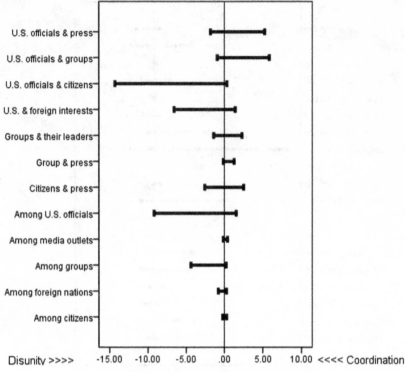

FIGURE 6.4 Descriptions of Coordination and Disunity

A letter (1) explains why things turn out as they do, (2) reinforces readers' inchoate perceptions, and (3) assures readers that someone similar to them understands their frustrations, that they are not alone. Politics is unpretty, but one can hardly blame the map maker for that.

It must also be remembered that there are a great many map makers operating in the public sphere and that they plot things out differently. These differences explain why letters to the editor are read so avidly. A map of Chicago based on tourist destinations, after all, looks quite different from a map featuring sewer lines. And a map of Chicago's politics looks different still. Consider, for example, two "maps" produced a week after the riots spawned by the 1968 Democratic Convention. Given the turbulence at the time, it is not surprising that the city was laid out differently by the two letter writers. In the excerpts below, the authors identify the same key players – city officials, protestors, police, and the press – but describe them in starkly different ways:

The Afro-Americans have learned for themselves that the only way to make America take notice of a minority's sad plight is to cause trouble. Maybe the white youths have taken note. The so-called "now generation" refuses to continue men's 50-year-old fashions and hair styles that show the skull with all its lumps and bumps. This apparently makes them qualify as hippies and scum to newspapermen. This type of reasoning should cause people to scorn George Washington, Thomas Jefferson and Ben Franklin who not only wore long hair but also ruffled shirts. My son is already a member of the Johnson-Humphrey slave army but I applaud the resistance of those who are still free. It is apparent that you have no son likely to lose his life in Vietnam.

(Mrs. Jimmy P., *Lake Charles American Press*, September 7, 1968)

* * * * * *

In the past week over coffee and in small groups of concerned citizens, I have heard time and again the remark that "these people have been cradled too long in the lap of ineffectual police procedures in other cities." We have seen Detroit burn, Watts fall apart, Cleveland explode in bursts of insane rioting. If you knew this could happen here, what would you do? To me the answer is what the Chicago police did. They acted and they were tough about it. To all of us who demand of our own children decent deportment, clean clothes and neat appearance, respect for law and order, and then have to listen to some sanctimonious news reporter call hard-working and harassed police "thugs," then it is time Americans got mad.

(John C., *Billings Gazette*, September 5, 1968)

In Saul Bellow's famed novel, *Herzog*, one of its minor characters, Geraldine Portnoy, has this to say about letters: "[They] give one a chance to consider – think matters over, and reach a more balanced view," instead of spewing forth love and hate simultaneously as lovers often do.[18] When viewed in the round, then, when viewed collectively, letters to the editor have a similar capacity. John C. and Mrs. Jimmy P. tell different stories because they see the world through different eyes. Accepting those differences, says Bernard Dauenhauer, is central to finding political hope, which is "incompatible with any claim to self-sufficiency" and can only be found by positing "interminable political amelioration."[19] In other words, civic hope is found through patience. Neither of our writers had all the truth needed to understand the Vietnam protests. Each drew an earnest but incomplete map.

Having a sense for the terrain, knowing what goes with what, is not everything, but it is something. Researchers tell us, for example, that reading a local newspaper increases consumers' (1) knowledge of politics, (2) confidence in their own opinions, (3) civic participation, and (4) willingness to monitor office holders.[20] Letters to the editor are filled with conflict but that, too, can be a plus. According to sociologist Richard Sennett, conflict clarifies issues for us even when we find it distasteful.[21] The fact that letter writers expose gaps between citizens and their leaders can also be beneficial. As Murray Levin pointed out many years ago, one of the greatest sources of political alienation is the notion of an all-powerful citizenry, a highly idealized vision that leads to frustration and, worse, to demoralization on the parts of voters.[22] It is better, says Levin, for us to assume that life is a journey requiring continued vigilance. People who write letters to the editor offer a map for that journey.

THE WRITER AS PRIEST

Maps are important but rarely interesting and almost never motivating. Letters to the editor would not have remained a staple in the nation's newspapers if they were solely topographical. It turns out that they are also sermonic. People write letters to get things off their chests, to set others straight, to get their juices flowing. A woman wakes up in the morning and decides over coffee that a great many people need to hear from her. That is intrusive on her part, but she does it anyway.

In his fine book *American Democracy: From Tocqueville to Town Halls to Twitter*, Andrew Perrin argues that democracies are sustained not by institutions but by culture. He provides this piece of evidence: When people are asked if they voted in a recent national election, 17 percent of those who say they did will be lying, a figure that has held constant for the past fifty years.[23] When people are asked that same question about local elections, 15 percent of those who say they voted will not be telling the truth, or, better, the truth they will be telling – that democracy is precious to them – trumps the inconvenient fact of their voting habits. Because politics is such a source of conflict, many do all they can to avoid it.[24] But conflict draws other people in nonetheless, and that is one more reason why people read letters.

Letter writers "rehearse" democratic values for their readers, often by detailing the nation's shortcomings. That is how it is in church as well. What is a sermon without sin, after all? In this connection, a fascinating study was done recently by political scientist Kevin Mullinix, who wondered what would happen if people were primed to think about democratic ideals. Would they become less small-minded when reminded of "good government" virtues? To answer that question, Mullinix ran an experiment in which he presented subjects with the following message:

We are going to ask you about a couple different issues, but first, please read what Dr. Mark Jenkins, a professor of public policy at Stanford University, recently stated: "When it comes to complex public policies, citizens have a duty to get informed. They need to openly evaluate the information from all sides and try to understand why other people have the opinions they do —independently forming opinions. Too often people just follow their party's lead, and when they do this they cannot be sure they picked the best policy position or justify their opinion. They should do this not only for themselves, but also because of a responsibility to make sure the government is making the best policies for the country, including those who are less fortunate. Even though I do not directly vote on the issue, I have a say in who gets elected. That is why I always vote. Plus, you can get involved in other ways, like simply talking about issues with friends and co-workers. Ultimately, we have to obey the laws that are made, so at the very least, we should be well informed about them."[25]

Surprisingly, Mullinix found that by invoking the language of civic norms, 80 percent of his subjects became more willing to question party-inflected positions. They also became more willing to discuss issues with people from the opposing party, to question partisan endorsements, and to incorporate new information into their decision-making. A similar study by Cindy Kam at UC-Davis found that subjects became more open-minded about a hypothetical political candidate when civic duty was cued.[26] Reflecting on his own study, Mullinix admits that using an alleged Stanford professor may have intimidated his subjects, hence producing an overly dramatic effect. But he also notes that variants of his stimulus message can be found in the real world, where they might have even more impact.

Nobody knows if consuming a steady diet of letters to the editor produces similar effects, but it is not implausible. Consider, for example, a letter to the editor written by Tanya B., an older-than-average student at Virginia Tech University. Tanya B. took up the same theme developed in the Mullinix passage, but she did so with greater innocence and considerably more personal investment:

Going to college is one of the single most important steps a person can take toward a fulfilling life. I am putting myself through school and I sometimes forget what a privilege it is to be here and how liberating it is to find knowledge and truth.

I was reminded with Ross Perot's recent visit to campus. Not only did the visit emphasize the numerous opportunities one has by being in school but emphasized also the importance of being open-minded to new and old ideas. This way of thinking was the essence of the American Dream.

I am not a history major but I know this country was not founded on one idea by one lawmaker but by a collection of visions and dreamers. Perot a manifestation of the American Dream used his graphs and lists to paint a picture of truth and history – not cynicism. I never once doubted what he said nor did I feel the need to read between the lines. Truth is logic. A president should be logical.

This revelation has led me to ask pessimistic questions: Has my generation been labeled "x" because we have had nothing to believe in? Can society accept logic? Perhaps a new Generation of dreamers and doers would come forth if we had someone like Perot to remind us of the believable again.

(*Roanoke Times*, November 11, 1996)

People who write letters to the editor are often preachy in this way. We see that tendency in Table 6.1, which rank-orders agents of hope and decline. Although only two campaign seasons are represented here, the hierarchy of actors never varied across the entire sixty-five-year timeline. These data show that letter writers are thorough-going institutionalists, focusing on those at the top of the pyramid. Voters are found at the bottom of the list but they are rarely the focus du jour, an odd outcome for a genre devoted to the vox populi. But when it comes to politicians, letter writers rev up their engines, as we see in the following letter:

I am voting for Trump. And here's why. First, I despise his vulgar mouth. And how he acts kind of stupid when he is angry. And his many other shortcomings. But I don't despise him nearly as much as I do the Washington crowd.

The Romneys, the McConnells, the Grahams, the Reids, the Obamas, the Clintons. The whole stinking bunch. Frankly, I despise them all. Because they have all looked out for their own interests, making tax loopholes for themselves and their rich friends while taxing me to the breaking point, and making my life very difficult.

That's why I want to give them the gift of Trump. Because they all hate him, and they all deserve him. And it's the only way I'll ever get even with that two-faced, back-stabbing crowd. I hope Trump gets up there and makes their lives as miserable as they have made mine.

(Lonnie M., *Roanoke Times*, March 10, 2016)

TABLE 6.1 *Rank of Most Referenced Agents: 1948 vs. 2012*

Agents	Hope: 1948	Hope: 2012	Decline: 1948	Decline: 2012
Presidential Candidate	1	1	1	1
Local Candidate/ Official	2	2	4	2
Federal Official	3	3	2	3
Former Public Official	4	4	6	4
US Citizen	5	–	5	5
Member of the Press	6	6	3	6
Historical Personage	–	5	–	–

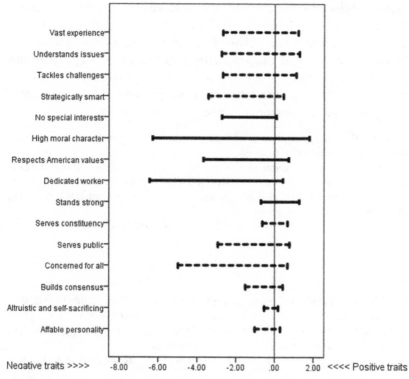

FIGURE 6.5 References to Positive and Negative Leadership Traits

Figure 6.2 revealed that writers identify three times as many *Agents of Decline* as *Agents of Hope*.[27] Figure 6.5 shows that they spot many more negative *Leadership Traits* than positive ones (i.e., the leftward tilt of the bars). Three clusters can be observed here. Gathered at the top of the figure are functional qualities (e.g., vast experience, etc.), with social outreach skills grouped at the bottom (e.g., build consensus, etc.). Characterological traits (those found in the middle of the chart) receive the greatest emphasis, suggesting that writers' agendas are quite different from those of the press. Letter writers feature personal strength more than affability, moral values more than tactical skills. For them, the modernist notion of charisma – interpersonal charm – distorts its meaning. They think of charisma in biblical terms, as an "anointing," as a near-spiritual quality.

Democratic letter writers were especially upset with leaders who showed little "concern for all Americans," while Republican writers decried those with insufficient "respect for American values." But those were the only partisan differences to be found among the sixteen Leadership Traits.[28] Whether praising or decrying politicians, writers from both parties focused on core values. Faced with a choice of going broad or deep, they went deep. Faced with a choice of attacking party positions or campaign platforms, they chose a third option – pointing out character flaws and clandestine motivations. Although the following passages were written many years apart, issues of human morality unite and animate them:

Is McCarthy trying to destroy the confidence of the people not only in the Democratic administration of government, but the Republican, as well? Is he trying to breed a revolution in this nation so that – maybe – communism or fascism can step in and take over? McCarthy is not a Republican, and certainly, not a Democrat. What is he? Is he a threat to our national way of life? Is he a king-pin of destruction to our nation?

(J.H.H., *Wichita Falls Times Record News*, October 22, 1952)

* * * * * *

It is Mr. Nixon and his war machine who now butcher large numbers with daily bombings and alleged attacks on the dikes and foreign missions in Hanoi plus a blockade that prevents food reaching the North, using the pretext of protecting the South Vietnamese from a Communist blood bath.

(G.T.H., *Provo Daily Herald*, October 19, 1972)

* * * * * *

Instead of learning from error, Carter digs in all the deeper, withdraws all the more from face-to-face argument and attacks the motives of his critics. Underneath that brittle mask of control one senses an uptight and agitated psyche, filled with anger and venom. His meanness of spirit and heart has come out in the campaign, especially in the pattern of cowardice displayed in his flight from debate and in his truly Nixonian facility for saying nasty things while piously denying that he is saying them.

(William B., *Springfield News-Sun*, October 22, 1980)

* * * * * *

It's a very sad commentary on the United States as a nation when a flag-waving incompetent will likely be elected by voters who have been deceived by name-calling and truth-twisting. Take a cold shower of reality, America! Ronald Reagan, George Bush and the rest of those bright Republicans in Washington have managed in eight short years to mortgage away the future of our nation for the benefit of the rich and corrupt.

(Jeffrey M., *Roanoke Times*, November 1, 1988)

In each of these passages, writers are essentialistic. While citing a bevy of undesirable outcomes – potential revolution, a communist bloodbath, an unwillingness to debate, a financially crippled nation – they bore deeply within the candidates themselves to find relevant causes: a compromised Self, hard-heartedness, sublimated anger, xenophobic incompetence. Long-distance observations of up-close matters such as these require an almost ecclesiastic sensibility.

Given their salty attitudes, how can letter writers be described as emissaries of hope? Five reasons: (1) they have a point of view, (2) they share it with others, (3) they do not shrink from conflict, (4) they are invested in the political process, and (5) they sometimes inspire readers to care about the polity. In other words, it is *the willingness to search for solutions*, not the writer's jauntiness, that is the sign of civic hope. As I stress throughout this book, buoyancy and hope are not the same thing at all. Buoyancy results in a smile; hope results in work.

This struggle for hope is a tack that social scientists also recommend. Joseph Gershtenson and Dennis Plane argue, for example, that excessive trust can be as dangerous to society as no trust at all, that "some distrust of government is in fact patriotic and healthy."[29] Gershtenson and Plane find that people with "excessive trust" usually do not vote, feel uninformed about government, and do not discuss politics with friends or family. Research by John Hibbing and Elizabeth Theiss-Morse makes an even more startling observation: the less people believe that politicians care, the more they vote.[30]

To hope well, says philosopher Victoria McGeer, "is to experience ourselves as agents of potential as well as agents in fact."[31] Letter writers, at least the inveterate ones, see themselves as the former, and probably as the latter as well. The surveys reported in Chapter 4 evidence those beliefs and the passion found in writers' letters evidences it as well. Psychologically, it is hard to know why some citizens become preachers while others do not. Imagination may play a role, with letter writers constantly envisioning how politics can be fixed. That is the third reason why their letters are read so avidly.

THE WRITER AS SEER

Fortune tellers, fantasy baseball, Wall Street projections, the Weather Channel, war gaming in the military. Everyone wants to know what they cannot know – the future. Some people make handsome salaries by boldly declaring what they cannot know. A physician tells a patient it will take six weeks for her broken arm to heal and pollsters forecast the final vote

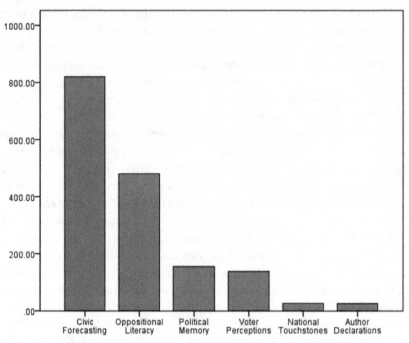

FIGURE 6.6 Use of Individual Civic Hope Variables

tally three days before the Michigan primary. The confidence shown by such experts makes it seem that they lead bi-temporal lives, and clients often genuflect in the presence of their clever guesswork.

Figure 6.6 shows that those who write letters to the editor also trade in the future. They do so relentlessly and with bravado. Passion, especially political passion, overtakes them, making them feel that what should happen *will* happen. Writers conflate the Actual with the Desired and rhetoric covers over the seams between them. Because the future is so tantalizing, writers and readers strike a bargain: Let us go together to a place free of our current annoyances.

Figure 6.6 shows that *Civic Forecasting* is, by far, the letters' stock-in-trade. The future is a safe place for several reasons: (1) a writer's predictions cannot be empirically dismissed, but only countered with alternative predictions; (2) the availability of evidence supporting a prediction is limited only by a writer's imagination; (3) talk of the future combines the rhetorical with the poetic, resulting in rich, lyrical depictions. Conceptually, one could dismiss all future-talk as mere hypothecation, but that becomes hard to do when the good people of Duluth take pen to paper:

- *Environmental disaster*: "We cannot, we must not, ignore the environmental realities of our time. If things continue as they are, the next battle in the Boundary Waters is bound to make motorboats a moot point [because] Mondale and others in pursuit of fish are sure to bypass the lakes there when they become devoid of life. A coal liquefaction plant to solve our energy and employment ills? Shall we continue to feed carcinogens to the cancer patient?" (Betsy G., *Duluth News Tribune*, September 14, 1980)
- *Nuclear holocaust*: The parties of big business have no cure for inflation, unemployment, pollution, poverty, racism and crime; yet these problems must be resolved if we are to survive. Sooner or later, the working people will have to build a new, independent labor party of their own, based on the working class, with a program for returning back to the people, placing people before profits and recognizing the right to a job with decent wages as a fundamental human right. But at the moment, our country and the world are being prepared for a nuclear holocaust which could end all life on this earth. (Andy J., *Duluth News Tribune*, October 5, 1980)
- *A federal Gestapo*: If the Equal Rights Amendment passes, it will be the law of the land and you will have no more choice but to conform your family to the image of those who have drawn up this amendment. If you disobey it you will have the federal Gestapo hammering on your door - what choice will my daughter have when they call her up for cannon fodder in another no-win war? What choice will I have but to have my tax money used for a final solution for unborn babies for those who will not exercise self-control and want the lazy way out? (Ellas L., *Duluth News Tribune*, August 22, 1980)

"Hoping," says philosopher Darrel Moellendorf, "is imaginative activity," a unique combination of belief and desire.[32] It is easy to tell what the Duluth writers believe and desire in the foregoing. Imagination adds a propulsive force to this mixture, a fleshing-out that helps to command readers' attention. Depictions like these can, however, make one time-confused: Are the fish dead yet? Have the nukes left the launch pads? Is the Gestapo at the door? While all talk of the future rests on fabrication, one forgets that when reading a well-crafted letter, especially if one believes – as many do – that dark forces skulk about.

"Although the presence of doubt is destructive of belief," says Moellendorf, "it is not destructive of hope."[33] That is, even as the Duluth writers laid out their worries, they made ready to offer solutions. When it comes to hope, says scholar Patrick Shade, one must distinguish between wishing – something we do when we have lost control – and planning – something we do "when means are determinate and within our reach."[34] Sour though they sometimes are, letter writers are also chronic planners, believing neither in Fate nor Folly. In their world, the present is known and the future controllable ... if only their remedies are adopted. The future – a place where belief and desire become one.

Figure 6.7 shows that the future looms ominously on multiple fronts – economic, legal, political, moral, intellectual. All of Maslow's needs can be found here and all are under siege. Occasionally, letter writers offer happier accounts (justice, morality, etc.), but those predictions take a back seat. Why do people read such unhappy stuff? Some readers do so because they share the writers' ideological predispositions, while others do so for comic relief, which is to say, to keep cognitive dissonance at a minimum. Between these poles one finds readers using the letters column as an exploratory place where they can expand their beliefs ever so

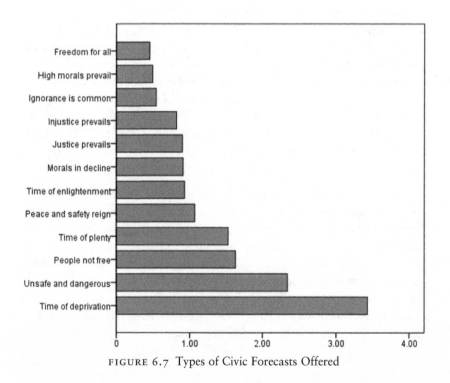

FIGURE 6.7 Types of Civic Forecasts Offered

slightly. People watch soap operas for the same reason, "trying on" alternative lifestyles without actually adopting those lifestyles.

The future is a fabrication but the past is a fabrication too. We live in the present; all else is invented. On the fourth of July, on Lincoln's birthday, on the eve of war, politicians resurrect past events so new plans can be advanced. Politicians are creative in these ways, but so are all people, which explains why so many people become better high school athletes (or debaters or banjo players) the further removed they are from their high school days. Media scholar Stephen Coleman expands on this point: "To be a democratic citizen is to belong to a community of memories. There is much to remember: what is law, what is custom, what is taboo; the professed differences between political parties; acknowledged repertoires of protest and affirmation; the names of the historically iconic and demonic; and countless mundane enactments of civic fidelity."[35]

Memory "teaches us to ourselves," says rhetorical scholar Susan Miller, but it does not do so passively. Direct human intervention is needed to wring meaning from the past. Letter writers work hard on these interventions. Figure 6.8 displays the choices they make and, once again, morality becomes their trump card. Morality is a flexible and

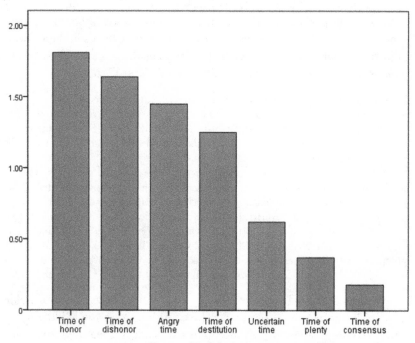

FIGURE 6.8 Types of Political Memories Recalled

generous friend, as is the past, validating what Terry Eagleton once said: "Like a work of art, the meaning of the past evolves over time."[36] One letter from the 2004 campaign shows how personal history, documented history, imagined history, and extrapolated history join together to create a smooth, clear contrivance:

> John Kerry become a turncoat to his fellow Vietnam veterans after leaving Vietnam. By his actions, he caused the increase of American and Vietnamese casualties. Kerry, Jane Fonda and others like them gave aid and comfort to the enemy. I served 33 months in Vietnam and supported naval river patrol boat operations in the Mekong Delta.
>   Kerry served only four months and left his boat crew to serve the normal 12-months tour of duty. It is not a good example of a naval officer to leave his crew and not complete a normal tour of duty. His wounds were too superficial to warrant leaving early. His statements about U.S. war crimes in Vietnam were inaccurate and exaggerated. Now he wants to become president? What he did was wrong and he should not be considered for the highest office.
>   (William H., *Salinas Californian*, October 26, 2004)

History is always *someone*'s story. That premise allowed "swift-boating" to become a new art form in the 2004 presidential campaign and resulted in the savaging of a war hero (John Kerry). Letters to the editor constantly take advantage of history like this, sometimes identifying a straight-line function between an imagined past, a confusing present, and a mythical future. Because of rhetoric, time bends in these ways, adjusting to whatever is needed at the moment. It bends one way in the *Salinas Californian* and another way in the *Billings Gazette*:

> I am proud that I honorably served my country when I was called. I am also proud that I dedicated myself to the struggle to end that war when I returned to the U.S. as a soldier in Vietnam Veterans Against the War. I believe the huge numbers of protesting vets turned the tide of America's opinion and forced Nixon to mealy mouth his way out.
>   Those who now claim that spoiled rich kids who used the corrupt system of wealth and family to duck out of Vietnam are somehow more worthy than John Kerry who chose not to hide behind privilege are both silly and dishonest. More than 50,000 poor young Americans died and countless others were wounded or emotionally scarred for life; more than a million Vietnamese, Cambodians and Laotians – mostly civilian – died as well. George Bush drank beer and waved pompoms with the other cheerleaders. Dick Cheney had other things to do.
>   (Michael B., *Billings Gazette*, October 20, 2004)

When commenting on letter writing as a social practice, literary scholar Charles Bazerman notes that, when first formulated in the Middle Ages, letters were designed to connect church leaders separated by great distances. That distance required something more elegant than the "U OK?" of twenty-first-century texting. It required a more complete story of what was going on, who was involved, what their motives were, and what it all meant. Letters to the editor recall that tradition, containing, in Bazerman's terms, a confection of "narrative of remarkable events, proselytizing, prayer, consolation, moral teachings, praise of the faithful and warnings against deceivers, philosophical thought, prophesy, and church organization."[37] Except for the last item on this list, Bazerman identifies the core components of today's letters to the editor.

CONCLUSION

As mentioned in Chapter 3, to be fully manifest, civic hope requires (1) belief in the democratic verities, (2) a willingness to stand with these values in public, and (3) the rhetorical skill to make others feel similarly. Civic hope is therefore undermined when a democracy goes silent and when nobody is available to defend its deeply felt but oft-disputed premises. Letter writers rarely let that happen, but that is not to say they always make the right stylistic choices. As we have seen here, letters to the editor are compelling for many reasons, but all letters are not equally compelling. Some are petulant and short-sighted. Others are daft or peculiar, turning readers away from the public sphere. When that happens, civic hope loses an ally.

For these reasons, letters to the editor are easy to parody. Their boldness alone justifies a parody or two. Letter writers are aware of the jibes directed at them and, while some get defensive, most understand that criticism comes with the territory. In that sense, they are rather like bloggers. Bloggers, says Andrew Barlow, are keenly aware of how they are seen, and it rankles them. Says Barlow: "For the most part, [bloggers] want to be taken seriously within the greater society, not dismissed as weirdo loners in their mother's suburban basements. Though most will stoutly defend the right of anyone to say anything they wish on the blogs, they still want their own blogs, both personal and group, to reflect well on them."[38]

Letter writers also have their pride, but they have more than that as well: They have civic hope. In modern parlance, they "lean into" political affairs, patiently waiting until it is their turn to send off another missive to straighten people out. While waiting, they pay more attention to political affairs than do most Americans, folding each new event into their ideological schemas. "Perhaps," they reason, "my next letter will cause a break-through; perhaps the sluggards will finally listen."

Given how frequently letter writers feature negative emotions, it is worth revisiting the distinction between optimism and hope. Optimism involves feeling good about the future, with or without evidence. Hope is a different matter entirely. Hope confronts the world's inadequacies with a willingness to do something about them. That willingness derives from a certain toughness of spirit but also from a set of ideals. Along these lines, Leonard Pitts, Jr., a columnist for the *Miami Herald*, wrote a fine essay during the 2016 presidential campaign describing how he, as an African-American, coped with the campaign's denigrations of minority citizens. After painfully detailing the remarks he had heard, Pitts explains his coping mechanism, a mechanism I refer to as civic hope:

So I write this letter for four reasons: The first is to say that some of us have been there. Some of us still are. The second is to remind you that Cruz and Trump do not represent the predominant opinion – only the loudest. The third is to say, on behalf of the rest of us: I'm sorry for what you're dealing with. The fourth is to point out that there is a difference between America and Americans.

"America" is simple. It's "liberty and justice for all." It's freedom. It's an ideal. "Americans" are the people charged with living up to that ideal. And very often, they fail to do so. Because of expedience. Because of bigotry. Because of cowardice. Truth to tell, sometimes, they don't even try.

But the failure of the people is not the failure of the ideal. This is a truth some of us hold to when our country disappoints and I commend it to you. America belongs to all of us. And America is worth believing in. Even when Americans let you down.[39]

The letter writers I studied are not nearly as eloquent as Leonard Pitts, Jr., but they understand his distinction between what is going on at present and how things might be changed. Letter writers also have their frustrations and they, too, will not give up the ghost. That is how it is with hope – if it gets a grip on you, it is hard to shake. In the meantime, perhaps, a hobby:

Hope is
folding paper cranes
even when your hands get cramped
and your eyes tired,
working past blisters and
paper cuts,
simply because something in you
insists on
opening its wings.[40]

Endnotes

1 Karlyn Kohrs Campbell and Kathleen Hall Jamieson, *Presidents Creating the Presidency: Deeds Done in Words* (Chicago: University of Chicago Press, 2008); James N. Druckman and Justin W. Holmes, "Does presidential rhetoric matter? Priming and presidential approval," *Presidential Studies Quarterly*, 34 (4) (2004) 755–78; Andrew B. Whitford and Jeff Yates, *Presidential Rhetoric and the Public Agenda: Constructing the War on Drugs* (Baltimore: The Johns Hopkins University Press, 2009).

2 Julia R. Azari, *Delivering the People's Message: The Changing Politics of the Presidential Mandate* (Ithaca, NY: Cornell University Press, 2014); Judi Atkins and Alan Finlayson, "'As Shakespeare so memorably said...': quotation, rhetoric, and the performance of politics," *Political Studies*, 64(1) (2014), 164–81.

3 Samuel Kernell, *Going Public: New Strategies of Presidential Leadership*, 4th edn. (Washington, DC: CQ Press, 2007) Thomas E. Patterson, "Political roles of the journalist," in Doris A. Graber, Denis McQuail, and Pippa Norris (eds.), *The Politics of News, The News of Politics*, 2nd edn. (Washington, DC: CQ Press, 2007), pp. 23–39.

4 Frank Esser, "Dimensions of political news cultures: sound bite and image bite news in France, Germany, Great Britain, and the United States," *International Journal of Press/Politics*, 13(4) (2008), 401–28.

5 Shanto Iyengar, Helmut Norpoth, and Kyu S. Hahn, "Consumer demand for election news: the horserace sells," *Journal of Politics*, 66(1) (2004), 157–75; Matthew A. Baum, "Circling the wagons: soft news and isolationism in American public opinion," *International Studies Quarterly*, 48(2) (2004), 313–38; Tim Groeling and Samuel Kernell, "Is network news coverage of the president biased?" *The Journal of Politics*, 60(4) (1998) 1063–87; Roderick P. Hart, *Seducing America: How Television Charms the Modern Voter* (New York: Oxford University Press, 1994); and Jeffrey S. Peake, "Presidents and front-page news: how America's newspapers cover the Bush administration," *The International Journal of Press/Politics*, 12(4) (2007), 52–70.

6 David Domke, *God Willing? Political Fundamentalism in the White House, the "War on Terror," and the Echoing Press* (London: Pluto Press, 2004); Shanto Iyengar, Mark D. Peters, and Donald R. Kinder, "Experimental demonstrations of the 'not-so-minimal' consequences of television news programs," *American Political Science Review*, 76(4) (1982), 848–58.

7 For the presidential perspective on this matter see Harold M. Zullow, Gabriele Oettingen, Christopher Peterson, and Martin E. Seligman, "Pessimistic explanatory style in the historical record: CAVing LBJ, presidential candidates, and east versus west Berlin," *American Psychologist*, 43(9) (1988), 673–82; Jean Schroedel, Michelle Bligh, Jennifer Merolla, and Randall Gonzalez, "Charismatic rhetoric in the 2008 presidential campaign: commonalities and differences," *Presidential Studies Quarterly*, 43(1) (2013), 101–28; Peter Drahos, "Trading in public hope," *The Annals of the American Academy of Political and Social Science*, 592(1) (2004), 18–38. For descriptions of press coverage see Michelle C. Bligh, Jeffrey C. Kohles, and James R. Meindl, "Charting the language of leadership: a methodological investigation of President Bush and

the crisis of 9/11," *Journal of Applied Psychology*, 89(3) (2004), 562–74; Stephen J. Farnsworth and S. Robert Lichter, *The Nightly News Nightmare: Television's Coverage of U.S. Presidential Elections, 1988–2004* (Lanham, MD: Rowman & Littlefield, 2007); Stuart Soroka and Stephen McAdams, "News, politics, and negativity," *Political Communication*, 32(1) (2015), 1–22.

8 For a tolerably complete list of research studies using the DICTION program see www.dictionsoftware.com/published-studies.

9 *Promote–Complain Ratio* for letters = 1.1995, for news reports = 1.0154, for political speeches = 1.4904; F [2, 34973] = 960.490, p < .000. For additional details see Roderick P. Hart and Alexander L. Curry, "The third voice of American politics," *Presidential Studies Quarterly*, 46(1) (2016), 73–97.

10 William P. Eveland and Ivan Dylko, "Reading political blogs during the 2004 election campaign: correlates and political consequences," in Mark Tremayne (ed.), *Blogging Citizenship, and the Future of Media* (New York: Routledge, 2007), pp. 114ff.

11 Carolyn R. Miller and Dawn Shepherd, "Blogging as social action: a genre analysis of the weblog," in Laura Gurak, Smiljana Jevic, Laurie Johnson, Clancy Ratliff, and Jessica Reyman (eds.), *Into the Blogosphere*, October 20, 2010. Accessed at www.researchgate.net/publication/274510648_Blogging_as_Social_Action_A_Genre_Analysis_of_the_Weblog.

12 Barbara K. Kaye, "Blog use motivations: an exploratory study," in Mark Tremayne (ed.) *Blogging Citizenship, and the Future of Media* (New York: Routledge, 2007), pp. 127–48.

13 For more demographic and psychographic information about bloggers see Susan C. Herring, Lois A. Scheidt, Inna Kouper, and Elijah Wright, "Longitudinal content analysis of blogs: 2003–2004," in Mark Tremayne (ed.), *Blogging, Citizenship, and the Future of Media* (New York: Taylor and Francis, 2007), pp. 3–20 and Aaron Barlow, *The Rise of the Blogosphere* (Westport: Praeger, 2007). For an exceptionally nuanced discussion of blogging see David D. Perlmutter, *Blogwars* (New York: Oxford University Press, 2008).

14 Aaron S. Veenstra, "Reconceptualizing political blogs as part of elite political media." Paper presented at the annual conference of the Association for Education in Journalism and Mass Communication, Denver, August 2010, 14.

15 For a fascinating discussion of related matters see Jeremy Black, *Maps and Politics* (Chicago: University of Chicago Press, 1998).

16 For Figures 6.2 and 6.6, corrected Density scores are shown. For Figures 6.1, 6.3, 6.4, 6.5, and 6.7, standardized scores are displayed.

17 David Brooks, "How to Fix Politics," *New York Times*, April 12, 2016, 15–16.

18 Saul Bellow, *Herzog* (Greenwich: Fawcett Crest, 1965), p. 19.

19 Bernard P. Dauenhauer, "The place of hope in responsible political practice," in Jaklin A. Eliott (ed.), *Interdisciplinary Perspectives on Hope* (New York: Nova Science Publishers, 2005) 91.

20 See Joshua P. Darr, "The news you use: political knowledge and the importance of local newspapers." Paper presented at the annual meeting of the Midwest Political Science Association, Chicago, IL., April, 2015; Danny

Hayes and Jennifer L. Lawless, "As local news goes, so goes citizen engagement: media, knowledge, and participation in U.S. house elections," *Journal of Politics*, 77(2) (2015), 447–62. Patricia Moy and her colleagues also find that readers of local newspapers participate more in political affairs but that those who watch local TV news do not. See Patricia M. Moy, Michael McCluskey, Kelley McCoy, and Margaret Spratt, "Political correlates of local news media use," *Journal of Communication*, 54 (2004), 532–46.

21 Richard Sennett, *The Corrosion of Character: The Personal Consequences of Work in the New Capitalism* (New York: Norton, 1998) 143. Lee Shaker worries that Americans' rapid transition to new media outlets "may have uniformly negative consequences for levels of local political knowledge." See Lee Shaker, "Citizens' local political knowledge and the role of media access," *Journalism & Mass Communication Quarterly*, 86 (2009) 809–26.

22 Murray Burton Levin, *The Alienated Voter: Politics in Boston* (New York: Holt, 1960), p. 73.

23 Andrew J. Perrin, *American Democracy: From Tocqueville to Town Halls to Twitter* (London: Polity, 2014), pp. 51–2.

24 Kate Krontitis, John Webb, and Chris Chapman, "Understanding America's 'interested bystander': a complicated relationship with civic duty." Accessed at http://googlepolitics.blogspot.com/2015/06/understanding-americas-interested.html

25 See Kevin J. Mullinix, "Civic duty and political preference formation." Paper presented at the annual meeting of the Midwest Political Science Association, Chicago, April 2016.

26 Cindy D. Kam, "When duty calls, do citizens answer?" *The Journal of Politics*, 69:1 (200) 17–29.

27 Throughout this study, I found very few differences between male and female letter writers. One exception was that men identified significantly more *Agents of Decline* (but neither more nor fewer *Agents of Hope*) than women: men = .03849; women = −.11616; F [1, 7824] = 44.241, p < .000. Men especially identified both current and former public officials as Agents of Decline.

28 Pattern for *Unconcerned for All Americans*: Democratic writers = 1.5603, Republican writers = −.02330; F [1, 5603] = 44.720, p < .000; for *Forsakes American Values*: Democratic writers = −.04676; Republican writers = .16161; F [1, 5603] = 47.993, p < .000.

29 Joseph Gershtenson and Dennis L. Plane, "In government we distrust: citizen skepticism and democracy in the United States," *The Forum*, 13(3) (2015), 486.

30 John R. Hibbing and Elizabeth Theiss-Morse, "How trustworthy politicians decrease mass political participation." Paper presented at the annual convention of the American Political Science Association, San Francisco, September 2001, 11.

31 Victoria McGeer, "The art of good hope," *Annals of the American Academy of Political and Social Science*, 592 (2004), 105.

32 Darrel Moellendorf, "Hope as a political virtue," *Philosophical Papers*, 35 (2006), 413.

33 Ibid, 416.

34 Patrick Shade, *Habits of Hope: A Pragmatic Theory* (Nashville: Vanderbilt University Press, 2001), p. 61.
35 Stephen Coleman, *How Voters Feel* (New York: Cambridge University Press, 2013), p. 76.
36 Terry Eagleton, *Hope without Optimism* (Charlottesville: University of Virginia Press, 2015), p. 32.
37 Charles Bazerman, "Letters and the social grounding of differentiated genres," in David Barton and Nigel Hall (eds.), *Letter Writing as a Social Practice* (Philadelphia: John Benjamins, 1999), p. 19.
38 Barlow, *The Rise of the Blogosphere*, p. 37.
39 Leonard Pitts, Jr., "Trump, Cruz ideas are just plain stupid," *Miami Herald*, March 25, 2016. Accessed at: www.miamiherald.com/opinion/opn-columns-blogs/leonard-pitts-jr/article68350122.html#storylink=cpy
40 Elizabeth Barrette, "Origami emotion," in Paul Rogat Loeb (ed.), *The Impossible Will Take a Little While: Perseverance and Hope in Troubled Times* (New York: Basic Books, 2014), p. 374.

7

Why Letters Are Irritating

This book argues that those who write letters to the editor help preserve the nation's civic hope, but that does not mean they are universally loved. In fact, letter writers are often downright irritating, minding other people's business instead of their own and implying that their fellow citizens are insufficiently virtuous. Who made such people our moral guardians? Why must we listen to their half-baked theories and endless carping? And why, especially, don't they edit themselves?

What I want to read is a well-expressed point. The problem with email is that one is more often apt to "write in haste, and regret at leisure." One feature of email that I think would help is a "delayed" send mail button. This would let you dash off the email, send it. And an hour later stop it from being delivered – saving you from making a fool of yourself. The act of writing a paper letter to the editor provided time to review and correct "your first draft." Sometimes the very best letters (from the reader's perspective) are those <u>not sent</u>!¹

Many people deal with letters to the editor by simply turning the page. Others, a considerable number in my opinion, read letters because they enjoy irritating themselves, thereby establishing their moral superiority over the writers. There is something of the self-flagellant in such readers, people who pick up new viewpoints by reading letters but who cannot admit to such perversions.

This is not to say that writers are intentionally irritating (although some no doubt are) but they are typically mournful. To inspire broader discussion and to jolly them up a bit, one editorial page editor – Michael Carey of the *Anchorage Daily News* (now the *Alaska Dispatch News*) – began hosting what became known as the "Letter Writers Ball." The first

such ball was held on February 21, 1990 and drew seventy-five of
Anchorage's most inveterate letter writers. They were served finger food
and mild libations, after which a Q&A session with the editor and an
open-mic segment were held. Given the mix of folks attracted to the Ball,
including "anarchists, atheists, prisoners, pro-lifers, gun toters, environmentalists, libertarians, Gingrich Republicans, animal rights activists, and
fathers at war with child-custody laws," the Ball produced a bouillabaisse
of argument.[2] The evening ended with door prizes being distributed,
consisting of books, mugs, tote bags, and a parchment replica of the
Constitution. Although Mr. Carey notes that the event "was a polite,
even fastidious affair," the writers often accused him of being "in the pay
of the oil companies, the military, the Republican Party, and President Bill
Clinton."

A number of other newspapers have held similar events over the years,
including the *Chicago Tribune*, the *San Jose Mercury News*, the *Tennes-
sean*, and the *Orlando Sentinel*. These, too, were colorful affairs. In
Orlando, for example, letter writers made the following observations:

- *On Florida transplants*: "If you tell me one more time how this is not
  like New York City, we will mug you and carjack you and make you
  feel right at home."
- *On telemarketers*: "I think [they] should be hung by their dialing
  fingers, and phone solicitation should be banned as a public nuisance."
- *On fat discrimination*: "It has always been OK to criticize the fat [and]
  the media does little to discourage this prejudice. We as a nation are in
  jeopardy of losing our melting-pot status to individual prejudices."[3]

For some Americans – the mild-mannered, the reticent, those striving
to fit in, social climbers – any sort of expressed opinion can be offensive,
trebly offensive if expressed loudly. For other Americans – the volatile, the
choleric, those suffering discrimination, those nursing grudges – letters to
the editor are considered too mild an intervention. Most Americans live
somewhere between these two poles. They like it when people mix it up
for good reason, when genuine evil is identified and decried, and yet they
too find letters to the editor irritating. Why?

I identify two main sources of irritation here. I will argue that writers'
self-projections, the roles they assign themselves, grate on readers. Writers
come across as too puffed-up, too willing to assign themselves to all beats,
local as well as international. They become ambassadors without port-
folio, self-appointed moral arbiters. Psychologists call this affliction

"illusory superiority" or, more colorfully, the "Lake Wobegon Effect," which presumes that writers' opinions – all of them – are above average.[4]

Letter writers' *social projections* are also off-putting. There is an undeniable paternalism in letters to the editor. Writers constantly identify their fellow Americans' inadequacies, accusing them of being easily duped and politically inert. Sometimes these judgments are offered explicitly but, even worse, sometimes they are offered nonchalantly: "As we all know, a good citizen must..." Remarks like these remind people of sermons delivered to them by their parents, sermons that can be effective until a child turns fourteen, at which point they reach for their ear buds, sensing a lecture coming on.

To say that letters to the editor are irritating is to be agnostic about the authors as people. No doubt, some writers intend to be offensive; others just mutter to themselves, while still others return to their formerly beatific state once they have written their letter. It is not so much the personalities of the writers that bring censure but rather their pronunciatory style that rubs readers the wrong way. That is how it is with strong opinions. Sharp-tongued people launched the American Revolution, after all, and now their descendants write letters to the editor. Same instinct, different modality.

To say that writers are irritating also does not mean that they have no effect. Indeed, the more irritating a letter is, the more impact it can have by giving readers a sense of "subordinate control" over the author. When that happens, a reader's surveillance capacities are lowered, adding a predictable unpredictability to letters columns: What manner of nonsense will be served up today? In short, reading a letter to the editor has its entailments. When added to readers' daily routines, letters can affect people's personal agendas without their being aware of that happening.

Letters to the editor have been around for a great many years and continue to thrive despite the irritations they produce. Web-based comment strings have a more recent provenance but generate far greater notoriety – and antipathy. When asked by a boss to add online curation to their duties, many an editor will leave their place of employment rather than oversee an endless stream of bile. Cooler heads argue that online commentary can help create a more robust public sphere, but others cannot get past its toxicities. For several reasons, then, the things that people find irritating about letters to the editor are helpfully contextualized by first examining their online offspring, a topic to which we now turn.

THE HAZARDS OF FAST DEMOCRACY

Some years ago, a Canadian journalist by the name of Carl Honoré wrote a bestseller entitled *In Praise of Slow: How a Worldwide Movement is Challenging the Cult of Speed*. The book is light reading but pulls together a number of cultural shifts related to "time sickness." "Thanks to speed, we live in the age of rage," Honoré proclaims – we jet from appointment to appointment and from city to city without calculating the toll it takes on our physical and emotional health.[5] Family members race past one another rather than sit down at the dinner table together; people take drugs to make them energetic, other drugs so they can go to sleep quickly, still other drugs to help them lose ten pounds by next Tuesday. The love of speed, says Honoré, has become idolatrous.

"We are so time-poor and time-sick that we neglect our friends, families, and partners," Honoré warns.[6] The solution? Slowing things down – collectively cooked meals instead of microwaved pizzas; neighborhood walks rather than twenty-minute exercise frenzies; Tantric sex instead of something quicker and less meaningful. "Simply resisting the urge to hurry is free," Honoré reports, so slowing things down can deliver what really counts: "good health, a thriving environment, strong communities and relationships, freedom from perpetual worry."[7]

Pop psychology aside, Honoré makes a good case for cutting ourselves some slack. Interestingly, though, while he surveys modern life broadly – fast food, crazy work schedules, inadequate leisure, raising children on the hustle – he never mentions that politics, too, moves more quickly because of new technologies. For example, when an exposé appears on the front page of the morning newspaper, it may by then be in its twelfth edition, having been constantly edited online the night before. It will generate thirty comments by 6 a.m. and a hundred more by noon. Online posters never sleep, it seems, with one scholar calculating that 250 news articles appearing in ten large US newspapers gave rise to 15,384 online posts. Only 14.2 percent of these posts added new information; 68.6 percent were negative and 34.6 percent bore no relationship to the news story to which they was responding.[8]

In the age of speed, says the University of Tempere's Ari Heinonen, readers have entirely different relationships with their local newspapers, becoming at once fellow news-gatherers, guardians of journalistic quality, pulse-takers, community discussants, and political pundits.[9] Not surprisingly, public affairs topics generate the greatest number of online comments, as do (1) continuing (vs. one-shot) stories, (2) evaluative vs. factual entries, and (3) stories focusing on demographic subgroups.[10] Young people in Western countries are especially drawn to online commentary, which is not to say they are a dependable political constituency.[11] While many online posters are vituperative, not all are, with some scholars arguing that "superposters" perform a range of positive roles, including storytelling, consultative dialogue, and personal disclosure, and with only a minority (15 percent) having a predilection to attack others.[12]

Because the study of online commentary is as new as online commentary itself, opinions range widely about "fast democracy." Jack Rosenberry of St. John Fisher College reports, for example, that online and offline commenters are often similar (loyal readers, a bit older, more likely to be male, interested in fostering dialogue, etc.), although he admits that online participation does *not* get people more involved in their "geographic communities" – a finding that differs from that of Susan Robinson and Cathy Deshano of the University of Wisconsin, who have linked online participation to greater volunteerism and offline civic investments.[13] Taking a somewhat median position are Penn State's Kyung Han You and his colleagues, who found that *writing* online comments produced greater civic engagement while *reading* them did not.[14]

Online commenters are often "loner populists" who believe in people more than institutions, who are anti-elitist but also distrustful of pluralism, who are drawn toward charismatics, and who operate out of a "simplified ideological core."[15] Not surprisingly, political elections sharply increase the number of online posts,[16] many of which will be authored by young males who, according to media scholar Jennifer Stromer-Galley, have few acquaintances with whom they discuss politics in person, but who "feel more in control, bolder, safer engaging in conversation online."[17] Strangely, while the world is now filled with online commenters, a transnational space for dialogue has not emerged, according to Bart Cammaerts of the London School of Economics and Leo Van Audenhove of the Free University of Brussels, who argue that xenophobia and racism make the notion of "unbounded citizenship" an empty concept.[18]

Two factors – anonymity and incivility – distinguish online commentary from letters to the editor. In all, 22 percent of online comments are uncivil, reports one group of scholars, with half of all commenters posting at least one uncivil comment and with frequent commenters producing far more than occasional posters.[19] Not surprisingly, online incivility is more likely to thrive on sites pitched to individuals of low socio-economic status.[20] Often, commenters will participate in a "spiral of incivility" that makes non-participants less likely to deliberate in the future and that increases political polarization for all.[21]

Comment columns attached to newspapers are more civil than those associated with other outlets. A study by Robin Blom and his colleagues found a considerable number of "outspoken" participants in the eighty newspaper columns they studied and, while these individuals were strongly opinionated and more than willing to attack one another's ideas, they engaged in very little flaming.[22] Still, such columns contained more claim-making than genuine argument and issues of identity constantly came to the surface. Highly personalized, and essentialized, remarks were directed at everyone – public officials, business leaders, media celebrities, and anyone else brave enough to enter the discussion. In short, the Web is not a place for the faint-hearted.

Issues related to anonymity have been especially problematic for the nation's newspapers. Goaded by the spirit of Publius, the *New York Times* habitually ran unsigned letters until 1973, when it instituted a "must sign" policy for legal and other reasons. By 1995, says journalism scholar Bill Reader, 84 percent of the newspapers he surveyed required their correspondents to identify themselves.[23] Given its reverence for the First Amendment and its concern to make all speech free and unfettered (especially for those in the minority), the press has stoutly resisted such strictures, fearing that reducing the "expression of diverse viewpoints" would make newspapers a place "where the voiceless can only watch in silence."[24]

The advent of the Web has sharpened this debate, with 90 percent of the nation's top 150 newspapers now hosting online comment sections. While the press is skeptical of such columns, they do get readers involved, hence contributing to a newspaper's bottom line.[25] Some observers have hoped that such user-generated content will tip off journalists to breaking news stories, a hope that is sometimes realized.[26] More often, though, reporters continue to think of their readers as consumers rather than co-producers. As a result, online comments (1) play "little or no role in newsroom discussions" and (2) rarely affect the stories being reported.[27] According to media critic Howard Rheingold, "flamers, bullies, bigots, charlatans, know-nothings and nuts" have turned the Web into a jour-nalistic wasteland.[28]

More progressive voices contend that online comments belong to the commenters and that journalists should steer clear of them entirely.[29] But a masthead is a masthead, so most newspapers try to find some way of moderating the columns even though it adds more overhead to a news-paper's budget.[30] An editor who was asked to take on such tasks declared his job "thankless" because it forced him to absorb commenters' "feelings of bitterness and hatred."[31] Independent news operations such as Slash-dot have had better luck "crowdsourcing civility," but such aggressive moderation can be prohibitively expensive.[32] Many news outlets, then, are confronted with a Hobson's choice: risk being marginalized by user media or risk doing damage to the newspaper's brand.[33] For a host of reasons, then, journalists greatly prefer to have their audiences imagined.[34]

When it comes to online participants themselves, 68 percent find comment columns to be too negative, but only 20 percent of those surveyed feel that the rules on anonymity should be lifted.[35] Commenters report liking the opportunity to disagree with formal authorities, to confront media bias, to blow off steam, and to be part of a "commu-nity."[36] And so we get what we get: fragmented political discussion, people re-exposed to viewpoints they already hold, and the *New York Times* publishing 100 letters to the editor versus 8,000 online comments each week.[37]

Fast democracy makes many journalists misty-eyed for those who write letters to the editor, because *living somewhere* and *having a name* act as disciplining agents. Not surprisingly, Michael McCluskey and Jay Hmielowski of Ohio State find that letter writers tend to be more "com-munity protective" than online commenters, more measured, and more institutionalist as well.[38] Letter writers prize their communal status but things are more perverse on the Web. One scholar reports, for example, that reproaches of online comments make guilty parties post more often, not less often, than before the censure.[39]

Stephen Coleman of the University of Leeds observes that modern citizens live a life of endless anticipation – waiting until they are old enough to vote, waiting in line to cast a ballot, waiting for election results, waiting for politicians to make good on their promises. We live in "the deferred moment," says Coleman," where our desires are "forever anticipated but rarely reached."[40] Perhaps that is why fast democracy appeals to so many – have a thought, share a thought; have a feeling, share a feeling. As we have seen, however, hyper-speed takes a toll on social capital. Although impa-tience can stir people to action, it can also stir them to anger, a commodity now in ample supply online. For these reasons, one brave editor, Neal Pattison of *The Daily Herald* in Everett, Washington, tried to slow things down with the following Yuletide request:

On Monday, *The Daily Herald* staff is hoping to remove some rancor from our corner of the world. We will be closing public comments on our website, *Heraldnet. com*, until early January – or, perhaps, longer ... [So] here is our wish for habitual commenters: Embrace the season. Use the hours you've been spending on social critiques to reconnect with friends and loved ones who don't hear from you enough. Channel your argumentative energy into caring for yourself, your family and our community. Public comments were meant to broaden and enrich civic discussions. Until we can get back on that track, *The Daily Herald* is taking a break.[41]

THE CONCEITS OF SLOW DEMOCRACY

If online commentary is a crashing thunderstorm, letters to the editor are a gentle spring rain. Letters to the editor are less spontaneous and less pyrotechnic than online commentary. While letters to the editor can be passionate and while they are not strangers to verbal excess, temporal forces slow them down. A writer may fire off a letter to the editor in a moment of anger, but then a week or more will pass before the letter is returned to the author's doorstep in printed form. In between, editing will have occurred, perhaps even a bit of negotiation, so the heat of the moment will not be the driving force it is for online commenters. When crafting their letters, writers factor in these delays and often pre-edit themselves. As a result, their letters are less reactive to others' viewpoints, and usually less churlish as well.

This is not to say, however, that ego is an irrelevancy. As we saw in Chapter 4, letter-writing is a very personal business. Writers take the world seriously, often over-seriously, for reasons both intellectual and psychological. Said one of my interviewees, Camilla T. of Springfield: "Writing letters helps me feel better. They help me get some of that churning emotion out of me and move it outwards so that I feel better. I feel purged. I feel less stressed afterwards. I feel better." Egos require therapy but they also make ideological demands. Said another inter- viewee, Susan V. of Duluth:

I don't like it when people say "Americans want." Well, how the hell could you know what Americans want? Who are you speaking for? I think we can all only speak for ourselves. I don't think somebody can tell me what Americans in general think or what people of religion believe or that we are a Christian nation. I think that we should be free to practice any religion we want. The people that I admire the most are people like my sister, who is very religious, but those are the people that live it. They're not the people that preach it. They live it.

Self-referential statements like these give letters to the editor their undeni- able charm, adding both immediacy and a sense of "presence." They also

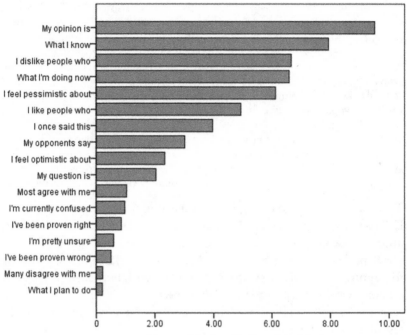

FIGURE 7.1 Types of Author Declarations Made

add boldness, a feeling that the author is "fully formed," that his or her opinions are deep-seated, that they know what they know. Self-references also make letters readable, serving as a public invitation to a private world. But the reverse is also true: When the "I" goes missing, an author can seem distanced, uncaring. People use communication to find one another. I-statements help them do so.

One of the great letter-writers in human history, Elizabeth Barret Browning, once declared that she habitually emptied her "heart out with a great splash on paper."[42] The letter writers in my twelve cities behaved similarly, although Figure 7.1 shows such writers often irritate people when doing so. The most common self-assertions are all about *me* – how smart I am, what I'm doing, what's wrong with other people, the beliefs I hold. Relegated to the bottom of the list are insecurities – where I've gone wrong, the questions I have, the people who disagree with me. There is no vulnerability here, no sense of interrogation either. Despite the legion complexities of politics, writers know what is right and know what is true.

Naturally, self-references are but one of many rhetorical devices, but, because they point so directly to an author, they heavily affect its tone. Consider, for example, an excerpt from one letter:

> All too often, in those legislative offices where Republican congressmen hold sway, I have noted an almost elitist attitude prevail and grow, which most certainly puts this average citizen on the defensive. I strongly suspect that were I to have walked into the Republican offices in the latest Brooks Brothers suits with a silk shirt and tie and booties by Gucci made of some rare South African animal's skin, I would have probably been given a much better reception. Unfortunately, as is the case with most of the people I have come across lately, gabardine and Good Will polyester and tennis shoes are the best I can afford.
>
> (Bill P., *Billings Gazette*, October 10, 1988)

This passage is part of a long letter delineating the corruptions found on K Street in the nation's capital, but one does not need those details to appreciate what the author is trying to do. Rhetorically, though, he fails. His hypothetical scenario is trite, inelegant. He works too hard, straining to capture the reader's sympathy. Ideally, self-references open up the author's world to the reader and thus become a sign of trust. Bill P.'s scenario, in contrast, is artificial, his gabardine and tennis shoes failing the test of authenticity.

Self-references also signal emotionality, and that is a blessing when it is not a curse. A personal story can instantly connect reader and writer, exciting their common feelings. It can, in critic Kenneth Burke's terms, build "identification" between them, helping them share their identities with one another.[43] But emotion can also be unruly, throwing authors off the track and making them forget their purpose. When that happens, a reader reasons this way: "Yes, I see you are concerned about this matter but what about me? Why should I care?" Emotion can also lead to hyperbole, and, while hyperbole is sometimes good, it is also sometimes bad. To wit:

> I hope we senior citizens will still be able to obtain clinic and hospital care in spite of Obamacare's reduction in Medicare and introduction of death panels to decide who is worthy of major medical care. I had harbored hopes of retiring in a few years but now I'm obligated to continue working to help support my "fair share" of those unfortunate welfare free-cell-phone-subsidized-housing food stamp recipients.
>
> I hope I can still afford gas as government-created shortages will soon be the norm. Since Obama has tightened regulations on exploration refining and drilling and nixed the Canadian pipeline we will soon be waiting in lines again for gasoline at $5.00 per gallon or more. In short, I hope all you Democrats get precisely what you voted for. Too bad the rest of us have to suffer for your inability to distinguish results from rhetoric.
>
> (Jim M., *Wichita Falls Times Record News*, November 8, 2012)

Jim M.'s self-references seem contrived here, unconnected to any real-world experience he has had. He seems more interested in blowing off steam than adding to the dialogue. He also exaggerates things: Was he really planning to retire soon? Will gasoline really get to $5 a gallon? Are death panels really in the offing? In other words, his self-references so strongly resemble the lamentations of Fox News that his text seems a cheat.

Because self-references so reliably point to a person's emotional state, and because it is hard to shut down one's emotional engine once it gets started, letters to the editor can run away with themselves. That makes them more charming but it also makes them seem over-indulgent, as we see in the following letter, a letter that will not stop:

I am sick, I will admit, of do-gooders who blame me and those who feel as I do for the action of crackpots. I am sick of television news commentators who blame all the ills of our nation on an inanimate gun and the lack of complete governmental control of same yet at the same time see the networks for whom they toil – programming shows of violence that I can't allow my children to see them.

I am sick of politicians who decry the ease of gun acquisition and the terrible violence that grips our citizens yet sit calmly by as rioters loot and burn our cities effectively tying the hands of our police until they are powerless to take steps to enforce our laws ... I am sick of movies that portray violence, sex perversion and crime as so glamorous that children believe Bonnie and Clyde were heroes hounded to death by the terrible police. I am sick of magazines and paperbacks that go even further – if that is possible – than the movies in lowering the morals of our youths to whom they are peddled and I am even more sick of a court that rules such trash as being freedom of the press.

(Hurley C., *Wichita Falls Time Record News*, June 28, 1968)

Hurley C.'s letter was written in June of 1968, a tumultuous year, so one can sympathize with his litany of worries. That year produced assassinations, riots, the war in Vietnam, a strife-torn Olympics, and much else. These events piled atop one another, quickly overwhelming the nation. They overwhelmed Hurley C. as well, hence his use of the run-on style. He ties his assertions together with a homely refrain ("I am sick") and, while he is earnest, he seems not to know how or when to stop (the letter goes on much longer). One senses a writer out of control here, one who cares deeply about issues but who has not yet sorted them out. His text is aimless and disjointed, sending off emotional sparks in a thousand directions.

Pronouncing an opinion is not the same thing as sharing an opinion, and that is why self-assertions must be handled carefully. Editors prefer letters that feature writers' experiences – not their abstract ideas, not their pet ideologies – because such experiences connect to the lives readers live.[44] Letter writers often violate that principle, assuming that readers will forgive them for rambling if they ramble from the heart. Sometimes readers do so, but more often they dismiss writers who conduct auto-therapy in public.

Editors like letters that are personalized and localized. The former quality grants them authenticity and the latter makes them feel familiar to readers. Astute letter writers position themselves within their geo-graphic community and their geographic community within the larger society.[45] Too much egocentricity gets in the way of their doing so, however, and that is especially true when letter writers appear "unhinged," when their self-references signal a lack of control.[46] Lin-guists Susana Sotillo and Dana Starace have also studied letters to the editor and found 42 percent of them to be pontifical, moralizing, and platitudinous.[47] While the researchers supported their conclusions with their own coding scheme, one wonders if their letter writers' unwise use of self-references may not also have contributed to such impressions.

In their study of online news discussions, Marc Ziegle and his col-leagues at the University of Mainz found that their participants were especially successful in getting others to participate in the conversation when they mentioned (1) their own experiences with the topic at hand and (2) their personal uncertainty about how to proceed.[48] As we saw in Figure 7.1, this is not the formula most letter writers follow, and that is often to their detriment. But when they do follow it, the effect can be powerful. I present three excerpts in support of that claim:

- *On dying*: Being a nurse, I saw people suffer for weeks, sometimes months. One patient had diabetes, then kidney failure; both legs and one arm were amputated, then he slipped into a coma. His fingertips and penis rotted off and his family was horrified. And I thought, if this horrifies you, what about when he lost three limbs (they insisted he continue dialysis). When his extremities rotted off his body, his family wanted him to continue dialysis and wanted doctors, nurses and EMTs to take measures to continue his life of suffering. I thought "You want a comatose torso to continue dialysis"? We don't let animals suffer like this but, humans, we do. (Sheila L., *Fall River Herald News*, November 1, 2012)
- *On poverty*: Today I saw a woman and her child. The woman was blonde and wore her hair matted, her face unwashed. Her child was a tall, lanky young girl, maybe 13, with the same bewildered face of her

mother ... I usually look away from these people because I don't want to see their pain, but as they walked in front of my car at the intersection, this child looked at me. Her eyes locked into mine and I was trapped. She was scared. She was hungry. She was angry. She was confused. And I was swept with guilt because I am unemployed and had no hope to offer her. All I could do was return her questioning eyes. (Susan C., *Lake Charles American Press*, October 17, 1988)

• *On freedom*: My mind and emotions recall the face of the most beautiful woman I have ever seen in my life – in the outskirts of Quang Tri city – firing her husband's rifle at the on-coming North Vietnamese tanks – with the bodies of her soldier husband and her child offering the only protection she had. My mind remembers swimmers who braved shark infested waters to seek the "freedom" they only knew through the remembrances of older people. I can still see the tears of my Marines as they pulled them from the surf at Guantanamo Bay. I wish you could have been there when 200 Cubans sought "liberty" under the gunfire of Castro's Frontier Brigade. (George R., *Provo Daily Herald*, November 22, 1980)

These three passages have remarkable force. In the first instance, Sheila L. takes us behind the scenes of nursing, leaving us with searing images that are at once foreign to us but also deeply human. Susan C.'s thoughts are arresting for a different reason: She is interrogative, even confused, unsure of what she has seen, even less sure of where she is going, but somehow knows that her experience has changed her in important ways. George R. takes us on a different journey. His anecdote provides sharp detail linked in a direct, almost clinical, way to his overall argument. None of these letters is easy to forget.

Letters to the editor offer a special window into the culture of a community and the people who live there. That is especially true when their authors bring themselves into the conversation. Sometimes doing so works out for them and sometimes it does not. Too much *me* can seem authoritarian; too much *you* can seem manipulative. Too little of *me* can seem cold-hearted; too little of *you* can seem selfish. Striking the right balance is therefore hard. When reading as many letters to the editor as I have over the years, though, I found myself paying special attention to writers who invested themselves in their letters. Sometimes their investments irritated me, but I listened nonetheless. I suspect that my experience was not unique.

THE PATERNALISM OF SLOW DEMOCRACY

When referring to themselves in letters to the editor, writers often come across as know-it-alls, as sermonic. That impression is heightened when they comment on their fellow citizens, which they do quite often. Sometimes writers upbraid voters, sometimes they counsel them, but almost always they know what is best for them. Most of us avoid making these large, glandular claims about the nation because we live in small communities – in family circles, in ethnic groups, in religious congregations, in work groups – many of which are class-defined. We let somebody else worry about Society Itself.

Letter writers, however, habitually reach past their micro-identities for something grander and more complete. "A place becomes a community," observes Richard Sennett of the London School of Economics, "when people use the pronoun 'we,'" although it is also a "dangerous pronoun" because it excludes others.[49] "A regime which provides human beings no deep reason to care about one another," says Sennett, "cannot long preserve its legitimacy."[50]

Figure 7.2 shows a steady increase in communal references in the letters studied here. This is a small fact but an important one. It stands as a talisman for why people write letters in the first place – to change other people. By nature, says legal scholar Mary Ann Glendon, "we roam at large in a land of strangers where we presumptively have no obligations towards others except to avoid the active infliction of harm."[51] This is a minimalist definition of society, and an unacceptable one for writers. Technically, though, Glendon is correct: We are born alone and we die alone. All else – family relations, ethical injunctions, societal bonds – must be invented. To identify with a nation is to reify it, to treat an abstraction as if it were real. When writing about their hometowns, that is, letter writers also construct them:

Fall Riverites have always felt and maintained a special bond with Ted Kennedy and that bond has been reflected in our overwhelming support for him in past elections. We are a city of workers and we are a community of compassion and caring toward each other. Senator Kennedy shares that sense of compassion and represents this community with intelligence integrity and sensitivity. For those of us who remain skeptical towards the ethereal theory that somehow "a thousand points of light" are going to solve America's problems I suggest that our best bet is to insure that the light voice and conscience of Ted Kennedy remain in the United States Senate for the next six years.

(James C., *Fall River Herald News*, October 29, 1988)

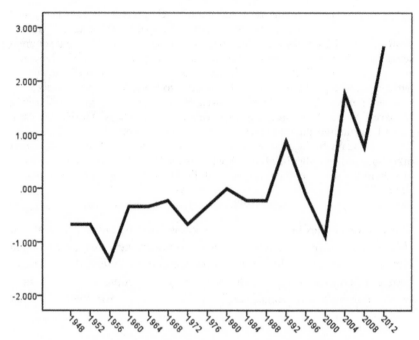

FIGURE 7.2 First-Person Plurals-per-Word over Time (Standardized Scores)

Journalists also construct the citizenry, although they are not always charitable when doing so. Justin Lewis and his colleagues at the University of Cardiff did an impressive study of how British citizens are described during nightly newscasts, finding them consistently framed as "childlike"; people with "moods, experiences, and emotions," but with virtually no deliberative skills. Broadcasters present citizens as "passive observers of a world constructed and defined by those more powerful than themselves."[52] Communication scholars Sharon Jarvis and Soo-hye Han also find that citizens are discussed in "thin ways" in news coverage, "subsumed under public opinion polls and depicted as pawns of strategists."[53] They also discovered that voting is depicted as a "choice" for voters, not as a "right," a "duty," or a "value."[54] With news coverage like this, ask Jarvis and Han, how can voters think well of themselves?

As we see in Figure 7.3, those who write letters to the editor are especially worried about the polity's lethargy and naiveté. In the passage below, for example, the writer never details his own credentials, nor does he provide evidence for his claims, but he finds ample time for finger-pointing and, implicitly, for self-puffery:

Despite today's heavy emphasis on education which seems not to have sharpened sensibilities one iota, the typical voter appears incapable of distinguishing right from wrong – the key elements consisting of personal responsibility and common sense based on the religious principles our founding fathers intended. Hypocrisy comes easy to Slick Willie because he has practiced it so much. Well-known as a left-winger, he typically poses as a conservative to boost his election chances.

Soon after his election Clinton showed his utter contempt for hardworking taxpayers by suddenly attacking their economic underbelly. During his campaign he promised the middle-class tax relief but reversed himself in the election's aftermath by increasing taxes to the highest level in history. Now that takes guts and describes in a nutshell what he really thinks of the people – which brings up the most pertinent question of all: Does the American public understand all this?

(William V., *Roanoke Times*, November 9, 1996)

Our author implies here that if voters knew what he knows, they would see the wisdom of his ways. That may seem arrogant but, as we see in Figure 7.3, writers also identify a fundamental unity among the American people. In political science terms, they judge the people low on "competence" but high on "consensus," so there is hope for them.[55] Letter

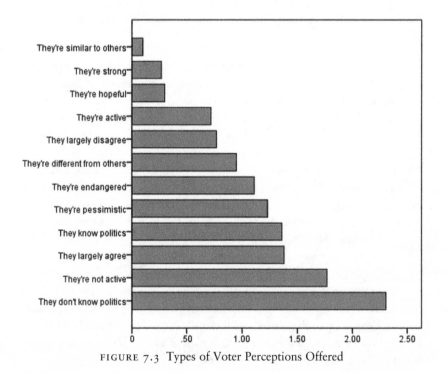

FIGURE 7.3 Types of Voter Perceptions Offered

writers offer a host of explanations for why the citizenry falls short, ranging from pop psychology to pop sociology to pop philosophy. Here are but a few of them:

- *Human selfishness*: "For the past 30 years we have been so engrossed in reaping the benefits of higher wages and a higher standard of living we have become extremely selfish inconsiderate leeches. And the only time we get concerned or hostile is if someone threatens our own private little self-made world – our home, our immediate family, our personal security." (Shirley O., *Provo Daily Herald*, August 13, 1980)
- *Social isolation*: "Some of the people don't ever go to school board, city council, police, jury, PTA or any kind of meetings. Some don't know where the meetings are being held. The time has come for women, poor people, the new poor (former blue collar workers) to unite. I don't care what color you are, if you're in this class of people you should get with people that are in this class because we need to help one another and share ideas because the Bible tells us the poor will be with us always." (Yvonne A., *Lake Charles American Press*, October 21, 1984)
- *Biased journalism*: "If Bush were the CEO of a company he would be sacked. It isn't happening, however, because he has Fox News' Joe Scarborough and Wolf Blitzer to distort the facts and spin a web of disinformation that would make O.J.'s lawyers look incompetent. What's happening in Iraq is being done with our tax dollars and in our name. The choice is to stand like a bewildered herd at the slaughterhouse gate or to rise up and be counted." (Ralph K., *Wichita Falls Times Record News*, September 19, 2004)
- *Intellectual shortcomings*: "We chose Reagan for the same reasons we choose our entertainment, our news, and most distressingly, our popular religion. He is slick, simplistic, unchallenging, and he offers easy answers which are totally divorced from the tough questions we ought to be asking. We will no doubt find Reagan's solutions to our nation's problems wholly inadequate and self-destructive. Jimmy Carter, we will miss you." (Glen H., *Duluth News Tribune*, November 8, 1980)

Given the size of the United States, virtually any generalization made about its people will be true. Letter writers take advantage of that fact with their easy cultural dissections and stern warnings. They altercast voters constantly, assigning to them opinions that may be minority opinions at best. That is a gratuity of living in a pluralistic democracy, where everyone gets to speak for everyone else – a gratuity that lets writers set the record straight:

I am writing about two recent "news" articles and now your editorial in the April 9 *Record News*. Your continued crying crocodile tears about zoning suggests that you are dissatisfied with the democratic process . . . Your claim that all people who voted against the proposal were ignorant of the facts and were misled is an insult to the intelligence of the citizens of this community. I prefer to believe that well-intentioned people on both sides of the issue exercised free choice in a free and open election.

(Henry D., *Wichita Falls Times Record News*, April 16, 1980)

Henry D. happened to be on the winning side of the issue in this case but, even if he had lost, he would have known what the voters really, really wanted. Such confidence comes naturally to letter writers; it is part of their birthright. They look at the world from a high perch, overseeing their fellow citizens while running a non-stop audit of them. Sometimes they speak kindly when doing so; sometimes they are stricter. But whether strict or kind, they know where the American people are headed. It takes an oracle to make such predictions. It irritates people as well.

CONCLUSION

Unlike citizens who offer online commentaries, those who write letters to the editor are separated in time and space from their audience. And their audience is an audience, a removed entity, not one that can snap back in nanoseconds with a cutting retort that then goes viral. Things are slower in the Land of Letters, and there is much to be desired in that: more thinking things through, more civility, fewer hit-and-run observations, less anonymity. When entering an online forum, one never really knows who is there. Letter writers, in contrast, may see their interlocutors in church tomorrow. That, too, slows things down.

People who read letters columns often get irritated, and with good reason: Their writers are too lordly too much of the time. They intrude into every conversation they can find and cluck loudly at the intellectual infirmities of those who disagree with them. They gloat too much, lecture too much, nag too much. Nobody appointed them king but they sit on a throne nonetheless, surveying the Kingdom of Billings and nattering about how its vassals have failed yet again. Letter writers are irritating in these ways, at least in part, at least some of the time.

But letters to the editor are also profoundly communitarian and that is a blessing. One Nebraska weekly, *The Papillion Times*, put in place a rule some years ago that only registered voters would be allowed in its letters column based on the premise that "if people don't vote, they don't have a right to complain."[56] According to the findings I report in Chapter 4, this was a needless imperative: letter-writers always vote. If allowed to, they would vote thrice. Letter writers are outfitted with a surplus of attitude but also a surplus of commitment. They care enough to be irritating.

All too often, however, letter writers are overlooked or trivialized by the media. In contrast, some members of the press now treat Twitter feeds as a "news beat," even though it is still hard to know who is Tweeting and for what reasons.[57] "Twitter offers journalists a rich, quick, and easy-to-access harvest of utterances," report two Dutch scholars; a "vox populi" that adds richness to their stories.[58] Even more disconcerting is a finding reported by the University of Oregon's Arthur Santana, who notes that online comments are changing not only what kinds of stories reporters cover but also how they tell their stories.[59]

Meanwhile, people-with-names, people with street addresses, are too often ignored. Perhaps letter writers bring that on themselves with their tendency to be, well, irritating. To my way of thinking, though, the Founders' irritations built the nation, and that is reason enough to give letter writers their due. Benjamin Franklin would agree. He wrote his first letter to the editor at the age of sixteen, but felt the need to use a pseudonym. That is no longer necessary. Except online.

Endnotes

1 Sometimes Thoughtful, "Response to Mike Mansick: "Do people still write letters to the editor?" *Tech Dirt* (August 22, 2008). Accessed at www.techdirt.com/articles/20080822/0140562057.shtml#comments

2 Michael Carey, "All sorts mingle at 'Letter Writers Ball,'" *The Masthead*, June 22, 1997. Accessed at www.thefreelibrary.com/All+sorts+mingle+at+'Letter+Writers+Ball.'+%28meeting+of+writers+of...-a021059906

3 As quoted in Julius Duscha, "Letters to the editor now come via many routes," *NewsInc*, October 11, 1999. Accessed at www.thefreelibrary.com/letters+to+editors+now+come+via+many+routes+%3a+One+of+the+best+read...-a057101806

4 See, for example, Ezra W. Zuckerman and John T. Jost, "What makes you think you're so popular? Self-evaluation maintenance and the subjective side of the 'friendship paradox,'" *Social Psychology Quarterly*, 64(3) (2001), 207–23.

5 Carl Honoré, *In Praise of Slow: How a Worldwide Movement is Challenging the Cult of Speed* (London: Orion, 2004), p. 13.

6 Ibid, p. 274.

7 Ibid, pp. 278, 279.

8 Danny Paskin, "Say what? An analysis of reader comments in bestselling American newspapers," *The Journal of International Communication*, 16 (2010), 67–83.

9 Ari Heinonen, "The journalist's relationship with users: new dimensions to conventional roles," in Jane Singer et al., eds., *Participatory Journalism: Guarding Open Gates at Online Newspapers* (Chichester: Wiley-Blackwell, 2011), p. 45.

10 Patrick Weber, "Discussions in the comments section: factors influencing participation and interactivity in online newspapers' reader comments," *New Media & Society*, 16(6) (2014), 943.

11 Michael Xenos, Ariadne Vromen, and Brian D. Loader, "The great equalizer? Patterns of social media use and youth political engagement in three advanced democracies," *Information, Communication & Society*, 17(2) (2014), 151–67.

12 Todd Graham and Scott Wright, "Discursive equality and everyday talk online: the impact of 'superparticipants,'" *Journal of Computer-Mediated Communication*, 19(3) (2014), 625–42.

13 See Jack Rosenberry, "Virtual community support for offline communities through online newspaper message forums," *Journalism & Mass Communication Quarterly*, 87 (2010), 154–69; Sue Robinson and Cathy Deshano, "Citizen journalists and their third places: what makes people exchange information online (or not)?" *Journalism Studies*, 12 (2011), 642–57.

14 Kyung H. You, Mi Sun Lee, and Sohyun Oh, "Why use online comments? Examining the relationship among online comments, civic attitudes, and participation intention." Paper presented at the annual meeting of the International Communication Association, Boston, May 2011.

15 Benjamin Krämer, "Media populism: a conceptual clarification and some theses on its effects," *Communication Theory*, 24 (2014), 46.

16 Pablo J. Boczkowski and Eeugenia Mitchelstein, "The prosumption practices of monitorial citizens: accounting for the most commented stories on leading online news sites during and after the U.S. 2008 presidential election." Paper presented at the annual meeting of the International Communication Association, Boston, May 2011.

17 Jennifer Stromer-Galley, "New voices in the public sphere: a comparative analysis of interpersonal and online political talk." *Javnost – The Public*, 9 (2) (2002), 36.

18 Bart Cammaerts and Leo Van Audenhove, "Online political debate, unbound citizenship, and the problematic nature of a transnational public sphere," *Political Communication*, 22 (2005), 194.

19 Kevin Coe, Kate Kenski, and Stephen Rains, "Online and uncivil? Patterns and determinants of incivility in newspaper website comments," *Journal of Communication*, 64(4) (2014), 658–79.

20 Chris J. Vargo and Toby Hopp, "Socioeconomic status, social capital, and partisan polarity as predictors of political incivility on Twitter: a congressional district-level analysis," *Social Science Computer Review*, 33 (2015), 1–23.

21 See Bryan T. Gervais, "Incivility online: affective and behavioral reactions to uncivil political posts in a Web-based experiment," *Journal of Information Technology & Politics*, 12(2) (2015), 167–85; Ashley A. Anderson, Dominique Brossard, Dietram A. Scheufele, Michael A. Xenos and Peter Ladwig,

"The 'nasty effect': online incivility and risk perceptions of emerging technologies," *Journal of Computer-Mediated Communication*, 19(3) (2014), 373–87.

22 Robin Blom, Serena Carpenter, Brian J. Bowe, and Ryan Lange, "Frequent contributors in U.S. newspaper comment forums: an examination of their civility and informational value." Paper presented at the annual meeting of the International Communication Association, London, June 2013.

23 Bill Reader, "A case for printing 'name withheld' letters," *The Masthead*, June 22, 2002. Accessed at www.thefreelibrary.com/A+case+for+printing+'name+withheld'+letters.-a089648658

24 Bill Reader, "An ethical 'blind spot': problems of anonymous letters to the editor," *Journal of Mass Media Ethics*, 20 (2005), 62–76.

25 Rodrigo Zamith and Seth C. Lewis, "From public spaces to public sphere: rethinking discursive spaces on news websites." Paper presented at the annual convention of the International Communication Association, London, June 2013.

26 Alfred Hermida, "Fluid spaces, fluid journalism: the role of the "active recipient" in participatory journalism," in Jane Singer et al., eds., *Participatory Journalism: Guarding Open Gates at Online Newspapers* (Chichester: Wiley-Blackwell, 2011), pp. 177–91.

27 Carolyn E. Nielsen, "Coproduction or cohabitation: are anonymous online comments on newspaper websites shaping news content?" *New Media & Society*, 16 (2014), 470–87.

28 Howard Rheingold, *Smart Mobs: The Next Social Revolution* (New York: Basic Books, 2004), p. 121. An interesting contrast to the often irresponsible remarks found in comment columns are those submitted to C-SPAN by its devotees, who are, not surprisingly, much more constructive. For details see David D. Kurpius and Andrew Mendelson, "A case study of deliberative democracy on television: civic dialogue on C-SPAN call-in shows," *Journalism and Mass Communication Quarterly*, 79 (2002), 587–601.

29 Nicholas Diakopoulos and Mor Naaman, "Towards quality discourse in online news comments," in Pamela Hinds, John C. Tang, and Jian Wang, eds., *Proceedings of the ACM 2011 Conference on Computer Supported Cooperative Work* (New York: Association for Computing Machinery, 2011), pp. 133–42.

30 For more on these dilemmas see Matthew W. Hughey and Jessie Daniels, "Racist comments at online news sites: a methodological dilemma for discourse analysis," *Media, Culture & Society*, 35 (2013), 332–47.

31 Quoted in Eugenia Mitchelstein, "Catharsis and community: divergent motivations for audience participation in online newspapers and blogs," *International Journal of Communication*, 5 (2011), 2025.

32 For more on this operation see Cliff Lampe, Paul Zube, Jusil Lee, Chul Hyun Park, and Erik Johnston, "Crowdsourcing civility: a natural experiment examining the effects of distributed moderation in online forums," *Government Information Quarterly*, 31(2) (2014), 325.

33 For a thoughtful discussion of such dilemmas see Alfred Hermida and Neil Thurman, "A clash of cultures: the integration of user-generated content

within professional journalistic frameworks at British newspaper websites," *Journalism Practice*, 2 (2008), 343–56.

34 Zvi Reich, "User comments: the transformation of participatory space," in Jane Singer et al., eds., *Participatory Journalism: Guarding Open Gates at Online Newspapers* (Chichester: Wiley-Blackwell, 2011), p. 99.

35 Jack Rosenberry, "Users support online anonymity despite increasing negativity," *Newspaper Research Journal*, 32(2) (2011), 6–19.

36 Mitchelstein, "Catharsis and community," 2020.

37 Kathleen McElroy, "Where old (gatekeepers) meets new (media): herding reader comments into print," *Journalism Practice*, 7(6) (2013), 755–71.

38 Michael McCluskey and Jay Hmielowski, "Opinion expression during social conflict: comparing online reader comments and letters to the editor," *Journalism*, 13(3) (2011), 303–19.

39 Joseph M. Reagle, *Reading the Comments: Likers, Haters and Manipulators at the Bottom of the Web* (Cambridge: MIT Press, 2015), p. 172. For more on the comparison of letter writers to online commenters see Jaime Loke, "Old turf, new neighbors: journalists' perspectives on their new shared space," *Journalism Practice*, 6(2) (2012), 233–49.

40 Stephen Coleman, *How Voters Feel* (New York: Cambridge University Press, 2013), p. 113.

41 Neal Pattison, "The din of online comments to fall silent," *HeraldNet*, December 20, 2015. Accessed at www.heraldnet.com/article/20151220/NEWS01/151229934

42 As quoted in Esther Milne, *Letters, Postcards, Email Technologies of Presence* (New York: Routledge, 2010), p. 13.

43 Kenneth Burke, *A Rhetoric of Motives* (Berkeley: University of California Press, 1950).

44 Karin Wahl-Jorgensen, "Letters to the editor as a forum for public deliberation: modes of publicity and democratic debate," *Critical Studies in Media Communication*, 18 (2001), 315.

45 Bill Reader and Kevin Moist, "Letters as indicators of community values: two case studies of alternative magazines," *Journalism & Mass Communication Quarterly*, 85 (2008), 834.

46 For more on the use of personal disclosure see Monique Mémet, "Letters to the editor: a multi-faceted genre," *European Journal of English Studies*, 9 (2005), 75–90.

47 Susana M. Sotillo and Dana Starace-Nastasi, "Political discourse of a working-class town," *Discourse and Society*, 10 (1999), 411–38.

48 Marc Ziegele, Timo Breiner, and Oliver Quiring, "What creates interactivity in online news discussions? An exploratory analysis of discussion factors in user comments on news items," *Journal of Communication*, 64 (2014), 1111–38.

49 Richard Sennett, *The Corrosion of Character: The Personal Consequences of Work in the New Capitalism* (New York: W. W. Norton & Company, 1998), pp. 137, 139.

50 Ibid, 148.

51 Mary Ann Glendon, *Rights Talk: The Impoverishment of Political Discourse* (New York: The Free Press, 1991), p. 77.

52 Justin Lewis, Karin Wahl-Jorgensen, and Sanna Inthorn, "Images of citizenship on television news: constructing a passive public," *Journalism Studies*, 5 (2) (2004), 154, 160. For an interesting comparison of traditional and online news coverage see Jeroen DeKeyser and Karin Raeymaeckers, "The printed rise of the common man: how Web 2.0 has changed the representation of ordinary people in newspapers," *Journalism Studies*, 13(5–6) (2012), 825–35.

53 Sharon E. Jarvis and Soo-Hye Han, "The mobilized voter: portrayals of electoral participation in print coverage of campaign 2008," *American Behavioral Scientist*, 55(4) (2011), 411, 432.

54 Sharon E. Jarvis and Soo-Hye Han, "From an honored value to a harmful choice: how presidential candidates have discussed electoral participation (1948–2012)," *American Behavioral Scientist*, 57(12) (2013), 1658.

55 For an interesting study along these lines see Stephen K. Medvic, "Explaining support for stealth democracy." Paper presented at the annual convention of the Midwest Political Science Association, Chicago, April 2016.

56 John Fulwider, "Newspaper requires letter writers to be registered voters," *AP Online*, May 19, 1998. Accessed at www.highbeam.com/doc/1P1-19723286 .html

57 Eli Skogerbø and Arne H. Krumsvik, "Newspapers, Facebook and Twitter: intermedial agenda setting in local election campaigns," *Journalism Practice*, 9 (3) (2015), 350–66.

58 Marcel Broersma and Todd Graham, "Social media as beat: Tweets as a news source during the 2010 British and Dutch elections," *Journalism Practice*, 6 (2012), 403–19.

59 Arthur D. Santana, "Online readers' comments represent new opinion pipeline," *Newspaper Research Journal*, 32 (2011), 66–81.

8

How Letters Have Changed

Letters to the editor are a chronograph; they tell a democracy's time. Having a database distributed across sixty-five years has allowed me to examine where the citizenry has been and where it is heading. This is, of course, speculative work, since all letter writers are not alike, nor are letter writers like all Americans. Letter writers do, however, pick up the argot of their age, and they do engage its issues in unique ways. But there is also something about people who write letters to the editor – their resoluteness, their intrusiveness – that never changes. Time determines much, but not everything.

Based as this chapter is on letters produced during seventeen presidential elections plus sixteen coding strategies containing several hundred sub-measures, thousands of temporal permutations could be studied. Doing so is impractical, but it may also be unnecessary, because the letters shifted in tone and temperament at three natural breakpoints: (1) *the Cold War Era: 1948 to 1964* – Berlin Blockade, Joe McCarthy, nuclear deterrent, Hungarian Revolution, blacklisting, Nikita Khrushchev, U2 spy plane, containment, the Cuban Missile Crisis; (2) *the Human Rights Era: 1968 to 1992 – Brown v. Board of Education*, busing, Martin Luther King Jr., NAACP, equal pay, *Roe v. Wade*, ecofeminists, Gloria Steinem, Stonewall Rebellion, gay rights; and (3) *the Partisan Politics Era: 1996 to 2012* – Clinton impeachment, Dick Cheney, the Tea Party, Fox News, congressional gridlock, Mitch McConnell, Birthers, affective polarization, Occupy Wall Street.

Admittedly, these are arbitrary markers. Politicians were, after all, highly partisan when debating entry into the Korean War, and Vladimir Putin currently seems to be ushering in a second Cold War. Too, advances in civil rights were made by Harry Truman when he integrated the army in 1948, and civil rights were advanced yet again by Barack Obama when he supported transgender Americans. Partisanship, discrimination, and foreign entanglements have bedeviled the United States from its very beginning, and these challenges have never abated. Still, this tripartite scheme makes historical sense, and, more important, it captures organic changes I noticed in the letters themselves.

To stimulate my thinking about these matters, I turned to a source of inspiration that college professors often draw upon – their students. I taught an undergraduate honors class in the fall of 2013 and wondered how my students would react to letters written many years before. So I asked them to examine a sheaf of letters from 1952 – when their grandparents were pre-adolescents – and compare them to letters written during the Obama–Romney campaign. My instructions to the students were sketchy: I asked them to compare the letters' tone in 1952 to that in 2012 and to explain what they found.

The students did not disappoint me. Rachel E. noted that letters from both eras concerned themselves with the deterioration of American values, the loss of liberties, lying politicians, excessive taxation, the sanctity of the Constitution, and the nation's religious heritage. Jenna C. also spotted continuities in the letters, especially with regard to the role of women. She noted that even though "the second and third waves of feminism crashed onto the shores of our country" between 1952 and 2012, the letter writers treated women as "specular objects" in both eras, as persons whose physical appearance (whether praised or blamed) occupied far too much attention.

Sarah E. approached her paper psychologically, identifying an undertone of fear in both eras. Some writers, she noted, externalized that fear – the Communists were coming – while others internalized it – Americans no longer trusted one another. The uneven distribution of wealth in society was also a source of fear, a fact that Sarah found interesting since a dollar in 1952 was worth $8.51 in 2012. Money is an inconstant thing, she noted, and that surprised her – a surprise visited on almost every twenty-year-old when he or she turns forty.

While the students noted an impressive number of similarities in the letters, most concentrated on the differences and were appalled by what they found. "There has been an exponential flight from the notion of our country as a unified body of like-minded people," Daniel A. wrote, to a nation featuring constant polarities, including "far greater dogma and far more disdain for the opposing political party." We are keener to condemn our adversaries, Daniel observed, "using harsher and more abrasive langue than several decades ago." Why has this happened? he asked. His answer: "with so many people in the world and so many different sources of social networking, finding a news source or a friend group that shares your beliefs is as easy as the click of a button on a TV remote or a computer mouse." "We humans can now choose whom and what to interact with on a day-to-day basis," he concluded. This leads to a situation in which familiarity breeds attraction yet again.

One of the most revealing aspects of this assignment emerged during class discussion. The students were dismayed by what they had read, embarrassed to be living in an age when petulance had become a sign of sophistication. The students said that the 1952 writers were earnest and passionate even if reserved, a sensibility that made further discussion possible. Cara G. contrasted this with today's tendency to "twist universal debates such as healthcare and gun control into personal – not political – issues," as if the writer's Self were an inviolate thing. "We are now more vocal," Cara noted, "but also more uneasy."

As it turned out, my students were prescient, handily capturing the changes to be reported in this chapter. I find, for example, a major decline in writers' references to *National Touchstones*, the nation's core beliefs. While religious traditions, the popular vote, and the right to bear arms have maintained their popularity, the remaining members of the pantheon have either dropped substantially (e.g., capitalistic ideals, family centrality, and personal freedoms) or precipitously (mass education, law and order, equal rights, civic volunteerism). Do these trends reflect the splintering of a nation, a distaste for vague abstractions, or a people grown tired of bloviation? Whatever the cause, the nation's discourse has changed, and not in ways always flattering to a robust, pluralistic society.

I also report that letter writers are now standing further back, making fewer personal disclosures. Their descriptions of politics are more antiseptic but their conclusions more judgmental. People who write letters to the editor have always been cranky, of course, but now they are also coarser and meaner. In addition, they are less able to identify collective forces – membership societies, business organizations, community groups, etc. – available for civic recruitment. There is a palpable loneliness in many of their letters, as if a friend has gone missing, a friend the writer no longer remembers. While writers continue to call for patriotic engagement, they seem less sure what makes the nation special, or even if being special is now an acceptable virtue.

There has also been a drop in *Oppositional Literacy*, in people's abilities to describe what their opponents believe. Although writers have no trouble laying out their own viewpoints, they seem unable to explain the deep structure of their differences with others. And that is odd since all human thought is now just a URL away. As a result, the inability to describe what others are thinking seems an antediluvian condition in the twenty-first century, and yet it exists. I also find that dialogue has turned into monologue for many of the writers.

When I asked my students why they were embarrassed by the 2012 letters their responses were vague. They declared the older letters more "respectful" and the recent letters somewhat craven. My students understood, of course, that democracy is always a tussle and that people's tastes – in what to value, in how to write – change from era to era. They also knew that such changes can be beneficial. My students were not prudes, after all, and they had the tattoos and piercings to prove it. Even as they wrote their papers, several of their icons – Lindsay Lohan, Fiona Apple, David Cassidy, Flavor Flav, and Stephen Baldwin – had been arrested for some kind of chemical indulgence, and some of my students may have sympathized with them. And yet they were embarrassed by letters to the editor. This chapter explains why.

A SHIFTING FOUNDATION

How to understand a nation? Through its people, its economy, or its geography? All these factors help, as do people's language habits, religious practices, sporting events, available technologies, and popular narratives. It also helps to know a nation's shared values, what I refer to as its National Touchstones. When clearly articulated, Touchstones provide people with a sense of authority (who speaks definitively), a sense of continuity (what connects past and present), a sense of community (who belongs, who does not), a sense of coherence (how different ideas fit together), and a sense of agreement (who can be trusted and who cannot).[1]

Touchstones are baked into a nation's discourse and their relative popularity tells us what "time" it is. The United States, for example, has had its angry moments when taking on the world in defense of liberty, but it has had quieter times too when launching some scientific or social experiment. Of the letters during the Cold War era, 54.5 percent contained one or more of these Touchstones, but that proportion slipped to 49.0 percent during the Human Rights era and to 35 percent during the Partisan Politics era. What does it mean when writers become less "preachy"? Is it a sign that the nation is less concerned with ultimate

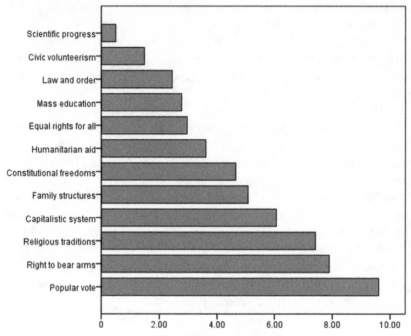

FIGURE 8.1 Overall Hierarchy of National Touchstones

values and more worried about bottom-line matters? We will explore that question shortly.

Figure 8.1 shows that the Touchstones are differentially popular, although each commands its own constituency. Not surprisingly, given the enormous complexity of the United States, these values are often counterpoised to one another. The abortion question, for example, is internally riven – religious traditions vs. constitutional freedoms vs. family structures vs. equal rights vs. scientific progress (e.g., the morning-after pill). Because Touchstones express a people's "life orientations," they are constantly being debated and ignored, rediscovered and debated once again.

The Capitalistic System, Religious Traditions, Family Structures, the Right to Bear Arms, and the Popular Vote are the most popular Touchstones, a finding that holds true over the years. Discourse surrounding the Popular Vote is especially interesting, as we saw during the 2016 primaries when everyone was angry with everyone else. Instead of sulking, however, voters surged to the polls, often standing in impossibly long lines in their precincts. The Popular Vote is therefore a complicated icon; it is something done but also something felt:

- *Voting as identity*: "I believe a Republican Party is on the way in Texas because of the many 'Democrats for Eisenhower' organizations. I too wish they would simply say they are Republicans. But for many especially older voters it is hard to make the change after so many years of regarding the Democratic Party as almost sacred. More voters are realizing that a political party is not a sacred thing and they may still get to heaven even after switching parties. I am for independence and individuality ... If we must vote the same each year as our fathers did why hold elections?" (C.J.B., *Wichita Falls Time Record News*, November 6, 1956)
- *Voting as relationship*: "In some parts of the country the situation is such that to vote for one man actually brings suspicion of insanity upon the voter while to vote for his opponent is the surest sign of superior intelligence and acumen. Certainly the present election process with all of its charges and counter-charges, its mudslinging, and its defamation of character adds color and drama to the election. But it also brings many hard feelings and hurt feelings. So much anger and bitterness does not heal easily. Yet we know that the day after the election we will all go on living – and what is more important we will all go on living in much the same way as before." (John E., *Lake Charles American Press*, November 10, 1956)
- *Voting as opportunity*: "All we hear is Bush vs. Kerry and people telling you you're throwing your vote away if you vote for anyone else... The more I listen to both of them, the more I fear that I cannot trust either one. So will I throw my vote away? No. Instead, I will let my true feelings be heard and vote for the Constitutional Party and Mike Peroutka for president. You say I'm throwing my vote away? I say I am not throwing my vote away but voting for the one candidate who best represents my beliefs values and passions rather than throwing my vote away on a compromise for the lesser of two evils as most Americas will do this coming Nov. 2." (Seth H., *Provo Daily Herald*, September 23, 2004)

National Touchstones are part of the nation's architecture, but they are also quite abstract, so writers can use them in diverse ways. "History will discover," says one writer, "that the final years of past societies have typically been marked by rampant homosexuality, abortion, and all forms of sexual permissiveness." "History has shown," says another, "that when a strong middle class exists and the wealthy contribute to help the poor out of poverty, everybody prospers." "In history," says a third, "when government grew in power, people lost freedom."[2] As we see here, history teaches us much, some of which is true and some of which is a guess.

Touchstones can become a loaded gun and, if handled carelessly, misfirings can occur, which is to say coherence can be lost. When a sentence begins with value triggers like "the Bible teaches" or "the law requires" or "our children demand," there is no telling where it will end up. And when Touchstones are *combined*, they take on special potency:

I viewed with some amusement the Mondale-Dole debate. Mondale stuck to issues while Dole tried his role as comedian. We've had too many comedians in the White House who have made a farce of our *Constitution* and have insulted the intelligence of the American voter. I know it would be too much to ask or expect but *Christ* would be my first choice and since [Communist] Gus Hall has no more chance than a snowball in a blast furnace of making it and since we're stuck with the idea that only two parties can do anything for *the American people* I feel Carter and Mondale may bring a fresh approach to the political scene.

(Erick T., *Duluth News Tribune*, November 4, 1976)

In the language of the eminent French sociologist Émile Durkheim, letters such as this combine the Sacred and the Profane, with the author moving fluidly from the ultimate to the quotidian.[3] "Some are trying to edit God out of the pledge and God Bless America," says a letter writer, who follows that up with "we have so much debt that we can't even pay the interest and going deeper in debt by $2 billion per day."[4] There is no transition between these two statements, perhaps because the relevant values – religious freedom and economic responsibility – have equivalent import for the writer. What works for the Right works equally well for the Left: "The ozone protection God gave us is being destroyed every day. It is time to take our planet Earth seriously and personally."[5]

Some years ago, historian Robert Lovell discovered a remarkable cache of Depression-era complaint letters written by ordinary Americans to the Justice Department in the late 1930s. When first reading the letters, Lovell noticed the writers' confidence in interpreting the law, especially the Constitution. "The letters reveal how deeply talk of law and rights is woven into every political activity and engagement" in the United States, Lovell noted, despite "the law's technical complexity and formality" and its ability to intimidate people into silence.[6] The "familiar symbols of American democracy," Lovell observed, let writers ground their "aspirational claims" in a widely shared set of values.[7] In a similar vein, journalism scholar Brian Goss notes that when writing to popular magazines, both liberals and conservatives embed themselves in "the American way of life," and do so instinctively.[8]

The ease with which Americans reference these core values is remarkable, given the size of the nation and the complexity of its socialization patterns. Identity rhetorics ("One nation under God") are especially popular, as are nativist rhetorics ("Are you a real American?").[9] Because the US pantheon has such breadth, citizens can repair to different aspects of it and still be on safe ground.[10] Philosopher Ernst Bloch's motion of "coming home," of transcending the given by returning to a set of core values, is therefore especially important in the United States.[11] An interesting result: Even those who distrust politicians retain high expectations for American ideals.[12]

Things may be changing, however. As we see in Figure 8.2, overall references to National Touchstones have dropped over the years, and that is true for most of the values in the pantheon. The only major exception is the Right to Bear Arms, which rose sharply during the 2004 presidential campaign because of the Bush administration's Iraq policy. Otherwise, both progressive values (Equal Rights, Mass Education, Humanitarian Aid) and conservative values (Capitalistic System, Family Structures, Law and Order) have been mentioned less often. The Greatest Generation has been replaced by the Generation Still Figuring Things Out.

Statistically speaking, this drop in Touchstones is not enormous,[13] but it does conform to other studies describing a hollowing-out of the citizenry. Based on survey data, Neil Nevitte and Stephen White found a widening gap between "citizens' expectations and evaluations of democracy," findings that were especially true for older Americans, the sorts of people who write letters to the editor.[14] Why has this gap occurred? Nevitte and White offer several possibilities: economic marginalization, too many demands made on government, less willingness to support the opposite political party, and, intriguingly, greater disappointment among idealists – people with a clear model of how government *should* operate – again pointing in the direction of those who write letters to the editor.[15]

Why have Touchstones lost some of their luster? Political scientist Aaron Wildavsky might explain it by citing an overall drop in institutional support starting in the 1960s. Writing in 1991, Wildavsky claimed that "every large-scale integrative institution, from parties to unions to churches, is weaker than it was."[16] Institutional regard has continued to decline since then: "69 percent believe the country's values have deteriorated since the 1970s," reports one pollster, and many forces are said to be

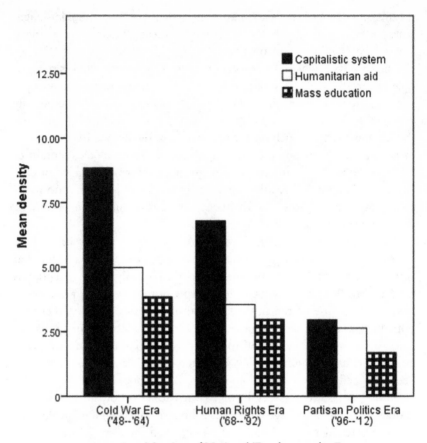

FIGURE 8.2 Mention of National Touchstones by Era

responsible – churches, the economic system, corporations, lobbyists, and, of course, government itself.[17]

If hierarchy is under siege, so too is diversity. In 2016, Donald Trump careened around the United States declaring he would make America great again, a code word for prizing some Touchstones (Constitutional Freedoms, Law and Order, the Right to Bear Arms) over others (Equal Rights, Mass Education, Humanitarian Aid). Many enlisted in the Trump brigade, some of whom blamed Mexicans for taking jobs they would never wish to work in. Skinheads, black separatists, and anti-Muslim groups joined long-standing haters and anti-Semites in a chorus of national decline. New websites sprang up to channel people's frustrations about an economy that had been especially unkind to middle-aged white men.

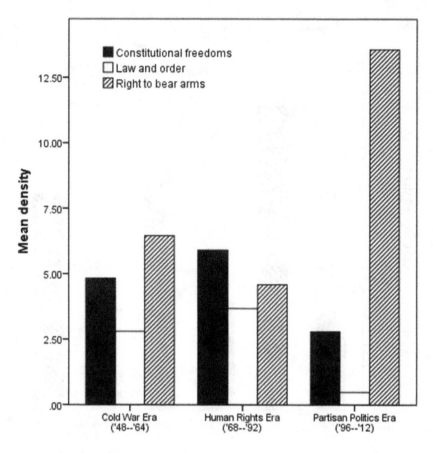

FIGURE 8.2 (*cont.*)

Others – educated women, traditional conservatives, non-whites, leftists of all stripes, and people with taste – were outraged, if not frightened, by Trump's rise to prominence. Those who took the long view of American history, however, had seen it all before – when Charles Coughlin, Joe McCarthy, and George Wallace had their moments in the sun. Touchstones become touchstones, after all, because they are touched repeatedly over a great many years and because they provide dependable emotional sustenance as a result. Touchstones can be abused, their popularity can wax and wane, but because they are so structurally integrated, so central to a child's socialization, and so persistently reinforced by cultural rituals, they return once the politicians of the moment have drifted away.

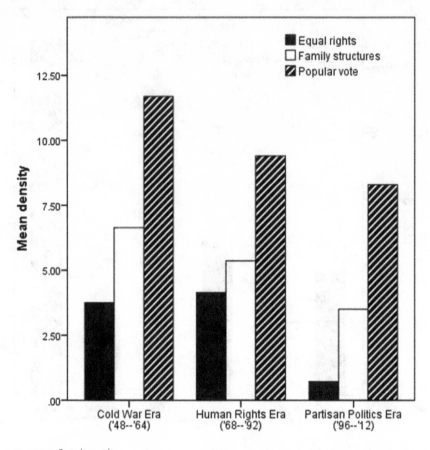

FIGURE 8.2 *(cont.)*

That, at least, is the traditionalist's story. But it is also possible that older Touchstones are being replaced by newer ones. Concepts such as Environmental Stewardship and Work–Life Balance, for example, are still vague and do not have the authoritative force needed to command legislation or stimulate mass emotion. But given enough time and enough generational replacement, they too may ascend the hierarchy, as might Sexual Equality, Rural Reclamation, Economic Fairness, and Techno-logical Determinism. These are as all indistinct concepts but if the old Touchstones can drop in popularity by 20 percent in sixty-five years, change may be in the offing.

A purely rhetorical explanation for the drop-off in Touchstones is also available: Letter writers may no longer feel comfortable speaking in such

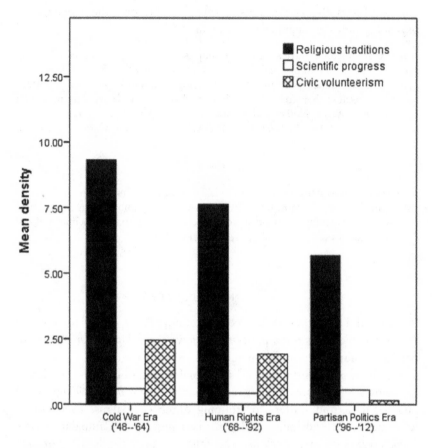

FIGURE 8.2 (*cont.*)

grand ways. The old, self-congratulatory style of writing may have run its course. In an egalitarian age when national boundaries have been rendered porous by convenient transportation systems and world-spanning media, a new national language may be emerging. If so, what will this sound like? Will it be humbler and less elitist? Will it abjure the pieties of the 1940s and 1950s, pieties which bound the nation together during two major wars but which seem too strident in a modern, multicultural nation?

In the language of Chapter 3, my findings here suggest that the *depth* with which civic hope is embraced may be slipping (vis-a-vis National Touchstones), but its *belief* and *action* components are still strong. Recent letter writers are snarkier and less reverential but they still engage one another forcefully, contentiously, often substituting the language of psychology for the language of democracy:

Any Christian should have seen who Trump is from the beginning. He is proud, boastful, greedy, a pathological liar and an angry man who stirs up others to be angry. His vocabulary is awful. We as Christians should know how important words are because they are an indication of what is in our heart. And now with this tape from Access Hollywood we see that he is a sexual predator.

(John M., *Wichita Falls Times Record News*, October 25, 2016)

* * * * * *

If Democrats think lying and corruption is a resume enhancement they got exactly what they deserve – the most untrustworthy, self-serving public figure in America! It's agonizing watching her blind surrogates crown this pariah. This image of evil occupying the people's house should sicken you!

(Tom W., *Utica Observer-Dispatch*, July 23, 2016)

THE LONELY POLITY

If National Touchstones have declined in popularity, what has replaced them? The picture is not a pretty one. As we see in Figure 8.3, the era of partisan politics is now very much with us, with Campaign Complaints having increased substantially.[18] Everyone is being blamed – politicians for being scallywags, voters for tuning out, the press for being superficial and negative, and staffers for running dumb campaigns. Even worse, letter writers are no longer trying to fix things, with Campaign Advice (which was never their stock in trade) falling through the floor.[19] For each piece of advice the writers offer, they register five complaints, many of which are essentialistic. The refrain that "candidates have no morals" is mentioned three times more often now than it was during the Cold War era, and "candidates' strategic ineptness" is cited six times more often than before.[20]

People who write letters to the editor have always complained about campaigns, of course, but their growing unwillingness to offer solutions implies a special loss of agency. "The biased coverage is absolutely disgusting and quite frankly should be illegal," said one writer in Fall River in 2012; "the elite media has basically called [Sarah Palin] white trash and not ready to be president." What to do about such matters? Irony is the author's only ally: "I simply ask for a little scrutiny of Obama and at least one negative story about him each week for the 100 negative stories about McCain and Palin. Is that too much to ask?"[21]

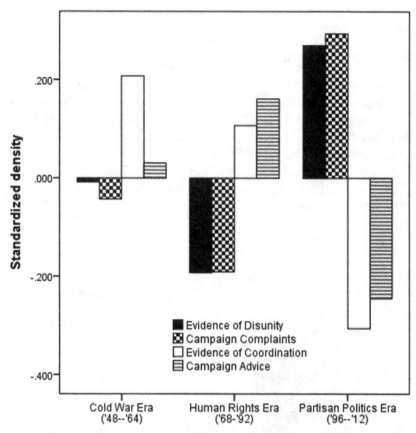

FIGURE 8.3 Commentary on Political Tensions across Eras

Writers' worries are also reflected in the societal discord they identify (Evidence of Disunity) and in people's inability to work with one another (Evidence of Coordination).[22] One senses genuine angst in such letters, a nation unable to pull itself together. Many of the letters are soulful as a result:

I have been deeply disturbed by the divisiveness and fear that have increasingly dominated our national vision. It seems we sorely lack the moral courage to stand by our Bill of Rights, to promote a dream of a more peaceful world, to build educational opportunities for young people, to tackle our nation's health care needs, and to work together with kindness and respect to build community ... We have record deficits, an America more divided between haves and have-nots, an increasing number of uninsured, the world's largest prison population, the certain devastating effects of global climate change, and less economic and educational opportunity for us all. Can't we do better than this?

               (Kathy M., *Duluth News Tribune*, September 15, 2004)

    Kathy M. is a cellist and a composer. Her letter is musical too, replete with rhythm, timing, and duration. It is philosophic and pragmatic, social but also highly personal. It draws on the spirit of the United States, its laws and expectations, and yet it seems sad, weary. Many years ago, Kathy M. might have ended her letter by harking back to grand American traditions, but she does not do so here. She implies that we can do better as a nation but she does not say how. She ends with a plaintive question, no Touchstones in sight.

    As we see in Figure 8.4, American exceptionalism has declined steadily over time – less boosterism in the letters, less self-satisfaction. Today's

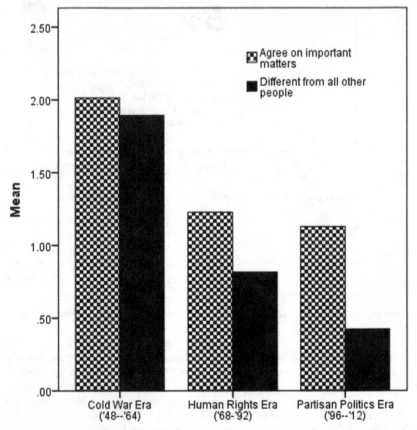

FIGURE 8.4 Characterizations of American Voters across Eras (Voter Perceptions)

writers are more sociologists than apologists. They are analytical in their thinking, and analytical in their feelings as well. When they find Americans agreeing on things they attribute it to luck, not to destiny or tradition. For these reasons, the following letter, filled as it is with indomitability, has an antique ring to it:

How very great America really is can only be fully measured by people who have once lived in a poor foreign country or who have left the heavy pressures of a dictatorship. If we should ask people in other countries where they would like to live if they had the choice America or Russia what do you think they would choose? The answer certainly would prove that America has still the highest prestige in the world and will continue to have it so long as faith in the greatness of American principles and accomplishments and are fully aware how fortunate they are to be citizens of the United States of America.

(Renate H., *Fall River Herald News*, November 11, 1960)

Figure 8.5 reveals another aspect of modernity – a pulling back of the Self, a distantiation.[23] This is a surprising finding, since people who write letters to the editor have considerable self-esteem. So why this avoidance of the first-person? For one thing, it might reflect the current scientific ethos, the need to stand back so one can generalize properly. It might also suggest an emotional tamping down, a need to keep one's ego-involvement in check. In addition, it could mean that the world has become so complicated that letter writers are now risk-averse. Most worrisome of all, it might signal that politics has become a mere game, a chessboard of moves and countermoves permitting observation and commentary but no existential involvement.

Whatever the reason, letter writers now sound more like pundits than citizens. It is as if the press agenda – emphasize leaders' idiosyncrasies, look for discontinuities, evaluate things dispassionately – has become the people's agenda. Table 8.1 captures the changing rhetorical texture over the years. The early letters are engaged, not coy, and their authors bring politics into their own experiences. Today's letters are different. They are informed and concerned but also cynical. Motive – that which cannot be observed – is featured prominently and evidence supporting the writers' claims is often anecdotal, personality-driven. Politics is thereby reduced to strategic maneuverings.

Harvard's Robert Putnam has famously told us that people are now "bowling alone," less likely to join social clubs or community organizations and more likely to sit at home with a gaggle of electronic devices.[24] To get an overall measure of the letters' rhetorical tone, Figure 8.6 collapses the group- and individual-based variables as well as the campaign- and

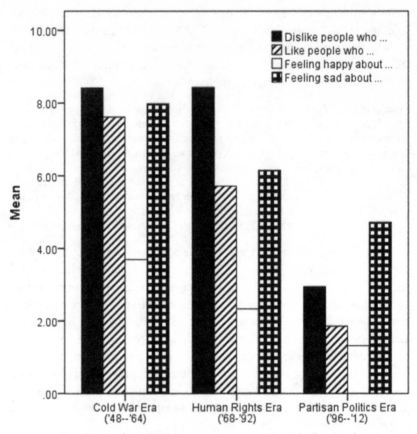

FIGURE 8.5 Sense of Personal Investment across Eras (Author Declarations)

idea-based measures (e.g., Political Memory, National Touchstones, etc.). The results are eerily reminiscent of Putnam's claims.[25] Even though, as we saw in Chapter 7, letter writers used the first-person plural more often over the years, it was an abstracted and unspecific *we*, more a rhetorical thrust than an identification of named groups and functioning organizations that could advance the political enterprise. The implications of these data are clear: If you want to understand contemporary politics, look to the people making the headlines, not to communities or their constituent groups; pay attention as well to campaign hoopla, not to the ideas and aspirations undergirding democratic governance. The age of celebrity is surely with us.

TABLE 8.1 *Tonal Differences in Letters: Cold War vs. Partisan Politics Eras*

Topic	1948–1964: Philosophical, Existential, Value-Centered	1996–2012: Personal, Characterological, Strategy-Centered
Tax Policy	It will take action – quick action – to win the coming war and while tax-conscious politicians will be in bomb range next time, our sons will still do the actual fighting. Taxes are high, but if we let tax worries cause our boys to train with wooden guns again, there will be no taxes or anything else to worry about – except spilled blood and communistic slavery. (J.B.B., *Wichita Falls Time Record News*, August 11, 1948)	Bill Clinton has given us Whitewater Bimbo eruptions, Travelgate, Cattlegate and, more recently, the FBI files scandals. Many of his friends and presidential appointees have had to resign are in jail or have been or will be indicted for fraud and conspiracy. Who backs him? Class-action and tort lawyers, Hollywood liberals, Socialists, the liberal media, and some minority groups that want special privileges. (John C., *Lake Charles American Press*, October 21, 1996)
Medical Care	America has progressed in the last 20 years; advances in the medical world and in science have expanded under the reign of the Democrats and I am not saying "we never had it so good," but looking at it from other than monetary aspects, we can see America has gone further in those last years than before, and I feel only a Democrat president can keep America headed that way. However whichever way you vote, let's vote Tuesday for this, the American way, and let us hope and pray that	Seniors who are living on a fixed income are hurting. Millions find it increasingly difficult to make ends meet. We have the high cost of gas and groceries. Seniors on Social Security get a raise and immediately Medicare and the insurance supplement get a big chunk … Palin and McCain will cut Medicare for seniors. They don't need it. McCain has 13 cars and nine houses and how many planes? Palin also has a seaplane, lives in a governor's mansion, and has a large house. They are not seniors on fixed

(continued)

TABLE 8.1 *(continued)*

Topic	1948–1964: Philosophical, Existential, Value-Centered	1996–2012: Personal, Characterological, Strategy-Centered
	whoever wins will be for the United States of America and keep America out of bondage and slavery. (M.I., *Lake Charles American Press*, November 3, 1952)	incomes. They are not Joe Six Pack. (Merle N., *Roanoke Times*, October 16, 2008)
Military Involvement	The people of the world say they do not want war. Then if that is so, why are we traveling down a path that will lead us to the cataclysm of war? A peace that can only be had through fear or the use of force is not the kind of peace the world needs ... If the mothers had the authority as to whether we had war or peace, war would be no more. Mothers who have raised their sons to manhood have no desire to see them suffer and die on a bloody battlefield. I may seem naive and idealistic when I write about world brotherhood but I am convinced that real peace and enduring peace can come only when a world brotherhood founded on faith, love, hope, and charity is established. (Clyde W., *Springfield News-Sun*, August 30, 1960)	We had four Americans killed because this administration ignored the call for more security at one of our embassies and, because of political reasons, did not acknowledge this as a terrorist attack until about a week or two later ... If none of this convinces you, let's look at the debates. Joe Biden looked like a complete idiot, mugging it up and showing complete disrespect for Paul Ryan. Obama's performance was not much better. In the first debate, he acted like he was somewhere else – maybe on the moon ... He has no vision for the nation other than continuing his vision of a socialistic society with his corrupt administration and his czars, not to mention Biden. (Bud D., *Lake Charles American Press*, October 27, 2012)

The contrasts between the early and recent letters are stark. Consider the following passage, which is dry and colorless. Filled as it is with groups and cabals, with the gray ghosts of government, it sounds, one is ashamed to admit, almost professorial:

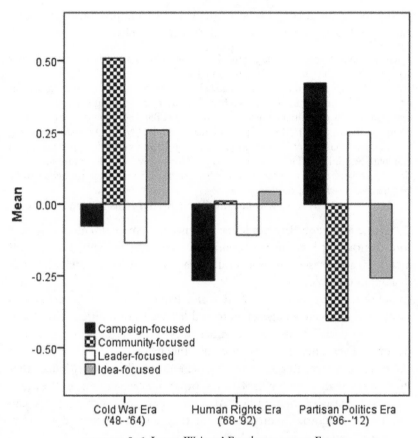

FIGURE 8.6 Letter Writers' Emphases across Eras

For more than 50 years, *the Democratic Party* has been the progressive and forward-looking party and *the Republicans* believe in standing-pat. The Democrats as early as 1896 advocated the election of our *United States senators* by a direct vote of *the people* rather than by *the legislatures* ... Then came *the Republican administration* with Warren G. Harding as President. It was so corrupt and incompetent that it was a disgrace to *the nation*. Such little things as "mink coats" and "deep freezers" were peanuts when compared to the give-away of our natural resources to *the big boys* who had contributed millions to the Republican campaign funds to elect Harding."

(John M., *Wichita Falls Times Record News*, November 2, 1956)

The following passage provides a sharp contrast. It is filled with bluster and bravado and it turns ad hominems into an art form. Its sprightliness drives us along – "I hate this; I hate this too" – making it sound a bit like reality television. It contains very little evidence and precious few qualifications but its rapid pace makes it darkly irresistible:

Then we have Joe Biden, a plagiarist of speeches who is a Washington insider but with no leadership history. Where was Joe during Vietnam? That's why I'm registered and voting the McCain ticket. I'd rather have him in office in a crisis and know his running mate who is a heartbeat away from being president has the leadership skills that Obama lacks. She blows Mr. Big Talk right out of the water. Kinda reminds me of Margaret Thatcher or Golda Meir. And that is a big compliment. Personally I'd like to see Mr. Big Talk shut up and put up – in a ring with Sarah Palin. He'd lose as he will in November. All talk and no substance doesn't go very far. And Obama doesn't have any of the things necessary to be commander-in-chief of our great country.

(Roy S., *Wichita Falls Times Record News*, October 11, 2008)

Energetic though Roy S.'s letter is, it is also remote, lonely. He battles foul demons by himself, no community resources in sight. He fires off assertion after assertion as if crafting a series of Tweets. His letter is disjointed but colorful.

Political scientists Patrick Miller and Pamela Conover have found a growing convergence between elite and lay views of politics, with "winning at all costs" being seen as more important than advancing public policy.[26] Everyone, it seems, not just the media, is caught up in the political horserace. Recent letters to the editor reflect New Media affinities – a fascination with personalities, rapid-fire castigations, bold declarations, a sense of derring-do. At times, perhaps, such features can promote democratic involvement, but they also have their downsides. We must keep them in our sights.

A TROUBLING MONOLOGUE

More than thirty years ago, philosopher Thomas Bridges observed that "a civic culture is a countervailing culture." Such a culture, Bridges observed, requires citizens "to step out of the perspectives from which they normally view the world and to see things from a different point of view."[27] That is happening less often today. The Pew Journalism Project, for example, reports that "in personal conversations about politics, those on the right and left are more likely to largely hear the views in line with their own thinking" because they get their information from entirely different media sources.[28] These informational divides have their consequences: Shanto Iyengar and Sean Westwood find, for example, that extreme partisans now discriminate against their adversaries "to a degree that exceeds discrimination based on race."[29] It gets worse: Sharing party membership draws people together more than does people's educational background, personality traits, smoking frequency, body type, religion, or ethnic views.[30]

This kind of "negative partisanship," whereby citizens despise members of the opposite party more than they embrace those in their own party, is a new phenomenon. Back in 1960, journalist Max Ehrenfreund reports, "only about 5 percent of Republicans and 4 percent of Democrats told pollsters they would be 'displeased' if their child married someone from the opposite party." By 2012, "49 percent of Republicans and 33 percent of Democrats said they would be at least 'somewhat unhappy' if one of their children had a bipartisan wedding."[31] As we see in Figure 8.7, letter writers are now less able to explain their opponents' views, even though the

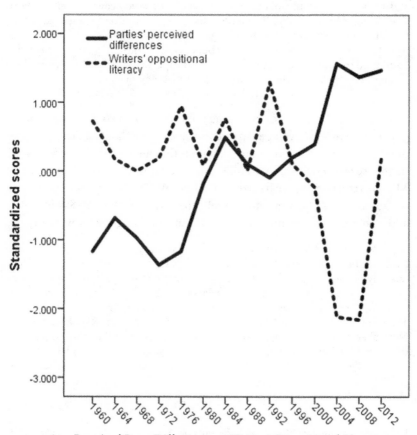

FIGURE 8.7 Perceived Party Differences vs. Writers' Oppositional Literacy
(Partially Adapted from ANES Cumulative File)

political information available to them has become a deluge. Antipathy seems to have spawned uninformed antipathy.

Things were different in Texas in 1956. Back then, the governor of the state was Allan Shivers, a Democrat, but a Democrat who was backing Republican presidential candidate Dwight Eisenhower, all of which set Texas jaws wagging. Mr. Eisenhower won the state that year with a plurality of 55 percent, an early sign that Texas might eventually turn red. But many Yellow-Dog Democrats were offended by the governor's shenanigans, especially those in Wichita Falls:

Governor Shivers at Houston, April 20th, stated "To be chairman of the Texas delegation should be a man who is not a candidate for any office." Why did he not follow the advice in 1942 when he was a candidate for Governor of Texas? He had no opposition that year, so that was all right, but he has opposition this year and he is crying about political and economic pressure being brought to bear. Does he not remember that he did the same thing in 1954 on the members of the legislature for them to endorse him for governor? He also made the statement that if we lost the fight in the precinct and county conventions this year we may never be allowed to hold any more unless we clear them with Mr. Sam [Rayburn], which he knows is not true as this country is larger than any one man.

(R.S.E., *Wichita Falls Times Record News*, April 30, 1956)

One need not know or care much about Texas history to see what is going on here – an average American engaging in classic dialectic, reproducing his opponents' arguments and refuting them point by point. None of this seems terribly remarkable until we contrast it with the state of Missouri forty-eight years later. George W. Bush was running for a second term at the time and, while the letter writers in St. Joe were admirably feisty, they mostly ignored what their opponents were saying:

Well, Northwest Missouri State University has sunk to a new low. What am I talking about? Inviting Michael Moore to speak on campus October 9th. While this may please the ultra-far left, I believe the majority of decent people should be outraged by inviting a lying, gross, overweight, hate-filled lunatic to speak his mind. Apparently there were some demonstrators outside protesting his presence and what was his response? Something about an impending Republican loss in November. Come on, the guy promised white undies and other stuff to people if they voted for John Kerry. Doesn't say much for his character does it?

(John B., *St. Joseph News-Press*, October 10, 2004)

* * * * *

I also am appalled at Bob Dole's recent comments about John Kerry's Purple Heart medals and whether he actually deserved them or not. I have the utmost respect for Bob Dole and his service in World War II. However, his latest comments are a low blow and just because John Kerry's injuries weren't as severe as the ones Bob Dole sustained, it doesn't mean that John Kerry shouldn't have been awarded his three Purple Hearts. I served in Vietnam and I know that any medal that was awarded had to be earned.

(William L., *St. Joseph News-Press*, September 3, 2004)

In many ways, these letters present citizens at their best, delivering stinging blows to their opponents and supporting their arguments with impassioned examples and asides. There is pace and form to their remarks, some deft rhetorical questions, and more than a bit of personal investment. The writers say what they mean and mean what they say. But they stand alone on stage, their opponents relegated to the wings. We learn nothing about Michael Moore's speech from John B. and nothing from William L. about John Kerry's detractors. These two writers may have known what their opponents were saying, but they do not wish to share it.

There are at least three possible explanations for this drop in Oppositional Literacy:

1. *Hearing but not engaging*: Journalism scholar Brian Weeks and his colleagues have found that citizens today have their own (narrow) modes of news acquisition, but many of them also peruse "general interest outlets" containing contrary viewpoints.[32] Broadly speaking, says the University of Pennsylvania's Diana Mutz, television has "the capacity to encourage greater awareness of oppositional perspectives" even when casting doubt on the legitimacy of those perspectives.[33] Northwestern University's Pablo Boczkowski and Eugenia Mitchelstein show that online consumers are especially open to new information during times of "heightened political activity" (e.g., political campaigns), although other researchers find that only 11 percent of online discussants actually *engage* the comments of other contributors.[34] In the offline world, BYU's Chris Karpowitz found that citizen deliberators were comfortable making value claims but avoided referencing their opponents' arguments.[35]

2. *Not hearing, not engaging*: Many researchers are concerned about the increasing fragmentation of the news, much of which is attributable to the rise in online sources. People can pick the news that suits them, says the University of Georgia's Barry Hollander, allowing many consumers to avoid contrary viewpoints.[36] Those who read print news appear to be less guilty of doing so, report Stacy Ulbig and Steven Perry, but it is still hard to find everyday citizens engaging in push–pull disputation.[37] In short, we now have

a curious phenomenon: While the Web delivers more political viewpoints to more people than ever before, the uptake of those comments is hardly guaranteed.

3. *Hearing but engaging badly*: Although many believed that the internet would give rise to enlightened dialogue, that has not always been the case. "Electronic talk participants are too frequently set in their own discussion ghettoes," reports political scientist Richard Davis, with flaming being one of the Web's most common commodities.[38] Even forums sponsored by newspapers are too often "an outlet for the loudest voices to be heard" rather than a genuine public sphere, says Florida State's Summer Harlow.[39] The more uncivil political elites have become, says Daniel Coffey and his colleagues, the more uncivil online commentators have become as well.[40] All too often, it appears, the Web has produced "a dialogue of the deaf."[41]

The worrisome thing about the decline in Oppositional Literacy is that the letter writers I studied are members of *geographical* communities. It is one thing to ignore others' viewpoints when writing a blog or commenting anonymously online. It is quite another to do so in print in a small-town newspaper and to sign one's name to the letter. The great worry, of course, is that the Web's hyper-partisanship and incivility will bleed into all discourse – classroom discussions, family conversations, letters to the editor, etc. That would be a sorry legacy for an invention with so much democratic potential.

There is one bright spot in Figure 8.7. For some reason, Oppositional Literacy rose dramatically during the 2012 presidential campaign, getting more than half-way back to its peak in 1992. The rise was widespread across all the cities studied and true for all discussion topics. Why the change? Did more lawyers write letters to the editor in 2012? Did the national recession encourage people to open up to one another? Were candidates Obama and Romney more civil, giving the electorate a model to follow? Was campaign coverage more responsible, reminding citizens what informed discussion looks like?

Only time will tell if the improvements of 2012 can be sustained. The vitriol manufactured prodigiously during the 2016 Republican primary on discussion boards suggests more dire possibilities. Given the importance of democratic give-and-take for the future, it is useful to be reminded what Oppositional Literacy looks like when it is thoughtful and articulate. Beverly S. obliges:

[Senator] Scott Brown is a Republican. He keeps calling himself an independent but his voting record shows he votes with his party 97 percent of the time. Scott says he supports women, the family and the middle class. He has co-sponsored several anti-choice bills, supported the "Blunt Amendment" to allow employers and insurers to deny women any health coverage they morally oppose. He voted to defund Planned Parenthood where many women get lifesaving medical tests.

Scott [also] voted against the Health Care Access and Affordability Act that stopped insurance companies from refusing to fund treatment for pre-existing conditions when someone had to change insurers. It is also providing health care for adults and children with serious medical issues that they could not afford otherwise. Evidently the average person doesn't need such things as health care, but we have to ensure that those millionaires have enough money for their multiple homes, their yachts and their horses. I don't know about you, but I am voting for Elizabeth Warren. She truly supports the middle class. It's not just talk.

(Beverly S., *Fall River Herald News*, September 20, 2012)

CONCLUSION

When my students contrasted the 1952 letters to those from 2012, they were dismayed. They knew little about the issues of the first election but they knew civility when they saw it, and they saw too little of it in 2012. I teased the students that they were becoming "young fogies" but they demurred. They said that democracy deserved better than it was getting and that prudence seemed a small price to pay for a better politics. They knew nothing about National Touchstones but they sensed that the letters from 1952 were more "important." They described recent letters as "nasty" (too many Campaign Complaints?) and "pessimistic" (not enough Evidence of Coordination? Too little Voter Agreement?). They also felt that today's writers "pontificated" a lot (too much Individual Agency?). My students were embarrassed by the 2012 letters, and they said so.

My students were idealists, as everyone should be at their age. I explained to them that politics is a contact sport and that the man in the arena is important precisely because he is in the arena and not lying on a beach somewhere. Civic hope, I argued, is based on contestation – on beliefs being performed – and that is ultimately more important than the rhetorical finesse with which those beliefs are manifested. The 2012 letter writers, I continued, were doing what engaged citizens have always done – punching out an argument, taking on all comers. Their rough edges signaled their passion, a necessary adjunct to political change.

The findings of this chapter dovetail with other evidence about the increasing polarization of the American polity. Such negativity drives many citizens underground, but not those who write letters to the editor, and that is an unalloyed blessing. "Through his chronic inability to forget," says sociologist Scott Lash, "the melancholic may be our best hope of retrieval of any sort of politics of value."[42] Politics exists, says the University of Sheffield's Matt Sleat, because people do *not* agree with one another, because it is so hard to identify abstract goals – liberty, equality, sufficiency – to which all subscribe.[43] When people do not win the lottery, says Lash, they do not get colossally disappointed because the odds are stacked against them. Why get so despondent about politics, he asks, when things do not go our way, since the odds of getting exactly what we want in a nation of 300 million people are equally atrocious.

Several years ago, Michael Dupre and David Mackey compared people who phoned the *Framingham Sun* to those who wrote letters to its editor. The callers turned out to be edgier, concerned primarily with immediate municipal concerns and media shortcomings. The letter writers were after bigger game – broad political principles, better standards of behavior, community pride and altruism.[44] Civic hope, I argue, finds its reservoir in people like this. As we have seen in this chapter, civic hope is not always expressed equivalently in all circumstances. That is because political issues are thorny and because people are, well, people. I told my students that those who wrote letters in 2012 still did everyone a service, despite their imperfections. They were, after all, standing in the arena, even if they did not use all of the civic hope strategies available to them. My students listened respectfully, but they were clearly hoping for more.

Endnotes

1 For more on these matters see Roderick P. Hart and Suzanne M. Daughton, *Modern Rhetorical Criticism*, 3rd edn. (Boston: Pearson, 2005), pp. 233–58.

2 Daniel S., *Salinas Californian*, October 17, 1984; Gilbert A., *Duluth News Tribune*, August 6, 2012; Duane F., *Wichita Falls Times Record News*, October 11, 2012.

3 See Émile Durkheim, *The Elementary Forms of the Religious Life*, ed. Mark S. Cladis; trans. Carol Cosman (New York: Oxford University Press, 2008).

4 Phyllis K., *Utica Observer-Dispatch*, August 1, 2012.

5 Elaine S., *Duluth News Tribune*, May 8, 1952.

6 George I. Lovell, *"This is Not Civil Rights": Discovering Rights Talk in 1939 America* (Chicago: University of Chicago Press, 2012), pp. 180–1, 134.

7 Ibid, 122.

8 Brian Michael Goss, "Online 'looney tunes': an analysis of reader-composed comment threads in The Nation," *Journalism Studies*, 8 (2007), 365–81.

9 For more on this matter see David Campbell, "Cold wars: securing identity, identifying danger," in Frederick M. Dolan and Thomas L. Dumm, eds., *Rhetorical Republic: Governing Representations in American Politics* (Amherst, MA: University of Massachusetts Press, 1993), pp. 39–60.

10 Political scientist Taeku Lee finds that different American values are embraced by different ethnic groups (e.g., "universal rights" for blacks and "anti-communism" for whites), with each value cluster being accessed effortlessly by the groups in question. See *Mobilizing Public Opinion: Black Insurgency and Racial Attitudes in the Civil Rights Era* (Chicago: University of Chicago Press, 2002), p. 177.

11 Peter Thompson, "Religion, utopia and the metaphysics of contingency," in Peter Thompson and Slavoj Žižek, eds., *The Privatization of Hope: Ernst Bloch and the Future of Utopia* (Durham: Duke University Press, 2013), pp. 82–105.

12 Sofie Marien, Marc Hooghe, and Jennifer Oser, "Great expectations: the effect of democratic ideals and evaluations on political trust; a comparative investigation of the 2012 European social survey." Paper presented at the annual meeting of the Midwest Political Science Association, Chicago, April 2015.

13 National Touchstones for Cold War era = 0.7340, for Human Rights era = 0.4024; for Partisan Politics era = 0.2871; F [2, 5345] = 51.785, p < .000.

14 Neil Nevitte and Stephen White, "Citizen expectations and democratic performance: the sources and consequences of democratic deficits from the bottom up," in Patti Tamara Lenard and Richard Simeon, eds., *Imperfect Democracies: The Democratic Deficit in Canada and the United States* (Vancouver: University of British Columbia Press, 2012), p. 52.

15 Amy Erica Smith finds a continuing decline in system support *within* the Partisan Politics era as well (from 2006 to 2014). See "Do Americans still believe in democracy? State of the 2016 race," *Monkey Cage/Washington Post*, April 9, 2016. Accessed at www.washingtonpost.com/news/monkey-cage/wp/2016/04/09/do-americans-still-believe-in-democracy.

16 Aaron Wildavsky, "Resolved, that individualism and egalitarianism be made compatible in America: political-cultural roots of exceptionalism," in Byron E. Shafer, ed., *Is America Different? A New Look at American Exceptionalism* (Oxford: Clarendon Press, 1991), p. 134.

17 Bob Cohn, "21 charts that explain American values today," *The Atlantic*, June 27, 2012. Accessed at www.theatlantic.com/national/archive/2012/06/21-charts-that-explain-american-values-today/258990/.

18 *Campaign Complaints* for Cold War era = –0.0428, for Human Rights era = 0.1908; for Partisan Politics era = 0.2939; F [2, 9594] = 220.106, p < .000; *Evidence of Coordination* for Cold War era = 0.2077, for Human Rights era = 0.1068; for Partisan Politics era = –0.3060; F [2, 9594] = 228.277, p < .000.

19 *Campaign Advice* for Cold War era = 0.0309, for Human Rights era = 0.1614; for Partisan Politics era = –0.2446; F [2, 9594] = 151.839, p < .000.

20 *Candidates without Morals* for Cold War era = 2.0760, for Human Rights era = 0.7430; for Partisan Politics era = 6.7081; F [2, 9594] = 128.991, p < .000; *Strategically Inept Candidates* for Cold War era = .7346, for Human Rights era = 0.4602; for Partisan Politics era = 4.5185; F [2, 9594] = 110.517, p < .000.

21 Unidentified author, *Fall River Herald News*, October 7, 2008.

22 *Evidence of Disunity* for Cold War era = –0.0083, for Human Rights era = 0.1923; for Partisan Politics era = 0.2695; F [2, 9594] = 196.277, p < .000; *Evidence of Coordination* for Cold War era = 0.2077, for Human Rights era = 0.1068; for Partisan Politics era = –0.3060; F [2, 9594] = 228.277, p < .000.

23 *Author Declarations* for Cold War era = –0.1601, for Human Rights era = 0.0146; for Partisan Politics era = –0.1432; F [2, 9594] = 62.822, p < .000.

24 Robert D. Putnam, *Bowling Alone: The Collapse and Revival of American Community* (New York: Simon & Schuster, 2001).

25 After standardizing the subaltern measures, the variables were combined as follows: **Idea-Focus** = Civic Forecasts + Author Declarations + Political Memory + National Touchstones + Oppositional Literacy; **Community-Focus** = Helpful and Non-Helpful Groups + Evidence of Coordination and Evidence of Disunity; **Leader-Focus** = Negative and Positive Leadership Traits + Agents of Hope and Decline; **Campaign-Focus** = Campaign Advice + Campaign Complaints. The statistical results were as follows: Campaign-Focus for Cold War era = –.0756, for Human Rights era = 0.2653; for Partisan Politics era = 0.4210; F [2, 9594] = 202.291, p < .000; Community-Focus for Cold War era = .5082, for Human Rights era = 0.0103; for Partisan Politics era = -0.4053; F [2, 9594] = 96.407, p < .000; Idea-Focus for Cold War era = .2576, for Human Rights era = 0.0434; for Partisan Politics era = –0.2577; F [2, 9594] = 190.868, p < .000; Leader-Focus for Cold War era = –0.1344, for Human Rights era = – 0.1072; for Partisan Politics era = 0.2500; F [2, 9594] = 25.916, p < .000.

26 Patrick R. Miller and Pamela J. Conover, "Winning is everything: the psychology of partisan competition." Paper presented at the annual convention of the Midwest Political Science Association, Chicago, April 2014.

27 Thomas Bridges, *The Culture of Citizenship: Inventing Postmodern Civic Culture* (Albany: SUNY Press, 1994), p. 25.

28 Amy Mitchell, Jeffrey Gottfried, Jocelyn Kiley, and Katerina Eva Matsa, "Political Polarization and Media Habits," *Pew Research Journalism Project*, October 21, 2014. Accessed at www.journalism.org/2014/10/21/political-polarization-media-habits/.

29 Shanto Iyengar and Sean J. Westwood, "Fear and loathing across party lines: new evidence on group polarization," *American Journal of Political Science*, 59(3) (2015), 690.

30 Shanto Iyengar, Tobias Konitzer, and Kent Tedin, "The Home as a political fortress: family agreement in an era of polarization." Working paper, Department of Communication, Stanford University (May 2016), 21.

31 Max Ehrenfreund, "These political scientists are discovering even more reasons U.S. politics are a disaster," *Washington Post*, November 3, 2015, 12. Accessed at www.washingtonpost.com/news/wonk/wp/2015/11/03/these-political-scientists-are-discovering-even-more-reasons-u-s-politics-are-a-disaster/.

32 Brian E. Weeks, Thomas B. Ksiazek, and R. Lance Holbert, "Partisan enclaves or common media experiences? A network approach to understanding citizens' political news environment." Paper presented at the annual meeting of the International Communication Association, London, June 2013.

33 Diana C. Mutz, "Effects of 'in-your-face' television discourse on perceptions of a legitimate opposition," *American Political Science Review*, 101(4) (2007), 621–35.

34 Pablo J. Boczkowski and Eugenia Mitchelstein, *The News Gap: When the Information Preferences of the Media and the Public Diverge* (Cambridge: MIT Press, 2013); Carlos Ruiz, David Domingo, Josep Lluís Micó, Javier Díaz-Noci, Koldo Meso, and Pere Masip, "Public sphere 2.0? The democratic qualities of citizen debates in online newspapers," *The International Journal of Press/Politics*, 16 (2011), 463–87.

35 Christopher F. Karpowitz, "Men, women, and Wal-Mart: citizen discourse at local public hearings." Paper presented at the annual meeting of the American Political Science Association, Chicago, September 2007.

36 Barry A. Hollander, "Tuning out or tuning elsewhere? Partisanship, polarization, and media migration from 1998 to 2006," *Journalism and Mass Communication Quarterly*, 85(1) (2008), 23–40.

37 Stacy Gwenn Ulbig and Steven Perry, "I virtually hate them: the differential impact of online and offline news sources on partisan sentiment." Paper presented at the annual meeting of the Midwest Political Science Association, Chicago, April 2014; Eric Lawrence, John Sides, and Henry Farrell, "Self-segregation or deliberation? Blog readership, participation, and polarization in American politics," *Perspectives on Politics*, 8 (2010), 141–57.

38 Richard Davis, *Politics Online: Blogs, Chatrooms, and Discussion Groups in American Democracy* (New York: Routledge, 2005), 123.

39 Summer Harlow, "Story-chatterers stirring up hate: racist discourse in reader comments on U.S. newspaper websites," *Howard Journal of Communications*, 26 (2015), 35.

40 Daniel J. Coffey, Michael Kohler, and Douglas M. Granger, "Sparking debate: campaigns, social media, and political incivility," in Victoria A. Farrar-Myers and Justin S. Vaughn, eds., *Controlling the Message: New Media in American Political Campaigns* (New York: New York University Press, 2015), p. 262.

41 Ruiz et al., "Public sphere 2.0," 480.

42 Scott Lash, "Being after time: towards a politics of melancholy," *Cultural Values*, 2 (1998), 318.

43 Matt Sleat, "Hope and disappointment in politics," *Contemporary Politics*, 19 (2013), 131–45.

44 Michael Dupre and David Mackey, "Letters and phone-mails to the editor: a comparison of reader input," *Newspaper Research Journal*, 23 (2002), 142–7.

9

How Letters Differ

Letters to the editor are homely things. They are written by ordinary people and published in ordinary newspapers. In that sense, letters are rather like sidewalks – people depend on them but rarely notice them until a crack appears and causes them to stumble. Similarly, letters to the editor are never newsworthy until they become newsworthy.

Dr. Starner Jones, an emergency room physician in Jackson, Mississippi, wrote one such letter, and it (and he) became a cause célèbre as a result. His letter included these sentiments:

During my last shift in the ER, I had the pleasure of evaluating a patient with a shiny new gold tooth, multiple elaborate tattoos and a new cellular telephone equipped with her favorite R&B tune for a ringtone. Glancing over the chart, one could not help noticing her payer status: Medicaid. She smokes a costly pack of cigarettes every day and, somehow, still has money to buy beer. And our president expects me to pay for this woman's health care?[1]

In a blog posting, Mountain Trail Runner took grievous exception to Dr. Jones' letter, decrying his violation of the Hippocratic Oath, his latent racism (e.g., the mention of R&B music), his classism, and, especially, his callousness: "I can just imagine him angrily and violently suturing a wound and muttering under his breath about the worthlessness of his patient."[2] Given the fractiousness of the debate over healthcare in the United States, it should not be surprising that Mountain Trail Runner kicked off a series of heated exchanges with Bandit 4, Harmonysmine, Sarah Terzo, Ol'Reb, TGonz, Coach Leslie, SouthernBelle, and four dozen other equally colorful characters. Dr. Jones did not participate in the resulting contretemps. Wisely, no doubt.

The Jones story was mostly a regional one, but Princeton grad Susan Patton made national news when writing a letter to her alma mater's newspaper (*The Daily Princetonian*) that strongly encouraged today's coeds to be sure to leave campus with an engagement ring. Given their vaunted intelligence, Ms. Patton argued, Princeton women would price themselves out of the market if they failed to find a guy of equal intelligence during their four-year stay in New Jersey.[3] Anne Spurzem, a Smith College alum, also made national news when claiming that her alma mater's admissions office was ignoring SAT scores so it could admit more black lesbians to the Northampton campus.[4] A bit further north, Ralph Coffman found a nationwide audience after writing a letter to the *Penobscot (Me.) Times* decrying the teaching of homosexual practices to elementary schoolchildren – an absurd claim on its face, but a special absurdity for a person who knew what was going on in the town's schools. Mr. Coffman was a member of the Penobscot School Board.[5]

Correspondents Patton, Spurzem, and Coffman were pikers, though, compared to W. Richard Stover of Lewisburg, Pennsylvania, who championed the killing of President Barack Obama in the pages of the *Sunbury (Pa.) Daily Item*. Mr. Stover began by apologizing for being excessively blunt, but then observed that, historically speaking, regime change was typically "accompanied by execution by guillotine, firing squad [or] public hanging," any one of which would, in his opinion, be suitable for the nation's chief executive.[6] Somewhat more charitably, Tom Perkins, a legendary venture capitalist from Silicon Valley, wrote a letter to the *Wall Street Journal* describing "a rising tide of hatred" directed at the nation's top 1 percent, epitomized by the "outraged public reaction to the Google buses carrying technology workers from the city to the peninsula high-tech companies which employ them." Such attitudes, Mr. Perkins declared, paralleled the hatred suffered by another despised minority – Jews during Nazi Germany – thereby exposing the nation's wealthiest citizens to a progressive version of Kristallnacht.[7]

When Chris Royse of Woodbridge, Virginia wrote a letter to the editor urging the nation's Catholic bishops to deny communion to any politician defending a woman's right to choose, he made news, but he, too, was an exception.[8] Despite the foregoing pyrotechnics, most letters to the editor are eminently forgettable. The letters I studied were earnest, passionate, and often thoughtful, but few were worthy of being reprised elsewhere. Their authors were sometimes frivolous but mostly they behaved themselves.

Why concentrate on such ordinary letters, rather than those making national news? That question returns us to sidewalks. Sidewalks are important, I argue, because they are so dependable: They help children and the elderly perambulate safely. They knit neighborhoods together. They make urban living possible. When sidewalks are being constructed in a community it is typically seen as a sign of progress. The smoothness of their surfaces, the regularity of their seams, help people walk in a predictable manner and make them feel safe. When sidewalks call attention to themselves – when a sinkhole swallows them or when they are being refurbished – people become irritated. Sidewalks are best when not noticed.

Most letters to the editor go unnoticed, and that makes them especially interesting. This chapter looks at (1) presidential campaigns, (2) political parties, and (3) geographic locations through the lens of letter-writing. Many other scholars have already examined such topics, so why bring letters to the editor into the picture? Once again, sidewalks offer a parallel. To describe a city, one could begin by noting the height of its skyscrapers, its network of highways and seaports, its economic strength, its ethnic neighborhoods and city parks, its political infrastructure and social enclaves. One could also study its sidewalks: How people get from the subway to the job and back again; how hot dog vendors and souvenir stands make cheap goods available to those of modest means; how sophisticates traverse the sidewalk when parading their latest finery and how teenagers do so while glued to their smartphones; how the sociology of the sidewalk changes from early morning (blue-collar workers, CEOs) to late in the evening (the glitterati, the homeless); how passersby calculate for whom eye contact is and is not appropriate.

Similarly, letters to the editor give us a pedestrian view of politics. It is one thing to examine presidential campaigns through the eyes of the candidates and quite another to examine what voters in Duluth are saying about them. Too, even though we are now awash in formal theories of party polarization and regional influences, such things look different at the ground level. Thus, while letters cannot tell us everything we need to know, they can be useful, teaching us the sorts of things former Philadelphia mayor Michel Nutter once learned about sidewalks: "When I shoveled the sidewalk my parents didn't let me stop with our house. They told me to keep shoveling all the way to the corner. I had a responsibility to my community."[9]

HOW CAMPAIGNS MATTER

Historian Gil Troy has described American presidential campaigns as "too lengthy, too costly, too nasty, and too silly."[10] Perhaps he understates the case. "I dread the next few months of campaign commercials and coverage," says one letter writer. "I am so sick of this campaign – the bickering among the candidates, the constant taped phone calls asking for money," says another. "The politics of fear, hatred, and division has only gotten worse since the reelection campaign began," says a third.[11] Popular sentiments all, but according to political scientist James Campbell, campaigns are important because they introduce citizens to would-be leaders and mobilize them as a result. Equally important, says Campbell, is the fact that "the parties, issues, the voters, and even many of the candidates do not go away after an election," thereby making the campaign part of a "continuing civil (and, marginally civilized) war for control of the government rather than a war unto itself."[12]

Campaigns also educate voters, especially when candidates and the press emphasize the same issues.[13] Oddly enough, say the University of Montreal's Richard Nadeau and his colleagues, voters' satisfaction with democracy noticeably increases after an election, even if voters were dismayed by the preceding campaign.[14] In addition, argue John Brehm and Wendy Rahn, campaigns increase voters' "efficacy," the sense that they are making a difference when voting.[15] Norman Luttbeg and Michael Gant found another intriguing fact: Even though only 55 percent of the American people voted in the 1992 presidential election, 75 percent of the electorate claimed to have done so when surveyed by pollsters.[16] These are pro-social lies, Luttbeg and Gant argue, proving that democratic norms remain vital.

Letters to the editor provide us with yet another way of looking at campaigns. Although most of the letters I collected were published during general election campaigns, 15 percent were written during primaries. As we see in Figure 9.1, the two seasons differ: Primaries focus voters on ideas, while the general election encourages them to pick sides, critique campaign behavior, and debate the contenders' resumes. Not all writers follow this seasonal schedule, but enough do to make things interesting.[17]

Consider a common stereotype of the letter writer: A lonely fellow in his garret, unhappy with the world, lashing out at politicians for being politicians. My findings suggest an alternative stereotype for the primaries: Someone setting the table for the general election, examining the

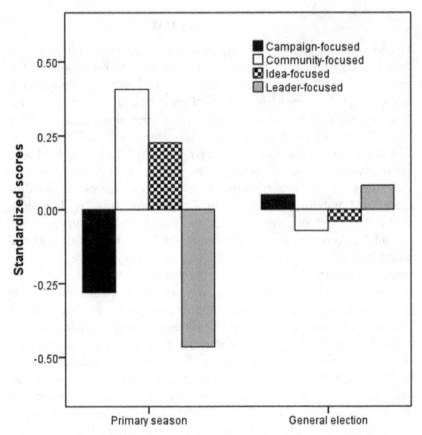

FIGURE 9.1 Letters Written during Primary and General Elections

proffered platforms and jousting about issues. The primary-season writer is not a fanatic but a wonk, someone committed to the politics of ideas:

This is to correct the inaccurate and misleading statement which appeared in your editorial of March 23 concerning presidential candidate Jimmy Carter's stand on tax reform, and especially the statement that he opposed the homeowner's interest deduction.

(Drew R., *Lake Charles American Press*, April 25, 1976)

* * * * *

Federal budget time is here again and it has come to my attention that the Food Stamp Program faces drastic consequences. The Senate Agriculture Committee Bill regarding food stamps will eliminate approximately one-sixth of the current program participants.

(Judy S., *Lake Charles American Press*, March 21, 1976)

* * * * *

My fellow citizens, the price of freedom and security has and will continue to be a very expensive thing, but our great congressmen would rather cut corners than supply the funds which have been the foundations for...

(Keith V., *Lake Charles American Press*, July 4, 1976)

Writers such as these are far more concerned with getting the facts straight than are most primary voters, who have become narrowly partisan over the years, focusing heavily on value propositions.[18] Political scientist Stephen Ansolabehere and his colleagues report that only 25 percent of statewide candidates now face serious opposition during primaries. As a result, they run on ideology, although that makes pivoting to the general election more arduous.[19] The mass media further complicate things. Scholars find that issue-oriented voters rely on newspapers while "values voters" depend on television (and, increasingly, cable stations), all of which makes political primaries volatile.[20]

Given these trends, Figure 9.1 may represent the waning of a democratic ideal for the primaries – sort through the issues, rally community groups, avoid getting caught up in campaign hoopla. But general elections are important too. Campaigns usually narrow as election day approaches, says James Campbell, as party loyalties take hold and as late-deciding voters make their decisions. Letter writers shift as well, replacing cool-headed deliberation with spirited name-calling:

There is now on the political scene one who is the personification of the Democratic Party. Endorsed by the Kremlin as the one most likely to pursue its programs, this man is vacuous, inconsistent, hypocritical, and a typification of the word "politician." His speeches must be written by Woody Allen because they are certainly comedic material. . .

Does the American public really want someone who is anxious to cut our defense budget, promote welfare programs, and who derides tax loop holes while using them himself? Someone who is supported by our political negative, Soviet Russia? Someone who has to ask what state he's in before he states his political views? Or do they just want a person untainted by the recent scandals? Jimmy Carter's no better than anyone else. He just didn't happen to be in Washington at the time. It's really unfortunate that Mr. Reagan wasn't nominated, but anybody is better than Jimmy Carter! Nixon, come back! Bring back the frying pan and take away the fire!

(Gary I., *Springfield News-Sun*, September 21, 1976)

Gary I. does not represent all letter writers, but he represents many. Six weeks before election day he is well into the campaign and the campaign is well into him. He uses every bludgeon in sight here, combining political culture with popular culture, micro-politics with macro-politics; he even resurrects Richard Nixon. That which is absent here – the Watergate scandal – is purified and Jimmy Carter's literal presence in Georgia becomes a metaphorical presence in the District of Columbia. Letters such as Gary's remind us that whereas primaries are a time for education, the general election is a time for persuasion.[21]

There is a second way in which letters to the editor help us understand campaigns. I found interesting differences between letters written during Open Elections (1952, 1968, 1980, 1992, 2000, and 2008) and those written during Incumbent Elections (1956, 1972, 1984, 1996, 2004, and 2012). This was not something I had anticipated but, upon reflection, the patterns make sense. Civic hope was advanced with greater depth during Open campaigns (more Agents of Hope, more Evidence of Coordination, more Campaign Advice) than during Incumbent campaigns, which featured Negative Leadership Traits, Evidence of Disunity, and Campaign Complaints.[22] The statistical effects were not overwhelming, but the tendencies were indeed tendencies.

My findings show that writers become nastier during incumbent campaigns, but one might have predicted the opposite. Because presidential incumbents can raise money easily, call in political debts, and exploit the perks of office, they almost always win.[23] Incumbents also have a better handle on legislative details than do Washington outsiders, are better versed in international diplomacy, and enjoy the emotional trappings of the Oval Office. Incumbents' unified party base lets them argue for both continuity and change, while challengers only have the latter option.[24]

The incumbency advantage has grown over the years, although that is less true for congressional and Senate races than for the presidential campaign.[25] Naturally, unexpected "campaign events" can undermine that advantage (e.g., the Iran hostage crisis during the latter portion of Jimmy Carter's presidency). Additionally, it is hard to dislodge voters' preferences the closer they get to election day, so if a sitting president has not made his case to the people by late September he will be in considerable difficulty.[26]

Christian Leuprecht and David Skillicorn report that presidential incumbents are much more positive when speaking on the stump than are challengers.[27] Why the opposite effect for letter writers? An obvious possibility is that the sitting president's popularity increases his detractors' ire. But I find a more complicated effect: Writers of all stripes "go negative" during incumbent elections, but they do so for different reasons: (1) the president's critics have stored up gripes for four long years and are primed to unload them; (2) the president's supporters, on the other hand, need to justify their prior electoral decision, and hence are both defensive and protective.

Consider, for example, one contribution from the 2000 presidential campaign exemplifying "open campaign" letters:

Regarding Gore and Joe Lieberman's attack on the movie industry, guess who sends tons of money to the Democratic National Committee? It's that industry from the Left Coast. About Gore's statement about George W. Bush's tax break for this country's wealthiest? Poor people don't create jobs. If you want to make money, there is only one way I know of – work.

Lieberman's home state of Connecticut pays the highest taxes per capita; taxes on personal property, cars and home are out of sight. Gasoline and home-heating oil are also the highest in the country. I got fed up and couldn't take the liberalism in Connecticut, so I moved to Virginia 14 months ago.

Before you vote, take a close look at these two individuals and their past performances. A past performance is always a good sign of what they will bring into our future.

(George H., *Roanoke Times*, October 24, 2000)

George H.'s letter is clear-cut and instructive. He tells us what he thinks, makes connections others may not have made before, and discloses his personal circumstances to show that he is not idly carping. His letter is mannerly but speculative: He does not know exactly what Al Gore would do as president or whether Joe Lieberman is responsible for all of Connecticut's sins. As a result, his conclusion is subdued: Think carefully before voting.

Things were different four years later. In early September of 2004, Linda L. of Archer City, Texas did not quite know how she would vote, but she *knew* John Kerry and she *knew* George Bush. Her letter has an empirical cast to it, descriptions of actions taken and not taken, promises kept and not kept. When she finally makes her decision, it will be for personal reasons:

I would like to say I have been voting for 20-plus years and I am a college graduate. Kerry did oppose the Vietnam War as did millions of other American people as it proved to be a useless war with far too many deaths. Many survivors were treated with very little respect and few benefits. At least John Kerry went and fought in Vietnam and did not take an honorable discharge to go to college like

President Bush did. President Bush would probably pass out at the sight of a three-car accident, God forbid.

(*Wichita Falls Times-Record-News*, September 5, 2004)

Patricia F. also lives in Texas, but she never doubted how she would vote in 2004. Two weeks after the election she still held a grudge against those who had savaged her president:

I have to tell you that I am really, really sick and tired of the many political cartoons that your paper runs bashing President Bush! I think I'm safe in saying that at least 95 percent of them either bash the President, the Vice-president, or the Republican party! What's fair and balanced about that?

The cartoon in Tuesday's paper was particularly sickening and like most of them so twisted and unjust! Also, these cartoonists try to make President Bush look so ugly; he isn't, but their images just reflect the ugliness inside themselves and their maliciousness. No wonder they don't sign their names in a recognizable way!

(*Wichita Falls Times-Record-News*, November 16, 2004)

Presidential campaigns in the United States are run by professionals for other professionals. People who write letters to the editor merely sit on the sidelines, so we do not know what effect their letters have on their fellow citizens. But letter writers may well be canaries in the coal mine, signaling what is good and bad about elections. Political campaigns – especially those at the presidential level – call citizens forward, offering political renewal. Letter writers stand at the front of the line when those calls are being issued.

HOW PARTIES MATTER

When it comes to political partisanship in the United States, two things seem true: (1) Republicans and Democrats have never been more internally cohesive than they are at present, and (2) they have never been more antagonistic to one another.[28] Party members know what their opposites stand for (i.e., they have staunch "partisan stereotypes"),[29] are politically distrustful,[30] watch different newscasts,[31] use rhetoric to disguise their partisanship,[32] and even have different brain structures, with Democrats showing more activity in the left insula and Republicans lighting up the right amygdala![33] According to two observers, the parties used to "stand for nothing" but now "stand for too much."[34]

The parties have also never been less popular. According to journalist Jennifer Agiesta, "more Americans now call themselves politically independent than at any point in the last 75 years," with 38 percent declaring themselves Independents, compared to 32 percent who identify as Democrats and 24 percent who claim the Republican mantle.[35] Independents are especially distressed by the parties' issue-ownership: Republicans cannot get beyond Obamacare and abortion, while Democrats are obsessed with income equality and gay marriage. Independents are also dismayed by the lack of cooperation in Washington. In contrast, partisan voters are more concerned that their representatives block bad legislation than pass good legislation.[36]

Many political scientists feel that there are actually very few "independents" among the citizenry, that most are Democratic and Republican "leaners" who choose to conceal their political alignments. Perhaps as a result, third parties have fared poorly at the polls. Between 1948 and 2012, only George Wallace, John Anderson, and Ross Perot have registered a political pulse on election day, garnering an average of 12 percent of the popular vote across their four runs for the White House.

Because partisanship is such a powerful force, one might assume that Republican and Democratic letter writers would differ sharply, but I found that not to be true. In my sample, 29.5 percent of the writers were Democrats and 29.9 percent Republicans, with another 36 percent giving no indication of their party affiliation and 4 percent overtly supporting third party candidates. Even though the civic hope codebook is quite extensive, very little distinguished Democratic and Republican authors. Democrats mentioned more Positive Leadership Traits and Campaign Complaints than Republicans, while the latter spent more time castigating Unhelpful Groups and offering more Campaign Advice.[37] But these differences were conceptually random and statistically modest. Republicans did not exclusively cling to National Touchstones and Political Memories as one might have expected, nor did Democratic populism result in more Voter Perceptions and Agents of Hope.

As Figure 9.2 shows, both Democratic and Republican letter writers praise their saviors, denigrate the rascals, and then rinse and repeat.[38] Parties are especially good at personifying political options, thereby reducing the social distance between politicians and their far-flung constituents. Because of television, especially, there is now a shocking intimacy between leaders and their followers. Whereas parties formerly focused on issue positions, the postmodern age has changed things, the result of which is this:

Imagine George W. Bush as the first sitting caricature of a president, the illusion of a president, a chimera of a president, a facsimile of a president lacking any of the necessary substance historically associated with the role.

(Michael Y., *Lake Charles American Press*, October 9, 2004)

* * * * *

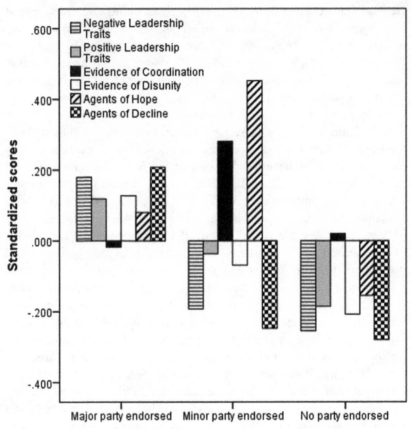

FIGURE 9.2 Rhetorical Correlates of Partisan Alignment

It is obvious that Mr. Dole is rambling. He has waffled on every issue from abortion to term limits. His obscure divorce and remarriage should deflate his ability to condemn the Clintons and thus claim the moral high ground. Uncomfortable in a contemporary setting, his campaign is contrived to avoid his archaic inclinations and project an image of fatherly certitude.

(John K., *Trenton Times*, August 22, 1996)

* * * * *

Carter digs in all the deeper, withdraws all the more from face-to-face argument and attacks the motives of his critics. Underneath that brittle mask of control, one senses an uptight and agitated psyche filled with anger and venom.

(William B., *Springfield News-Sun*, October 22, 1980)

* * * * *

Well, [Hillary's] done it again. The stalwart of the Democratic Party continues traditions that make the Clintons the darlings of American politics and about as trustworthy as a pit bulldog. No disrespect intended towards pit bulldogs, although many of the physical characteristics and appearances are strikingly similar.

(Roy B., *Wichita Falls Times-Record-News*, October 25, 2008)

To the best of my knowledge, none of the foregoing letters was written by a practicing psychiatrist, but they produce psychodrama nonetheless. Such boldness can be traced to the parties, which work hard to sell personalities. Parties also sell ideology, giving them a template for identifying which truths are being honored, which ignored, and by whom. Ideology appeals to a bifurcated world of "true believers" having totalistic mindsets. As a result, even though they spring from sharply different moral universes, religious and political extremism often go hand in hand.[39]

In odd ways, then, even though they adopt radically different – and opposed – philosophical positions, the parties promote a kindred psychology. But what about third party writers? Their job is considerably simpler. As we see in Figure 9.2, they make but two arguments: (1) well-resourced scoundrels abound, and (2) we need a new leader to dispatch them.[40] These arguments appear in virtually all of the 360 third party letters in my collection. Table 9.1 excerpts six of them and, while the conspirators change over time – sometimes the major parties are the enemy, sometimes lobbyists – the formula is dependable. The Agents of Hope identified in Table 9.1 are a diverse lot, but each champions the one and only thing – states' rights, New Age libertarianism – that will solve the nation's problems. Tiny though they are, third parties are attractive to those who like slender lines of argument.

A full third of the authors I studied admitted no party affiliation, but they wrote letters nonetheless. Table 9.2 provides a sampling of their remarks plus a provisional category system. These non-party writers ranged across the landscape, calling attention to matters rarely discussed and reminding readers of values forsaken, opportunities lost. Such writers present themselves as honest brokers unburdened by party loyalties. They are also pragmatists who cling to middle-class morality and who make business-like decisions. That, at least, is their self-conception.

Middlebury College's Matthew Dickinson has examined all of the commentary on political polarization, but he is not convinced.[41] He admits that there is a growing divide between Republicans and Democrats but he does not believe that this means the nation is riven. Instead, he says, "partisan

TABLE 9.1 *The Dependable Sound of Third Party Supporters*

Evidence of Coordination	Agents of Hope
As President of our country, Mr. [Henry] Wallace has no intentions whatever – and will not by any means – lead our country to Communism as our two older parties are now leading it slowly but surely to fascism.	We certainly have made a mess of our leadership but fortunately, we still have statesmen truly worth of the name. Mr. Wallace is one such statesman. (F.F.C., *Utica Observer-Dispatch*, October 11, 1948)
Nixon was a yes-man for Eisenhower the same as Humphrey has been for Johnson. So you see Nixon and Humphrey are carbon copies of their respective parties.	If we don't elect George Wallace president this time we may as well forget trying to save the land that I and countless other thousands like me love. (P.L.B., *Roanoke Times*, October 5, 1968)
Back in 1973, David Rockefeller set up the Rockefeller Tri-Lateral Commission to coordinate the foreign and economic policies of U.S., Western Europe, and Japan into a worldwide imperialist policy to serve the interests of the Rockefellers and other U.S. based trans-national corporations.	In the coming election, the best we can do is to help get the Communist party candidates – Gus Hall for president and Angela Davis for vice president on the ballot so the voters who have been hurt by inflation, unemployment, and the draft would at least have a chance to fight back. (Andy J., *Duluth News Tribune*, July 21, 1980)
"We need true statesmen with the quality of statesmanship – men and women – who will uphold the original Constitution of the United States. We need to be ever mindful of the changing faces of the Council on Foreign Relations, Trilateral Commission and the Aspen Institute.	Col. James "Bo" Gritz the most decorated Green Beret is one of America's greatest living heroes and may well be this country's best hope to continue as a free and virile nation. Let's wake up, America, and give our rousing support to Col. Gritz, the Populist Party's candidate. (Ray S., *Provo Daily Herald*, July 27, 1992)
Mr. Dole worked so hard to exclude Mr. Perot. This seems to confirm the worst stereotype we have of the "Grand Old Party" – a small faceless elite giving the rest of us the shaft.	Even though Mr. Perot met all the objective criteria of the Debate Commission, they say he failed when it came to their very subjective consideration that he had no chance to win. (Norris C., *Trenton Times*, October 12, 1996)
Working together, the Republicans and Democrats have also passed NAFTA and GATT, and got the United States to join the WTO. These trade deals sent hundreds of thousands of U.S. jobs to Third World countries that have low wages and no environmental standards.	Independents are free to vote third-party. If you lean conservative, vote for Buchanan. If you lean liberal, give Nader your vote. This year you have the liberty to vote your conscience. (B.K., *Trenton Times*, November 5, 2000)

TABLE 9.2 *Available Stances for Non-Party Letter Writers*

Stance	Example
Eternal Idealists	I believe Bush, Perot, or even Clinton can become good presidents. But my question is: Can we survive any of these guys? We the people of the United States must take a good look at ourselves and choose to work hard with whoever the next president of this country will be. If we do not do this, who can we blame as the Union slips from our sights? Whoever wins I wish them well. (Steve W., *Lake Charles American-Press*, June 7, 1992)
Single-Issue Specialists	What hypocrites people can be! All we ever hear is about "welfare" – all those pregnant mothers on welfare (they keep having more than one baby) using our tax money. And yet those same people make a big deal against Dan Quayle for speaking out about Murphy Brown (an unwed TV mother). Wouldn't it have been great if Murphy Brown had played up a daddy instead of making it sound "glorious" to not have a husband? What an example for all our teens! (Rose G., *Duluth News Tribune*, June 8, 1992)
Local Sentinels	I thought carpetbaggers disappeared in the 1800s. Apparently not. We now have a candidate for Congress, Phil Herwig, imported from Brooklyn N.Y. Herwig has been running around the Eighth District for months trying to persuade us [that] no one knows more about Minnesota and what we need than he does. To top it off, he's brought his New York-style campaigning with him: Sneak around, talk non-issues, make personal attacks – whatever it takes to get publicity. (Andrew F., *Duluth News Tribune*, September 30, 1992)
Campaign Referees	I am responding to John Guehlstorff's letter in Monday's *News-Press*. His letter is word-for-word a copy of a false e-mail that has been circulating about Barack Obama ... None of the men mentioned in Mr. Guehlstorff's letter are presently affiliated with the Obama campaign much less in charge. Both the *News-Press* and Mr. Guehlstorff should verify claims before printing them. (Mike E., *St. Joseph News-Press*, October 7, 2008)
Dogged Centrists	As long as the Republican Party panders to the apostles of greed, to the impositions of religious fundamentalists, and to the dictates of the National Rifle Association, it does not represent our country's citizens. As long as the Democratic Party panders to featherbedding unions, to entrenched bureaucrats, and to greedy trial lawyers, neither does it.

(continued)

TABLE 9.2 *(continued)*

Stance	Example
	Therein lies the public's apathy to the political process. (E. A. W., *Roanoke Times*, August 17, 2000)
Prophets of Doom	I must admit that I've gotten somewhat cynical this election season in my older age as I approach senior citizen status. Being asked to vote for either George W. Bush or John Kerry is about the same as being asked to vote on whether I'd like to have cancer or heart disease. Where are you, Daffy Duck and Kermit the Frog, when we really need you? (M. W., *Roanoke Times*, November 11, 2004)

sorting" has resulted in people identifying with one party or another, but without changing their fundamental beliefs. The nation is not divided into two ideological camps, Dickinson declares, because both parties are more internally varied than ever before. Most Americans continue to be centrists, he claims, which is why party apparatchiks pitch their wares to the median voter.[42] In short, party politics has never been more complicated than it is today, and letters to the editor often reflect those complications.

HOW PLACE MATTERS

The cities from which my letters originated stretch from the Atlantic (Fall River) to the Pacific Oceans (Salinas) and from Lake Superior (Duluth) to the Gulf of Mexico (Lake Charles). The cities have roots in both mining (Billings) and manufacturing (Springfield). George Washington's first military victory occurred in Trenton; the Pony Express began in St. Joseph. Provo lies at the foot of the Wasatch Mountains, Utica at the foot of the Adirondacks. The Cherokees once lived in Roanoke; wildcatters put Wichita Falls on the map. Each city has a unique history; each has struggled with modernity.

Issue Focus

I cannot tell all of these stories here, but I can present some findings about how place matters. Consider, for example, what happens when writers discuss local vs. national issues. Figure 9.3 is based on 3,300 letters not focused on presidential campaigns. These letters discuss what is happening locally – road construction, economic development, dogs

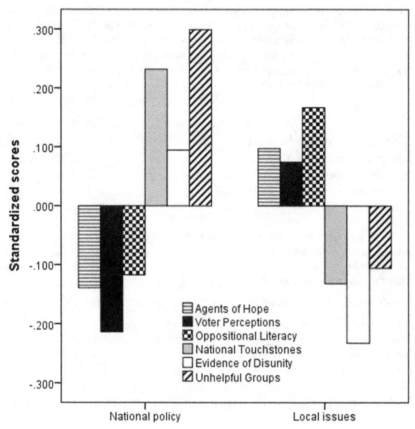

FIGURE 9.3 Letters Featuring Local vs. National Issues

without leashes – as well as issues facing the nation as a whole – the Vietnam War, the Great Recession, Monica Lewinsky.

Figure 9.3 is rather busy, but its point is simple. When writers focus on local matters, they speak directly to their fellow citizens, confront alternative viewpoints, and draw on community resources.[43] Consider the following letter, which is provincial and nativistic but also custodial. The author makes her point repeatedly, earnestly:

These out-of staters interfering in Montana politics are incredible ... In 1978, Larry Williams – only in Montana for three years – ran against Max Baucus, vigorously attacking Max. When Montanans discovered the true nature of this California flimflam man (who sported long hair and love beads), they sent him packing ... Now comes Chuck Cozzens, fresh from Wyoming via Minnesota who hires campaign leadership out of Virginia (NCPAC's home base) and who attended campaign schools sponsored by the Committee for the Survival of a Free Congress (NCPAC's sister group). This group of out-of staters has produced a series of radio ads that hit a new low in Montana politics. This direct and offensive name-calling is not acceptable to Montanans and Montanans are going to tell Cozzens and his out-of-state cronies what they've told similar GOP candidates over the years: "We don't want any part of you."

(Margie C., *Billings Gazette*, July 30, 1984)

Montanans become the key players in Margie C.'s drama here. She altercasts them as beleaguered yet canny. Her discussion also brings her antagonists to life, giving her letter a conversational feeling. She focuses not on the opposition's issues but on her geosocial relationships.

Robert M.'s letter was also written in 1984 but, in it, he reached well past his local community:

Perhaps you have read about a tea party that this land had many years ago. I would guess you know why this came about. I am one of many who go vote for persons who run our government. This past week or so one of these people said that the government should force the people to go out and vote.

South American people stand in line for hours to vote; some even die.

In our land many have given their lives and bodies so that we could do the same but we have something different. We send people to look out for us but when they get into office they work for the party, special interests, and themselves – all but the people who sent them to Washington or Baton Rouge.

I ask you, why should one go vote? Give us a choice! Have you ever heard of anyone wanting taxes? I pray that the party will someday think of us, the people, instead of a few.

(*Charles American Press*, April 22, 1984)

Technically speaking, this author's letter is paratactic. He thinks in sentences, not paragraphs, abandoning syntactic connections so things will move quickly. Jumping as he does from one Touchstone to another – Liberty, Voting, Patriotism – his prose becomes heady, searching. Angst, not propositional logic, propels his argument. Unlike Margie C., Robert M.'s enemies are vague and his solutions vaguer.

Sociologist Andrew Perrin has found that people who write about local issues are less inclined to pillory public officials or to use a "superior" tone – findings similar to mine.[44] Perrin suggests that national and local politics exist in separate spheres as a result.[45] He finds local letters to be more respectful, as do I. While the Local reminds people that they live in a specific somewhere, the National sends them on holiday, inviting them to over-indulge – on abstract values, on vitriol – because no one is watching. Naturally, a civil society must attend to both local and national issues, although some scholars find that the new media frequently turn local news into national news.[46] Other scholars worry that small newspapers are more concerned with making grand statements than with being a community asset.[47] Hyper-cosmopolitanism, that is, is not an unalloyed bounty.

City Strength

The twelve cities I examined are highly diverse, but they also have much in common. In Richard Dagger's terms, each is an "independent city" with distinct boundaries and unique political cultures.[48] The University of Chicago's Eric Oliver finds that mid-sized, middle-income cities like these enjoy somewhat higher rates of civic participation. Such cities, says Oliver, "have greater competition for public resources, which stimulates political conflict, and sparks citizen interest in public affairs; homogeneous, poor and affluent cities have less conflict, less citizen engagement, and lower participation rates."[49]

But it is not only economics that drives a city. People's imaginations play a role as well. "It is through the recollections of its people," says Dagger, "that a city comes to be something more than a bewildering agglomeration of streets and buildings and nameless faces. Their memories give it its working identity."[50] Other factors also advance civic health: Citizens' willingness to stay informed and to petition their government plays an especially important role, says economist Stephen Knack, as do their exposure of patronage practices and political malfeasance, their concern for public education, their volunteerism rates, and their participation in "good government" groups.[51] These forces place a check on elite power, build interpersonal trust, create norms of reciprocity, and advance less extreme city initiatives.

In an important series of studies exploring some fifty-five US cities, the University of Minnesota's Wendy Rahn found that political trust was not determined only by citizens' average age, education level, gender balance, or length of residence, but also by soft factors like their newspaper readership, their satisfaction with community life, their possibility of effecting change, their racial harmony, and their perceived economic advancement.[52] Rahn and her colleagues found that residents often "constructed" the same community in different ways depending on their age, ethnicity, and interpersonal experiences. Experiencing a city is thus both an empirical and a psychological event, say Rahn and colleagues: "Some places are safe, others are scary, some are nice, others are hostile, some are clean, and others are dirty because of what people actually do or do not do. But reality isn't everything, for communities are also psychological ideas ... To put it another way, social trust is both 'hardware' and 'software' for such cities.[53]

How a city is imagined, then, has consequences. Consider, for example, how differently just one city – St. Joseph, Missouri – has been framed by its residents at different times:

- *An historic city?* "St. Joseph is as rich in history as the Mother Lode country of California back in the Gold Rush days. Buildings like the old ones here would be considered historical monuments in the Mother Lode country." (William M., *St. Joseph News-Press*, August 17, 1972)
- *An antiquated city?* "In some respects St. Joseph is a bright and growing city. However, in other areas such as open burning we seem archaic. I can hardly believe St. Joseph allowed the burning of trash and yard debris as long as it did." (Sarah P., *St. Joseph News-Press*, May 21, 1980)
- *A dynamic city?* "St. Joseph is growing and needs to continue to grow. Let's not let a local company and 175 of our fellow citizens and their families down by refusing to permit them to build on a tract of land which in the city's own master plan has already been set aside for industrial development." (Bruce R., *St. Joseph News-Press*, November 11, 1972)
- *A timid city?* "I am beginning to believe that St. Joseph is never going to get ahead because everything that is attempted by the city seems to go in reverse. Specifically, I am referring to the upcoming events to be held at the Civic Arena. Why hasn't there been some publicity about these events either on the radio or in the paper?" (Barbara S., *St. Joseph News-Press*, October 5, 1980)

To better understand how location and letter-writing intersect, I rank-ordered the cities on forty different social, economic and historical indices, resulting in three overall groupings as seen in Figure 9.4 (see Appendix D for details): *Robust Cities* (Salinas, Billings, Roanoke, and Provo); *Challenged Cities* (Fall River, Lake Charles, Duluth, St. Joseph, and Wichita Falls); and *Distressed Cities* (Utica, Trenton, and Springfield).[54] Admittedly, these are gross measures and all these cities have had their ups and downs.

How do these quantitative markers relate to a city's manifestations of civic hope? Figure 9.5 provides a hint based on my cache of letters. To be sure, we are dealing with highly abstracted and theoretically uncertain

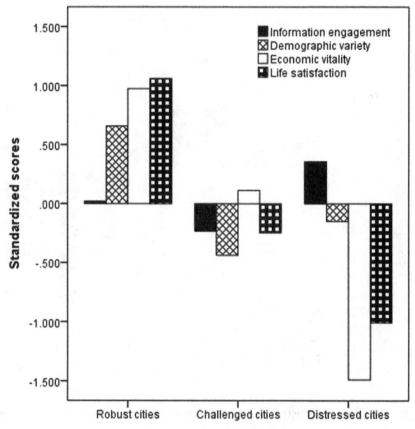

FIGURE 9.4 Comparative Dimensions of City Strength

matters here. Figure 9.5 is based on data spanning a great many years, a great many measures, and a great many letters, thereby affording only a rough estimation of how a city's circumstances affect its citizenry. Quali-fications aside, here are my findings: (1) writers in *Distressed Cities* seem heavily influenced by the difficulties they face; (2) writers in *Robust Cities* have greater civic energy but other issues (building a business, raising a family) suppress their zeal; (3) writers in *Challenged Cities* are the most spirited, drawing, it seems, on extant communal ties.

These are speculative claims, not conclusions, and worthy of further testing. Nevertheless, civic hope seems to be pursued in greater depth in Challenged Cities, where writers get more involved in their arguments (high Author Declarations), acknowledge alternative perspectives (high Oppositional Literacy), draw on storied values and traditions (high

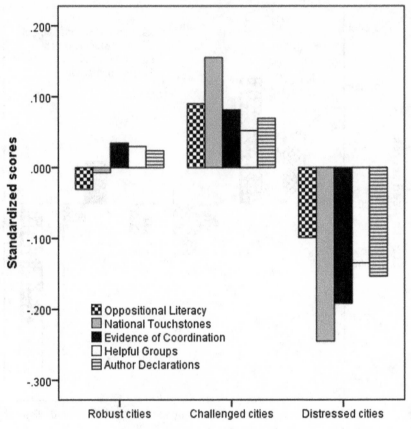

FIGURE 9.5 Letter Writers' Emphases and City Strength

National Touchstones), and reference community resources more frequently (high Helpful Groups and Evidence of Coordination).[55] Naturally, not all writers at all times behave in these ways. Too, letter writers do not speak for everyone living in Challenged communities. Without question, writers in Robust and Distressed Cities also draw on reservoirs of civic hope, but writers in Challenged Cities are bolder. Why?

Two explanations seem possible. As mentioned earlier, Eric Oliver's "conflict model" posits that when city residents are hard pressed – but not over-pressed – they become more competitive, more actively engaged in civic affairs. This is a good description of those living in Challenged Cities. Its writers keep "punching it out" when the going gets tough, drawing on communal energy built up over the years. In contrast, those resources may have waned in Distressed Cities because of economic downturns and social transformations. Alternatively, people living in Robust Cities may be too busy to stay on top of civic and community trends. In Michael Schudson's terms, citizens in Challenged Cities become "active monitors," constantly scanning the landscape. Those living in Robust Cities seem to be "standby monitors," focusing on a narrower set of bottom-line issues. Writers in Distressed Cities act like "defensive monitors," husbanding existing resources and trying to resist becoming too cynical.[56]

Clearly, all of this is conjectural. We do not yet know why civic hope presents itself differently from time to time or from place to place. And despite these differences, all twelve newspapers publish a great many letters each day written by people trying to make a difference. My repeated visits to these cities over the years show that all of them have struggled but that thousands of elected officials and civic-minded residents are working hard to push back the onslaught. The findings presented in Figure 9.5 are tantalizing at best. We need to know more about such matters.

CONCLUSION

This chapter has argued that political campaigns look different when seen through the eyes of letter writers, as do political parties, as does governance in the nation's cities and towns. Other scholars have used public opinion polls, network sociology, and historical archives to examine such matters, but letter writers teach us something new, something different. I find that letters ask us to think harder about political primaries and the transition to the general campaign. Letters also shed light on why incumbent campaigns are noisier than open campaigns and why the former so often leave the electorate in a sour mood. I find that Democratic and Republican letter writers are often alike, an interesting effect since partisan differences have commanded so much attention recently. And what do people say when freed from party orthodoxies? I find that they have a great deal to say, thereby raising new questions about lay politics in the United States.

When 10,000 letters are spread across sixteen presidential elections and examined with so many content categories, there is no end to the stories they can tell. Rather than trace all of them here I have looked for broader trends, finding that local and national politics are discussed quite differently by letter writers. Given the dominance of money and media in national campaigns – and the acrimony they generate – we might well look to the Local for a more salvific brand of politics. We should also ask why citizens in some towns are more politically engaged than those living elsewhere. Civic energy, I find, is not dictated by region or affluence or history alone, but also by shared resolve, a refusal to abandon politics when things become difficult. Some places have more resolve than others and this affects how their citizens talk about things.

I continue to wonder why letters columns are read so avidly. What are people hoping to find there? Do they read letters to feel better about themselves, to prove they are smarter and less weird than the writers? Do they read letters to learn something new or to confirm their existing biases? If the former, why read letters? If the latter, why read letters? Most of the people I have encountered readily admit that they read letters, but when I ask them why they get stumped. Some say they do so to pass the time; some do so out of curiosity. But what are they curious about and, if they want to pass the time, why not play solitaire? As for me, I read letters because the world looks different through the eyes of their authors. They teach me things I have not noticed and make me ask new questions. They have more to teach, in my opinion.

Endnotes

1 "Starner Jones," *Jackson Clarion-Ledger*, June 29, 2009. Accessed at http://clarionledger.newspapers.com/.

2 Ibid.

3 Aidan Orly, "Elite doesn't mean more intelligent," *The Student Life*, April 26, 2013. Accessed at http://tsl.news/opinions/3156/.

4 "Anne Spurzem, Smith College alum writes controversial letter to the editor," *Huffington Post*, February 27, 2012. Accessed at www.huffingtonpost.com/2012/02/24/smith-college-alum-writes-too-many-poor_n_1300279.html.

5 John Ripley, "Colleagues criticize Coffman for writing letter to editor," *BDN Archive: Penobscot/Bangor Daily News*, October 3, 1991. Accessed at http://archive.bangordailynews.com/1991/10/03/colleagues-criticize-coffman-for-writing-letter-to-editor/.

6 Nikki Krize, "Controversial letter to the editor calls for execution of president," WNEP – The News Station, May 28, 2015. Accessed at http://wnep.com/2015/05/28/letter-to-the-editor-reads-controversy/.

7 Thomas Perkins, "Progressive Kristallnacht coming?" *Wall Street Journal*, January 24, 2014. Accessed at www.wsj.com/articles/SB10001424052702304549504579316913982034286.

8 Alanna, "Chris Royse's controversial letter to the editor re. Christmas, abortion," *Moonhowlings: A Place for Civil Debate*, December 8, 2008. Accessed at www.moonhowlings.net/index.php/2008/12/08/chris-royses-letter-to-the-editor/.

9 Michael Nutter, "Speech at the Democratic National Convention," Charlotte, NC, September 7, 2012. Accessed at www.youtube.com/watch?v=VTE8tvzu XUQ.

10 Gil Troy, *See How They Run* (Cambridge: Harvard University Press, 1996) 4.

11 Michael S., *Trenton Times*, August 24, 2012; Ruby C., *Provo Daily Herald*, July 5, 2012; Judith R., *Utica Observer Dispatch*, September 4, 2012.

12 James Campbell, *The American Campaign: U.S. Presidential Campaigns and the National Vote* (College Station: Texas A&M Press, 2000) 100.

13 Kim Fridkin Kahn and Patrick J. Kenney, *The Spectacle of U.S. Senate Campaigns* (Princeton: Princeton University Press, 1999).

14 Richard Nadeau, Andre Blais, Neil Nevitte, and Elisabeth Gidengil, "Elections and Satisfaction with Democracy." Paper presented at the annual convention of the American Political Science Association, September 2000.

15 John Brehm and Wendy Rahn, "Individual-level evidence for the causes and consequences of social capital," *American Journal of Political Science*, 41 (1997), 999–1023.

16 Norman R. Luttbeg and Michael M. Gant, *American Electoral Behavior: 1952-1992* (New York: Peacock, 1994).

17 *Campaign-Focus* for primary season = –0.2795, for general election season = 0.0493; $F[1, 9595] = 60.277$, $p < .000$; *Community-Focus* for primary season = 0.4074, for general election season = –0.0718; $F[1, 9595] = 47.988$, $p < .000$; *Idea-Focus* for Primary season = 0.2267, for general election season = –0.0400; $F[1, 9595] = 87.697$, $p < .000$; *Leader-Focus* for primary season = –0.4648, for general election season = 0.0819; $F[1, 9595] = 67.222$, $p < .000$.

18 David W. Brady, Hahrie Han, and Jeremy C. Pope, "Primary elections and candidate ideology: out of step with the primary electorate," *Legislative Studies Quarterly*, 32(1) (2007), 79–105.

19 Whether or not presidential primary voters really are more extreme is still an open question. Barbara Norrander argues, for example, that rather than being grossly unrepresentative of the electorate, primary voters are rather like general election voters who don't vote in the primaries. See "Ideological representativeness of presidential primary voters," *American Journal of Political Science*, 33(3) (1989), 570–87.

20 See, for example, Nancy B. Lowden, Peter A. Andersen, David M. Dozier, and Martha M. Lauzen, "Media use in the primary election: a secondary medium model," *Communication Research*, 21(3) (1994), 293–304; David Tewksbury, "Exposure to the newer media in a presidential primary campaign," *Political Communication*, 23(3) (2006), 313–32.

21 For more on this latter point see Robert S. Erikson and Christopher Wlezien, *The Timeline of Presidential Elections: How Campaigns Do (and Do Not) Matter* (Chicago: University of Chicago Press, 2012).

22 *Agents of Hope* for open campaigns = 0.0598, for incumbent campaigns = –0.0626; $F[1, 6914] = 24.986$, $p < .000$; *Evidence of Coordination* for open campaigns = 0.0697, for incumbent campaigns = –0.1358; $F[1, 6914] = 73.884$, $p < .000$; *Campaign Advice* for open campaigns = 0.0113, for incumbent campaigns = –0.1371; $F[1, 6914] = 32.628$, $p < .000$; *Negative Leadership Traits* for open campaigns = –0.0481, for incumbent campaigns =

0.0631; F [1, 6914] = 20.674, p < .000; *Evidence of Disunity* for open campaigns = 0.0083, for incumbent campaigns = 0.2051; F [1, 6914] = 55.246, p < .000; *Campaign Complaints* for open campaigns = −0.0057, for incumbent campaigns = 0.1469; F [1, 6914] = 35.055, p < .000.

23 David R. Mayhew, "Incumbency advantage in U.S. presidential elections: the historical record," *Political Science Quarterly*, 123(2) (2008), 201–28; Herbert F. Weisberg, "Partisanship and incumbency in presidential elections," *Political Behavior*, 24(4) (2002), 339–61.

24 For more on the issue of continuity see James E. Campbell, "The miserable presidential election of 2012: a first party-term incumbent survives," *The Forum*, 10(4) (2012), 25.

25 See Jamie Carson, Joel Sievert, and Ryan Williamson, "Assessing the rise and development of the incumbency advantage in Congress." Paper presented at the Congress and History Conference held at Vanderbilt University, May 22–23, 2015; Steven D. Levitt and Catherine D. Wolfram, "Decomposing the sources of incumbency advantage in the U.S. House," *Legislative Studies Quarterly*, 22(1) (1997), 45–60; and Stephen Ansolabehere and James M. Snyder Jr., "Rules, politics, and policy," *Election Law Journal*, 1(3) (2004), 315–38.

26 Erickson and Wlezien figure that "as the campaign progresses over the timeline, voters behave less like Independents and more like committed partisans," with all but 5 percent of them having made up their minds by late September. See Erickson and Wlezien, *The Timeline of Presidential Elections*, 142, 162.

27 Christian Leuprecht and David Skillicorn, "Incumbency effects in U.S. presidential campaigns: language patterns matter," *Electoral Studies*, May 2016. Accessed at www.researchgate.net/publication/303917215_Incumbency_effects_in_US_presidential_campaigns_Language_patterns_matter.

28 For more on the reasons for party asymmetry see Matt Grossman and David A. Hopkins, "Ideological Republicans and group interest Democrats: the asymmetry of American party politics," *Perspectives on Politics*, 13(1) (2015), 119–39.

29 Wendy M. Rahn, "The role of partisan stereotypes in information processing about political candidates," *American Journal of Political Science*, 37(2) (1993), 472–96.

30 Marc Hooghe and Jennifer Oser, "Partisan identity, civic associations and the development of trust in the United States: an analysis of the General Social Survey, 1972–2012." Paper presented at the annual meeting of the Midwest Political Science Association, Chicago, April 2014.

31 Jonathan McDonald Ladd, "The role of media distrust in partisan voting," *Political Behavior*, 32 (2010), 567–85.

32 Jesse H. Rhodes and Zachary Albert, "The transformation of partisan rhetoric in presidential campaigns, 1952–2012: partisan polarization and the rise of bipartisan posturing among Democratic candidates." Paper presented at the annual meeting of the Midwest Political Science Association, Chicago, April 2015.

33 Darren Schreiber, Greg Fonzo, Alan N. Simmons, Christopher T. Dawes, Taru Flagan, James H. Fowler, and Martin P. Paulus, "Red brain, blue brain: evaluative processes differ in Democrats and Republicans," *PLoS ONE*, 8(2)

(February 13, 2013). Accessed at http://journals.plos.org/plosone/article?id= 10.1371/journal.pone.0052970.

34 Jeffrey M Stonecash and Mark D. Brewer, *Dynamics of American Political Parties* (New York: Cambridge University Press, 2009), pp. 208–9.

35 Jennifer Agiesta, "Poll: political independents outweigh partisans," *Huffington Post*, June 4, 2012. Accessed at www.huffingtonpost.com/huff-wires/ 20120604/us-independent-voters-poll/.

36 Susan Page and Kendall Breitman, "Divided we still stand – and getting used to it: long on dissatisfaction, divided about solutions," *USA Today*, March 23, 2014. Accessed at www.usatoday.com/story/news/politics/2014/03/23/con gress-divided-poll/6792585/.

37 *Positive Leadership Traits* for Democrats = 0.1956, for Republicans = 0.0391; $F [1, 5603] = 27.275$, $p < .000$; *Campaign Complaints* for Democrats = 0.0396, for Republicans = -0.0576; $F [1, 5603] = 15.560$, $p < .000$; *Unhelpful Groups* for Democrats = -0.0787, for Republicans = 0.0128; $F [1, 5603] = 17.782$, $p < .000$; *Campaign Advice* for Democrats = -0.0351, for Republicans = 0.0534; $F [1, 5603] = 13.125$, $p < .000$.

38 *Negative Leadership Traits* for Major Party = 0.1795, for Minor Party = -0.1926, for No Party = -0.2548; $F [2, 9347] = 212.517$, $p < .000$; *Positive Leadership Traits* for Major Party = 0.1180, for Minor Party = 0.0371, for No Party = -0.1854; $F [2, 9347] = 99.415$, $p < .000$; *Evidence of Disunity* for Major Party = 0.1271, for Minor Party = -0.2475, for No Party = -0.2800; $F [2, 9347] = 122.481$, $p < .000$; *Agents of Decline* for Major Party = 0.2079, for Minor Party = -0.1926, for No Party = -0.2548; $F [2, 9347] = 276.747$, $p < .000$.

39 The classic meditation on these matters is Eric Hoffer's *The True Believer: Thoughts on the Nature of Mass Movements* (New York: Harper and Row, 1951). See also Roderick P. Hart, "The rhetoric of the true believer," *Communication Monographs*, 38(4) (1971), 249–61.

40 *Evidence of Coordination* for Major Party = -0.0174, for Minor Party = 0.2811, for No Party = 0.0202; $F [2, 9347] = 15.275$, $p < .000$; *Agents of Hope* for Major Party = 0.0799, for Minor Party = 0.4522, for No Party = -0.1552; $F [2, 9347] = 95.383$, $p < .000$.

41 Matthew Dickinson, "No, America's not divided: what everyone gets wrong about political polarization," *Politico Magazine*, June 20, 2014. Accessed at www.politico.com/magazine/story/2014/06/no-americas-not-divided-108119#ixzz4CRAjabNC.

42 For more on this matter of party convergence see Roderick P. Hart, Jay P. Childers, and Colene J. Lind, *Political Tone: How Leaders Talk and Why* (Chicago: University of Chicago Press, 2013), pp. 59–88; Quentin Kidd, "The real (lack of) difference between Republicans and Democrats: a computer word score analysis of party platforms, 1996–2004," *PS: Political Science & Politics*, 41(3) (July 2008), 519–25.

43 *Agents of Hope* for National Policy = -0.1391, for Local Issues = 0.0971; $F [1, 3275] = 42.723$, $p < .000$; *Voter Perceptions* for National Policy = -0.2135, for Local Issues = 0.0742; $F [1, 3275] = 54.262$, $p < .000$; *Oppositional Literacy* for National Policy = -0.1173, for Local Issues = 0.1667; $F [1, 3275] = 63.164$, $p < .000$; *National Touchstones* for National Policy = 0.2319, for

Local Issues = −0.1318; F [1, 3275] = 80.779, p < .000; *Unhelpful Groups* for National Policy = 0.2991, for Local Issues = −0.1055; F [1, 3275] = 102.337, p < .000; *Evidence of Disunity* for National Policy = 0.0944, for Local Issues = −0.2327; F [1, 3275] = 76.551, p < .000.

44 Andrew J. Perrin, "Since this is the editorial section I intend to express my opinion," *The Communication Review*, 19(1) (2016), 55–76.

45 Andrew J. Perrin and Stephen Vaisey. "Parallel public spheres: distance and discourse in letter to the editor," *American Journal of Sociology*, 114 (2008), 785.

46 Rasmus L. Nielsen, "Local newspapers as keystone media: the increased importance of diminished newspapers for local political information environments," in R. K. Nielsen (ed.), *Local Journalism: The Decline of Newspapers and the Rise of Digital Media* (London: Tauris & Co., 2015), pp. 51–72.

47 Marcus Funk, "Imagined commodities? Analyzing local identity and place in American community newspaper website banners," *New Media & Society*, 5 (2012), 584.

48 Richard Dagger, "Metropolis, memory and citizenship," *American Political Science Review*, 25 (1981), 725.

49 J. Eric Oliver, "The effects of metropolitan economic segregation on local civic participation," *American Journal of Political Science*, 43 (1999), 198.

50 Dagger, "Metropolis," 729.

51 Stephen Knack, "Social capital and the quality of government: evidence from the States," *American Journal of Political Science*, 46(4) (2002), 772–85.

52 Wendy Rahn and Thomas J. Rudolph, "A tale of political trust in American cities," *Public Opinion Quarterly*, 69(4) (2005), 530–60. Tom W. Rice and Alexander F. Sumberg also find that newspaper readership is of pivotal importance in community life. See "Civic culture and government performance in the American States," *Publius: The Journal of Federalism*, 27(1) (1997), 99–114.

53 Wendy M. Rahn, Kwang Suk Yoon, Michael Garet, Steven Lipson, and Katherine Loflin, "Geographies of trust," *American Behavioral Scientist*, 52 (12) (2009), 1649.

54 To produce the master scores, rank orders for individual variables were calculated, directionally sorted, standardized, and combined as follows: *Information Engagement* (college graduates, educational workers, library circulation, television centrality, homes with television, homes with cable, newspaper subscriptions, newspaper circulation per capita, letters to the editor written, high school graduates); *Demographic Variety* (ethnic diversity, multiple languages spoken, religious dominance, new US arrivals, religious openmindedness, white dominance, children under eighteen, people over sixty-five, foreign-born citizens, MSA population rank); *Economic Vitality* (jobs available, new home construction, houses for sale, family income, homes in good repair, retail sales, percent poverty, financial workers, work satisfaction scores, population differentials); *Life Satisfaction* (crime rate, length of commute, hospital admissions, hospital workers, well-being score, air quality, happiness rank, emotional satisfaction rank, ease-of-life score, cost of living).

55 *Evidence of Coordination* for Robust Cities = 0.0344, for Challenged Cities = 0.0814, for Distressed Cities = −0.1916; F [2, 9594] = 56.008, p < .000;

Occupational Literacy for Robust Cities = −0.0305, for Challenged Cities = 0.0899, for Distressed Cities = −0.0987; F [2, 9594] = 27.698, p < .000; *National Touchstones* for Robust Cities = −0.0070, for Challenged Cities = 0.1549, for Distressed Cities = −0.2451; F [2, 9594] = 114.047, p < .000; *Helpful Groups* for Robust Cities = 0.0295, for Challenged Cities = 0.0519, for Distressed Cities = −0.1348; F [2, 9594] = 27.004, p < .000; *Author Declarations* for Robust Cities = 0.0235, for Challenged Cities = 0.0692, for Distressed Cities = −0.1535; F [2, 9594] = 36.413, p < .000.

56 For more on monitorial citizens see Michael Schudson, *The Good Citizen: A History of American Civic Life* (New York: Free Press, 1998).

PART IV

THE FUTURE OF CIVIC HOPE

IO

Sustaining a Culture of Argument

Abraham Lincoln wrote the most famous letter to the editor in US history. He did so in August of 1862, with a draft of the Emancipation Proclamation lying in his desk drawer. Mr. Lincoln wrote his letter to Horace Greeley, editor of the influential *New York Tribune*, in response to an editorial Greeley had written implying that the Lincoln administration was adrift conceptually and politically. Mr. Lincoln's letter went like this:

I have just read yours of the 19th addressed to myself through the New-York Tribune. If there be in it any statements, or assumptions of fact, which I may know to be erroneous, I do not, now and here, controvert them. If there be in it any inferences which I may believe to be falsely drawn, I do not now and here, argue against them. If there be perceptable in it an impatient and dictatorial tone, I waive it in deference to an old friend, whose heart I have always supposed to be right.

As to the policy I "seem to be pursuing" as you say, I have not meant to leave any one in doubt.

I would save the Union. I would save it the shortest way under the Constitution. The sooner the national authority can be restored; the nearer the Union will be "the Union as it was." If there be those who would not save the Union, unless they could at the same time save slavery, I do not agree with them. If there be those who would not save the Union unless they could at the same time destroy slavery, I do not agree with them. My paramount object in this struggle is to save the Union, and is not either to save or to destroy slavery. If I could save the Union without freeing any slave I would do it, and if I could save it by freeing all the slaves I would do it; and if I could save it by freeing some and leaving others alone I would also do that. What I do about slavery, and the colored race, I do because I believe it helps to save the Union; and what I forbear, I forbear because I do not believe it would help to save the Union. I shall do less whenever I shall believe what I am doing hurts the cause, and I shall do more whenever I shall believe doing more will help the cause. I shall try to correct errors when shown to be errors; and I shall adopt new views so fast as they shall appear to be true views.

I have here stated my purpose according to my view of official duty; and I intend no modification of my oft-expressed personal wish that all men every where could be free.[1]

Lincoln's letter is respectful and diplomatic but leaves no doubt where he stands on the two most pressing issues of the day – the union's preservation and the institution of slavery. Lincoln's letter has no false buoyancy and yet it is filled with the sort of civic hope discussed in this book. His letter is a paean to the National Touchstones of human freedom and constitutional rights. Lest anyone doubt Lincoln's resolve, each sentence contains an Author Declaration, ensuring that this most public of all documents will be seen by others as deeply personal. Lincoln speaks directly to the Evidence of Disunity surrounding the issue of slavery and his statements of Oppositional Literacy ("if there be those who would not save the Union...") make it clear that he knows he leads a divided nation.

The letter is also interesting for what it does *not* contain. No easy solutions are proposed, no Agents of Hope identified, no staid Political Memories drawn upon. Equally, no interpersonal blame is cast even though Lincoln surely had a great many Unhelpful Groups in mind when writing his letter. There is also no sociology here; what citizens are currently doing or not doing goes unmentioned by him. Lincoln eschews the hoary trick of putting his ideas in the people's mouths (via Voter Perceptions) and he offers no cheery Civic Forecasts either. There is no falseness in Lincoln's letter. It is a tortured document. And yet there is a glimmer of hope: Despite the divisions in the nation – because of the divisions in the nation – its leader has taken a stand.

Hope is such a happy word by itself, bringing to mind the birth of a child, the first day of kindergarten, high school graduation. We find *hope* again at weddings, on the first day of the job, at the retirement party. But something dark, something foreboding, happens when the words *civic* and *hope* are coupled. The *civic* instantly brings to mind other people's odd personalities, strange belief systems, and incessant demands. The *civic* reminds us of strangers required to share the same physical space and of their conflicts over limited resources.

Former New York governor Mario Cuomo has said that politicians campaign in poetry and govern in prose, which is another way of saying that *civic hope* is a contradiction in terms. The *civic*, with its rules and regulations, its constant surveillance, and its interest groups, conflicts with *hope*'s idyllic sensibility. The *civic* requires learning, listening, bargaining, compromising, and the resiliency needed to do it all over again. *Hope*, that which poet Emily Dickinson terms "the thing with feathers that perches in the soul," seems tawdry when the *civic* is appended to it. Civic hope is constantly being lost, requiring that it constantly be found anew.

My argument is that American democracy is shot through with imperfections, one of which is that power be both centralized and distributed, resulting in endless disputes between local and national government. Enforceable laws often vary from region to region – pot is acceptable in Colorado; abortion rights are abridged in Mississippi. Political leadership is also bewildering. Becoming the CEO of General Motors requires a fifty-page resume but Donald Trump can run for president fortified only with gumption. Some citizens actively participate in local governance while others live to be ninety without ever casting a ballot. Restrictive laws can change tomorrow or remain unaltered for three hundred years. Democracy – an impossible thing.

And yet democracies function, and yet democracies thrive. How? Why? I have argued here that US democracy is preserved by its laws and institutions, by its leaders and social structures, by its military and economic might, but also by its people's willingness to argue with one another endlessly. I have used letter writers to show what that looks like. While civic hope may seem a foggy brand of idealism, letter writers bring it to life each day, demonstrating that starting an argument and keeping it going is the nation's best strategy for sustainability. The cure for politics is more politics.

Those who write letters to the editor are a distinctive lot – true individuals, unremittingly themselves. They may seem an odd choice to represent the people-at-large, but where else could one turn to find them? Most people, after all, exit their lives without leaving an historical trace except in the hearts of their loved ones. Finding a *record* of the people's voice is therefore hard, so I sought out letter writers for practical reasons. But I was also attracted to them because they are such superb strugglers. Some of them peddle a mean brand of politics and some of them cling to ancient biases and impossible schemes. Collectively, though, they nudge democracy forward. They are the archangels of civic hope.

This book has covered considerable territory, so this chapter will offer a series of meditations on the journey taken. We will begin by reprising the book's key findings, including reflections on the nature of letter writers and letter-writing. I will then ask two questions: (1) What qualities must a person have to become a credible witness to the nation? and (2)

What conveyances can best sustain democratic ideas? Finally, I will inquire into the future of civic hope.

HOPE'S STORY

Psychologist Martin Seligman reports that 46,000 scholarly articles have been published on depression, compared to only 400 on joy.[2] Things are no happier when it comes to politics. In laying out potential sources of hope, for example, scholar Patrick Shade mentions history and tradition, education, popular narratives, voluntary communities, and even new technologies, but he says little about politics.[3] Hope must reckon with life's unpredictability, says philosopher Judith Andre, so it requires a lot of work.[4] The best way to avoid too much hope, says Luc Bovens, is to balance it off with fear.[5] Forget the hazy future, says literary theorist Terry Eagleton; for there to be genuine hope "the future must be anchored in the present."[6] Scholars are rarely lyrical when discussing hope.

Perhaps I should be ashamed to admit it, but I have fallen in love with letter writers. I love their earnestness and relentlessness. I love their persnicketiness and their love of dialectic. I love their off-the-shoulder solutions to complex problems and I love the darkness of their imaginations. I love how they care for their communities and how they expose local villains. I love their respect for newspapers and their distrust of newspaper editors. I love their willingness to step into the curveball.

Graeme Turner says that there has been a "demotic turn" in recent years, with ordinary people gaining visibility via reality TV, online blogs, talk radio, etc. Such visibility is not without its detriments, however, as people are commodified and turned into a form of "white trash celebrity" that makes them neither respected nor influential.[7] My letter writers are not thrust into the limelight in these ways. That makes them especially interesting because they are goaded by ideas, not by celebrity. Unless a nation can produce "promiscuous" political sites where people can discuss dissonant ideas, says Toby Miller, it cannot generate the democratic energy needed to make popular decisions popular.[8]

The letters column is one such site and, by its very existence, it makes these declarations: (1) ordinary people are important; (2) all ideas are contestable; (3) opinions are as least as important as facts; (4) your opinion must be balanced by the opinions of others; and (5) the sponsoring newspaper subscribes to all of the foregoing. The result is what Morris Janowitz has called the "democratization of expertise."[9] "We 'think' with the objects we use," says André Nusselder, "and our media 'teach us how to desire' as well."[10] Letters columns teach us the desires of democracy.

The letter writers I investigated cannot tell us everything, but they can tell us much. In Chapter 6 I reported that letters are reliably pugnacious, sending out alarms and holding politicians' feet to the fire. At the same time, they raise the nation's values aloft, reminding readers who is saint and who is sinner. Nobody asked them to perform these routines, but they do so instinctively. That can be nettlesome for readers who feel little need of moral cleansing, but the writers provide an offset: a steady stream of prognostications. Do readers actually believe these predictions? Probably not, but guesswork is hard to resist, since all of us want to know that which we cannot know – what will happen next. Writers and readers collude in these ways, and do so with impressive regularity.

In prior research I found that letter writers were consistently more optimistic than members of the press, but more pessimistic than national politicians. Writers have maintained this middle ground from 1948 to the present, and that may explain why letters columns are read so avidly. Readers find in them a place devoid of politicians' bloviations and reporters' attractions to the abyss. But, as reported in Chapter 7, letters are also irritating, with their authors implying that they have special knowledge and special experiences. Writers puff up their chests in these ways even as they offer running commentaries on their fellow citizens, showing where they have failed and where they have met the mark. Perversely enough, these self-indulgences seem to draw readers in, in part because they are low-level irritations and in part because they let readers feel superior to the writers.

As seen in Chapter 8, letters to the editor have changed over the years in two concerning ways. For one thing, writers' willingness to discuss National Touchstones – the nation's core beliefs – has diminished. They have become analytical instead, framing the country's leaders as tacticians rather than moral leaders. Equally worrisome is a decline in Oppositional Literacy. Today's writers are either less able or less willing to discuss others' perspectives. These findings track what scholars are learning about political polarization and partisans' abandonment of the middle ground. In short, modernity has taken its toll on letter writing. Recent letters are colder and more self-satisfied than their predecessors.

Chapter 9 reported several main differences in the letters. For one thing, I found that letters written during primaries differed from those penned during the general election. Writers wrestle with ideas during the primary, paying special attention to their local implications. Then things become personal. Candidates take center stage in the general election, with writers sounding more like handicappers than voters, more like psychologists than philosophers. Another surprising finding was that Democratic and Republican writers were more alike than different when compared to those endorsing third party candidates or declaring no party affiliation. Third party supporters followed an especially simple formula: A vast conspiracy is engulfing the nation and only Candidate X can stave it off. Ds and Rs opt for broader arguments, varying only in the conclusions they draw. These structural similarities might have been missed had not party endorsers been compared to those with narrower political tastes.

When starting this project, I took pains to gather letters from a variety of US cities. The cities I chose were middle-class, middle-of-the-road places distinguished by comparatively little. Because the editors in these towns published virtually every letter submitted to them, my collection resulted in a breadth of perspectives. A different story could be told about each of these cities but I settled for a bigger picture. I found, for example, that writers focusing on local issues were more hopeful than those discussing national policy – a finding that parallels the "incumbency lock" whereby national candidates are savaged and individual members of Congress are returned to Washington regularly. I also found that local conditions affect the kinds of letters written, with Challenged Cities generating more civic hope than Robust or Distressed Cities, suggesting a "Goldilocks effect" in which civic hope buoys up communities facing significant, but not overwhelming, obstacles.

The story of civic hope told in this book is but one of many that might be told. I focused on letters to the editor because they existed "in the wild." Nobody asked their authors to write their letters and nobody supervised their doing so. They wrote on their own timetables, discussing whatever topics interested them. They did so for reasons of their own making, some of which they disclosed and some of which they did not.

But letters to the editor can only tell us so much. It would be interesting to learn, for example, how civic hope might be manifested in James Fishkin's deliberative opinion polls or in Ned Crosby's citizen juries or in the Kettering Foundation's National Issues Forums.[11] Civic hope might look different in these larger, face-to-face meetings. Whatever the location, we must learn more about the people's voice. As Howard Zinn has argued, things look different when the Constitution is examined from the standpoint of the African-American slave, or when the biography of Andrew Jackson is written from a Cherokee perspective, or when industrialization is linked to the lives of young women working in the Lowell textile mills. In writing a people's history, says Zinn, "we must not accept the memory of states as our own."[12] For similar reasons, we must learn more about how civic hope is managed at the grassroots level.

HOPE'S WITNESSES

One of the major breakthroughs in modern science has been the discovery of dependable biomarkers – chemical traces, organic features, or even geological formations that "point toward" normal or pathological conditions. Considerable research is now being done to identify molecules, acids, tissue properties, etc. that signal abnormalities in the human body, in plants and animals, and in the environment. Some biochemical oddities are just that – oddities of nature – while others serve as early warning signs of danger.

This book has treated letters to the editor as just such pointers, but is my faith in them justified? The people who write these letters are different from others, after all, in that they care more about their communities and follow politics more closely. They are also not shy, constantly looking for a chance to have their say. Some writers make hurtful statements while others over-react to every small thing. Some draw crazy inferences from facts and others construct facts out of whole cloth. Some writers find perdition everywhere.

Letter writers are also constrained by their demography. As reported in Chapter 4, they are a bit older than their neighbors and are more likely to be male than female, to have lived in town longer, to care more about governance, and to be overwhelmingly Anglo. My surveys show, however, that newspaper readers see writers as mostly like themselves. Analysis of the letters also calls into question stereotypes of writers. While writers tend to be older citizens, they discuss the future four times more often than the past. They are also not ego-obsessed, their letters containing three times as many references to the citizenry as to themselves. Writers are not especially prideful, as seen by their low levels of political efficacy. Writers are not sure they can change things, but they must try.

While letter writers are not truly "representative" of the nation's voters, they are nonetheless ordinary. They have ordinary jobs in ordinary towns and they write ordinary letters published in ordinary newspapers. For the most part, they address ordinary topics and make ordinary arguments and, after shuffling off that mortal coil, they are replaced by younger, still ordinary, letter writers. For all of these reasons, letter writers are good witnesses to the polity. While public opinion surveys are also informative, they are largely silent about *why* people feel what they feel. Letter writers, in contrast, are never silent.

In a sense, letter writers are Shakespearean. Shakespeare, after all, was not a practicing social scientist advantaged by a toolkit of charts and indices. And yet he opened up Elizabethan England to us in profound ways, treating small things – a courtier's laugh, an old man's pride, a young Dane's desires – as markers of some broad social condition. Shakespeare was a fine witness because he did so much with so little. Letter writers, too, specialize in small things – an unkempt city park, a belligerent policeman – using them to tell a larger story of declining values, a put-upon citizenry. Like Shakespeare, they take literary license when doing so, but their lived, local experience gives them a kind of authority that even Shakespeare might envy.

Any credible witness, of course, must be able to get beyond themselves to report things truly. Can letter writers do that? They can indeed. To identify the topics discussed in the letters, I conducted a series of word searches (see Appendix F for details), finding that the writers reacted promptly to new issues, with the Communist menace peaking in the 1950s/1960s and declining steadily thereafter, and with civil rights rising in prominence in the 1960s/1970s and then trailing off. Similarly, letters focused on agricultural matters were common in the1950s but quickly disappeared, a fate also suffered by industrial manufacturing after the 1970s.

In contrast, other topics rose without stopping once they arrived on the scene: women's rights, right to life, and elder care got their starts in the 1960s and have not abated since, a trend also seen with environmental concerns and gay rights beginning in the 1970s. In other words, even white, middle-aged, small-town writers have wrestled vigorously with issues facing people quite unlike themselves and they continue to do so.

The letters also point up thoughts adawning, drawing attention to matters that will later generate widespread public concern. Letters written in 2004, for example, showed sudden anxiety about illegal immigration, a matter that Donald Trump would exploit a decade later. Interest in the space program had waned in the 1970s and 1980s but, oddly enough, popped up again in the late 1990s, perhaps suggesting a new constituency for greater scientific exploration. Religious beliefs, in contrast, have risen and fallen rhythmically over time, identifying an issue that excites some and irks others, but that never subsides for long. Drug addiction, a major concern in the 1970s and 1980s, suddenly dropped off the radar after 1996. From a progressive vantage point, its lower profile today may indicate a new willingness to decriminalize certain drugs. On the other (more conservative) hand, it may signal an electorate grown disgusted with the matter.

Despite their quirks, despite their animadversions, then, letter writers reveal themselves to be tribunes of the people when their letters are read carefully. But letter writers are not the only option for this. Markets, not letters, are the voice of the people, declares economist Steven Horwitz.[13] Political and corporate elites drown out citizens and, de facto, become the people's voice, says political scientist V. O. Key.[14] The voice of the people is a pure construction of the mass media, argue journalism scholars Matt Carlson and Eran Ben-Porath.[15] If you want to find the voice of the people, say Scott Wright and Todd Graham, look to convivial gathering spots where people go to enjoy themselves and forget about weighty matters.[16] The voice of the people, says William Tecumseh Sherman, is the voice of humbug!

With all due respect to the good General, I disagree. So do the people of Duluth, Minnesota and Roanoke, Virginia. They read letter columns each day and, to them, the letter writers sound like people they know. This is not to say that such letters always have "recommending force," for letter writers are trapped in their own skins and can only see what they can see. This is a restriction, but not a fatal one.

HOPE'S CONVEYANCES

This book began with two premises: (1) that letters to the editor reflect the relative depth of civic hope in a community, and (2) that letters written in small cities are especially revealing. The locations I chose were not garden spots but they had long-standing newspapers and a phalanx of local letter writers. Although Peter Dahlgren says that the modern public sphere has a "fluid and sprawling quality" to it, things become stickier and more restrictive in small cities.[17] The case can be made that the attitudes I studied were provincial, but calling someone provincial only says that they live in some province, a condition everyone shares.

The cities I studied were similar to a hundred others of their size in the United States and their overall demography compares fairly well to the nation as a whole. While the cities were indeed small (75,000 people on average), they were bountiful. Two Supreme Court justices (Samuel Alito and Antonin Scalia) were born in Trenton. Broadcasters George Stephanopolous and Vern Lundquist started in Fall River and Duluth, respectively. Roanoke and Provo produced two Nobel scientists (John Mather and Paul Boyer). Lake Charles gave birth to famed heart surgeon Michael

DeBakey, Utica to national pollster John Zogby, and Salinas, famously, to novelist John Steinbeck. Pop star Eminem was born in St. Joseph, Broadway's Tommy Tune hails from Wichita Falls, ten-time Grammy winner John Legend is from Springfield, and rock philosopher Bob Dylan got his start in Duluth. To the best of my knowledge, none of these notables wrote a letter to the editor of the local paper.

Karin Wahl-Jorgensen reports that people generally believe that "politicians have no access to their ideas," but newspapers work diligently to change that.[18] Unfortunately, newspapers are facing hard times because of economic and technological disruptions. Scholar Joshua Darr reports, for example, that educated Americans are switching to national newspapers for their news and that declining advertising revenues are making it difficult for newspapers to cover local politics adequately.[19] Letters to the editor constitute a particularly good site, say Susana Sotillo and Dana Starace-Nastasi, to "detect the presence of emerging discourses," but that becomes tougher when newspapers are hard pressed.[20]

For civic hope to flourish, it needs a conveyance that is (1) dialogical, (2) continuous, (3) pluralistic, (4) flexible, and (5) anticipatory of change – qualities attendant to any good letters to the editor column. But what happens when newspapers come a cropper, when editorial page staffers are cut and the news hole shrinks? What happens to civic hope when newspapers respond excessively to the "logic of the market" or "the logic of the occupation" by sidelining citizens' voices?[21] Traditionally, letter writers have served the newspapers that serves them, acting as newsgatherers, guardians of newspaper quality, and community pulsetakers.[22] When newspapers face hard times, then, everyone suffers.

Digital optimists urge us not to worry. By becoming Web-based, they say, newspapers will offer writers greater visibility as well as real participation – immediate, active, continuous participation.[23] According to scholars, "incidental learning" occurs in online forums, inadvertently exposing people to different ideas.[24] In addition, news organizations confer their own status on participants when agreeing to publish their thoughts.

When everyone becomes their own reporters, however, separating fact from fiction becomes harder and an era of "fake news" dawns. Freelance journalist and internet activist Josh Wolf has crafted an interesting description of what newspapers looks like when the world turns digital:

Imagine if a newspaper white-washed the side of its building every morning and encouraged strangers to tag it with their response to the day's news. Now imagine that printed in each edition of this paper is a photo of that wall just before it was painted over again. Although the experiment might yield interesting results, most of the messages on the wall would probably do little to contribute to the conversation about the news of the day and much of it would be little more than graffiti.[25]

The solution to Wolf's concern is ensuring that online comments are moderated by the sponsoring newspaper, but therein lies a problem – in fact, several of them. The editors I interviewed detest reading, never mind overseeing, the comment columns. They hate the sulfurous remarks they are forced to read but they hate the commenters' anonymity even more. While some editors see comment columns "as an effective way to engage readers and drive people to online content, others find it disgraceful to give misinformed, ignorant, and sometimes blatantly inflammatory opinion a public stage."[26]

News organizations have adopted a variety of strategies for handling online comments, with some carefully monitoring them while others shuttle them off to Facebook sites. Still others "wait for complaints from readers before considering removing a comment or a whole thread."[27] Other organizations make up rules on the fly. The *Minneapolis Star*, for example, automatically excludes comments on "crime, Muslims, suicides, homosexuals and race."[28] Progressives decry such a priori censorship, asking how civic hope can thrive when some voices are automatically excluded. But diversity cuts both ways. Summer Harlow has found, for example, that stories mentioning race spike the number of [negative] anonymous comments which, ipso facto, caused "more minorities to lose faith in newspapers."[29] Political scientists Jason Gainous and Kevin Wagner make an even larger claim, concluding that "the Internet is a major contributor to the polarized climate in the United States today."[30]

I began gathering letters to the editor for this study over twenty years ago, when the Web was a young and awkward thing. It is now older, more sophisticated, and infinitely more capacious. The core concepts of this study – that place-based opinions are of special importance and that civic hope thrives best in local communities – have been undercut by a medium that has turned "neighborhood" into a theoretical construct. As a result, there are now questions galore: Can people stay in touch with one another in an era of distantiation and information overload? Will news organizations continue to house readers' impassioned discussions? With "place" now being radically reconfigured, can cities and towns, states and nations, find practical ways of maintaining community bonds? Will candidates for office be able to draw on shared Political Memories and National Touchstones in an era of constant change, of constant cultural replacement? Will citizens feel safe sharing their opinions with one another when The Trolls move to town? Civic hope will continue to need multiple conveyances. What will they be?

HOPE'S FUTURE

Letters to the editor are not the only repositories of civic hope. Elected leaders work each day to reinforce core beliefs and explain their contemporary implications. Schools teach the fundaments of self-governance to the nation's children while youth groups (Girl Scouts, Future Farmers of America, the YMCA, etc.) follow up with more tailored messages. Fraternal and religious groups, business and civic associations, do their parts as well. Key democratic refrains are sounded during the nation's holidays, replete with fireworks and bunting. The "hegemonic themes" of the Republic are also woven into popular music, into news broadcasts, and into the storylines of TV sitcoms and Hollywood blockbusters. In the United States, one cannot escape the voice of democracy.

Given these reinforcements, will letters to the editor persist? Will they be needed? I believe they will, for two reasons: (1) the American people have always had fundamental disagreements with one another, and (2) they cannot keep quiet. Both conditions have existed since the nation's founding and seem unlikely to change. Here is one reason why:

> I would like to say that I think everything George Bush stands for is dirt. He's got the poor people starving and he's taking money out of their pockets. I have two sisters with two young boys. They are not making it. Get Bill Clinton in there. If we had more people fighting for Clinton than getting Bush out, I think we would stand a chance.
>
> (Darla T., *Salinas Californian*, October 8, 1992)

Somehow, through some medium, the Darla T.'s of the world will persist. Because they are Americans, they will link basic values (in this case, economic equality) to pragmatic solutions (putting Bill Clinton in office) and do so in short, crisp sentences. At some point in the future, friends may try to convince Darla T.'s granddaughter that she has been deluded by her culture's grand narratives, that she will never control the means of production, and that she should abandon politics as a result. But if she is anything like her grandmother, she will decry the machinations of George P. Bush and vote for Chelsea Clinton anyway.

Civic hope can never rest easy, however. "Much of what passes for public debate," says Karin Wahl-Jorgensen, "is actually intolerant, narrow-minded, uncivil, and sometimes downright hateful."[31] Until now, newspapers have been able to enforce modes of civility but what will happen if the Wild West continues to invade the World Wide Web? Will online forums drive people out of the public square, replacing their sense of agency with a hard and bitter cynicism? What will nurture local attachments in a nation constantly on the move? What will help Americans stay connected to their storied past? What will encourage them to think beyond the moment, to give new and untested policies a chance?

When operating at their best, letter writers have assumed many of the foregoing duties. But they have not always been at their best. Letters to the editor are filled with "negative othering," says Sheffield University's John Richardson – a mentality that helped drive the United Kingdom out of the European Union and fueled Donald Trump's run for the White House.[32] What will happen to a sense of the whole if sectarianism continues? Although broadcast news serves up brilliantly etched depictions of individual citizens and their individual lives, it "de-centers" the news when so doing, making shared problems and collective remedies harder to imagine.[33] By consuming so many of these little cameos, warns Lilie Chouliaraki of the London School of Economics, we risk being caught up in a "therapeutic discourse of community" rather than a "participatory discourse of citizenship."[34]

I have used letters to the editor to shed light on these broader cultural issues. Given US heterogeneity, that is asking a great deal of them. At the same time, though, says Vanderbilt University's Vanessa Beasley, it is precisely because the nation is such a patchwork of ethnicities, lifestyles, and class-based tensions that these *discursive realities* – how people talk and write – may be all that is available for understanding the nation.[35] So we have a lot to learn. In James Q. Wilson's terms, we must ask what will be lost and what gained if political discourse in the United States takes on an increasingly technocratic vs. a moral sound.[36] In Juvenal's terms, we must ask if displays of civic friendship are becoming harder to find as people retreat behind their digital walls. In Natalie Deckard and Irene Browne's terms, we must ask if market-based criteria – home ownership, time in a community, language-readiness, technological skills – are supplanting traditional, political notions of citizenship.[37] In Julie Firmstone and Stephen Coleman's terms, we must ask if people's vocalizations result in their being heard.[38]

This book has been about the United States as seen by fifty- to seventy-year-old adults. They have told us much but they have not told us everything. It would be interesting to know, for example, how citizen politics is practiced in other Western democracies. Gabrina Pounds of the

University of East Anglia has started us on that journey by comparing British and Italian letter writers. She found that, even today, Italians are constrained by the powerful ownership groups controlling the news-papers, as well as by the Roman Catholic church. Perhaps as a result, the Italian letters came across as victim-centered, often appealing to the editors to solve their problems. The Italian letters were also more per-sonal, hailing readers as fellow human beings rather than as potential activists. The British letters, in contrast, were bolder and more demanding of immediate action.[39] Using letters to the editor to tease out such cultural nuances holds great promise, in my opinion.

The whole concept of "authorship" must also be examined in a new media world. Digitization means speed, anonymity, and space-transcendence, all three of which affect how citizens address one another. In the paper-based letters I studied, authenticity was never much of a problem, with writers sending along their names, addresses, and phone numbers with their submissions. Sometimes, though, "astroturf" letters slip through the net, especially during political campaigns. For example, one enterprising Detroit teenager named Kyle sent out 14,000 letters to different newspapers in an attempt to get "cool stuff" from the cam-paigns.[40] Mass reproduction of this sort "can erode individualism and promote group think," says journalism scholar Bill Reader, but it also "allows those who are uncomfortable with writing their own letters to participate in debate."[41] An interview with one serial plagiarist, Greg Wheeler, personified a new and dangerous ethic: (1) he had permission to use the original author's letter, (2) he agreed with its contents, (3) he wanted his/their views promulgated, (4) so what's the problem?[42] To flourish, civic hope requires mass participation like this, but it also requires transparency. How these two qualities will accommodate one another remains to be seen.

Perhaps the most pregnant questions of all center on how the Millen-nial Generation will change things. According to social critic Paul Taylor, they are much less likely than Boomers or Xers to be socially trusting, to contact public officials, or to work on social or political causes.[43] Because they are still young and unsettled, millennials are also "spatially unattached" and, hence, unlikely to have neighborhood-based loyalties. On the other hand, millennials are more likely to see themselves as global citizens, a fine thing in an era of profound international tensions. Millen-nials are also more idealistic and more willing to push the boundaries, indicators that they will enter the political lists when the time is right. Because civic hope – and all else – depends on how these young people engage with the world, we must ask what lessons they will teach those of us who came before.

The concept of civic hope assumes that the American people have a voice and that things work out best when they use it. In this book, I have argued that one version of the people's voice – a very good version, in my opinion – arrives in letters to the editor. Such letters put citizens in touch with one another, on a daily basis, about matters of importance. Sometimes letter writers do not know what they are talking about and sometimes they get the facts wrong or draw improper inferences from perfectly good facts. Sometimes they posture, sometimes they wail, and sometimes they lose the thread of their arguments. But they also listen and learn, embrace the commonweal, and take ideas seriously. Civic hope depends on these things most of all.

CONCLUSION

This book has examined how political values are negotiated at the grass-roots level. My argument has been that democracy is an unsteady form of government shot through with contrary ideas leading to disputes over money, power, and human rights. In the United States, at least, every democrat knows what democracy means until he or she meets another democrat. Then they argue, sometimes find a resolution, and then argue about something else. Politics never stops.

In the book, I have treated letter writers as special witnesses. From the nation's very beginnings, their letters have built a clear, empirical record of American sentiments – not all of them but many of them. The letter writers I have gotten to know when writing this book are, to put it mildly, characters. They lead with their chin when laying out claims and they counter-punch pretty well too. Some of them are deadly serious about life while others are ironists; some write letters because they are vengeful, some because they cannot sleep. They all encounter one another on the pages of the local newspaper.

Some argue that the real voice of the American people lies elsewhere, among its silent majorities. Rather than look to argument, they suggest, we should study Americans' silent assumptions and uncontested beliefs. People do not argue about which side of the road to drive on, they observe, so we should look for the nation's true feelings in the unspoken. I disagree. Although American drivers are now loyal right-siders, that was not always true. At one point in history, the few who had automobiles drove wherever they pleased. Then Congress stepped in to fix things by building roads and erecting traffic signs, after which people wrote letters to the editor complaining about governmental overreach.

While the kind of hope profiled in this book does not have the gentle uplift found in church, we must not forget that all hope emerges from darkness. Christian hope, for example, began with the Crucifixion, Jewish hope from the Exodus, Muslim hope from felt social injustices. So hope is not just the presence of happiness. Happiness is the presence of happiness. Hope is the belief that happiness will emerge out of tribulation. Civic hope is the belief that certain political ideals will cause the dawn to break if those ideals are constantly nurtured.

As this book was being put to bed, columnist David Brooks of the *New York Times*, an eminently thoughtful and even-tempered fellow, wrote a short piece entitled "Are We on the Path to National Ruin?" In it, he ran through the depressing facts of US history, including racism and poverty, political corruption, immigration problems, economic dislocations, and two wildly unpopular 2016 presidential candidates. Brooks' essay deals largely with deficiencies among the nation's leaders and even his conclusion lionizes the importance of local mayors. "The healthy growth on the forest floor," Brooks opines, is ultimately "more important than the rot in the canopy."[44]

Scuttling about with the mayors on the forest floor are the people. This book celebrates their willingness to engage with politics and never stop. Letter writers have never been truly chipper, so they could not hope if they could not write. Norman Corwin, a journalist once known as the poet laureate of radio, might have been thinking of such people when crafting these lines at the end of World War II:

Let the singing fade, the celebrants go home. The bowl is drained and empty and the toasts are drunk. The guns are still, the tanks garaged, the planes rest in the hangar. Only the night remains. Outside the dew of morning glistens like a hope.[45]

Endnotes

1 Accessed at www.abrahamlincolnonline.org/lincoln/speeches/greeley.htm.
2 Quoted in John Braithwaite, "Emancipation and hope," *American Academy of Political and Social Science*, 592 (2004), 82.
3 Patrick Shade, *Habits of Hope: A Pragmatic Theory* (Nashville: Vanderbilt University Press, 2001), pp. 205–8.
4 Judith Andre, "Open hope as a civic virtue: Ernst Bloch and Lord Buddha," *Social Philosophy Today*, 29 (2013), 95.

5 Luc Bovens, "The value of hope," *Philosophy and Phenomenological Research*, 59 (1999), 672.

6 Terry Eagleton, *Hope Without Optimism* (Charlottesville: University of Virginia Press, 2015), p. 38.

7 Graeme Turner, *Ordinary People and the Media: The Demotic Turn* (Los Angeles: Sage, 2010), p. 34.

8 Toby Miller, *The Well-Tempered Self: Citizenship, Culture and the Postmodern Subject* (Baltimore: Johns Hopkins University Press, 1993), p. 19.

9 Morris Janowitz, *The Community Press in an Urban Setting* (Glencoe: Free Press, 1952), p. 165.

10 André Nusselder, "Twitter and the personalization of politics," *Psychoanalysis, Culture & Society*, 18 (2013), 93.

11 For more on these experiments in democracy see James S. Fishkin, *When the People Speak: Deliberative Democracy and Public Consultation* (New York: Oxford University Press, 2011) and Ned Crosby, *Healthy Democracy: Bringing Trustworthy Information to the Voters of America Paperback* (Edina: Beavers Pond Press, 2003). For reports on the National Issues Forum see www.nifi.org/en/reports.

12 Howard Zinn, *A People's History of the United States* (New York: HarperCollins, 1999), p. 10.

13 Steven Horwitz, "Markets are the voice of the people: modern populists have it all backwards," *Foundation for Economic Education* (May 12, 2016). Accessed at https://fee.org/articles/markets-are-the-voice-of-the-people/.

14 V. O. Key, *The Responsible Electorate* (Cambridge: Harvard University Press, 1966).

15 Matt Carlson and Eran Ben-Porath. "'The People's Debate': the CNN/YouTube debates and the demotic voice in political journalism," *Journalism Practice*, 6 (2012), 308.

16 Scott Wright and Todd Graham, "Discursive equality and everyday talk online: the impact of 'superparticipants'," *Journal of Computer-Mediated Communication* (2013), 1–18.

17 Peter Dahlgren, "The public sphere and the net: structure, space and communication," in E. Lance Bennett and Robert M. Entman (eds.), *Mediated Politics: Communication in the Future of Democracy* (New York: Cambridge University Press, 2001), pp. 33–55.

18 Karin Wahl-Jorgensen, "Coping with the meaninglessness of politics: citizen-speak in the 2001 British general elections." Paper presented at the annual meeting of the International Communication Association, Seoul, South Korea, July 2002, 26.

19 Joshua P. Darr, "The news you use: political knowledge and the importance of local newspapers." Paper presented at the annual meeting of the Midwest Political Science Association, Chicago, April 2015, 4, 7.

20 Susana Sotillo and Dana Starace-Nastasi, "Political discourse of a working-class town," *Discourse and Society*, 10 (1999), 435.

21 Pablo Boczkowski and Eugenia Mitchelstein, *The News Gap: When the Information Preferences of the Media and the Public Diverge* (Cambridge: MIT Press, 2013), p. 78.

22 For more on these roles see Ari Heinonen, "The journalist's relationship with users: new dimensions to conventional roles," in Jane B. Singer et al. (eds.), *Participatory Journalism: Guarding Open Gates at Online Newspapers* (Chichester: Wiley-Blackwell, 2011), pp. 34–55.

23 Generating an actual response, however, is not guaranteed because the Web is vast and readers' attention over-saturated. For more on this matter see Slavko Splichal, *Principles of Publicity and Press Freedom* (Lanham: Rowman & Littlefield, 2002), pp. 194–5.

24 Jennifer Brundidge, "Encountering 'difference' in the contemporary public sphere: the contribution of the internet to the heterogeneity of political discussion networks," *Journal of Communication*, 60 (2010), 680–700. Diana Mutz finds similar effects for television viewing. See "Effects of 'in-your-face' television discourse on perceptions of a legitimate opposition," *American Political Science Review*, 101(4) (2007), 621–35.

25 Josh Wolf, "Moderation matters for online commenting," *Journalism that Matters*, December 13, 2013. Accessed at http://journalismthatmatters.net/blog/2013/12/13/moderation-matters-for-online-commenting/.

26 Chris Puglia, "Do online comments bring newspapers value?" *St. Albert Gazette*, January 9, 2016. Accessed at www.stalbertgazette.com/article/Do-online-comments-bring-newspapers-value-20160109.

27 Arthur D. Santana, "Controlling the conversation: the availability of commenting forums in online newspapers," *Journalism Studies*, 17(2) (2016), 143.

28 Ibid, 143–4.

29 Summer Harlow, "Story-chatterers stirring up date: racist discourse in reader comments on U.S. newspaper websites," *Howard Journal of Communication*, 26 (2015), 37.

30 Jason Gainous and Kevin M. Wagner, "Surfing to the extremes: the polarization of public opinion." Paper presented at the annual meeting of the Midwest Political Science Association, Chicago, April 2015, 1.

31 Karin Wahl-Jorgensen, *Journalists and the Public: Newsroom Culture, Letters to the Editor, and Democracy* (Cresskill, NJ: Hampton Press, 2007), p. 159.

32 John E. Richardson, "'Now is the time to put an end to all this': argumentative discourse theory and 'letters to the editor,'" *Discourse & Society*, 12 (2001), 150.

33 For more on this see Lilie Chouliaraki, "Ordinary witnessing in post-television news: towards a new moral imagination," *Critical Discourse Studies*, 7 (2010), 316.

34 Lillie Chouliaraki, "Self-mediation: new media and citizenship," *Critical Discourse Studies*, 7 (2010), 229.

35 Vanessa Beasley, *You, the People: American National Identity in Presidential Rhetoric* (College Station: Texas A&M University Press, 2003), p. 45.

36 James Q. Wilson, *The Moral Sense* (New York: Free Press, 1997).

37 Natalie Delia Deckard and Irene Browne, "Constructing citizenship: framing unauthorized immigrants in market terms," *Citizenship Studies*, 19(6–7) (2015), 664–81.

38 Julie Firmstone and Stephen Coleman, "Rethinking local communicative spaces: implications of digital media and citizen journalism for the role of

local journalism in engaging citizens," in Rasmus K. Nielsen (ed.), *Local Journalism: The Decline of Newspapers and the Rise of Digital Media* (London: Tauris & Co., 2015), p. 133.

39 Gabrina Pounds, "Democratic participation and letters to the editor in Britain and Italy," *Discourse and Society*, 17(1) (2006), 29–63.

40 Ron Dzwonkowski, "It's a cheap form of propaganda: now they are offering prizes to people who trick newspapers into publishing fake letters," *The Masthead*, September 2004, www.thefreelibrary.com/It%27s+a+cheap+form +of+propaganda%3A+now+they+are+offering+prizes+to...-a0123078809

41 Bill Reader, "Who's really writing those 'canned' letters to the editor?" *Newspaper Research Journal*, 26 (2005), 53, 54.

42 Gilbert Cranberg, "Genuine letters help democratize our debate: letters give a window into how regular folks see the events of the day," *The Masthead*, September 2004, http://connection.ebscohost.com/c/letters/13221265/got-something-you-want-say

43 Paul Taylor, *The Next America: Boomers, Millennials, and the Looming Generational Showdown* (New York: Public Affairs, 2014), p. 27.

44 David Brooks, "Are we on the path to national ruin?" *New York Times*, July 12, 2016, 17. Accessed at www.nytimes.com/2016/07/12/opinion/are-we-on-the-path-to-national-ruin.html?_r=0.

45 Norman Corwin, "On a note of triumph," CBS Radio, May 8, 1945. Reprinted in Studs Terkel, *Hope Dies Last: Keeping the Faith in Difficult Times* (New York: New Press, 2003), p. xxi.

Appendix A

Civic Hope Codebook

WHAT IS CIVIC HOPE?

Civic hope is a set of expectations (1) that enlightened leadership is possible despite human foibles; (2) that productive forms of citizenship will result from cultural pluralism; (3) that democratic traditions will yield prudent governance; (4) but that none of this will happen without constant struggle.

WHAT DOES CIVIC HOPE REQUIRE?

1. Be able to cite instances of social cooperation (vs. social disunity)
2. Have a suitably generous understanding of why politicians behave as they do
3. Have a suitably generous understanding of why people disagree with one another
4. Have a balanced understanding of why campaigns succeed or fail
5. Have a complex understanding of who has political influence
6. Be willing to make a personal investment in the issues of the day
7. Be in touch with the historical past but not dominated by it
8. Be able to contemplate a workable future time
9. Express faith in democratic agents and institutions
10. Have a complex understanding of American cultural distinctiveness.

GENERAL CODING RULES

1. Coding occurs when a passage is highlighted and then "deposited" in the database with a distinct tag. When a textual fragment is deposited, two kinds of data are recorded: (1) *frequency* (a count of 1 for each deposit made) and (2) *density* (the number of words within the deposited fragment).

2. A given clause may be coded into as many content categories as appropriate (e.g., "I always liked Ike because of his war record" would be included both in *Author Declarations* and in *Positive Leadership Traits*)

3. When highlighting phrases or sentences, select only the textual fragments that are directly relevant to the construct being tapped.

4. In expert-based coding, there is a natural tendency for individual coders to "over-claim" textual fragments. Avoid this temptation by claiming only those fragments that follow the coding rules for your category.

5. The independent clause is the recording unit. Thus, highlight nothing less than a single independent clause.

6. When highlighting successive clauses or sentences, highlight as much material as necessary to make the coding designation meaningful to another person.

7. If two or more instances of the same subcategory are included in a given clause (e.g., if two separate *Agents of Hope* are mentioned), deposit only one textual fragment.

SECTOR 1: BASIC IDENTIFIERS

TEXTUAL FOCUS

1. *Presidential campaign* (major candidates, their families, campaign platforms, campaign strategies, etc.)

2. *National politics* (issue-centered letters on gun control, the United Nations, health care, social services, budget, taxes, immigration, abortion, etc.)

3. *Local politics* (mayoral race, environmental groups, city council, etc.)

4. *Non-political matters* (e.g., "I am disgusted how dogs roam freely downtown")

AUTHOR GENDER

1. *Male*
2. *Female*
3. *Gender unclear*

Candidate endorsement: If an endorsement is made, deposit the entire text with one coding. If no overall endorsement is made or if the author's endorsement is unclear, enter a code of "o." *Note*: An endorsement can be implicit. For example, a writer may bash Adlai Stevenson but not explicitly endorse Dwight Eisenhower.

0. *None made*
1. *Republican*
2. *Democrat*
3. *Independent*
4. *Third party candidate*
5. *Non-voting urged* (e.g., "Tweedledee vs. Tweedledum. Why bother voting?")

SECTOR 2: POLITICAL GOALS

National Touchstones: Highlight all clauses tapping basic US political traditions and institutions. Include only global statements (e.g., "this is the land of the free, isn't it?") rather than specific instantiations of those institutions (e.g., "Ronald Reagan will lead us to the promised land"). Note that national touchstones can be framed positively (e.g., "where but in America are the poor guaranteed an education?") as well as negatively (e.g., "What will happen to us all if the family is destroyed?"). *Key to coding*: Look for statements which use historically sanctioned "measuring devices" to assess the current landscape. Typically, National Touchstones are used (1) to show that fundamental issues are at stake and (2) to elevate mundane events to a grander level of importance.

0. *No commentary*
1. *Capitalistic system* (full employment; free trade vs. communism; "rags to riches")
2. *Mass education* (dedicated teachers; public universities; educational crisis)

3. *Scientific progress* (universal WiFi; medical advances; space exploration)
4. *Right to bear arms* (national security; military deployment; universal service; Star Wars)
5. *Popular vote* (right to campaign; online registration; illegal suffrage)
6. *Law and order* (safe streets; Miranda rights, Three Strikes legislation)
7. *Family structures* (two parents at home; gay rights; family values)
8. *Religious traditions* (Judeo-Christian heritage; in God we trust; freedom to worship)
9. *Civic volunteerism* (neighborhood clean-up; Thousand Points of Light; national service)
10. *Constitutional freedoms* (Bill of Rights; free speech; Fourth Estate; speedy trial)
11. *Equal rights for all* (desegregation; affirmative action; comparable worth)
12. *Humanitarian aid* (food stamps; social security; Peace Corps; developing nations)

Political Memory: Highlight all evaluative clauses referring to the non-immediate past (i.e., a decade or more removed from the current day). Incorporate both factual claims (e.g., "I remember when there wasn't enough food on the table") as well as injunctive or hortatory claims (e.g., "We don't want to turn this into another Vietnam.") *Note*: A passing reference to World War II or the Constitution, for instance, should not be coded unless it is *characterized* in some explicit way.

0. *No commentary*
1. *It was a time of destitution* (soaring gas prices; low wages; high interest rates)
2. *It was an angry time* (World War II; civil disturbances; etc)
3. *It was a time of dishonor* (slavery in the South; rampant immorality; Communist infiltration)
4. *It was an uncertain time* (no leadership; continued inflation; international tensions)
5. *It was a time of honor* (superior leaders; high moral standards; human rights flourished)
6. *It was a time of consensus* (peace among nations; no ethnic strife; cooperation among rivals)
7. *It was a time of plenty* (a chicken in every pot; high employment rate)

Civic Forecasting: Highlight all clauses referring to the future and its consequences. Do not include injunctive or hortatory statements (e.g., "We must double our efforts in the days ahead") unless they make "empirical" claims about what the future will be like (e.g., "We must double our campaign efforts lest the Democrats spend us into the poor house"). *Key to coding*: Look for bold predictions having clear societal implications. Hypotheticals can be coded as well.

0. *No commentary*
1. *Peace and safety will reign* (decrease in arms race; no border skirmishes; no threat to national defense)
2. *It'll be a time of plenty* (high standard of living; no mass starvation; lower taxes)
3. *There will be justice for all* (everyone gets a fair trial; no search and seizure; right to an attorney; joint custody arrangements)
4. *High moral standards will prevail* (family values; work ethic; compassion toward others; religious values; patriotism)
5. *It will be a time of enlightenment* (equal education for all; computers in every home; informed citizen participation)
6. *Freedom will flourish* (personal liberty; women's right to choose; don't ask, don't tell)
7. *It'll be a time of moral decline* (no Christian ideals; no prayer in the schools; promiscuity; draft-dodging; drug use, etc.)
8. *Freedoms will be trampled* (Communist enslavement; no right to privacy; loss of free speech; gun-control legislation)
9. *Ignorance will be common* (eroding education standards; TV generation; political apathy)
10. *It'll be an unsafe and dangerous time* (terrorism; drug wars; violent crimes; gangs)
11. *It'll be a time of deprivation* (poverty; hunger; substandard housing; higher taxes)
12. *Injustice will prevail* (segregation; minorities in jail; soak-the-rich tax schemes)

SECTOR 3: POLITICAL ACTORS

Agents of Hope: Highlight all clauses containing (1) given names, (2) pronominal designations (his, she), or (3) categorical names (e.g., "the head of the NAACP") of those who, in the author's opinion, positively affect the community. Include those explicitly described (e.g., "Ralph Nader had it right when he said...") and those referenced by indirection (e.g., "why don't we have an FDR today"?). *Key to coding*: Ignore persons who are mentioned but *uncharacterized* by the author.

0. *No commentary*
1. *Presidential/V-P candidate* (includes oblique references – "our opponent," "the Democratic candidate")
2. *Local candidate/official* (includes explicit names and titled persons – "the mayor," "Congressman Jones")
3. *Federal official/candidate* (includes military leaders, judges, cabinet members)
4. *Social/civic leader* (school principals; physicians; United Way director; "titled" citizens)
5. *US citizen* (average person; named voters; untitled citizens – "my corner grocer")
6. *Former public official* (former presidents/vice-presidents; other political figures who have *served within fifty years* of the current election)
7. *Historical personage* (famous person, alive or dead, who is at least fifty years removed from the current moment)
8. *Political celebrity/professional* (non-officeholders currently in the spotlight; includes political spouses, Jon Stewart, Angelina Jolie, etc.)
9. *Non-political celebrity* (movie stars; athletes; viral YouTubers)
10. *Political expert* (non-press pundits; pollsters; think-tank people – Peter Hart, Larry Sabato, Garry Wills)
11. *Member of the press* (TV anchors; reporters; columnists; editor of the local paper)
12. *Corporate leader* (Bill Gates; Meg Whitman; Michael Dell)
13. *Special interest/movement leader* (includes activists and spokespersons – Harvey Milk, Bob Geldof, Gloria Steinem)
14. *Foreign leader* (ambassadors; heads of state; etc.)
15. *Foreign citizen* (citizens without political titles)
16. *Unidentified individual* (a hypothetical person or someone *labeled* as unidentified: "I want to thank the wonderful woman who tried to save my cat.")

Agents of Decline: Use same coding rules as above. Highlight all commentary describing or evaluating people who *adversely* affect the community.

Helpful Groups: Highlight all clauses containing specifically named groups (e.g., the Veterans of Foreign Wars) or generic groups (e.g., Hispanics, Southerners) that have contributed positively to local, state, or national affairs. These contributions may be framed factually (e.g., "The NRA is backing Romney") or polemically (e.g., "Where would our campaign be without the Young Democrats?"). *Key to coding*: The coder should *adopt the author's viewpoint* of "helpfulness" and key on any overt evaluations made ("the good Christian people"). *Note #1*: Do not treat "the Administration" or "the White House" as a Helpful Group. *Note #2*: Complex entities such as Irish Catholics or Muslims should be coded in both the religious and ethnic categories.

0. *No commentary*
1. *International alliances* ("the Allies;" NATO; UN)
2. *Specific nation* (the French; the Bosnian people; etc.)
3. *Federal government* (the Justice Department; Capitol Hill; HHS. Do *not* code "the White House" or "the Administration")
4. *State/local government* (City Hall; school board; Governor's Office),
5. *Geographical region* (code any state or region followed by an active verb – "the Midwest is crazy about Elizabeth Warren")
6. *The military* (Army veterans; Navy headquarters; "our men and women in uniform")
7. *Corporate groups* (Silicon Valley; Wall Street)
8. *Ethnic/racial groups* (hyphenated Americans; civil rights activists; Black Caucus)
9. *Lobby groups* (Sierra Club; NEA; AFL-CIO)
10. *Political professionals* (strategists; polling companies; etc.)
11. *Mass media* (NBC; election pundits; news bloggers)
12. *Religious groups* (Christian Coalition; B'nai B'rith; the Vatican)
13. *Gender groups* (feminists; gays; lesbians; NOW)
14. *Age-based groups* (millennials; baby boomers; the elderly)
15. *Educational groups* (student protestors; academic researchers; school boards)
16. *Ideological groups* (liberals; environmentalists; pro-lifers)
17. *Major political party* (Democrats; GOP)
18. *Minor political party* (Libertarians; third parties; etc.)
19. *Service groups* (the United Way; Meals on Wheels; Boy Scouts)

Unhelpful Groups: Use same coding rules as above. Highlight all commentary describing or evaluating groups that *adversely* affect the community.

SECTOR 4: POLITICAL ATTRIBUTIONS

Author Declarations: Highlight all clauses containing first-person pronouns or their conjunctions. These codes are designed to capture authors' feeling states, knowledge states, and behavioral states as well as their ability to step back and look at themselves.

0. *No self-commentary*
1. *I have mainstream beliefs* ("Like everyone else I want lower taxes")
2. *My beliefs are unpopular* ("I'm the only one on my block who...")
3. *I have special knowledge* (includes both "expert" and "hearsay" knowledge – "I've been told that...")
4. *My knowledge is incomplete* ("I don't pretend to know everything but...")
5. *Here's what I did in the past* ("I've been a long-time supporter of President Obama and...")
6. *Here's what I'm now doing* (short-term action, less than five years: "I've already sent in my check. How about the rest of you?")
7. *Here's an opinion I hold* ("I'm convinced we should abandon both parties. They've failed us completely")
8. *Here's what I'll soon do* (long-term action, five or more years: "I'll never forsake the ACLU")
9. *I'm genuinely confused.* ("I'm at a loss as to what we should do with the homeless." *Note*: A literal question mark is not necessary here.)
10. *I have a question* ("So I ask you this: Who in their right mind would...?")
11. *I've heard opponents say* ("I don't understand why people think Clinton is innocent of this Whitewater business")
12. *I dislike people who* (a particular person or group must be referenced: "I'm sick and tired of the media making fun of the President")

13. *I like people who* (expressions of gratitude toward, or similarity to, specific persons/groups: "Right-to-Lifers are the only true Christians")
14. *I've been wrong before* ("I was naive then, but now I...")
15. *I've been proven right* ("my worst fears have now materialized")
16. *I'm feeling optimistic* (*impersonal* indications of contentment: "I trust that tomorrow will be a better day")
17. *I'm feeling pessimistic* (*impersonal* indications of disapproval: "the new bicycle helmet ordinance is driving me crazy")

Voter perceptions: Highlight all global references to the citizenry when they serve as the *subject* of a sentence (e.g., "America never stands by while others suffer"). Include factual-sounding statements (e.g., "We single-handedly saved the people of Vietnam") as well as evaluative phrasings (e.g., "people have been just sitting there and doing nothing"). *Key to coding*: Be sure that voters are linked to active, not passive, verbs; do not include subsets of the population (e.g., "the elderly"). *Note #1*: Code descriptive statements (e.g., "we are an opinionated people") rather than *injunctive statements* (e.g., "we must do all that we can to ..."). *Note #2*: Do not highlight statements using the "papal we" (e.g., "we will push through Congress a bill that ...")

0. *No commentary*
1. *They're different from all other people* ("We're still the last hope of the free world")
2. *They're similar to all other people* ("We must remember our place within the brotherhood of man")
3. *They typically disagree with one another* ("Scott Walker is taking advantage of a fundamental cleavage in American society")
4. *Typically agree on important matters* (Key phrases: "everyone knows that," "it's common sense that ...")
5. *They're actively involved in governance* (people are energized by the campaign; campaign volunteers are plentiful)
6. *They're not as active as they should be* ("Americans too often take their freedom for granted")
7. *They're intelligent about political matters* ("America will not trade inept management of complexity for doctrinaire assertions of simplicity")
8. *They're easily duped by political forces* ("Communist tricks," "falling for political rhetoric")

9. *They remain hopeful about politics* ("People are really energized by this campaign")
10. *They're pessimistic about the political future* ("the polls keep showing that voters' expectations are low")
11. *They're the strongest people on earth* ("We're not going to be bossed around by China")
12. *They could be dominated by others* ("Columbians are a powerful threat to jobs in this country")

Positive Leadership Traits: Highlight all clauses explaining how or why a particular politician promotes the social good (either practical or moral; either actual or potential). The key here is to uncover the author's "theory" of what makes a politician effective. Do not code praiseworthy statements (e.g., "Ross Perot rescued his men in the Middle East") that fail to explain *why* a given politician succeeded. *Key to coding*: Look for personal – versus systemic – reasons for success. *Note #1*: Be on the lookout for causal language. *Note #2*: Do not highlight tautological constructions implying that a person is successful because he has succeeded.

0. *No commentary*
1. *Can't be pushed around by others* (has vision, determination; takes on challengers)
2. *Strategically smart* (good speaker; street savvy; no TV gaffes)
3. *Real need to serve the public* (citizen-legislator; a grassroots person)
4. *Serves an important constituency* (connected to influentials – the urban vote, farmers, women, senior citizens)
5. *Has an affable personality* (charismatic; positive; presses the flesh; humorous)
6. *Enviable moral character* (no skeletons; clean record; family man; can be trusted)
7. *Vast political experience* (good résumé; incumbent; "has been around the block")
8. *Deep understanding of issues* (really knows foreign policy, federal budget, civil rights legislation)
9. *Altruistic and self-sacrificing* ("not in it for herself"; puts others first; cares for poor, sick, homeless)
10. *Genuine American values* (throws out first pitch; "God bless America," served in military)
11. *Well-financed* (family money, legacy; endorsed by powerful legislators, celebrities)

12. *Concerned for all Americans* (not trapped by special interests; "he won't leave anyone behind")
13. *A hard, dedicated worker* (puts in long hours; history of public service; no shortcuts)
14. *Builds consensus across factions* (cooperative; has good relations "across the aisle")
15. *Tackling new challenges* (fresh ideas; bold plans; "part of the solution, not part of the problem")

Negative Leadership Traits: Highlight all clauses explaining how or why a particular politician has failed – either practically or morally, either actually or potentially. The key here is to uncover the author's "theory" of what caused a person to fail. Do not code evaluative statements (e.g., "We can't possibly support Frank Calhoun for office") that fail to explain *why* a given politician is inadequate. *Key to coding*: Look for personal – versus systemic – reasons for failure. *Note #1*: Be on the lookout for causal language. *Note #2*: Do not highlight tautological constructions implying that a person has failed because he has not succeeded.

0. *No commentary*
1. *Seeks personal financial gain* (high speaker fees; "they all get rich at City Hall")
2. *Seeks only ego-gratification* (power-hungry; "hot-shot"; publicity hound)
3. *Has no clear purpose or vision* (doesn't have a plan; "the politics of yesterday")
4. *Likes to manipulate others* (looking for an angle; a "brown-noser"; a "sharper")
5. *Buckle under to the opposition* ("no backbone"; "under their thumb")
6. *Has important character flaws* (immoral; greedy; cheats on taxes)
7. *An unyielding doctrinaire* (can't find a way to cut a deal; "her only line is the party line")
8. *No strategic message skills* (flustered; mistake-prone; "silver foot in his mouth")
9. *Controlled by special interests* ("communist puppet," "takes his orders from. . .")
10. *Forsakes true American values* (an atheist; "never worked a day in his life")
11. *Devoid of intellectual substance* (shallow; hollow; "gives empty answers")

12. *Raised in another environment* ("not one of us"; "got his values from the European community")

13. *Not concerned for all Americans* ("keeps the little man down"; "no friend of women's rights")

14. *Has no real-life experience* ("never washed a dish"; "completely out of touch")

15. *Failed to take definitive action* (can't act when asked; "couldn't bring home the hostages")

16. *Not a competent manager* (undisciplined staff; "lost control of his own party")

SECTOR 5: POLITICAL TENSIONS

Oppositional Literacy: Highlight all clauses in which the author demonstrates an understanding of those with whom he or she disagrees. The "evidence" cited can be concrete (e.g., "Their value-added tax proposal didn't work the last time either") or projective ("The next thing he'll be saying is that same-sex marriage is OK for Christians"). *Key to coding*: Focus on *issue positions* here. Thus, a statement like "Jones used another one of his sleazy tactics again yesterday" would not be coded because the statement shows no understanding of Jones' ideas, programs, or philosophies.

0. *No commentary*
1. *Opponent explained*

Evidence of Coordination: Highlight all clauses in which actual or potential cooperation is depicted. Include behavioral statements (e.g., "in Congress, they scratch each other's backs") and injunctive statements (e.g., "we've all got to get out and vote next Tuesday." Be sure that at least two distinct entities (individuals or groups) are identified in the statement, neither of which is the author. *Key to coding*: Ignore the author's attitude about the coordination described. That is, a statement like "the damned labor unions have sold out to the Democratic party" should be included even though the author is decrying the linkage. *Note #1*: Mere mention of two groups in the same sentence is not evidence of their coordination; some form of overt action – real or projected – is required. *Note #2*: Ironic linkages can be included (e.g., "What? Dole is suddenly going to embrace Generation X?").

0. *No commentary*
1. *Among US officials* ("The President is finally working with Congress on a budget compromise")

2. *Between US officials and group leaders* ("The Gay Lobby is in the Obama camp on this one")

3. *Among ordinary citizens* ("The neighborhood watch program has proved to be effective")

4. *Between US officials and citizens* ("Voters clearly turned out to support the mayor's bridge proposal")

5. *Among domestic groups* ("The people of this city simply must support Greenpeace")

6. *Between groups and their leaders* ("Ryan's people finally rallied House Republicans today")

7. *Foreign/US relations* ("this reminds me of when the Allies brought Hitler to his knees")

8. *Among foreign nations* ("NAFTA helped Canada and Mexico but what about the US?")

9. *Between US officials and press* ("Limbaugh is rallying support for Ted Cruz. Can this marriage last?")

10. *Between group leaders and press* ("terrorists' media exposure only encourages more atrocities")

11. *Between citizens and the press* ("letters to the editor have become a major force in State politics")

12. *Among various media outlets* ("the *Wall Street Journal* today echoed the charges made on Friday by NBC's reporters in Haiti")

13. *Between groups and citizens* ("Now the locavores want us to boycott California broccoli!")

Evidence of Disunity: Use same coding rules as above. Highlight all commentary describing or evaluating linkages that *adversely* affect the community.

Campaign Advice: Highlight all clauses providing global explanations of how a given campaign (or campaigns in general) can be more successful. Such explanations may comment on what people "already know" and some may provide examples of some larger trend (e.g., "The Rand Paul campaign will bring out a new kind of voter"). Some of these comments may be "factual" in nature (e.g., "the folks in New Hampshire liked her stand on gun control") while others may be more projective (e.g., "People will jump on the Gore bandwagon. Just watch."). *Key to coding*: Look for three things: (1) *positive language* (i.e., certain strategies make the political process more efficient, respectable); (2) *cause–effect language*; and (3) *trend language* – the current campaign has features that will become widespread. *Note #1*: Key on concrete activities and tactics;

look for references to "campaigns" and "platforms." *Note #2:* Success assessments often appear after a series of factual assertions.

0. *No commentary*
1. *Maximize message opportunities* (get better speechwriters; use satellite feeds; MTV interviews)
2. *Maximize fund-raising opportunities* (targeted solicitations; "the chicken-and-peas circuit")
3. *Appeal to key political sub-groups* (the Religious Right; Marco Rubio supporters)
4. *Attend to regional politics* (California's electoral votes; "can't lose the South," etc.)
5. *Emphasize the incumbent advantage* ("Bush looked Iran in the eye. People respected his courage")
6. *Emphasize outsider status* ("We must get back to basics; no more tax-and-spend")
7. *Transcend intra-party disputes* (gender divide for Republicans; Blacks for Democrats)
8. *Bring new voters into the process* ("She appeals to the fence-sitters")
9. *Set a high moral tone for the campaign* ("Hillary is successful because she doesn't prevaricate")
10. *Address substantive issues* (the education crisis; the deficit; "meaningful choices")
11. *Cultivate favorable press coverage* (coffee with Oprah; good photo ops)
12. *Recruit a professional campaign staff* (better mobile aps; avoid "dirty tricks")
13. *Keep party faithful enthusiastic* ("appealing to the base"; "stirring up the troops")
14. *Emphasize your strengths, not their weakness* (no personal attacks; "people want clean campaigns")
15. *Stay up-to-date on domestic issues* (*meta-comments* about candidate emphases – "Hillary knows that people are fed up with the welfare state")
16. *Stay up-to-date on international issues* (*meta-comments* about candidate emphases – "Jeb Bush is smart to realize we don't want another Gulf War")

Campaign Complaints: Highlight all clauses providing global explanations of why a given campaign (or campaigns in general) are flawed. Some explanations may be brief asides (e.g., "Where have all the good candidates gone?") and some may provide examples of a larger trend (e.g., "Santorum fell victim to our lousy campaign finance laws"). *Key to Coding*: Look for three things: (1) *negative language* (i.e., that which degrades the political process); (2) *cause-effect language* and *trend language* – e.g., "gerrymandering has killed the honest election." *Note*: Failure assessments often appear after a series of factual assertions.

0. *No commentary*
1. *Campaign costs are too high*
2. *Campaign is poorly managed* (poor media decisions, hired the wrong people)
3. *Campaign is focusing on superficial issues* (e.g., "the Gennifer Flowers matter wastes our time")
4. *Candidates have questionable morals* (adulterer; political sleaze; Tricky Dick)
5. *Candidates are too negative* (mud-slinging; name-calling; "taking the low road")
6. *Candidates are strategically inept* (key verbs: fumbling, faltering, wavering)
7. *Candidates are overwhelmed by domestic issues* (often an incumbent problem – recession, Watergate, Iran–Contra, health care crisis)
8. *Candidates are overwhelmed by international issues* (often an incumbent problem – war, terrorism, communist takeovers)
9. *Candidates are too insulated from voters* (out of touch; too old; inside the Beltway)
10. *Most important issues are being ignored* (cities are burning; rivers polluted; nobody cares about the elderly)
11. *Electorate is divided* (suburbs vs. inner city; undecided voters; North vs. South)
12. *Electorate is unmotivated* (voter apathy; low turnout; online anger)
13. *Press is too negative* (media unfair; press ganging up on candidates)
14. *Press coverage is too superficial* (horserace stories; candidate can't get his message through)
15. *Party has been purchased* (unions pull Democrats' strings; business groups own Republican candidates)
16. *Parties have internal strife* (key terms: squabbling, in-fighting, bickering)

Appendix B

Survey of Writers vs. Non-Writers

**Campaign Experience: Please answer each of these questions by placing an
X in the appropriate space.**

1. Did you vote in the 2012 presidential election? ____ Yes ____ No

2. If yes, for whom did you vote? ____ Romney/Ryan ____ Obama/Biden ___ Other

3. Did you talk about the campaign frequently with family and friends? ____ Yes ____ No ___ Unsure

4. Did you work as a volunteer in one of the presidential campaigns? ____ Yes ____ No ____ Unsure

5. Did you contribute money to one of the campaigns? ____ Yes ____ No ____ Unsure

6. Did you listen to radio call-in shows more often during the campaign? ____ Yes ____ No ____ Unsure

7. Did you pay special attention to the 2012 campaign advertisements? ____ Yes ___ No ____ Unsure

8. Did you watch the evening news more often during the campaign? ____ Yes ___ No ____ Unsure

9. Did you watch portions of the Democratic or Republican conventions? ____ Yes ____ No ____ Unsure

10. Did you watch any of the 2012 presidential debates? ____ Yes ____ No ____ Unsure

11. Did you see the candidates on shows like *Today* or *Meet the Press*? ____ Yes ____ No ____ Unsure

12. Did you write a letter to the editor of your local paper about the campaign? ____ Yes ___ No ____ Unsure

Media Evaluation: Please think how the mass media (radio, TV, newspapers, etc.) covered the 2012 campaign and then give your opinion about each of the following statements.

13. In general, the news media increased my political knowledge during the campaign.

    ____ Strongly agree ____ Agree ____ Unsure ____ Disagree
    ____ Strongly disagree

14. The major TV networks (ABC, CBS, CNN, NBC) did a good job of covering the campaign.

    ____ Strongly agree ____ Agree ____ Unsure ___ Disagree
    ____ Strongly disagree

15. *The Billings Gazette* did a good job of covering the campaign.

    ____ Strongly agree ____ Agree ____ Unsure ____ Disagree
    ____ Strongly disagree

16. Having the major political candidates appear on talk shows like *Good Morning America* was helpful.

    ____ Strongly agree ____ Agree ____ Unsure ____ Disagree
    ___ Strongly disagree

17. Having ordinary citizens (rather than reporters) question the candidates on TV was a good idea.

    ____ Strongly agree ____ Agree ____ Unsure ____ Disagree
    ____ Strongly disagree

18. Reporters talked too much about the candidates' personal lives during the campaign.

    ____ Strongly agree ____ Agree ____ Unsure ____ Disagree
    ____ Strongly disagree

19. In general, the mass media treated the Democratic candidates better than the Republican candidates.

    ____ Strongly agree ____ Agree ____ Unsure ____ Disagree
    ____ Strongly disagree

General Political Assessment: Please give your frank reactions to each of the following statements.

20. The people we elect to public office usually keep the promises they make during the election.

    ____ Strongly agree ____ Agree ___ Unsure ____ Disagree
    ____ Strongly disagree

21. I often don't feel sure of myself when talking to others about politics and government.

____ Strongly agree ____ Agree ____ Unsure ____ Disagree
____ Strongly disagree

22. I feel I could do as good a job in public office as most other people.
____ Strongly agree ____ Agree ____ Unsure ____ Disagree
____ Strongly disagree

23. The people of the US have the final say about how the country is run, no matter who is in office.
____ Strongly agree ____ Agree ____ Unsure ____ Disagree
____ Strongly disagree

24. People like me really don't have a say about what government does.
____ Strongly agree ____ Agree ____ Unsure ____ Disagree
____ Strongly disagree

25. If public officials don't care what people think, there is no way to make them listen.
____ Strongly agree ____ Agree ____ Unsure ____ Disagree
____ Strongly disagree

26. When government leaders make public statements to the American people, they often mislead them.
____ Strongly agree ____ Agree ____ Unsure ____ Disagree
____ Strongly disagree

Background Information: Please respond to each of these items quickly before returning your survey.

27. What is your age? _____ (years)

28. What is the highest level of education you have completed?
____ 9th grade or less ____ High school ____ Vocational school
____ College ____ Graduate school

29. What is your gender? ____ Female ____ Male

30. Are you of Hispanic origin? ____ Yes ____ No

31. What is your race? ____ White ____ Black ____ Asian ____
Native American ____ Other

32. If born in the US, where were you born?
_____ (state)

33. How long have you lived in the Billings area? _____ (years)

34. What sort of home do you live in? ____ Own my own home ____ Renting a house or apartment

35. Which of the following categories best describes your occupation?
____ Student ____ Retired ____ Homemaker ____ Clerical/service worker ____ Laborer/craftsman

_____ Farmer _____ Manager/administrator _____ Sales/ marketing _____ Teacher _____ Public Service
_____ Professional (law, medicine, etc.) _____ Unemployed

36. Which category comes closest to your *family's* overall income?
    _____ Under $15,000 per year _____ $16,000 to $25,000 per year _____ $26,000 to $35,000 per year
    _____ $36,000 to $45,000 per year _____ $46,000 to $55,000 per year _____ $56,000 to $65,000 per year
    _____ $66,000 to $75,000 per year _____ $76,000 to $85,000 per year _____ Over $85,000 per year

37. Do you ever record TV shows at home? _____ Yes _____ No

38. Do you subscribe to cable television? _____ Yes _____ No

39. Approximately how much television do you watch each day? _____ (hours)

40. Do you subscribe to *The Billings Gazette*? _____ Yes _____ No

Have You Answered the Questions on the Front Side?
If So, Please Return Your Survey Immediately. Many Thanks!!

Appendix C

Survey of Readers' Attitudes

Media Habits: Please fill in the blanks below or put an X in the appropriate space.

1. Approximately how much television do you watch each day? _____ (hours)

2. Do you watch the *national* news on a regular basis? ____ Yes ____ No

3. Do you watch the *local* news on a regular basis? ____ Yes ____ No

4. Do you ever record TV shows at home? ____ Yes ____ No

5. Do you subscribe to cable television? ____ Yes ___ No

6. Which sorts of TV shows do you watch on a regular basis? (place an *X* next to as many as you'd like)

    _____ educational documentaries (e.g., on PBS) _____ interview shows (e.g., *Anderson Cooper 360*) _____ weekly news magazines (e.g., *60 Minutes*) _____ sports programming _____ daytime dramas (e.g., *Young and the Restless*) _____ network or cable movies _____ weekly comedy shows (e.g., *Big Bang Theory*) _____ weekly dramatic shows (e.g., *NCIS*) _____ early morning shows (e.g., *Today show*) _____ late-night programs (e.g., *David Letterman*)

7. Do you listen to the radio regularly? ____ Yes ___ No

8. What sorts of radio shows do you listen to on a regular basis? (place an *X* next to as many as you'd like)

    ____ rock or rap music ____ country-western music ___ easy-listening music

____ political call-in shows ____ sports call-in shows ____ weather or stock reports

____ hourly news broadcasts ____ advice programs (e.g., finances, gardening, etc.)

9. Do you regularly read *The Billings Gazette*? ____ Yes ____ No

10. Which of the following statements describes how you read a newspaper (place an *X* next to your choice):

_____ I read almost everything in the paper from start to finish

_____ I read one or more sections regularly (e.g., local events, the sports page)

_____ I skip around a lot, depending on my mood

_____ I read the headlines and nothing else

_____ I spend very little time reading the newspaper

11. Do you make it a point to read the letters to the editor in your local paper? ____ Yes ____ No

12. Have you yourself ever written a letter to the editor of your paper? ____ Yes ____ No

13. Do you often find when reading the paper that you know the letter-writers? ____ Yes ____ No

Media Attitudes: Please answer each of these questions by placing an X in the appropriate space.

14. Today's TV programs seem to be undermining the morals of the American people.

____ Strongly agree ____ Agree ____ Unsure ____ Disagree
____ Strongly disagree

15. In general, today's TV shows are more entertaining than they were ten years ago.

____ Strongly agree ____ Agree ____ Unsure ____ Disagree
____ Strongly disagree

16. TV does a better job broadcasting sporting events today than it did ten years ago.

____ Strongly agree ____ Agree ____ Unsure ____ Disagree
____ Strongly disagree

17. In general, TV commentators seem to treat Democratic politicians better than Republican politicians.

____ Strongly agree ____ Agree ____ Unsure ____ Disagree
____ Strongly disagree

18. The people who present the news on TV seem genuinely concerned about the American people.
    ____ Strongly agree ____ Agree ___ Unsure ____ Disagree ____ Strongly disagree

19. The people who call in to talk radio shows are better informed about current affairs than me.
    ____ Strongly agree ___ Agree ____ Unsure ____ Disagree ____ Strongly disagree

20. The people who call in to talk radio shows sometimes seem pretty unstable to me.
    ____ Strongly agree ____ Agree ___ Unsure ____ Disagree ____ Strongly disagree

21. The publishers of my local newspaper are genuinely concerned about my community.
    ____ Strongly agree ____ Agree ____ Unsure ____ Disagree ____ Strongly disagree

22. Think for a moment about the people who write letters to the editor of *The Billings Gazette*. Then place *X's* next to the statements that best describe the letter-writers:
    a) They prefer sounding off to being constructive ___ Str. agree ___ Agree ___ Unsure ___ Disagree ___ Str. Disagree
    b) They seem better educated than most people ___ Str. agree ___ Agree ___ Unsure ___ Disagree ___ Str. disagree
    c) Their views are fairly similar to my own ___ Str. agree ___ Agree ___ Unsure ___ Disagree ___ Str. disagree
    d) They seem pretty egotistical to me ___ Str. agree ___ Agree ___ Unsure ___ Disagree ___ Str. disagree
    e) They seem to want to help the community ___ Str. agree ___ Agree ___ Unsure ___ Disagree ___ Str. disagree
    f) Their views are fairly similar to people I know ___ Str. agree ___ Agree ___ Unsure ___ Disagree ___ Str. disagree
    g) They seem more liberal than conservative ___ Str. agree ___ Agree ___ Unsure ___ Disagree ___ Str. disagree

Background Information: Please respond to each of these items quickly before returning your survey.

23. What is your age? _____ (years)
24. What is your marital status? ____ Married ____ Divorced ____ Separated ____ Widowed ____ Never married

25. What is the highest level of education you have completed?
___ Grade school   ___ High school   ___ Vocational school
___ Some college   ___ College   ___ Graduate school
26. What is your gender?   ___ Female   ___ Male
27. What is your usual political affiliation?   ___ Democrat
___ Republican   ___ Independent   ___ Other
28. What is your race?   ___ White   ___ Black   ___ Asian
___ Native American   ___ Other
29. How long have you lived in the Billings area?   _____ (years)
30. Which of the following categories best describes your occupation?
___ Student   ___ Retired   ___ Homemaker   ___ Clerical/
service worker   ___ Laborer/craftsman
___ Farmer   ___ Manager/administrator   ___ Sales/marketing
___ Teacher   ___ Public service
___ Professional (law, medicine, etc.)   ___ Unemployed
31. Which category comes closest to your *family's* overall income?
___ Under $15,000 per year   ___ $16,000 to $25,000 per
year   ___ $26,000 to $35,000 per year
___ $36,000 to $45,000 per year   ___ $46,000 to $55,000 per
year   ___ $56,000 to $65,000 per year
___ $66,000 to $75,000 per year   ___ $76,000 to $85,000 per
year   ___ Over $85,000 per year

Have You Answered the Questions on the Front Side?
If So, Please Return Your Survey Immediately. Many Thanks!!

Appendix D

TABLE D.1 *Selective Population Data for Twelve-City Sample*

City Data for:	1950 Population	2010 Population	Population % Change
Fall River, MA	111,963	88,857	−20.64
Trenton, NJ	128,009	84,913	−33.67
Utica, NY	101,531	62,235	−38.70
Roanoke, VA	91,921	97,032	5.56
Lake Charles, LA	41,272	71,993	74.44
Wichita Falls, TX	68,042	104,553	53.66
St. Joseph, MO	78,588	76,780	−2.20
Springfield, OH	78,508	60,608	−22.80
Duluth, MN	104,511	86,265	−17.45
Provo, UT	28,937	112,488	288.73
Salinas, CA	13,917	115,441	729.49
Billings, MT	31,834	104,170	227.22
12-City Sample	*879,033*	*1,065,335*	*21.19*
US Total/Mean	*154,233,234*	*308,745,538*	*101.18*

Sources: 1950 Census of Population: Vol. 1, Number of Inhabitants (Washington, DC: US Government Printing Office, 1952); US Census Bureau; "American FactFinder" Census 2010; Table DP-1, http://factfinder2.census.gov; www.city-data.com

TABLE D.2 *Selective Ethnic Data for Twelve-City Sample*

City Data for:	% White Residents	% Black Residents	% Asian Residents	% Hispanic Residents	% Non-ethnic Identifiers*
Fall River, MA	97.2	3.9	2.6	7.4	7.0
Trenton, NJ	26.6	52.0	0.7	33.7	9.1
Utica, NY	69.0	15.3	0.3	10.5	9.7
Roanoke, VA	64.2	28.5	1.8	5.5	16.4
Lake Charles, LA	47.0	47.7	1.7	2.9	9.1
Wichita Falls, TX	73.2	12.7	2.4	18.9	14.1
St. Joseph, MO	87.8	6.0	0.9	5.7	17.6
Springfield, OH	75.2	18.1	0.8	3.0	20.6
Duluth, MN	90.4	2.3	1.5	1.5	12.5
Provo, UT	84.8	0.7	2.5	15.2	10.8
Salinas, CA	45.8	2.0	6.3	75.0	4.8
Billings, MT	89.6	0.8	0.7	5.2	11.9
12-City Sample	*70.9*	*15.9*	*1.9*	*15.4*	*11.9*
US Total	*72.4*	*12.6*	*4.8*	*16.3*	*6.2*

* Persons providing no/non-classifiable designation of ancestry.
Source: US Census Bureau; "American FactFinder" Census 2010; Tables DP-1 and B04001, http://factfinder2.census.gov

TABLE D.3 *Selective Demographic Data for Twelve-City Sample*

City Data for:	Median Age	% Persons Living Alone	% Persons 65 & Older	% Persons with Multiple Ancestry	% Persons Speaking English Only
Fall River, MA	38.1	34.9	15.1	2.8	66.2
Trenton, NJ	33.0	30.8	8.8	4.1	63.0
Utica, NY	34.8	36.5	14.8	4.0	73.4
Roanoke, VA	38.4	37.1	14.3	2.8	91.7
Lake Charles, LA	35.1	32.4	13.9	2.1	90.4
Wichita Falls, TX	32.5	31.0	12.4	3.2	85.1
St. Joseph, MO	35.6	30.7	13.8	2.7	94.1
Springfield, OH	36.0	34.1	15.3	4.0	95.6
Duluth, MN	32.8	35.1	13.8	3.0	95.1
Provo, UT	23.5	12.8	5.8	3.4	79.1
Salinas, CA	28.6	17.1	7.5	5.1	31.7
Billings, MT	37.6	32.6	15.0	2.9	95.1
12-City Mean	*33.8*	*29.0*	*12.5*	*3.3*	*80.0*
US Mean	*36.8*	*27.5*	*13.1*	*2.9*	*79.4*

Sources: US Census Bureau; "American FactFinder" Census 2010; Tables DP-1; http://factfinder2.census.gov; US Census Bureau; "American FactFinder"; "2008–2012 American Community Survey"; Table S1601; *65+ in the United States: 2010* (www.census.gov/content/dam/Census/library/publications/2014/demo/p23-212.pdf)

TABLE D.4 *Selective Residency Data For Twelve-City Sample*

MSA Data for:	% Persons Native to State	% Long-Term Residents	% Religious Adherents	Crime Rate
Fall River, MA	81.5	38.3	56.8	455.6
Trenton, NJ	76.9	30.1	52.6	625.9
Utica, NY	82.3	36.0	48.3	388.2
Roanoke, VA	93.5	33.8	54.0	387.8
Lake Charles, LA	96.4	33.7	70.7	432.2
Wichita Falls, TX	91.8	32.1	66.3	371.2
St. Joseph, MO	96.4	35.8	44.7	422.7
Springfield, OH	97.4	35.7	51.7	577.5
Duluth, MN	97.0	37.0	46.9	382.5
Provo, UT	88.0	19.3	90.8	144.1
Salinas, CA	63.0	32.2	49.4	400.2
Billings, MT	98.2	32.3	39.3	316.2
12-City Mean	*72.8*	*33.0*	*56.0*	*408.7*
US Mean	*87.1*	*37.6*	*50.1*	*298.5*

Sources: US Census Bureau; "American FactFinder" Census 2010; Table DP02; http://factfinder2.census.gov; C. Grammich, K. Hadaway, R. Houseal, D. E. Jones, A. Krindatch, R. Stanley, and R.H. Taylor (2012), *2010 U.S. Religion Census: Religious Congregations & Membership Study.* Association of Statisticians of American Religious Bodies; www.city-data.com

TABLE D.5 *Selective Employment Data for Twelve-City Sample*

City Data for:	% Unemployment, 2010	% Women in Work Force, 2010	Average Commuting Time, 2010
Fall River, MA	15.3	56.5	22.5
Trenton, NJ	17.9	51.2	23.3
Utica, NY	12.7	47.7	17.1
Roanoke, VA	7.7	54.5	18.6
Lake Charles, LA	10.0	53.2	17.3
Wichita Falls, TX	6.6	53.7	14.7
St. Joseph, MO	8.6	56.3	16.4
Springfield, OH	13.8	49.3	19.9
Duluth, MN	9.0	58.6	16.6
Provo, UT	7.7	58.3	16.7
Salinas, CA	11.8	53.3	22.6
Billings, MT	4.9	60.3	17.1
12-City Mean/ Median	*10.5*	*54.4*	*18.6*
US Mean/Median	*6.9*	*59.4*	*25.4*

Source: US Census Bureau; "American FactFinder" Census 2010; DP03; http://factfinder2.census.gov

TABLE D.6 *Selective Occupational Data for Twelve-City Sample*

City Data for:	% Government Workers	% Mining & Agriculture	% Construction & Manufacturing	% Transportation	% Wholesale & Retail Trade	% Finance, Insurance & Real Estate	% Service Workers
Fall River, MA	4.0	1.0	19.7	2.7	17.1	4.8	13.4
Trenton, NJ	10.3	1.3	15.8	4.0	12.7	4.3	13.4
Utica, NY	5.8	0.4	14.2	2.6	14.9	6.9	14.1
Roanoke, VA	2.4	4.4	4.4	3.5	10.0	10.5	21.1
Lake Charles, LA	4.4	1.5	14.5	3.4	14.0	4.7	14.5
Wichita Falls, TX	7.1	2.2	14.1	3.5	16.5	4.9	15.3
St. Joseph, MO	4.3	1.0	23.5	4.4	14.6	6.0	13.2
Springfield, OH	3.6	1.0	18.9	3.0	16.2	5.4	13.7
Duluth, MN	3.7	1.9	10.2	3.6	14.5	5.5	15.1
Provo, UT	2.0	0.7	11.2	1.3	13.4	3.7	13.9
Salinas, CA	5.1	21.0	11.3	3.2	15.0	3.6	11.2
Billings, MT	4.1	3.1	11.6	4.6	17.5	7.3	15.4
12-City Mean	*4.7*	*3.3*	*14.1*	*3.3*	*14.7*	*5.6*	*14.5*
US Mean	*15.3*	*1.2*	*14.5*	*3.6*	*13.2*	*7.0*	*48.6*

Sources: US Census Bureau; "American FactFinder" Census 2010; Table DP03; http://factfinder2.census.gov; "American FactFinder"; 2010 American Community Survey; Table CB1000A1; http://factfinder2.census.gov. "American FactFinder" Census 2010; Table DP03; http://factfinder2.census.gov

TABLE D.7 *Selective Housing Data for Twelve-City Sample*

City Data for:	% Recent Construction*	% Low-Cost Housing**	% Homes Vacant	% Householders Renting
Fall River, MA	2.7	1.2	10.0	64.3
Trenton, NJ	3.3	1.7	19.7	59.5
Utica, NY	1.8	1.3	13.4	51.5
Roanoke, VA	5.6	1.4	10.0	45.2
Lake Charles, LA	13.9	2.4	14.5	43.4
Wichita Falls, TX	9.3	4.1	13.5	40.1
St. Joseph, MO	7.5	1.4	12.6	37.4
Springfield, OH	3.9	4.3	15.0	46.5
Duluth, MN	7.2	1.2	6.1	40.4
Provo, UT	14.2	1.0	5.8	57.5
Salinas, CA	10.0	0.6	5.5	56.2
Billings, MT	13.5	1.3	4.8	35.7
12-city Mean	*7.7*	*1.8*	*10.9*	*48.1*
US Mean	*0.3*	*34.9*	*12.5*	*34.5*

*Homes built 2000–2010 (and later). ** Proportion of all housing units requiring less than 20% of householder's income
Source: US Census Bureau; "American Factfinder"; Census 2010; Table S2503; http://factfinder2.census.gov

TABLE D.8 *Selective Economic Data for Twelve-City Sample*

City Data for:	Median Household Income	Median Home Value	Retail Sales Per Capita	Cost of Living index
Fall River, MA	47,898	247,600	931,222	139.9
Trenton, NJ	36,727	122,500	402,335	113.2
Utica, NY	21,918	88,400	580,076	101.9
Roanoke, VA	38,265	134,300	2,039,763	87.6
Lake Charles, LA	36,316	119,500	1,507,469	87.6
Wichita Falls, TX	44,390	91,300	148,001	84.3
St. Joseph, MO	42,248	99,800	1,419,083	81.7
Springfield, OH	33,333	83,000	914,843	93.6
Duluth, MN	41,311	148,600	1,294,660	99.2
Provo, UT	40,288	210,300	1,202,471	87.1
Salinas, CA	50,587	279,000	194,873	102.1
Billings, MT	48,074	178,300	219,817	89.9
12-City Median	*40,799*	*128,400*	*93,303*	*91.7*
US Median	*50,046*	*181,400*	*1,200,000*	*100.0*

Sources: US Census Bureau; "American FactFinder" 2008–2012 American Community Survey. Table S1901; http://factfinder2.census.gov; US Census Bureau; "American FactFinder" 2008–2012 American Community Survey. Table DP04; http://factfinder2 .census.gov; *Palm Beach Post*, Emily Minor, ACCENT; Pg. 1D, via LexisNexis Academic; US Census Bureau; "American FactFinder"; 2010 Census; Table DP03; www.city-data.com

TABLE D.9 *Selective Educational Data for Twelve-City Sample*

City Data for:	% Private School Enrollees	% Persons with High School Diploma	% Persons with College Degrees
Fall River, MA	9.0	37.0	8.1
Trenton, NJ	8.2	31.6	2.4
Utica, NY	4.3	30.3	6.8
Roanoke, VA	6.2	35.2	7.5
Lake Charles, LA	10.3	24.6	7.7
Wichita Falls, TX	5.7	36.4	6.2
St. Joseph, MO	10.6	34.0	8.1
Springfield, OH	12.5	30.8	4.3
Duluth, MN	7.0	14.9	9.9
Provo, UT	3.7	11.0	3.1
Salinas, CA	3.0	29.7	1.6
Billings, MT	8.7	36.4	8.7
12-City Mean	*14.9*	*29.3*	*6.2*
US Mean	*10*	*29.4*	*9.2*

Sources: US Census Bureau; "American FactFinder" Census 2010; Table S1401; http://factfinder2.census.gov; "American FactFinder" Census 2010; Table S1501; http://factfinder2.census.gov; "American FactFinder" Census 2010; Table 2403; http://factfinder2.census.gov

TABLE D.10 *Selective Library Data for Twelve-City Sample*

City Data for:	Library Holdings	Library Circulation	Library Expenditures Per Capita
Fall River, MA	200,235	200,235	1.31
Trenton, NJ	375,000	196,949	2.25
Utica, NY	142,914	175,493	0.55
Roanoke, VA	315,368	1,141,376	4.49
Lake Charles, LA	231,666	1,008,544	22.94
Wichita Falls, TX	135,000	377,807	4.46
St. Joseph, MO	247,495	470,960	2.38
Springfield, OH	436,634	1,014,667	9.83
Duluth, MN	417,110	901,928	3.30
Provo, UT	240,000	1,471,000	30.41
Salinas, CA	204,665	727,227	28.74
Billings, MT	267,332	979,928	9.38
12-City Mean	*267,785*	*772,176*	*10.00*
US Mean	*N/A*	*N/A*	*20.71*

Sources: Beverly McDonough, ed., *American Library Directory: 2001–2; 2003–4; 2010–2011; 2011–12* (Medford, NJ: Information Today Inc.)

TABLE D.11 *Selective Media Data For 12-City Sample*

MSA and City Data for:	DMA Television Ranking*	% Households with Cable Services	Newspaper Subscriptions Per Capita (2012)
Fall River, MA	51	83.3	0.24
Trenton, NJ	4	79.3	0.74
Utica, NY	169	79.9	0.81
Roanoke, VA	68	52.2	0.93
Lake Charles, LA	175	67.2	0.50
Wichita Falls, TX	146	54.8	0.28
St. Joseph, MO	201	64.3	0.46
Springfield, OH	32	69.5	0.45
Duluth, MN	137	43.3	0.50
Provo, UT	35	40.7	0.27
Salinas, CA	124	62.0	0.11
Billings, MT	170	51.7	0.44
12-City Median/Mean	*109.3*	*62.4*	*0.49*
US Median/Mean	105.0	58.4	0.14

*DMA= Dominant Market Area as defined by Nielsen Market Research.
Sources: SRDS TV & Cable Source, Vol. 83 (Spring/Summer 2011); US Census, Special Edition, May 29, 2008, "American FactFinder"; Tables CB08-FFSE.03; http://factfinder2.census.gov; Gale Reference Library at www.cengage.com/search/showresults.do?N=197 +4294904997; SNL Financial and Media Services; Nielsen's Local Television Estimates, www.nielsen.com

TABLE D.12 *Selective Medical Data For 12-City Sample*

MSA Data for:	# Hospital Admissions	# Hospital Personnel (Per Capita)	Average Inpatients Per Day
Fall River, MA	63,514	7,131	298,139
Trenton, NJ	60,168	7,793	323,985
Utica, NY	36,836	5,771	258,750
Roanoke, VA	58,372	7,478	337,353
Lake Charles, LA	27,362	3,693	142,004
Wichita Falls, TX	18,399	2,138	84,739
St. Joseph, MO	19,424	2,911	87,779
Springfield, OH	108,704	1,267	544,765
Duluth, MN	42,052	8,638	288,418
Provo, UT	36,802	4,648	141,347
Salinas, CA	33,616	4,105	166,903
Billings, MT	26,361	4,822	153,591
12-City Mean	*44,300*	*5,032*	*235,648*
US Mean	*36,565*	*5,196*	*187,072,013*

Source: Hospital Statistics, 2013 edn. (Chicago: American Hospital Association, 2013)

TABLE D.13 *Selective Turnout Data for Twelve-City Sample*

County Data For:	1952 Presidential Turnout	2008 Presidential Turnout	% Change in Voter Activity
Fall River, MA	50.3	55.7	5.4
Trenton, NJ	47.3	55.8	8.5
Utica, NY	51.3	50.6	−0.7
Roanoke, VA	30.9	69.7	38.8
Lake Charles, LA	30.0	56.1	26.1
Wichita Falls, TX	26.1	45.1	19.0
St. Joseph, MO	43.4	56.7	13.3
Springfield, OH	43.2	62.1	18.9
Duluth, MN	50.1	72.3	22.2
Provo, UT	44.2	45.4	1.2
Salinas, CA	35.6	41.9	6.3
Billings, MT	47.2	60.7	13.5
12-City Mean	*41.6*	*56.0*	*+14.4*
US Mean	*39.9*	*53.4*	*+13.5*

Sources: America at the Polls: The Vote for the President, 1920–1964 (Pittsburgh: University of Pittsburgh Press, 1965); *America Votes Vol. 24: A Handbook of Contemporary American Election Statistics*, ed. R. Scammon and A. McGillivray (Washington: Congressional Quarterly, 2000); local county election offices; US Census Bureau; 2010 Census; "American Factfinder," http://factfinder2.census.gov Table QT-P1; www.cnn.com/ELECTION/2008/results/president/

TABLE D.14 Selective Partisanship Data for Twelve-City Sample*

County Data for:	1948 Democratic Vote	1948 Republican Vote	2008 Democratic Vote	2008 Republican Vote	D/R Change, 1948 vs. 2008
Fall River, MA	61.9	36.6	61.0	38.0	−0.9
Trenton, NJ	55.6	42.3	68.0	31.0	12.4
Utica, NY	49.5	47.9	46.0	52.0	−3.5
Roanoke, VA	38.6	53.5	39.0	60.0	0.4
Lake Charles, LA	56.9	15.6	37.0	61.0	−19.9
Wichita Falls, TX	77.1	18.2	30.0	69.0	−47.1
St. Joseph, MO	63.8	36.1	49.0	49.0	−14.8
Springfield, OH	48.0	51.6	48.0	51.0	0.0
Duluth, MN	64.3	29.3	66.0	33.0	1.7
Provo, UT	54.2	44.8	19.0	78.0	−35.2
Salinas, CA	46.1	50.6	68.0	30.0	21.9
Billings, MT	47.7	50.7	45.0	52.0	−2.7
12-City Mean	*55.4*	*39.5*	*47.0*	*53.0*	*−8.4*
US Mean	*49.6*	*45.1*	*53.0*	*47.0*	*3.4*

Source: "Election Center 2008," CNNPolitics.com

TABLE D.15 *Selective Fitness Data for Twelve-City Sample*

Congressional District Data for:	% Overall Well-being	% Obesity Rate	% Exercise Frequently	% Eat Produce	% Smokers	% Report Stress	% Not Insured	Air Quality Index
Fall River, MA	64.5	26.5	48.3	56.9	20.9	53.8	10.2	29.1
Trenton, NJ	65.4	25.0	49.3	56.4	15.9	60.4	12.7	29.0
Utica, NY	65.8	31.5	49.1	55.3	25.6	61.7	11.0	38.0
Roanoke, VA	67.0	23.4	52.5	59.1	23.5	60.5	19.8	32.6
Lake Charles, LA	65.7	28.7	50.4	55.6	23.4	62.7	21.8	26.9
Wichita Falls, TX	67.1	27.8	49.9	55.2	18.7	60.8	25.9	45.0
St. Joseph, MO	67.1	27.9	52.9	56.4	22.3	60.8	15.9	34.2
Springfield, OH	63.5	30.8	48.5	50.2	24.3	57.0	16.0	31.3
Duluth, MN	66.9	26.3	53.0	59.4	21.9	62.4	11.6	26.1
Provo, UT	71.4	21.4	56.5	57.6	7.0	53.4	12.5	34.9
Salinas, CA	68.2	26.1	59.5	64.0	16.5	66.5	26.2	25.1
Billings, MT	69.6	24.8	54.2	64.9	18.1	63.3	15.7	4.2
12-City Mean	*66.9*	*26.7*	*52.0*	*57.6*	*19.8*	*60.3*	*16.6*	*29.7*
US Mean	*66.5*	*26.5*	*52.8*	*58.0*	*21.0*	*59.3*	*17.0*	*32.0*

Sources: Gallup/Healthways Well-Being Index: www.gallup.com/poll/168230/boulder-colo-residents-least-likely- obese.aspx?utm_source=alert&utm_medium=email&utm_campaign=syndication&utm_content=morelink&utm_term=Well-Being; Air Quality Index, www.city-data.com

TABLE D.16 *Selective Fulfillment Data for Twelve-City Sample*

MSA and City Data for:	Twitter-Based Happiness Rank (1–388)	Religious Adherence Rank (1–941)	Ease-of-Living Rank (1–3,136)
Fall River, MA	270	28	1,200
Trenton, NJ	279	121	503
Utica, NY	340	159	1,362
Roanoke, VA	168	144	118
Lake Charles, LA	342	162	1,990
Wichita Falls, TX	246	210	1,645
St. Joseph, MO	179	332	1,813
Springfield, OH	318	107	1,987
Duluth, MN	84	170	885
Provo, UT	33	55	73
Salinas, CA	268	114	552
Billings, MT	142	305	395
12-City Median	*257*	*151*	*1,044*
US Median	*194*	*471*	*1,568*

Sources: L. Mitchell, M. R. Frank, K. D. Harris, P. S. Dodds, and C.M. Danforth, *The Geography of Happiness*, http://arxiv.org/pdf/1302.3299.pdf; *2010 U.S. Religion Census: Religious Congregations & Membership Study*, www.rcms2010.org/; A. Flippen, *Where Are the Hardest Places to Live?* www.nytimes.com/2014/06/26/upshot/where-are-the-hardest-places-to-live-in-the-us.html?_r=o

TABLE D.17 *Selective Well-Being Data for Twelve-City Sample*

Congressional District Data for:	Overall Well-Being Rank	Life Evaluation	Emotional Health	Physical Health	Healthy Behavior	Work Environ.	Basic Access
Fall River, MA	155	145	184	108	112	167	89
Trenton, NJ	112	116	125	51	79	122	131
Utica, NY	179	183	161	147	160	168	120
Roanoke, VA	66	171	17	34	124	13	76
Lake Charles, LA	104	75	143	25	189	53	114
Wichita Falls, TX	61	43	70	40	143	47	130
St. Joseph, MO	63	77	74	70	136	56	73
Springfield, OH	170	174	147	169	153	131	132
Duluth, MN	51	34	14	76	49	134	65
Provo, UT	4	5	9	43	60	27	8
Salinas, CA	28	26	25	20	1	30	181
Billings, MT	81	148	72	144	48	54	22
12-City Means	89.5	99.8	86.8	77.3	104.5	83.5	95.1
Means for All Congr. districts	66.2	48.2	79.2	76.4	63.7	48.0	81.9

Source: Gallup-Healthways Well-Being Index for 2012, www.well-beingindex.com/

308

TABLE D.18 Selective Religiosity Data for Twelve-City Sample

County Data for:	Pop.	Evangel. Prot.	%	Main. Prot.	%	Roman Catholic	%	Other	%	Religious Dominance*
Fall River, MA	548,285	18,765	3.4	20,322	3.7	286,113	52.2	7,807	1.4	48.5
Trenton, NJ	366,513	17,274	4.7	36,744	10.0	121,650	33.2	17,115	4.7	23.2
Utica, NY	234,878	9,119	3.9	19,384	8.3	86,750	36.9	4,616	2.0	28.6
Roanoke, VA	92,376	35,738	38.7	21,715	23.5	5,367	5.8	8,593	9.3	15.2
Lake Charles, LA	192,768	51,570	26.8	18,419	9.6	64,050	33.2	1,527	0.8	6.4
Wichita Falls, TX	131,500	61,669	46.9	12,306	9.4	11,699	8.9	2,472	1.9	37.5
St. Joseph, MO	89,201	24,772	27.8	7,891	8.8	8,934	10.0	2,298	2.6	17.8
Springfield, OH	138,333	18,482	13.4	14,369	10.4	9,130	6.6	1,508	1.1	3.0
Duluth, MN	200,226	19,017	9.5	33,296	16.6	38,757	19.4	2,760	1.4	2.8
Provo, UT	516,564	2,540	0.5	634	0.1	6,792	1.3	459,847	89.0	87.7
Salinas, CA	415,057	23,624	5.7	13,083	3.2	150,040	36.1	18,309	4.4	30.5
Billings, MT	147,972	20,845	14.1	12,143	8.2	17,155	11.6	7,761	5.2	2.5
12-City Mean	256,139	25,285	16.3	17,526	9.3	67,203	21.3	44,551	10.3	25.3
National Mean	150,596,792	50,013,107	33.1	28,501,860	18.9	58,934,906	39.1	13,146,919	8.7	6.0

* % primary denomination minus % secondary denomination

Sources: Association of Religion Data Archives for 2010; Religious Tradition of the Respondent: Baylor Religion Survey, Wave 2, 2007, www.thearda .com/rcms2010/r/c/3o/rcms2010_30111_county_name_2010.asp

Appendix E

Historical Snapshot of Twelve-City Newspapers

Paper	Origin	Legacies and Mergers	1948 Ownership	Subsequent Owner	Subsequent Owner	2015 Ownership	2015 Daily Circulation
Fall River Herald News	1892	News + Daily Herald + Globe	???	1960: Mark Goodson	2006: GateHouse Media	Northeast Publishing, Inc.	11,877
Trenton Times	1882	None	Kerney Family	1974: Washington Post	1981: Allbritton Communications	1986: Newhouse	30,374
Utica Observer-Dispatch	1817	Observer + Dispatch	1922: Gannett Co.			2007: GateHouse Media	28,071
Springfield News-Sun	1817	Daily News + Daily Sun	1925: James M. Cox	Seaton Publ.		2011: Cox Media Group	15,120
St. Joseph News-Press	1845	Gazette + News + Post	1889: Charles M. Palmer	1951: Henry D. Bradley		Bradleys & Missouri Press Services	22,411
Duluth News Tribune	1869	Minnesotian + Herald + Tribune + News	1936: Knight-Ridder		2006: McClatchy.	2006: Forum Communications	24,771
Roanoke Times	1886	News + World	1931: Times-World Corp.	1969: Landmark Communications		2013: Berkshire Hathaway	62,619
Lake Charles American Press	1893	American + Daily Press	1945: Thomas B. Sherman			Sherman Corp.	25,686
Wichita Falls Times Record News	1907	Weekly Times + Record News	1928: Ed Howard	1976: Harte Hanks Inc.		1997: Scripps Inc.	17,670
Billings Gazette	1885	Herald + Post + Evening Journal	1916: Anaconda Copper Mining	1959: Lee Enterprises		Lee Enterprises	32,663
Salinas Californian	1871	Index	1936: Merritt C. Speidel			1977: Gannett Corp.	7,364
Provo Daily Herald	1873	Post + Times + Herald	1926: James G. Scripps		1996: Pulitzer Co.	2005: Lee Enterprises	17,901

Appendix F

Keywords Used for Topical Determinations

ABORTION

abortion, abortions, anti-abortion, birth control, contraception, contraceptive, contraceptives, fetus, pregnancy, pro-choice, pro-life, rape or incest, reproductive, reproductive rights, right-to-choose, right-to-life, *Roe* v. *Wade*, *Roe* vs. *Wade*, sanctity-of-life

ADDICTION

addict, addiction, addictions, addictive, addicts, alcohol, alcoholism, beer, booze, cocaine, drugs, drugs, drunk, drunks, heroin, marijuana, pot, rehabilitation, smoke, smoking, whiskey, wine, withdrawal

AGRICULTURE

agriculture, animal, animals, breed, breeding, cattle, crop, crops, cultivate, cultivation, farm, farmers, farmer, farming, farms, fertilizer, forest, forests, grain, grains, harvest, harvesting, hay, livestock, planting, ranch, rancher, ranchers, ranches, ranching, rural, soil, tractor, tractors, vegetable, vegetables

CIVIL RIGHTS

African-American, African-Americans, Black Power, Blacks, civil rights, colored, desegregation, discrimination, fair housing, Freedom Ride, inner-city, KKK, Klan, Martin Luther King Jr., MLK, NAACP, negro, negroes, race, racial, racism, racist, racists, segregation, sit-in, Voting Rights Act, White flight

COMMUNISM

anti-communism, anti-communists, communism, communists, dictatorship, dictatorships, evil empire, Marxists, McCarthyism, Reds, Red China, Russia, Russians, Russians, socialism, socialist, socialists, Soviet, Soviets, spies, spy, spying, subversive, totalitarian, un-American

ELDERCARE

401K, AARP, ageing, ageism, Alzheimer's, assisted living, boomer, boomers, centenarians, dementia, elderly, feeble, frail, geriatric, gerontology, grandchild, grandchildren, grandchildren's, grandfather, grandmother, grandparent, grandparents, Greatest Generation, hospice, IRA, life expectancy, long-term care, Medicare, middle-aged, nursing care, nursing home, nursing homes, old age, older Americans, older citizens, pension, pensions, retire, retired, retiree, retirees, retirement, senior citizen, senior citizens, seniors, Social Security

ENVIRONMENT

air quality, atmosphere, contamination, environment, environmental, fertilizer, global warming, greenhouse, industrial waste, litter, nuclear waste, pesticides, pollute, pollutes, pollution, smog, toxic waste, trash

GAY RIGHTS

bisexual, bisexuals, bullying, Don't ask don't tell, gay, gay marriage, Gay rights, Gays, gender, hate crime, homophobia, homosexual, homosexuals, human rights, lesbian, lesbians, LGBT, queer, same-sex, sexual orientation, sexual rights, sodomy laws

IMMIGRATION

assimilation, border, borders, citizenship, citizenship's, emigration, ethnic, ethnicity, foreign-born, foreign workers, genocide, immigrant, immigrants, immigration, migrant, migrants, migration, nation's borders, naturalized, open border, open borders, refugee, refugees, US border, US borders

MANUFACTURING

AFL-CIO, arbitration, assembly line, bargain, bargaining, corporation, corporations, engineer, engineering, industrial, industry, iron, labor, machine, machinery, machines, management, manager, manufacture, manufacturing, mill, mills, package, packaging, product, production, products, Right-to-work, ship, shipping, ships, steel, steelworkers, strike, strikes, striking, Teamsters, technology, trade, transport, transportation, truck, trucking, trucks, UAW, unionism, unions, worker, workers

RELIGION

Allah, atheism, atheist, atheists, Baptist, Baptists, Bible, Bibles, Bible's, bishop, bishops, Catholic, Catholicism, Catholics, Christian, Christians, church, churches, church's, congregation, congregations, evangelical, evangelicals, faith, God, holy, Islam, Islamic, Jesus, Jew, Jewish, Jews, LDS, Lutheran, Lutherans, Methodist, Mormon, Mormons, Muslim, Muslims, New Testament, Old Testament, pastor, piety, pious, pray, prayer, prayers, preach, preacher, preaches, preaching, Presbyterian, Presbyterians, priest, priests, Protestant, Protestants, rabbi, religion, religions, religious, sacred, scripture, worship, worships, worshiping

SPACE PROGRAM

aerospace, Apollo, astronaut, atmosphere, exploration, flight, flights, John Glenn, landing, launch, launching, lunar, manned, Mars, Mercury, mission, moon, moon's, NASA, orbit, orbital, orbiting, pilot, pilots, planet, planet's, probe, probes, rocket, rockets, satellite, satellites, Saturn, shuttle, solar system, space, Sputnik, stars, wings

WOMEN'S RIGHTS

Affirmative Action, equal rights, gender, glass ceiling, sexism, sexist, sexual harassment, suffrage, woman's, woman's right, women's, women's lib, women's liberation, women's rights

Bibliography

"Anne Spurzem, Smith College alum writes controversial letter to the editor," *Huffington Post*, February 27, 2012. Accessed at www.huffingtonpost.com/2012/02/24/smith-college-alum-writes-too-many-poor_n_1300279.html.

"It is Donald Trump's Washington now – what's next?" *Denver Post*, November 9, 2016. Accessed at www.denverpost.com/2016/11/09/how-donald-trump-won-and-why-the-media-missed-it/.

Abramowitz, Alan I. and Morris P. Fiorina. "Polarized or sorted? Just what's wrong with our politics anyway?" *The American Interest*, 2013. Accessed at www.the-american-interest.com/2013/03/11/polarized-or-sorted-just-whats-wrong-with-our-politics-anyway/.

Lincoln, Abraham. "Letter to Horace Greeley," August 12, 1862. Accessed at www.abrahamlincolnonline.org/lincoln/speeches/greeley.htm.

Agiesta, Jennifer, "Poll: political independents outweigh partisans," *Huffington Post*, June 4, 2012. Accessed at www.huffingtonpost.com/huff-wires/20120604/us-independent-voters-poll/.

Ahn, Toh-Kyeong, Robert Huckfeldt, Alexander K. Mayer, and John Barry Ryan, "Expertise and bias in political communication networks," *American Journal of Political Science*, 57(2) (2013), 357–373.

Alanna, "Chris Royse's controversial letter to the editor re. Christmas, abortion," *Moonhowlings: A Place for Civil Debate*, December 8, 2008. Accessed at www.moonhowlings.net/index.php/2008/12/08/chris-royses-letter-to-the-editor/.

Althaus, Scott L., Anne M. Cizmar, and James G. Gimpel, "Media supply, audience demand, and the geography of news consumption in the United States," *Political Communication*, 26 (2009), 249–77.

Anderson, Benedict, *Imagined Communities: Reflections on the Origin and Spread of Nationalism*, rev. edn. (London: Verso, 1991).

Anderson, Ashley A., Dominique Brossard, Dietram A. Scheufele, Michael A. Xenos, and Peter Ladwig, "The 'nasty effect': online incivility and risk perceptions of emerging technologies," *Journal of Computer-Mediated Communication*, 19(3) (2014), 373–87.

Andre, Judith, "Open hope as a civic virtue: Ernst Bloch and Lord Buddha," *Social Philosophy Today*, 29 (2013), 95, 97.

Andrews, Molly, *Lifetimes of Commitment: Aging, Politics, Psychology* (Cambridge: Cambridge University Press, 1991).

Ansolabehere, Stephen and James M. Snyder Jr., "Rules, politics, and policy," *Election Law Journal*, 1(3) (2004), 315–38.

Ardelt, Monika, "Wisdom as expert knowledge system: a critical review of a contemporary operationalization of an ancient concept," *Human Development*, 47 (2004), 257–85.

Ashraf, Hina, "Letters to the editor: a resistant genre of unrepresented voices," *Discourse & Communication*, 1 (2013), 1–19.

Atkins, Judi and Alan Finlayson, "'As Shakespeare so memorably said…': quotation, rhetoric, and the performance of politics," *Political Studies* 64(1) (2014), 164–81.

Atkinson, Lucy, "The public sphere in print: do letters to the editor serve as a forum for rationale-critical debate?" Paper submitted to the Cultural and Critical Studies Division, Association for Education in Journalism & Mass Communication, Washington, DC, 2007.

Austin, John L., *How to Do Things with Words*, 2nd edn. (Cambridge: Harvard University Press, 1975).

Azari, Julia R., *Delivering the People's Message: The Changing Politics of the Presidential Mandate* (Ithaca: Cornell University Press, 2014).

Barbazon, Tara, *Unique Urbanity? Rethinking Third Tier Cities, Degeneration, Regeneration and Mobility* (Singapore: Springer, 2015).

Barlow, Aaron, *The Rise of the Blogosphere* (Westport: Praeger, 2007), p. 37.

Barrette, Elizabeth, "Origami emotion," in Paul Rogat Loeb (ed.), *The Impossible Will Take a Little While: Perseverance and Hope in Troubled Times* (New York: Basic Books, 2014).

Baruch, Yehuda and Brooks C. Holtom, "Survey response rate levels and trends in organizational research," *Human Relations*, 61(8) (2008), 1139–60.

Baum, Matthew A., "Circling the wagons: soft news and isolationism in American public opinion," *International Studies Quarterly*, 48(2) (2004), 313–38.

Bazerman, Charles, "Letters and the social grounding of differentiated genres," in David Barton and Nigel Hall (eds.), *Letter Writing as a Social Practice* (Philadelphia: John Benjamins, 1999), pp. 15–30.

Beasley, Vanessa, *You, the People: American National Identity in Presidential Rhetoric* (College Station: Texas A&M University Press, 2003).

Bellah, Robert N., "Citizenship, diversity, and the search for the common good," in Robert E. Calvert (ed.), *"The Constitution of the People": Reflections on Citizens and Civil Society* (Lawrence: University Press of Kansas, 1991), p. 47–63.

Bellah, Robert N., Richard Madsen, William M. Sullivan, Ann Swidler, and Steven M. Tipton, *Habits of the Heart: Individualism and Commitment in American Life* (Berkeley: University of California Press, 2007).

Bellow, Saul, *Herzog* (Greenwich: Fawcett Crest, 1965).

Bennett, Stephen Earl, *Apathy in America, 1960–1984: Causes and Consequences of Citizen Political Indifference* (Dobbs Ferry: Transnational, 1986).

Bennett, W. Lance, "Changing citizenship in the digital age," in W. Lance Bennett (ed.), *Civic Life Online: Learning How Digital Media Can Engage Youth* (Cambridge: MIT Press, 2008), p. 1–24.

"The uncivic culture: communication, identity, and the rise of lifestyle politics," *PS: Political Science and Politics*, 31 (1998), 740–61.

Berry, Wendell, *Home Economics* (San Francisco: North Point Press, 1987).

Bertsou, Eri, "Disentangling political distrust: what do citizens mean and think when expressing distrust towards political institutions and politicians?" Paper presented at the annual meeting of the Midwest Political Science Association, Chicago, April 2014.

Black, Jeremy, *Maps and Politics* (Chicago: University of Chicago Press, 1998).

Blais, André, *To Vote or Not to Vote? The Merits and Limits of Rational Choice Theory* (Pittsburgh: University of Pittsburgh Press, 2000).

Bligh, Michelle C., Jeffrey C. Kohles, and James R. Meindl, "Charting the language of leadership: a methodological investigation of President Bush and the crisis of 9/11," *Journal of Applied Psychology*, 89(3) (2004), 562–74.

Blom, Robin, Serena Carpenter, Brian J. Bowe, and Ryan Lange, "Frequent contributors in U.S. newspaper comment forums: an examination of their civility and informational value," Paper presented at the annual meeting of the International Communication Association, London, June 2013.

Blumenthal, Paul, "Crowdpac helps small donors find a perfect match in politics," *Huffington Post*, October 7, 2014, 2. Accessed at www.huffingtonpost.com/2014/10/07/crowdpac-donors_n_5943022.html.

Boczkowski, Pablo J. and Eugenia Mitchelstein, *The News Gap: When the Information Preferences of the Media and the Public Diverge* (Cambridge: MIT Press, 2013).

Boczkowski, Pablo J. and Eeugenia Mitchelstein, "The prosumption practices of monitorial citizens: accounting for the most commented stories on leading online news sites during and after the U.S. 2008 presidential election," Paper presented at the annual meeting of the International Communication Association, Boston, May 2011.

Bogart, Leo, "The public's use and perception of newspapers," *Public Opinion Quarterly*, 48 (1984), 709–719.

Bovens, Luc, "The value of hope," *Philosophy and Phenomenological Research*, 59 (1999), 667–681.

Brabazon, Tara, *Unique Urbanity: Rethinking Third Tier Cities, Degeneration, Regeneration and Mobility* (London: Springer, 2015).

Brady, Emily and Arto Haapala, "Melancholy as an aesthetic emotion," *Contemporary Aesthetics*, 1 (2003), 10. Accessed at http://hdl.handle.net/2027/spo.7523862.0001.006.

Brady, David W., Hahrie Han, and Jeremy C. Pope, "Primary elections and candidate ideology: out of step with the primary electorate," *Legislative Studies Quarterly*, 32(1) (2007), 79–105.

Braithwaite, John, "Emancipation and hope," *The Annals of the American Academy of Political and Social Science*, 592 (2004), 179–198.

Braithwaite, Valerie, "The hope process and social inclusion," *The Annals of the American Academy of Political and Social Science*, 592 (2004), 128–151.

Bramlett, Brittany H., "Aged communities and political knowledge," *American Politics Research*, 41 (2013), 674–98.

Brehm, John and Wendy Rahn, "Individual-level evidence for the causes and consequences of social capital," *American Journal of Political Science*, 41 (1997), 999–1023.

Bridges, Thomas, *The Culture of Citizenship: Inventing Postmodern Civic Culture* (Albany: SUNY Press, 1994).

Broersma, Marcel and Todd Graham, "Social media as beat: Tweets as a news source during the 2010 British and Dutch elections," *Journalism Practice*, 6 (2012), 403–19.

Bromley, Michael, "'Watching the watchdogs'? The role of readers' letters in calling the press to account," in Hugh Stephenson and Michael Bromley (eds.), *Sex, Lies and Democracy: The Press and the Public* (New York: Longman, 1998), pp. 147–62.

Brookhart, Jennifer L. and Alexander Moss Tahk, "The origin of ideas," Paper presented to the 72rd Annual Meeting of the Midwest Political Science Association, Chicago, April 2015.

Brooks, Arthur C., "We need optimists," *New York Times*, July 25, 2015. Accessed at www.nytimes.com/2015/07/26/opinion/sunday/arthur-c-brooks-we-need-optimists.html?_r=0.

Brooks, David, "Are we on the path to national ruin?" *New York Times*, July 12, 2016, 17. Accessed at www.nytimes.com/2016/07/12/opinion/are-we-on-the-path-to-national-ruin.html?_r=0.

"How to fix politics," *New York Times*, April 12, 2016, 15–16.

Brown, Sarah, "A scholar of racial equity describes his 'painful gratitude' for Donald Trump," *Chronicle of Higher Education*, January 20, 2017, A22.

Brundidge, Jennifer, "Encountering 'difference' in the contemporary public sphere: the contribution of the internet to the heterogeneity of political discussion networks," *Journal of Communication*, 60 (2010), 680–700.

Bryan, Frank M., *Real Democracy: The New England Town Meeting and How It Works* (Chicago: University of Chicago Press, 2004).

Buell, Emmett H. "Eccentrics or gladiators? People who write about politics in letters-to-the-editor," *Social Science Quarterly*, 56 (1975–6), 440–449.

Burgess, Jean, "Hearing ordinary voices: cultural studies, vernacular creativity and digital storytelling," *Continuum: Journal of Media & Culture Studies*, 20 (2006), 201–214.

Burke, Kenneth, *A Rhetoric of Motives* (Berkeley: University of California Press, 1950).

Burkeman, Oliver, "The power of negative thinking: both ancient philosophy and modern psychology suggest that darker thoughts can make us happier," *Wall Street Journal*, December 7, 2012, 5, 8. Accessed at www.wsj.com/articles/SB10001424127887324705104578147333270637790.

Burn, Stephen (ed.), *Conversations with David Foster Wallace* (Jackson: University Press of Mississippi, 2012).

Butler, Daniel M. and Emily Schofield, "Were newspapers more interested in pro-Obama letters to the editor in 2008? Evidence from a field experiment," *American Politics Research*, 38 (2010), 356–71.

Byers, Dylan, "How politicians, pollsters and media missed Trump's ground-swell," *CNN Media*, November 9, 2016. Accessed at http://money.cnn .com/2016/11/09/media/polling-media-missed-trump.

Cammaerts, Bart and Leo Van Audenhove, "Online political debate, unbound citizenship, and the problematic nature of a transnational public sphere," *Political Communication*, 22 (2005), 179–196.

Campbell, David, "Cold wars: securing identity, identifying danger," in Frederick M. Dolan and Thomas L. Dumm (eds.), *Rhetorical Republic: Governing Representations in American Politics* (Amherst: University of Massachusetts Press, 1993), pp. 39–60.

Campbell, James, *The American Campaign: U.S. Presidential Campaigns and the National Vote* (College Station: Texas A&M Press, 2000).

Campbell, James E., "The miserable presidential election of 2012: a first party-term incumbent survives," *The Forum*, 10(4) (2012), 20–28.

Campbell, Karlyn Kohrs and Kathleen Hall Jamieson, *Presidents Creating the Presidency: Deeds Done in Words* (Chicago: University of Chicago Press, 2008).

Canovan, Margaret, *The People* (Cambridge: Polity, 2005).

Carey, Michael, "All sorts mingle at 'Letter Writers Ball,'" *The Masthead*, June 22, 1997. Accessed at www.thefreelibrary.com/All+sorts+mingle+at+'Letter +Writers+Ball.'+%28meeting+of+writers+of...-a021059906.

Carlin, Diana B., Dan Schill, David G. Levasseur, and Anthony S. King, "The post-9/11 public sphere: citizen talk about the 2004 presidential debates," *Rhetoric & Public Affairs*, 8 (2005), 617–638.

Carlson, Matt and Eran Ben-Porath, "'The People's Debate': the CNN/YouTube debates and the demotic voice in political journalism," *Journalism Practice*, 6 (2012), 302–316.

Carson, Jamie, Joel Sievert, and Ryan Williamson, "Assessing the rise and development of the incumbency advantage in Congress," Paper presented at the Congress and History Conference held at Vanderbilt University, May 22–23, 2015.

Chabot, Dana, "In defense of 'moderate' relativism and 'skeptical' citizenship," Paper presented at the annual convention of the American Political Science Association, Washington, DC, 1993.

Chamberlain, Adam, "The (dis)connection between political culture and external efficacy," *American Politics Research*, 41(5) (2013), 761–82.

Chouliaraki, Lilie, "Ordinary witnessing in post-television news: towards a new moral imagination," *Critical Discourse Studies*, 7 (2010), 305–319.

Chouliaraki, Lillie, "Self-mediation: new media and citizenship," *Critical Discourse Studies*, 7 (2010), 227–232.

Civettini, Andrew J. W., "Hope and voting: exploring the usefulness of hope scales in examining political participation," Paper presented at the annual meeting of the Midwest Political Science Association, Chicago, 2010.

Clark, April K., "Rethinking the decline in social capital," *American Politics Research*, 43(4) (2015), 569–601.

Clarke, John, "Enrolling ordinary people: governmental strategies and the avoidance of politics?" *Citizenship Studies*, 14(6) (2010), 637–650.

Coe, Kevin, Kate Kenski, and Stephen Rains, "Online and uncivil? Patterns and determinants of incivility in newspaper website comments," *Journal of Communication*, 64(4) (2014), 658–79.

Coffey, Daniel J., Michael Kohler, and Douglas M. Granger, "Sparking debate: campaigns, social media, and political incivility," in Victoria A. Farrar-Myers and Justin S. Vaughn (eds.), *Controlling the Message: New Media in American Political Campaigns* (New York: New York University Press, 2015), 245–269.

Cohn, Bob, "21 charts that explain American values today," *The Atlantic*, June 27, 2012. Accessed at www.theatlantic.com/national/archive/2012/06/21-charts-that-explain-american-values-today/258990/.

Coleman, Stephen, "Beyond the po-faced public sphere," in Stephen Coleman, Giles Moss, Katy Parry, John Halperin, and Michael Ryan (eds.), *Can the Media Serve Democracy? Essays in Honor of Jay G. Blumler* (London: Palgrave, 2015), pp. 184–193.

How Voters Feel (New York: Cambridge University Press, 2013).

Cooper, Christopher A. and H. Gibbs Knotts, "Voice of the people? Analyzing letters to the editor in North Carolina newspapers," Paper presented at the annual meeting of the American Political Science Association, Washington, DC, September 2005.

Cooper, Christopher, H. Gibbs Knotts, and Moshe Haspel, "The content of political participation: letters to the editor and the people who write them," *Political Science & Politics*, 42(1) (2009), 131–7.

Corwin, Norman, "On a note of triumph," CBS Radio, May 8, 1945. Reprinted in Studs Terkel, *Hope Dies Last: Keeping the Faith in Difficult Times* (New York: New Press, 2003), p. xxi.

Craig, Stephen C. and Michael A. Maggiotto, "Measuring political efficacy," *Political Methodology*, 8 (1982), 85–109.

Cramer, Katherine, *The Politics of Resentment: Rural Consciousness in Wisconsin and the Rise of Scott Walker* (Chicago: University of Chicago Press, 2016).

Cranberg, Gilbert, "Genuine letters help democratize our debate: letters give a window into how regular folks see the events of the day," *The Masthead*, September 22, 2004.

Crosby, Ned, *Healthy Democracy: Bringing Trustworthy Information to the Voters of America Paperback* (Edina: Beavers Pond Press, 2003).

da Silva, Marisa Torres, "Newsroom practices and letters-to-the-editor: an analysis of selection criteria," *Journalism Practice*, 6 (2012), 250–263.

"Professional views on letters-to-the-editor as a means of audience participation," *Participations: Journal of Audience & Reception Studies*, 10 (2013), 430.

Dagger, Richard, "Metropolis, memory and citizenship," *American Journal of Political Science*, 25 (1981), 715–737.

"Metropolis, memory and citizenship," *American Political Science Review*, 25 (1981), 725, 729.

Dahlgren, Peter, "The public sphere and the net: structure, space and communication," in E. Lance Bennett and Robert M. Entman (eds.), *Mediated Politics: Communication in the Future of Democracy* (New York: Cambridge University Press, 2001), pp. 33–55.

Darr, Joshua P., "The news you use: political knowledge and the importance of local newspapers," Paper presented to the 73rd annual meeting of the Midwest Political Science Association, Chicago, April 2015.

Data, Daily, "The most liberal and conservative cities in America," December 15, 2015. Accessed at www.crowdpac.com/blog/the-most-liberal-and-conserva tive-cities-in-america.

Dauenhauer, Bernard P., "The place of hope in responsible political practice," in Jaklin A. Eliott (ed.), *Interdisciplinary Perspectives on Hope* (New York: Nova Science Publishers, 2005), 81–97.

Davidson, William B. and Patrick R. Cotter, "Psychological sense of community and newspaper readership," *Psychological Reports*, 80 (1997), 659–65.

Davis, Richard, *Politics Online: Blogs, Chatrooms, and Discussion Groups in American Democracy* (New York: Routledge, 2005).

Deckard, Natalie Delia and Irene Browne, "Constructing citizenship: framing unauthorized immigrants in market terms," *Citizenship Studies*, 19(6–7) (2015), 664–81.

DeKeyser, Jeroen and Karin Raeymaeckers, "The printed rise of the common man: how Web 2.0 has changed the representation of ordinary people in newspapers," *Journalism Studies*, 13(5–6) (2012), 825–35.

Diakopoulos, Nicholas and Mor Naaman, "Towards quality discourse in online news comments," in Pamela Hinds, John C. Tang, and Jian Wang (eds.), *Proceedings of the ACM 2011 Conference on Computer Supported Cooperative Work* (New York: Association for Computing Machinery, 2011), pp. 133–42.

Dickinson, Greg, *Suburban Dreams: Imaging and Building the Good Life* (Tuscaloosa: University of Alabama Press, 2015).

Dickinson, Matthew, "No, America's not divided: what everyone gets wrong about political polarization," *Politico Magazine*, June 20, 2014. Accessed at www.politico.com/magazine/story/2014/06/no-americas-not-divided-108119#ixzz4CRAjabNC.

Dillard, James Price and Steven J. Backhaus, "An exploration into emotion and civic deliberation," Paper presented at the annual meeting of the National Communication Association, Chicago, November, 1997.

Dinesen, Peter Thisted, Aasbjørn Sonne Nørgaard, and Robert Klemmensen, "The civic personality: personality and democratic citizenship," *Political Studies*, 62(1) (2014), 134–152.

Dionne, Eugene Joseph Jr., "The good that could come from a Trump presidency," *Washington Post*, December 28, 2016. Accessed at www.washingtonpost.com/opinions/the-good-that-could-come-from-a-trump-presidency/2016/12/28/63f5c 82e-cdoe-11e6-a87f-b91706733 1bb_story.html?utm_term=.e08b97dff23e.

Domke, David, *God Willing? Political Fundamentalism in the White House, the "War on Terror," and the Echoing Press* (London: Pluto Press, 2004).

Donnelly, Daria, "The power to die: Emily Dickinson's letters of consolation," in Rebecca Earle (ed.), *Epistolary Selves: Letters and Letter-Writers, 1600–1945* (Farnham: Ashgate, 1999), 134–151.

Drahos, Peter, "Trading in public hope," *The Annals of the American Academy of Political and Social Science*, 592(1) (2004), 18–38.

Druckman, James N. and Justin W. Holmes, "Does presidential rhetoric matter? Priming and presidential approval," *Presidential Studies Quarterly*, 34(4) (2004) 755–78.

Dunkelman, Marc, *The Vanishing Neighbor: The Transformation of American Community* (New York: Norton, 2014).

Dupre, Michael and David Mackey, "Letters and phone-mails to the editor: a comparison of reader input," *Newspaper Research Journal*, 23 (2002), 142–7.

Durkheim, Émile, *The Elementary Forms of the Religious Life*, Mark S. Cladis (ed.); trans. Carol Cosman (New York: Oxford University Press, 2008).

Duscha, Julius, "Letters to the editor now come via many routes," *NewsInc*, October 11, 1999. Accessed at www.thefreelibrary.com/letters+to+editors+now+come +via+many+routes+%3a+One+of+the+best+read...-a057101806.

Dzwonkowski, Ron, "It's a cheap form of propaganda: now they are offering prizes to people who trick newspapers into publishing fake letters," *The Masthead*, 56, September 22, 2004, 12. Accessed at www.highbeam.com/ doc/1G1-123078809.html.

Eagleton, Terry, *Hope without Optimism* (Charlottesville: University of Virginia Press, 2015).

Earle, Rebecca, "Introduction: letters, writers and the historian," in Rebecca Earle (ed.), *Epistolary Selves: Letters and Letter-Writers, 1600–1945* (Aldershot: Ashgate, 1999), 1–14.

Edelstein, Alex S. and Otto N. Larsen, "The weekly press' contribution to a sense of urban community," *Journalism & Mass Communication Quarterly*, 37(4) (1960), 489–98.

Edwards, Lee, "Accommodating agency and reflexivity in Bourdieu's analysis of language and discourse," Paper presented at the annual meeting of the International Communication Association, Boston, May 2011.

Ehrenfreund, Max, "These political scientists are discovering even more reasons U.S. politics are a disaster," *Washington Post*, November 3, 2015, 12. Accessed at www.washingtonpost.com/news/wonk/wp/2015/11/03/these-pol itical-scientists-are-discovering-even-more-reasons-u-s-politics-are-a-disaster/.

Emerson, Ralph Waldo, "Second centennial of Concord," in J. E. Cabot (ed.), *Emerson's Complete Works: Miscellanies* (Boston: Houghton Mifflin, 1883).

Erikson, Robert S. and Christopher Wlezien, *The Timeline of Presidential Elections: How Campaigns Do (and Do Not) Matter* (Chicago: University of Chicago Press, 2012).

Esser, Frank, "Dimensions of political news cultures: sound bite and image bite news in France, Germany, Great Britain, and the United States," *International Journal of Press/Politics*, 13(4) (2008), 401–28.

Eveland, William P. and Ivan Dylko, "Reading political blogs during the 2004 election campaign: correlates and political consequences," in Mark Tremayne (ed.), *Blogging Citizenship, and the Future of Media* (New York: Routledge, 2007), pp. 114ff.

Farnsworth, Stephen J. and S. Robert Lichter, *The Nightly News Nightmare: Television's Coverage of U.S. Presidential Elections, 1988–2004* (Lanham: Rowman & Littlefield, 2007).

Finkel, Steven E., "Reciprocal effects of participation and political efficacy: a panel analysis," *American Journal of Political Science*, 29 (1985), 891–913.

Firmstone, Julie and Stephen Coleman, "Rethinking local communicative spaces: implications of digital media and citizen journalism for the role of local journalism in engaging citizens," in Rasmus K. Nielsen (ed.), *Local Journalism: The Decline of Newspapers and the Rise of Digital Media* (London: Tauris & Co., 2015), pp. 117–40.

Fishkin, James S., *When the People Speak: Deliberative Democracy and Public Consultation* (New York: Oxford University Press, 2011).

Flatley, Johnathan, *Affective Mapping: Melancholia and the Politics of Modernism* (Cambridge: Harvard University Press, 2008).

Fowler, Robert Booth, *The Dance with Community: The Contemporary Debate in American Political Thought* (Lawrence: University of Kansas Press, 1991).

Fox, Richard J., Melvin R. Crask, and Jonghoon Kim, "Mail survey response rate: a meta-analysis of selected techniques for inducing response," *Public Opinion Quarterly*, 52(4) (1988), 467–91.

Freud, Sigmund, "Mourning and melancholia," in James Strachey (trans.), *Complete Psychological Works of Sigmund Freud*, vol. 14 (London: Hogarth Press, 2016), p. 243–258.

Frisinger, Jim and Luanne Traud, "An e-mail conversation: how to deal with letter-planters; let's try the town square rule for determining legitimate letters," *The Masthead* (56), September 22, 2004. Accessed at www.highbeam.com/doc/1G1-123078816.html.

Fryrear, Andrea, "Survey response rates," *Survey Gizmo*, July 27, 2015. Accessed at www.surveygizmo.com/survey-blog/survey-response-rates/.

Fulwider, John, "Newspaper requires letter writers to be registered voters," *AP Online*, May 19, 1998. Accessed at www.highbeam.com/doc/1P1-19723286.html.

Funk, Marcus, "Imagined commodities? Analyzing local identity and place in American community newspaper website banners," *New Media & Society*, 5 (2012), 574–595.

Gainous, Jason and Kevin M. Wagner, "Surfing to the extremes: the polarization of public opinion," Paper presented at the annual meeting of the Midwest Political Science Association, Chicago, April 2015.

Gans, Herbert, *Middle American Individualism: The Future of Liberal Democracy* (New York: Free Press, 1988).

Garfield, Simon, *To the Letter: A Celebration of the Lost Art of Letter Writing* (New York: Gotham, 2013).

Gastil, John and Michael Xenos, "Of attitudes and engagement: clarifying the reciprocal relationship between civic attitudes and political participation," *Journal of Communication*, 60 (2010), 318–43.

Gershtenson, Joseph and Dennis L. Plane, "In government we distrust: citizen skepticism and democracy in the United States," *The Forum*, 13(3) (2015), 481–505.

Gervais, Bryan T., "Incivility online: affective and behavioral reactions to uncivil political posts in a Web-based experiment," *Journal of Information Technology & Politics*, 12(2) (2015), 167–85.

Ghadessy, Mohsen, "Information structure in letters to the editor," *International Review of Applied Linguistics in Language Teaching*, 21 (1983), 46–56.

Gibson, Ginger and Chris Kahn, "America's angry voters divvied by Trump and Sanders: poll," *Reuters*, January 30, 2016. Accessed at www.reuters.com/article/us-usa-election-anger-idUSMTZSAPEC1USEXIB3.

Glaeser, Edward, *Triumph of the City: How our Greatest Invention Makes Us Richer, Smarter, Greener, Healthier, and Happier* (New York: Penguin, 2011), p. 64.

Glendon, Mary Ann, *Rights Talk: The Impoverishment of Political Discourse* (New York: The Free Press, 1991).

Goldman, Loren, "What is political hope? Kantian reflections on practical philosophy," Paper presented at the annual meeting of the Midwest Political Science Association, Chicago, April 2008, p. 8.

Goss, Brian Michael, "Online 'looney tunes': an analysis of reader-composed comment threads in *The Nation*," *Journalism Studies*, 8 (2007), 365–81.

Goyanes, Manuel, "The value of proximity: examining the willingness to pay for online local news," *International Journal of Communication*, 9 (2015), 1507, 1505–1522.

Graham, Todd and Scott Wright, "Discursive equality and everyday talk online: the impact of 'superparticipants,'" *Journal of Computer-Mediated Communication*, 19(3) (2014), 625–42.

Gray, Sean W. D., "Mapping silent citizenship: how democratic theory hears citizens' silence and why it matters," *Citizenship Studies*, 19(5) (2015), 474–91.

Grey, David L. and Brown, Trevor R., "Letters to the editor: hazy reflections of public opinion," *Journalism and Mass Communication Quarterly*, 47 (1970), 450–471.

Groeling, Tim and Samuel Kernell, "Is network news coverage of the president biased?" *The Journal of Politics*, 60(4) (1998) 1063–87.

Gross, Kimberly, Paul R. Brewer, and Sean Aday, "Confidence in government and emotional responses to terrorism after September 11, 2001," *American Politics Research*, 37 (2009), 107–28.

Grossman, Matt and David A. Hopkins, "Ideological Republicans and group interest Democrats: the asymmetry of American party politics," *Perspectives on Politics*, 13(1) (2015), 119–39.

Gutman, Amy and Dennis Thompson, *Democracy and Disagreement: Why Moral Conflict Cannot Be Avoided in Politics, and What Should Be Done About It* (Cambridge: Harvard University Press, 1996).

Habermas, Jürgen, "Citizenship and national identity," in Bart Van Steenbergen (ed.), *The Condition of Citizenship* (London: Sage, 1994), 20–35.

Hagner, Paul, Linda Maule, and Janine Alisa Parry, "Political culture and information supply and consumption," Paper presented at the annual meeting of the Midwest Political Science Association, Chicago, April 1996.

Haidt, Jonathan, "The positive emotion of elevation," *Prevention & Treatment*, 3 (2000), 1–5.

Harlow, Summer, "Story-chatterers stirring up hate: racist discourse in reader comments on U.S. newspaper websites," *Howard Journal of Communications*, 26 (2015), 21–42.

Hart, Roderick P., "The rhetoric of the true believer," *Communication Monographs*, 38(4) (1971), 249–61.

Seducing America: How Television Charms the Modern Voter (New York: Oxford University Press, 1994).

Hart, Roderick P., Jay P. Childers, and Colene J. Lind, *Political Tone: How Leaders Talk and Why* (Chicago: University of Chicago Press, 2013), pp. 59–88.

Hart, Roderick P. and Alexander L. Curry, "The third voice of American politics," *Presidential Studies Quarterly*, 46(1) (2016), 73–97.

Hart, Roderick P. and Suzanne M. Daughton, *Modern Rhetorical Criticism*, 3rd edn. (Boston: Pearson, 2005).

Hart, Stephen, *Cultural Dilemmas of Progressive Politics: Styles of Engagement among Grassroots Activists* (Chicago: University of Chicago Press, 2001).

Hauser, Gerard A., *Vernacular Voices: The Rhetoric of Publics and Public Spheres* (Columbia: University of South Carolina Press, 1999).

Hawken, Paul, "You are brilliant and the earth is hiring," in Paul Loeb (ed.), *The Impossible Will Take a Little While: Perseverance and Hope in Troubled Times* (New York: Basic Books, 2014), 54–59.

Hayes, Andrew F., Dietram A. Scheufele, and Michael E. Huge, "Nonparticipation as self-censorship: publicly observable political activity in a polarized opinion climate," *Political Behavior*, 28 (2006), 259–283.

Hayes, Danny and Jennifer L. Lawless, "As local news goes, so goes citizen engagement: media, knowledge, and participation in U.S. house elections," *The Journal of Politics*, 77(2) (2015), 447–62.

Heinonen, Ari, "The journalist's relationship with users: new dimensions to conventional roles," in Jane B. Singer et al. (eds.), *Participatory Journalism: Guarding Open Gates at Online Newspapers* (Chichester: Wiley-Blackwell, 2011), pp. 34–55.

Herbst, Susan, *Reading Public Opinion: How Political Actors View the Democratic Process* (Chicago: University of Chicago Press, 1998).

Hermida, Alfred, "Fluid spaces, fluid journalism: the role of the "active recipient" in participatory journalism," in Jane Singer et al. (eds.), *Participatory Journalism: Guarding Open Gates at Online Newspapers* (Chichester: Wiley-Blackwell, 2011), pp. 177–91.

Hermida, Alfred and Neil Thurman, "A clash of cultures: the integration of user-generated content within professional journalistic frameworks at British newspaper websites," *Journalism Practice*, 2 (2008), 343–56.

Herring, Susan C., Lois A. Scheidt, Inna Kouper, and Elijah Wright, "Longitudinal content analysis of blogs: 2003–2004," in Mark Tremayne (ed.), *Blogging, Citizenship, and the Future of Media* (New York: Taylor and Francis, 2007), pp. 3–20.

Hibbing, John R. and Elizabeth Theiss-Morse, "Americans' desire for stealth democracy: how declining trust boosts political participation," Paper presented at the annual convention of the Midwest Political Science Association, Chicago, April 2001.

"How trustworthy politicians decrease mass political participation," Paper presented at the annual convention of the American Political Science Association, San Francisco, September 2001.

Congress as Public Enemy: Public Attitudes toward American Political Institutions (Cambridge: Cambridge University Press, 1995).

Hill, David B., "Letter opinion on ERA: a test of the newspaper bias hypothesis," *Public Opinion Quarterly*, 45(3) (1981), 384–92.

Hoffer, Eric, *The True Believer: Thoughts on the Nature of Mass Movements* (New York: Harper and Row, 1951).

Hoffman, Lindsay H. and William P. Eveland Jr., "Assessing causality in the relationship between community attachment and local news media use," *Mass Communication and Society*, 13 (2010), 174–195.

Hogan, Jackie, "Letters to the editor in the 'War on Terror': a cross-national study," *Mass Communication & Society*, 9 (2006), 63–83.

Hollander, Barry A., "Tuning out or tuning elsewhere? Partisanship, polarization, and media migration from 1998 to 2006," *Journalism and Mass Communication Quarterly*, 85(1) (2008), 23–40.

Honoré, Carl, *In Praise of Slow: How a Worldwide Movement is Challenging the Cult of Speed* (London: Orion, 2004).

Hooghe, Marc and Jennifer Oser, "Partisan identity, civic associations and the development of trust in the United States: an analysis of the General Social Survey, 1972–2012," Paper presented at the annual meeting of the Midwest Political Science Association, Chicago, April 2014.

Hopkins, Dan J., "The increasingly United States," Paper prepared for the Annual Meeting of the American Political Science Association, Washington, DC, August 2014.

Horwitz, Steven, "Markets are the voice of the people: modern populists have it all backwards," *Foundation for Economic Education*, May 12, 2016. Accessed at https://fee.org/articles/markets-are-the-voice-of-the-people/.

Huckfeld, Robert and John Sprague, *Citizens, Politics, and Social Communication: Information and Influence in an Election Campaign* (New York: Cambridge, 1995).

Hudson, Wayne, "Bloch and a philosophy of the proterior," in Peter Thompson and Slavoj Žižek (eds.), *The Privatization of Hope: Ernst Bloch and the Future of Utopia* (Durham: Duke University Press, 2013), pp. 21–36.

Hughey, Matthew W. and Jessie Daniels, "Racist comments at online news sites: a methodological dilemma for discourse analysis," *Media, Culture & Society*, 35 (2013), 332–47.

Ingraham, Chris, "Talking (about) the elite and mass: vernacular rhetoric and discursive status," *Philosophy and Rhetoric*, 46 (2013), 6, 14.

Iyengar, Shanto, Mark D. Peters, and Donald R. Kinder, "Experimental demonstrations of the 'not-so-minimal' consequences of television news programs," *American Political Science Review*, 76(4) (1982), 848–58.

Iyengar, Shanto, Helmut Norpoth, and Kyu S. Hahn, "Consumer demand for election news: the horserace sells," *Journal of Politics*, 66(1) (2004), 157–75.

Iyengar, Shanto and Sean J. Westwood, "Fear and loathing across party lines: new evidence on group polarization," *American Journal of Political Science*, 59(3) (2015), 690–707.

Iyengar, Shanto, Tobias Konitzer, and Kent Tedin, "The home as a political fortress: family agreement in an era of polarization," Working paper, Department of Communication, Stanford University, May 2016.

Janowitz, Morris, *The Community Press in an Urban Setting* (Glencoe: Free Press, 1952).

Jarvis, Sharon E. and Soo-Hye Han, "The mobilized voter: portrayals of electoral participation in print coverage of campaign 2008," *American Behavioral Scientist*, 55(4) (2011), 419–436.

"From an honored value to a harmful choice: how presidential candidates have discussed electoral participation (1948–2012)," *American Behavioral Scientist*, 57(12) (2013), 1650–1662.

Jeffres, Leo W., Jean Dobos, and Mary Sweeney, "Communication and commitment to community," *Communication Research*, 14(6) (1987), 619–643.

Jeffres, Leo W., David Atkin, and Kimberly A. Neuendorf, "A model linking community activity and communication with political attitudes and involvement in neighborhoods," *Political Communication*, 19 (2002), 387–421.

Jennings, M. Kent and Gregory B. Markus, "Political involvement in the later years: a longitudinal survey," *American Journal of Political Science*, 32 (1988), 320–316.

Johnson, Timothy and Linda Owens, "Survey response rate reporting in the professional literature," Paper presented at the annual meeting of the American Association for Public Opinion Research, Nashville, May 2003. Accessed at www.srl.uic.edu/publist/Conference/rr_reporting.pdf.

Jones, Starner, *Jackson Clarion-Ledger*, June 29, 2009. Accessed at http://clarionledger.newspapers.com/.

Kaase, Max, Kenneth Newton, and Elinor Scarbrough, "A look at the beliefs in government study," *Political Science & Politics*, 29 (1996), 226.

Kahn, Kim Fridkin and Patrick J. Kenney, *The Spectacle of U.S. Senate Campaigns* (Princeton: Princeton University Press, 1999).

Kam, Cindy D., "When duty calls, do citizens answer?" *The Journal of Politics*, 69 (1) (2007), 17–29.

Kapoor, Suraj and Carl Botan, "Editors' perceptions of the letters to the editor column," Paper presented at the annual meeting of the International Communication Association, San Francisco, May 1989.

Kapoor, Suraj, "Most papers receive more letters," *The Masthead*, 47, Summer 1995, 18–21.

Karpowitz, Christopher F., "Extremists or good citizens? The political psychology of public meetings and the dark side of civic engagement," Paper presented at the annual meeting of the Midwest Political Science Associate, Chicago, April 2006.

"Men, women, and Wal-Mart: Citizen Discourse at Local Public Hearings," Paper presented at the annual meeting of the American Political Science Association, Chicago, September 2007.

"A theory of local public talk and deliberative reform," Paper presented at the annual meeting of the American Political Science Association, Washington, DC, September 2005.

Karpowitz, Christopher F. and Tali Mendelberg, *The Silent Sex: Gender, Deliberation, and Institutions* (Princeton: Princeton University Press, 2014).

Krontiris, Kate, John Webb, Charlotte Krontiris, and Chris Chapman, "Understanding America's 'interested bystander': a complicated relationship with civic duty," June 3, 2015. *Politics and Election Blog.* Accessed at http://googlepolitics.blogspot.com/2015/06/understanding-americas-interested.html.

Kaye, Barbara K., "Blog use motivations: an exploratory study," in Mark Tremayne (ed.), *Blogging Citizenship, and the Future of Media* (New York: Routledge, 2007), pp. 127–48.

Kelley, Mark, "For democracy and the bottom line: goals United States newspapers hold for their letters to the editor section," Paper presented at the Association for Education in Journalism and Mass Communication convention, San Francisco, August 2006.

Keren, Michael, "Blogging and the politics of melancholy," *Canadian Journal of Communication,* 29 (2004), 5–23.

Kernell, Samuel, *Going Public: New Strategies of Presidential Leadership*, 4th edn. (Washington, DC: CQ Press, 2007).

Key, V. O., *The Responsible Electorate* (Cambridge: Harvard University Press, 1966).

Kidd, Quentin, "The real (lack of) difference between Republicans and Democrats: a computer word score analysis of party platforms, 1996–2004," *PS: Political Science & Politics,* 41(3) (July 2008), 519–25.

Kim, Joohan, Robert O. Wyatt, and Elihu Katz, "News, talk, opinion, participation: the part played by conversation in deliberative democracy," *Political Communication,* 16 (1999), 361–85.

Klein, Daniel B., "The people's romance: why people love government (as much as they do)," *The Independent Review,* 10 (2005), 5–37.

Klofstad, Casey, *Civic Talk: Peers, Politics, and the Future of Democracy* (Philadelphia: Temple University Press, 2011).

Knack, Stephen and Martha E. Kropf, "For shame! The effect of community cooperative context on the probability of voting," *Political Psychology,* 19 (1998), 585–99.

Knack, Stephen, "Social capital and the quality of government: evidence from the States," *American Journal of Political Science,* 46(4) (2002), 772–85.

Kornberg, Alan and Harold D. Clarke, *Citizens and Community: Political Support in a Representative Democracy* (New York: Cambridge University Press, 1992).

Krämer, Benjamin, "Media populism: a conceptual clarification and some theses on its effects," *Communication Theory*, 24 (2014), 42–60.

Krize, Nikki, "Controversial letter to the editor calls for execution of president," *WNEP – The News Station*, May 28, 2015. Accessed at http://wnep.com/2015/05/28/letter-to-the-editor-reads-controversy/.

Krontitis, Kate, John Webb, and Chris Chapman, "Understanding America's 'interested bystander': a complicated relationship with civic duty," (2015). Accessed at http://googlepolitics.blogspot.com/2015/06/understanding-amer icas-interested.html.

Kurpius, David D. and Andrew Mendelson, "A case study of deliberative democracy on television: civic dialogue on C-SPAN call-in shows," *Journalism and Mass Communication Quarterly*, 79 (2002), 587–601.

Ladd, Jonathan McDonald, "The role of media distrust in partisan voting," *Political Behavior*, 32 (2010), 567–85.

Lampe, Cliff, Paul Zube, Jusil Lee, Chul Hyun Park, and Erik Johnston, "Crowdsourcing civility: a natural experiment examining the effects of distributed moderation in online forums," *Government Information Quarterly*, 31(2) (2014), 317–326.

Landert, Daniela and Andreas H. Jucker, "Private and public in mass media communication: from letters to the editor to online commentaries," *Journal of Pragmatics*, 43 (2011), 1422–34.

Lane, Robert E., "The joyless polity: contributions of democratic process to ill-being," in Stephen L. Elkin and Karol Edward Soltan (eds.), *Citizen Competence and Democratic Institutions* (University Park: Pennsylvania State University Press, 1999), p. 329–370.

Lash, Scott, "Being after time: towards a politics of melancholy," *Cultural Values*, 2 (1998), 316–18.

Lawrence, Eric, John Sides, and Henry Farrell, "Self-segregation or deliberation? Blog readership, participation, and polarization in American politics," *Perspectives on Politics*, 8 (2010), 141–57.

Lee, Taeku, *Mobilizing Public Opinion: Black Insurgency and Racial Attitudes in the Civil Rights Era* (Chicago: University of Chicago Press, 2002).

Lemert, James B. and Jerome P. Larkin, "Some reasons why mobilizing information fails to be in letters to the editor," *Journalism Quarterly*, 56 (1979), 504–12.

Lepenies, Wolf, *Melancholy and Society*, Jeremy Gaines and Doris Jones (trans.) (Cambridge: Howard University Press, 1992).

Leuprecht, Christian and David Skillicorn, "Incumbency effects in U.S. presidential campaigns: language patterns matter," *Electoral Studies*, May 2016. Accessed at www.researchgate.net/publication/303917215_Incumbency_ effects_in_US_presidential_campaigns_Language_patterns_matter.

Levi, Margaret and Laura Stoker, "Political trust and trustworthiness," *Annual Review of Political Science*, 3 (2000), 475–507.

Levin, Murray Burton, *The Alienated Voter: Politics in Boston* (New York: Holt, 1960).

Levitt, Steven D. and Wolfram, Catherine D., "Decomposing the sources of incumbency advantage in the U.S. House," *Legislative Studies Quarterly*, 22(1) (1997), 45–60.

Lewis, Justin, Karin Wahl-Jorgensen, and Sanna Inthorn, "Images of citizenship on television news: constructing a passive public," *Journalism Studies*, 5(2) (2004), 153–164.

Lindquist, Julie, *A Place to Stand: Politics and Persuasion in a Working-Class Bar* (New York: Oxford University Press, 2002).

Loeb, Paul Rogat, "Hope, voting and creating the world you want to live in: getting to the polls is just the first step," *The Nation*, September 10, 2014, 7. Accessed at www.thenation.com/article/hope-voting-and-creating-world-you-want-live/.

Loke, Jaime, "Old turf, new neighbors: journalists' perspectives on their new shared space," *Journalism Practice*, 6 (2012), 233–49.

Lovell, George I., *"This Is Not Civil Rights": Discovering Rights Talk in 1939 America* (Chicago: University of Chicago Press, 2012).

Lowden, Nancy B., Peter A. Andersen, David M. Dozier, and Martha M. Lauzen, "Media use in the primary election: a secondary medium model," *Communication Research*, 21(3) (1994), 293–304.

Luks, Samantha, "Stability of citizenship values over time and the life cycle," Paper presented at the annual meeting of the Midwest Political Science Association, San Francisco, April 1996.

Luttbeg, Norman R. and Michael M. Gant, *American Electoral Behavior: 1952–1992* (New York: Peacock, 1994).

Magnet, Anne and Didier Carnet, "Letters to the editor: still vigorous after all these years? A presentation of the discursive and linguistic features of the genre," *English for Specific Purposes*, 25 (2006), 173–99.

Mansick, Mike, "Do people still write letters to the editor?" *Tech Dirt*, August 22, 2008. Accessed at www.techdirt.com/articles/20080822/0140562057.shtml# comments.

Marcus, George E. and Michael B. MacKuen, "Anxiety, enthusiasm, and the vote: the emotional underpinnings of learning and involvement during presidential campaigns," *American Political Science Review*, 87 (1993), 672–685.

Marcus, George E., *The Sentimental Citizen: Emotion in Democratic Politics* (University Park: Pennsylvania State University Press, 2002).

Marien, Sofie, Marc Hooghe, and Jennifer Oser, "Great expectations: the effect of democratic ideals and evaluations on political trust: a comparative investigation of the 2012 European Social Survey," Paper presented at the annual meeting of the Midwest Political Science Association, Chicago, April 2015.

Markus, Gregory B., "Causes and consequences of civic engagement in America: initial report of the civic engagement project," Paper presented at the annual convention of the Midwest Political Science Association, Chicago, IL, April 2001.

Masnick, Mike, "Too much free time: do people still write letters to the editor?" *TechDirt*, August 22, 2008, 7:38 p.m. Accessed at www.techdirt.com/art icles/20080822/0140562057.shtml.

Mataconis, Doug, "38% of congressmen represent 'safe' districts," *Outside the Beltway*, October 7, 2013, 7. Accessed at www.outsidethebeltway.com/38-of-congressmen-represent-safe-districts/.

Matthews, David, *Politics for People: Finding a Responsible Public Voice* (Urbana: University of Illinois Press, 1994).

Maybin, Janet, "Death row penfriends: some effects of letter writing on identity and relationships," in David Barton and Nigel Hall (eds.), *Letter Writing as a Social Practice* (Philadelphia: John Benjamins, 1999), 151–177.

Mayhew, David R., "Incumbency advantage in U.S. presidential elections: the historical record," *Political Science Quarterly*, 123(2) (2008), 201–28.

McCluskey, Michael and Jay Hmielowski, "Opinion expression during social conflict: comparing online reader comments and letters to the editor," *Journalism*, 13(3) (2011), 303–19.

McCormick, Samuel, "Neighbors and citizens: local speakers in the now of their recognizability," *Philosophy & Rhetoric*, 44 (2011), 424–45.

McDaniel, James P. and Bruce E. Gronbeck, "Through the looking glass and back: democratic theory, rhetoric, and Barbiegate," in Karen Tracy, James P. McDaniel, and Bruce E. Gronbeck (eds.), *The Prettier Doll: Rhetoric, Discourse, and Ordinary Democracy* (Tuscaloosa: University of Alabama Press, 2007), 22–44.

McElroy, Kathleen, "Where old (gatekeepers) meets new (media): herding reader comments into print," *Journalism Practice*, 7(6) (2013), 755–71.

McGeer, Victoria, "The art of good hope," *The Annals of the American Academy of Political and Social Science*, 592 (2004), 100–127.

McGillis, Alec, "Who turned my blue state red: why poor areas vote for politicians who want to slash the safety net," *New York Times*, November 20, 2015. Accessed at www.nytimes.com/2015/11/22/opinion/sunday/who-turned-my-blue-state-red.html?_r=0.

McLeod, Jack M., Dietram A. Scheufele, and Patricia Moy, "Community, communication, and participation: the role of mass media and interpersonal discussion in local political participation," *Political Communication*, 16 (1999), 315–36.

Medvic, Stephen K., "Explaining support for stealth democracy," Paper presented at the annual convention of the Midwest Political Science Association, Chicago, April 2016.

Mémet, Monique, "Letters to the editor: a multi-faceted genre," *European Journal of English Studies*, 9 (2005), 75–90.

Mencken, Henry Louis, "The cult of hope," in *Prejudices: Second Series* (New York: Alfred A. Knopf, 1920).

Mencken, Henry Louis, *Prejudices: Second Series* (New York: Alfred A. Knopf, 1920), pp. 211–18.

Miller, Toby, *The Well-Tempered Self: Citizenship, Culture and the Postmodern Subject* (Baltimore: Johns Hopkins University Press, 1993).

Miller, Susan, *Assuming the Positions: Cultural Pedagogy and the Politics of Commonplace Writing* (Pittsburgh: University of Pittsburgh Press, 1998).

Miller, Carolyn R. and Dawn Shepherd, "Blogging as social action: a genre analysis of the weblog," in Laura Gurak, Smiljana Jevic, Laurie Johnson, Clancy Ratliff, and Jessica Reyman (eds.), *Into the Blogosphere*, October 20, 2010. Accessed at www.researchgate.net/publication/274510648_Blogging_as_Social_Action_A_Genre_Analysis_of_the_Weblog.

Miller, Michael K., Guanchun Wang, Sanjeev R. Kulkarni, H. Vincent Poor, and Daniel N. Osherson, "Citizen forecasts of the 2008 U.S. presidential election," *Politics & Policy*, 40 (2012), 1019–52.

Miller, Patrick R. and Pamela J. Conover, "Winning is everything: the psychology of partisan competition," Paper presented at the annual convention of the Midwest Political Science Association, Chicago, April 2014.

Milne, Esther, *Letters, Postcards, Email Technologies of Presence* (New York: Routledge, 2010).

Mitchell, Amy, Jeffrey Gottfried, Jocelyn Kiley, and Katerina Eva Matsa, "Political polarization and media habits," *Pew Research Center*, October 21, 2014. Accessed at www.journalism.org/2014/10/21/political-polarization-media-habits/.

Mitchell, Amy, Jesse Holcomb, and Dana Page, "Local news in a digital age," *Pew Research Center*, March 2015. Accessed at www.journalism.org/2015/03/05/local-news-in-a-digital-age/.

Mitchelstein, Eugenia, "Catharsis and community: divergent motivations for audience participation in online newspapers and blogs," *International Journal of Communication*, 5 (2011), 2014–2034.

Moellendorf, Darrel, "Hope as a political virtue," *Philosophical Papers*, 35 (2006), 413–433.

Morrell, Michael E., "Survey and experimental evidence for a reliable and valid measure of internal political efficacy," *Public Opinion Quarterly*, 67 (2003), 589–602.

Moy, Patricia M., Michael McCluskey, Kelley McCoy, and Margaret Spratt, "Political correlates of local news media use," *Journal of Communication*, 54 (2004), 532–46.

Mulgan, Geoff, *Politics in an Antipolitical Age* (Cambridge: Polity Press, 1994).

Mullinix, Kevin J., "Civic duty and political preference formation," Paper presented at the annual meeting of the Midwest Political Science Association, Chicago, April 2016.

Mutz, Diana C., "Effects of 'in-your-face' television discourse on perceptions of a legitimate opposition," *American Political Science Review*, 101(4) (2007), 621–35.

Nadeau, Richard, Andre Blais, Neil Nevitte, and Elisabeth Gidengil, "Elections and Satisfaction with Democracy," Paper presented at the annual convention of the American Political Science Association, September 2000.

Nader, Ralph and Steven Gold, "Letters to the editor: how about a little down-home glasnost?" *Columbia Journalism Review*, 27 (1988), 53–4.

Nakajo, Miwa, "The role of civic engagement in local political trust," Paper presented at the annual meeting of the Midwest Political Science Association, Chicago, April 2015.

Neblo, Michael A., Kevin M. Esterling Ryan P. Kennedy, David M. J. Lazer, and Anand E. Sokhey, "Who wants to deliberate – and why?" Working paper, Harvard University, John F. Kennedy School of Government, 2009.

Neveu, Catherine, "Of ordinariness and citizenship processes," *Citizenship Studies*, 19(2)(2015), 141–54.

Nevitte, Neil and Stephen White, "Citizen expectations and democratic performance: the sources and consequences of democratic deficits from the bottom up," in Patti Tamara Lenard and Richard Simeon (eds.), *Imperfect*

Democracies: The Democratic Deficit in Canada and the United States (Vancouver: University of British Columbia Press, 2012), p. 52.

Newhagen, John E., "Media use and political efficacy: the suburbanization of race and class," Paper presented at the annual meeting of the International Communication Association, Washington, DC, 1993.

Newport, Frank, Lydia Saad, and Michael Traugott, "Informed Americans rate both parties in Congress worse," *Gallup*, October 5, 2015. Accessed at www.gallup.com/poll/186011/informed-americans-rate-parties-congress-worse.aspx.

Nielsen, Carolyn E., "Coproduction or cohabitation: are anonymous online comments on newspaper websites shaping news content?" *New Media & Society*, 16 (2014), 470–87.

Nielsen, Rasmus K., "Introduction: the uncertain future of local journalism," in Rasmus K. Nielsen (ed.), *Local Journalism: The Decline of Newspapers and the Rise of Digital Media* (London: Tauris & Co., 2015), pp. 1–30.

"Participation through letters to the editor: circulation, considerations, and genres in the letters institution," *Journalism*, 11 (2010), 21–35.

Nielsen, Rasmus L., "Local newspapers as keystone media: the increased importance of diminished newspapers for local political information environments," in R. K. Nielsen (ed.), *Local Journalism: The Decline of Newspapers and the Rise of Digital Media* (London: Tauris & Co., 2015), pp. 51–72.

Nietzsche, Friedrich, *Human, All Too Human: A Book for Free Spirits*, Marion Faber and Stephan Lehmann (trans.) (Lincoln, NB: Bison Books, 1996), section 70.

Niven, David, "The other side of optimism: high expectations and the rejection of status quo politics," *Political Behavior*, 22(1) (2000), 1–88.

Norrander, Barbara, "Ideological representativeness of presidential primary voters," *American Journal of Political Science*, 33(3) (1989), 570–87.

Norris, Andrew, "Becoming who we are: democracy and the political problem of hope," *Critical Horizons: A Journal of Philosophy and Social Theory*, 9 (2008), 77–89.

Nusselder, André, "Twitter and the personalization of politics," *Psychoanalysis, Culture & Society*, 18 (2013), 91–100.

Nutter, Michael, "Speech at the Democratic National Convention," Charlotte, NC, September 7, 2012. Accessed at www.youtube.com/watch?v=VTE8tvzuXUQ.

Oldenburg, Ray, *The Great Good Place: Cafes, Coffee Shops, Bookstores, Bars, Hair Salons, and Other Hangouts at the Heart of a Community* (New York: Da Capo Press, 1999), p. 77.

Oliver, Eric, "The influence of social context on patterns of political mobilization," Paper presented at the annual meeting of the American Political Science Association, San Francisco, August 1996.

Local Elections and the Politics of Small-Scale Democracy (New Jersey: Princeton University Press, 2012).

Oliver, J. Eric, "The effects of metropolitan economic segregation on local civic participation," *American Journal of Political Science*, 43 (1999), 186–212.

Orly, Aidan, "Elite doesn't mean more intelligent," *The Student Life*, April 26, 2013. Accessed at http://tsl.news/opinions/3156/.

Page, Susan and Kendall Breitman, "Divided we still stand – and getting used to it: long on dissatisfaction, divided about solutions," *USA Today*, March 23, 2014. Accessed at www.usatoday.com/story/news/politics/2014/03/23/congress-divided-poll/6792585/.

Paskin, Danny, "Say what? An analysis of reader comments in bestselling American newspapers," *The Journal of International Communication*, 16 (2010), 67–83.

Pasternak, Steve, "Editors and the risk of libel in letters," *Journalism and Mass Communication Quarterly*, 60 (1983), 311–328.

Pasternak, Steve and Suraj Kapoor, "The letters boom," *The Masthead*, Fall 1980, 23–25.

Patterson, Thomas E., "Political roles of the journalist," in Doris A. Graber, Denis McQuail, and Pippa Norris (eds.), *The Politics of News, The News of Politics*, 2nd edn. (Washington, DC: CQ Press, 2007), pp. 23–39.

Pattison, Neal, "The din of online comments to fall silent," *HeraldNet*, December 20, 2015. Accessed at www.heraldnet.com/article/20151220/NEWS01/151229934.

Peake, Jeffrey S., "Presidents and front-page news: how America's newspapers cover the Bush administration," *The International Journal of Press/Politics*, 12(4) (2007), 52–70.

Perkins, Thomas, "Progressive Kristallnacht coming?" *Wall Street Journal*, January 24, 2014. Accessed at www.wsj.com/articles/SB10001424052702304549504579316913982034286.

Perlmutter, David D., *Blogwars* (New York: Oxford University Press, 2008).

Perrin, Andrew J. and Stephen Vaisey, "Parallel public spheres: distance and discourse in letters to the editor," *American Journal of Sociology*, 114 (2008), 781–810.

Perrin, Andrew J., *American Democracy: From Tocqueville to Town Halls to Twitter* (London: Polity Press, 2014).

"'Since this is the editorial section I intend to express my opinion': inequality and expressivity in letters to the editor," *The Communication Review*, 19(1) (2016), 20.

"Since this is the editorial section I intend to express my opinion," *The Communication Review*, 19(1) (2016), 55–76.

Peters, Jeremy W., "Gloomy Republican campaigns leave behind Reagan cheer," *New York Times*, September 12, 2015. Accessed at www.nytimes.com/2015/09/13/us/politics/gloomy-republican-campaigns-leave-behind-reagan-cheer.html.

Pettit, Philip, "Hope and its place in mind," *The Annals of the American Academy of Political and Social Science*, 592 (2004), 152–165.

Pew Research Center, "Political polarization in the American public: how increasing ideological uniformity and partisan antipathy affect politics, compromise and everyday life," June 12, 2014. Accessed at www.people-press.org/2014/06/12/political-polarization-in-the-american-public/.

Pinkleton, Bruce E. and Erica Weintraub Austin, "Individual motivations, perceived media importance, and political disaffection," *Political Communication*, 18 (2001), 321–334.

Pitts Jr., Leonard, "Trump, Cruz ideas are just plain stupid," *Miami Herald*, March 25, 2016. Accessed at: www.miamiherald.com/opinion/opn-columns-blogs/leonard-pitts-jr/article68350122.html#storylink=cpy.

Pollock III, Philip H., "The participatory consequences of internal and external political efficacy: a research note," *Western Political Quarterly*, 36(3) (1983), 400–9.

Pounds, Gabrina, "Democratic participation and letters to the editor in Britain and Italy," *Discourse and Society*, 17(1) (2006), 29–63.

Pranger, Robert J., *The Eclipse of Citizenship: Power and Participation in Contemporary Politics* (New York: Holt, 1968).

Pritchard, David and Dan Berkowitz, "How readers' letters may influence editors and news emphasis: a content analysis of 10 newspapers, 1948–1978," *Journalism & Mass Communication Quarterly*, 68 (1991), 388–95.

Prothro, James W. and Grigg, Charles M., "Fundamental principles of democracy: bases of agreement and disagreement," *Journal of Politics*, 22 (1960), 276–294.

Puglia, Chris, "Do online comments bring newspapers value?" *St. Albert Gazette*, January 9, 2016. Accessed at www.stalbertgazette.com/article/Do-online-comments-bring-newspapers-value-20160109.

Putnam, Robert D., *Bowling Alone: The Collapse and Revival of American Community* (New York: Simon & Schuster, 2001).

Radmacher, Dan, "A look at the perpetrators: the list of interest groups encouraging 'astroturf' is as long as the list of interest groups," *The Masthead*, 56, September 22, 2004. Accessed at www.thefreelibrary.com/A+look+at+the+perpetrators%3A+the+list+of+interest+groups+encouraging. . .-a0123078810.

Raeymaeckers, Karin, "Letters to the editor: a feedback opportunity turned into a marketing tool: an account of selection and editing practices in the Flemish daily press," *European Journal of Communication*, 20 (2005), 199–221.

Rahn, Wendy M., "The role of partisan stereotypes in information processing about political candidates," *American Journal of Political Science*, 37(2) (1993), 472–96.

Rahn, Wendy and Thomas J. Rudolph, "A tale of political trust in American cities," *Public Opinion Quarterly*, 69(4) (2005), 530–60.

Rahn, Wendy M., Kwang Suk Yoon, Michael Garet, Steven Lipson, and Katherine Loflin, "Geographies of trust," *American Behavioral Scientist*, 52(12) (2009), 1646–1663.

Reader, Bill, "A case for printing 'name withheld' letters," *The Masthead*, June 22, 2002. Accessed at www.thefreelibrary.com/A+case+for+printing+'name+withheld'+letters.-a089648658.

"An ethical 'blind spot': problems of anonymous letters to the editor," *Journal of Mass Media Ethics*, 20 (2005), 62–76.

"New research on the nature of letters and their writers," *The Masthead*, June 22, 2005, 17.

"Who's really writing those 'canned' letters to the editor?" *Newspaper Research Journal*, 26 (2005), 43–56.

Reader, Bill and Kevin Moist, "Letters as indicators of community values: two case studies of alternative magazines," *Journalism & Mass Communication Quarterly*, 85 (2008), 823–840.

Reader, Bill and Dan Riffe, "Survey supports publication of controversial letters," *Newspaper Research Journal*, 27 (2006), 74–90.

Reader, Bill, Guido H. Stempel, and Douglass K. Daniel, "Age, wealth, education predict letters to the editor," *Newspaper Research Journal*, 25 (2004), 55–66.

Reagle, Joseph M., *Reading the Comments: Likers, Haters and Manipulators at the Bottom of the Web* (Cambridge: MIT Press, 2015).

Reich, Zvi, "User comments: the transformation of participatory space," in Jane Singer et al. (eds.), *Participatory Journalism: Guarding Open Gates at Online Newspapers* (Chichester: Wiley-Blackwell, 2011).

Renfro, Paula Cozort, "Bias in selection of letters to editor," *Journalism Quarterly*, 56 (1979), 822–6.

Rheingold, Howard, *Smart Mobs: The Next Social Revolution* (New York: Basic Books, 2004).

Rhine, Staci, Stephen E. Bennett, and Richard Flickinger, "Patterns of media exposure in the U.S. and their impact on knowledge of foreign affairs," Paper presented at the annual meeting of the Midwest Political Science Association, Chicago, April 1996.

Rhodes, Jesse H. and Zachary Albert, "The transformation of partisan rhetoric in presidential campaigns, 1952–2012: partisan polarization and the rise of bipartisan posturing among Democratic candidates," Paper presented at the annual meeting of the Midwest Political Science Association, Chicago, April 2015.

Rice, Tom W. and Alexander F. Sumberg, "Civic culture and government performance in the American States," *Publius: The Journal of Federalism*, 27(1) (1997), 99–114.

Richardson, John E., "'Now is the time to put an end to all this': argumentative discourse theory and 'letters to the editor,'" *Discourse & Society*, 12 (2001), 143–168.

Richardson, John E. and Bob Franklin, "'Dear editor': race, reader's letters and the local press," *The Political Quarterly*, 74 (2003), 184–92.

"Letters of intent: election campaigning and orchestrated public debate in local newspapers' letters to the editor," *Political Communication*, 21 (2004), 459–78.

Ricoeur, Paul, "The political paradox," in Hwa Yol Jung (ed.), *Existential Phenomenology and Political Theory: A Reader* (Chicago: Henry Regnery, 1972), 414–427.

Ripley, John, "Colleagues criticize Coffman for writing letter to editor," *BDN Archive: Penobscot/Bangor Daily News*, October 3, 1991. Accessed at http://archive.bangordailynews.com/1991/10/03/colleagues-criticize-coffman-for-writing-letter-to-editor/.

Robinson, Sue and Cathy Deshano, "Citizen journalists and their third places: what makes people exchange information online (or not)?" *Journalism Studies*, 12 (2011), 642–57.

Rodden, Jonathan, "This map will change how you think about American voters – especially small-town, heartland white voters," *Monkey Cage: The Washington Post*, October 31, 2016. Accessed at http://atlas.esri.com/Atlas/VoterAtlas.html?t=1&m=1&x=-94.69&y=38.62&l=5.

Roper Social and Political Trends Data, 1973–1994. The Roper Center for Public Opinion Research, Ithaca, NY. Accessed at http://ropercenter.cornell.edu/CFIDE/cf/action/catalog/abstract.cfm?Ext=1&Archno=USRoper1994-Trends.

Rorty, Richard, *Contingency, Irony and Solidarity* (Cambridge: Harvard University Press, 1989).

Rosenberry, Jack, "Users support online anonymity despite increasing negativity," *Newspaper Research Journal*, 32(2) (2011), 6–19.

"Virtual community support for offline communities through online newspaper message forums," *Journalism & Mass Communication Quarterly*, 87 (2010), 154–69.

Rosenblum, Nancy L., "Navigating pluralism: the democracy of everyday life (and where it is learned)," in Stephen L. Elkin and Karol Edward Soltan (eds.), *Citizen Competence and Democratic Institutions* (University Park: Pennsylvania State University Press, 1999), 67–88.

Rosenstone, Steven and John Mark Hansen, *Mobilization, Participation and Democracy in America* (New York: Macmillan, 1993).

Rosenthal, Irving, "Who writes the 'letters to the editor'?" *Saturday Review*, September 13, 1969, 116.

Rothenbuhler, Eric W., Lawrence J. Mullen, Richard DeLaurell, and Choon Ryul Ryu, "Communication, community attachment, and involvement," *Journalism and Mass Communication Quarterly*, 73 (1996), 445–66.

Ruiz, Carlos, David Domingo, Josep Lluís Micó, Javier Díaz-Noci, Koldo Meso, and Pere Masip, "Public sphere 2.0? The democratic qualities of citizen debates in online newspapers," *The International Journal of Press/Politics*, 16 (2011), 463–87.

Sampson, Robert J., "Local friendship ties and community attachment in mass society: a multilevel systemic model," *American Sociology Review*, 53 (1988), 766–79.

Sandel, Michael J., "America's search for a new public philosophy," *The Atlantic Monthly*, March (1996), 57–74.

Santana, Arthur D., "Online readers' comments represent new opinion pipeline," *Newspaper Research Journal*, 32 (2011), 66–81.

"Controlling the conversation: the availability of commenting forums in online newspapers," *Journalism Studies*, 17(2) (2016), 141–158.

Scheufele, Dietram A. and Matthew C. Nisbet, "Being a citizen online: new opportunities and dead ends," *International Journal of Press/Politics*, 7 (2002), 55–75.

Scheufele, Dietram A., James Shanahan, and Sei-Hill Kim, "Who cares about local politics? Media influences on local political involvement, issue awareness, and attitude strength," *Journalism and Mass Communication Quarterly*, 79 (2002), 427–444.

Schreiber, Darren, Greg Fonzo, Alan N. Simmons, Christopher T. Dawes, Taru Flagan, James H. Fowler, and Martin P. Paulus, "Red brain, blue brain: evaluative processes differ in Democrats and Republicans," *PLoS ONE*, 8 (2) (February 13, 2013). Accessed at http://journals.plos.org/plosone/article?id=10.1371/journal.pone.0052970.

Schroedel, Jean, Michelle Bligh, Jennifer Merolla, and Randall Gonzalez, "Charismatic rhetoric in the 2008 presidential campaign: commonalities and differences," *Presidential Studies Quarterly*, 43(1) (2013), 101–28.

Schudson, Michael, *The Good Citizen: A History of American Civic Life* (New York: Free Press, 1998).

Schultz, Lucille M., "Letter-writing instruction in 19th century schools in the United States," in David Barton and Nigel Hall (eds.), *Letter Writing as a Social Practice* (Philadelphia: John Benjamins, 1999), 109–130.

Seigel, Kalman, *Talking Back to the New York Times: Letters to the Editor, 1851–1971* (New York: Quadrangle, 1972).

Sennett, Richard, *The Corrosion of Character: The Personal Consequences of Work in the New Capitalism* (New York: W. W. Norton & Company, 1998).

Shade, Patrick, *Habits of Hope: A Pragmatic Theory* (Nashville: Vanderbilt University Press, 2001).

Shaker, Lee, "Citizens' local political knowledge and the role of media access," *Journalism & Mass Communication Quarterly*, 86 (2009), 809–26.

Sharot, Tali, "Optimism bias: why the young and the old tend to look on the bright side," *The Washington Post*, December 31, 2012. Accessed at www.washingtonpost.com/national/health-science/optimism-bias-why-the-young-and-the-old-tend-to-look-on-the-bright-side/2012/12/28/ac4147de-37f8-11e2-a263-foebffed2f15_story.html.

The Optimism Bias: A Tour of the Irrationally Positive Brain (New York: Pantheon Books, 2011).

Shklar, Judith N., *American Citizenship: The Quest for Inclusion* (Cambridge: Harvard University Press, 1991).

Siebel, Catherine, "Gender on the page: letters to the editor and the tobacco debate," *Feminist Media Studies*, 8 (2008), 408–423.

Siegel, Beth and Andy Waxman, *Third-Tier Cities: Adjusting to the New Economy* (Washington, DC: US Economic Development Administration, 2001). Accessed at www.mtauburnassociates.com/pubs/Third_Tier_Cities.pdf.

Sigelman, Lee and Barbara J. Walkosz, "Letters to the editor as a public opinion thermometer: the Martin Luther King holiday vote in Arizona," *Social Science Quarterly*, 73 (1992), 938–46.

Singletary, Michael, "How public perceives letters to the editor," *Journalism and Mass Communication Quarterly*, 53 (1976), 535–7.

Singletary, Michael W. and Marianne Cowling, "Letters to the editor of the non-daily press," *Journalism Quarterly*, 56 (1979), 165–8.

Skey, Michael, "The mediation of nationhood: communicating the world as a world of nations," *Communication Theory*, 24 (2014), 1–20.

Skogerbø, Eli and Arne H. Krumsvik, "Newspapers, Facebook and Twitter: intermedial agenda setting in local election campaigns," *Journalism Practice*, 9(3) (2015), 350–66.

Sleat, Matt, "Hope and disappointment in politics," *Contemporary Politics*, 19 (2013), 131–45.

Smith, Aaron, Kay Lehman Scholzman, Sidney Verba, and Henry Brady, "The current state of civic engagement in America," *Pew Research Center*,

September 1, 2009. Accessed at www.pewinternet.org/2009/09/01/the-cur rent-state-of-civic-engagement-in-america.

Smith, Amy Erica, "Do Americans still believe in democracy? State of the 2016 race," *Monkey Cage/Washington Post*, April 9, 2016. Accessed at www.washingtonpost.com/news/monkey-cage/wp/2016/04/09/do-americans-still-believe-in-democracy.

Snyder, Charles Richard, "Hope theory: rainbows in the mind," *Psychological Inquiry*, 13 (2002), 249–275.

Soltan, Karol Edward, "Civic competence, attractiveness, and maturity," in Stephen L. Elkin and Karol Edward Soltan (eds.), *Citizen Competence and Democratic Institutions* (University Park: Pennsylvania State University Press, 1999), p. 17–38.

Soroka, Stuart and Stephen McAdams, "News, politics, and negativity," *Political Communication*, 32(1) (2015), 1–22.

Sotillo, Susana M. and Dana Starace-Nastasi, "Political discourse of a working-class town," *Discourse and Society*, 10 (1999), 411–38.

Splichal, Slavko, *Principles of Publicity and Press Freedom* (Lanham: Rowman & Littlefield, 2002).

Stamm, Keith R., *Newspaper Use and Community Ties: Toward a Dynamic Theory* (Norwood: Ablex, 1986).

Steinbeck, John, *Travels with Charley in Search of America* (New York: Penguin, 1961).

Stonecash, Jeffrey M. and Mark D. Brewer, *Dynamics of American Political Parties* (New York: Cambridge University Press, 2009).

Stotsky, Sandra, "Writing in a political context: the value of letters to legislators," *Written Communication*, 4 (1987), 394–410.

Stromer-Galley, Jennifer, "New voices in the public sphere: a comparative analysis of interpersonal and online political talk," *Javnost – The Public*, 9(2) (2002), 23–42.

Stropnicky, Gerard, "Foreword," in Gerard Stropnicky, Tom Byrn, James Goode, and Jerry Matheny (eds.), *Letters to the Editor: Two Hundred Years in the Life of an American Town* (New York: Simon and Schuster, 1998), p. iii.

Tarrant, William D., "Who writes letters to the editor?" *Journalism Quarterly*, 34 (1957), 501–2.

Taylor, Paul, *The Next America: Boomers, Millennials, and the Looming Generational Showdown* (New York: Public Affairs, 2014).

Tewksbury, David, "Exposure to the newer media in a presidential primary campaign," *Political Communication*, 23(3) (2006), 313–32.

Thelen, David, *Becoming Citizens in the Age of Television: How Americans Challenged the Media and Seized Political Initiative During the Iran-Contra Debate* (Chicago: University of Chicago Press, 1996).

Thompson, Peter, "Religion, utopia and the metaphysics of contingency," in Peter Thompson and Slavoj Žižek (eds.), *The Privatization of Hope: Ernst Bloch and the Future of Utopia* (Durham: Duke University Press, 2013), pp. 82–105.

Thornton, Brian, "Heroic editors in short supply during Japanese internment," *Newspaper Research Journal*, 23 (2002), 99–113.

"Rejecting the eloquence of hate: 1972 magazine letters to the editor," *Journal of Magazine & New Media Research*, 12 (2011), 1–25.

"Subterranean days of rage: how magazine letters to the editor in 1952 foretold a generation of revolution," *American Journalism*, 24 (2007), 59–88.

"Telling it like it is: letters to the editor discuss journalism ethics in 10 American magazines, 1962–1972–1982–1992," *Journal of Magazine and New Media Research*, 1 (1999), 1–15.

Times Mirror Survey, *The Vocal Minority in American Politics* (Washington, DC: Times Mirror Center, 1993).

Townsend, Rebecca M., "Town meeting as a communication event: democracy's act sequence," *Research on Language and Social Interaction*, 42 (2009), 68–89.

Trachtenberg, Zev M., *Making Citizens: Rousseau's Political Theory of Culture* (London: Routledge, 1993).

Tracy, Karen, *Challenges of Ordinary Democracy: A Case Study in Deliberation and Dissent* (University Park: Penn State University Press, 2010).

Troy, Gil, *See How They Run* (Cambridge: Harvard University Press, 1996).

Turner, Bryan S., "Outline of the theory of human rights," in Bryan S. Turner (ed.), *Citizenship and Social Theory* (London: Sage, 1993), p. 162–190.

"Silent citizens: reflections on community, habit, and the silent majority in political life," *Citizenship Studies*, 19(5) (2015), 507–519.

Turner, Graeme, *Ordinary People and the Media: The Demotic Turn* (Los Angeles: Sage, 2010).

Twenge, Jean M., W. Keith Campbell, and Nathan T. Carter, "Decline in trust in others and confidence in institutions among American adults and late adolescents, 1972–2012," *Psychological Science*, 25(10) (2014), 1914–23.

Ulbig, Stacy Gwenn and Steven Perry, "I virtually hate them: the differential impact of online and offline news sources on partisan sentiment," Paper presented at the annual meeting of the Midwest Political Science Association, Chicago, April 2014.

Vacin, Gary L., "A study of letter-writers," *Journalism Quarterly*, 42 (1965), 464–5, 510.

Vargo, Chris J. and Toby Hopp, "Socioeconomic status, social capital, and partisan polarity as predictors of political incivility on Twitter: a congressional district-level analysis," *Social Science Computer Review*, 33 (2015), 1–23.

Vasquez, Francisco and Thomas Eveslage, "Newspapers' letters to the editor as reflections of social structure," Paper presented at the annual meeting of the Association for Education in Journalism and Mass Communication, Corvallis, Oregon, August 1983.

Vedlitz, Arnold and Eric P. Veblen, "Voting and contacting: two forms of political participation in a suburban community," *Urban Affairs Quarterly*, 16(1) (1980), 31–48.

Veenstra, Aaron S., "Reconceptualizing political blogs as part of elite political media," Paper presented at the annual conference of the Association for Education in Journalism and Mass Communication, Denver, August 2010.

Verba, Sidney, Richard A. Brody, Edwin B. Parker, Norman H. Nie, Nelson W. Polsby, Paul Ekman, and Gordon S. Black, "Public opinion and the war in Vietnam," *American Political Science Review*, 61 (1967), 317–33.

Verba, Sidney and Norman H. Nie, *Participation in America: Political Democracy and Social Equality* (New York: Harper, 1972).

Verba, Sidney, Kay Lehman Schlozman, and Henry E. Brady, *Voice and Equality: Civic Voluntarism in American Politics* (Cambridge: Harvard University Press, 1995).

Verba, Sidney, "Culture, calculation, and being a pretty good citizen: alternative interpretations of civil engagement," Eckstein Lecture, University of California, Irvine (January 2001).

Volgy, Thomas J., Margaret Krigbaum, Mary Kay Langan, and Vicky Moshier, "Some of my best friends are letter writers: eccentrics and gladiators revisited," *Social Science Quarterly*, 58 (1977), 321–7.

Wahl-Jorgensen, Karin, "Coping with the meaninglessness of politics: citizen-speak in the 2001 British general elections," Paper presented at the annual meeting of the International Communication Association, Seoul, South Korea, July 2002.

"Letters to the editor," *Peace Review*, 11 (1999), 56.

"Letters to the editor as a forum for public deliberation: modes of publicity and democratic debate," *Critical Studies in Media Communication*, 18 (2001), 303–320.

"Letters to the editor in local and regional newspapers: giving voice to the readers," in Bob Franklin (ed.), *Local Journalism and Local Media: Making the Local News* (London: Routledge, 2006), p. 231–241.

Journalists and the Public: Newsroom Culture, Letters to the Editor, and Democracy (Cresskill: Hampton Press, 2007), pp. 54, 91, 137, 159.

"Understanding the conditions for public discourse: four rules for selecting letters to the editor," *Journalism Studies*, 3 (2002), 69–81.

Walsh, Katherine Cramer, *Talking about Politics: Informal Groups and Social Identity in American Life* (Chicago: University of Chicago Press, 2004).

"Putting inequality in its place: rural consciousness and the power of perspective," *American Political Science Review*, 106 (2012), 517–32.

Walsh, Katherine Cramer and David S. Lassen, "Rural vs. urban coverage in newspapers across an upper Midwestern state," Paper presented at the annual meeting of the Midwest Political Science Association, Chicago, April 2012.

Walzer, Michael, "Civility and civic virtue in contemporary America," *Social Research*, 41 (1974), 593–611.

"Citizenship," in Terence Ball, James Farr, and Russell L. Hanson (eds.), *Political Innovation and Conceptual Change* (New York: Cambridge University Press, 1989), p. 216.

Warner, Michael, *The Letters of the Republic: Publications and the Public Sphere in Eighteenth-Century America* (Cambridge: Harvard University Press, 1990).

Weaver, Jerry L., "The elderly as a political community: the case of national health policy," *Western Political Quarterly*, 29 (1976), 610–619.

Weber, Patrick, "Discussions in the comments section: factors influencing participation and interactivity in online newspapers' reader comments," *New Media & Society*, 16(6) (2014), 941–957.

Weeks, Brian E., Thomas B. Ksiazek, and R. Lance Holbert, "Partisan enclaves or common media experiences? A network approach to understanding citizens' political news environment," Paper presented at the annual meeting of the International Communication Association, London, June 2013.

Weinschenk, Aaron C., "Personality traits and the sense of civic duty," *American Politics Research*, 42 (2014), 90–113.

Weisberg, Herbert F., "Partisanship and incumbency in presidential elections," *Political Behavior*, 24(4) (2002), 339–61.

West, Cornel, "The moral obligations of living in a democratic society," in David Bartstone and Eduardo Mendieta (eds.), *The Good Citizen* (New York: Routledge, 1999), p. 5–12.

Whitford, Andrew B. and Jeff Yates, *Presidential Rhetoric and the Public Agenda: Constructing the War on Drugs* (Baltimore: The Johns Hopkins University Press, 2009).

Whyman, Susan, "'Paper visits': the post-restoration letter as seen through the Verney family archive," in Rebecca Earle (ed.), *Epistolary Selves: Letters and Letter-Writers, 1600–1945* (Aldershot: Ashgate, 1999), p. 15–36.

Wildavsky, Aaron, "Resolved, that individualism and egalitarianism be made compatible in America: political-cultural roots of exceptionalism," in Byron E. Shafer (ed.), *Is America Different? A New Look at American Exceptionalism* (Oxford: Clarendon Press, 1991), p. 117–137.

Wilson, James Q., *The Moral Sense* (New York: Free Press, 1997).

Wolf, Josh, "Moderation matters for online commenting," *Journalism that Matters*, December 13, 2013. Accessed at http://journalismthatmatters.net/blog/2013/12/13/moderation-matters-for-online-commenting/.

Wright, Scott and Todd Graham, "Discursive equality and everyday talk online: the impact of 'superparticipants'," *Journal of Computer-Mediated Communication*, 19 (3) (2013), 1–18.

Xenos, Michael, Ariadne Vromen, and Brian D. Loader, "The great equalizer? Patterns of social media use and youth political engagement in three advanced democracies," *Information, Communication & Society*, 17(2) (2014), 151–67.

You, Kyung H., Mi Sun Lee, and Sohyun Oh, "Why use online comments? Examining the relationship among online comments, civic attitudes, and participation intention," Paper presented at the annual meeting of the International Communication Association, Boston, May 2011.

Zamith, Rodrigo and Seth C. Lewis, "From public spaces to public sphere: rethinking discursive spaces on news websites," Paper presented at the annual convention of the International Communication Association, London, June 2013.

Ziegele, Marc, Timo Breiner, and Oliver Quiring, "What creates interactivity in online news discussions? An exploratory analysis of discussion factors in user comments on news items," *Journal of Communication*, 64 (2014), 1111–38.

Zinn, Howard, *A People's History of the United States* (New York: HarperCollins, 1999).

Žižek, Slavoj, "Preface: Bloch's ontology of not-yet-being," in Peter Thompson and Slavoj Žižek (eds.), *The Privatization of Hope: Ernst Bloch and the Future of Utopia* (Durham: Duke University Press, 2013), 1–20.

Zuckerman, Ezra W. and John T. Jost, "What makes you think you're so popular? Self-evaluation maintenance and the subjective side of the 'friendship paradox,'" *Social Psychology Quarterly*, 64(3) (2001), 207–23.

Zullow, Harold M., "American exceptionalism and the quadrennial peak in optimism," in Arthur H. Miller and Bruce E. Gronbeck (eds.), *Presidential Campaigns and American Self-Images* (Boulder: Westview, 1994), 214–230.

Zullow, Harold M., Gabriele Oettingen, Christopher Peterson, and Martin E. Seligman, "Pessimistic explanatory style in the historical record: CAVing LBJ, presidential candidates, and east versus west Berlin," *American Psychologist*, 43(9) (1988), 673–82.

Index